Sign Language Phonology

A concise overview of key findings and ideas in sign language phonology and its contributions to related fields, including historical
linguistics, morphology, prosody, language acquisition, and language creation. Working on sign languages not only provides important new insights on familiar issues, but also poses a whole new set
of questions about phonology, because of the use of the visual
communication modality. This book lays out the properties needed
to recognize a phonological system regardless of its modality.
Written by a leading expert in sign language research, the book
describes the current state of the field and addresses a range of
issues that students and researchers will encounter in their work,
as well as highlighting the significant impact that the study of sign
languages has had on the field of phonology as a whole. It includes
lists of further reading materials, and a full glossary, as well as
helpful illustrations that demonstrate the important aspects of
sign language structure, even to the most unfamiliar of readers.
A text that will be useful to both specialists and general linguists,
this book provides the first comprehensive overview of the field.

DIANE BRENTARI is the Mary K. Werkman Professor in the
Department of Linguistics at the University of Chicago. She is author
or editor of six books including *Shaping Phonology* (co-edited with
Jackson Lee, 2018), *Sign Languages: A Cambridge Language Survey*
(Cambridge University Press, 2010), *A Prosodic Model of Sign Language
Phonology* (1998) and *Foreign Vocabulary in Sign Languages: A Cross-
linguistic Investigation of Word Formation* (2001).

Windsor and Maidenhead

KEY TOPICS IN PHONOLOGY

Key Topics in Phonology focuses on the main topics of study in phonology today. It consists of accessible yet challenging accounts of the most important issues, concepts and phenomena to consider when examining the sound structure of language. Some topics have been the subject of phonological study for many years and are re-examined in this series in light of new developments in the field; others are issues of growing importance that have not so far been given a sustained treatment. Written by leading experts and designed to bridge the gap between textbooks and primary literature, the books in this series can either be used in courses and seminars, or as one-stop, succinct guides to a particular topic for individual students and researchers. Each book includes useful suggestions for further reading, discussion questions and a helpful glossary.

Already Published in the Series:

Neutralization by Daniel Silverman

Underlying Representations by Martin Krämer

Intonation and Prosodic Structure by Caroline Féry

Phonological Tone by Lian-Hee Wee

Sign Language Phonology by Diane Brentari

Sign Language Phonology

DIANE BRENTARI

University of Chicago

CAMBRIDGE
UNIVERSITY PRESS

University Printing House, Cambridge CB2 8BS, United Kingdom

One Liberty Plaza, 20th Floor, New York, NY 10006, USA

477 Williamstown Road, Port Melbourne, VIC 3207, Australia

314-321, 3rd Floor, Plot 3, Splendor Forum, Jasola District Centre, New Delhi - 110025, India

103 Penang Road, #05-06/07, Visioncrest Commercial, Singapore 238467

Cambridge University Press is part of the University of Cambridge.

It furthers the University's mission by disseminating knowledge in the pursuit of education, learning and research at the highest international levels of excellence.

www.cambridge.org
Information on this title: www.cambridge.org/9781107534094
DOI: 10.1017/9781316286401

First published 2019
First paperback edition 2022

A catalogue record for this publication is available from the British Library

Library of Congress Cataloging in Publication data
Names: Brentari, Diane, author.
Title: Sign language phonology / Diane Brentari.
Description: New York, NY : Cambridge University Press, 2019. | Series: Key topics in phonology
Identifiers: LCCN 2019010022 | ISBN 9781107113473 (hardback)
Subjects: LCSH: Sign language. | American Sign Language. | Grammar, Comparative and general – Phonology. | BISAC: LANGUAGE ARTS & DISCIPLINES / Linguistics / Phonetics & Phonology.
Classification: LCC HV2474 .B724 2019 | DDC 419–dc23
LC record available at https://lccn.loc.gov/2019010022

ISBN 978-1-107-11347-3 Hardback
ISBN 978-1-107-53409-4 Paperback

Contents

Contents   ix

Figures

Tables

Acknowledgments

I would like to thank my colleagues who provided support while I was preparing this manuscript by reading chapters or helping with the manuscript preparation itself (in alphabetical order): Iris Berent, Rain Bosworth, Marie Coppola, Karen Emmorey, Jordan Fenlon, Laura Horton, Aurora Martinez del Rio, Kathryn Montemurro, and Gary Morgan. Also, special thanks to my sign language phonology seminar in the fall of 2018 that helped me iron out the final kinks of the text and to Petra Eccarius who assisted with excellent comments, as well as editorial and logistical help. All of you helped to make the text clearer and more readable. All of the mistakes are my own.

I'd like to acknowledge my funding sources that helped support this work over the years from NSF grants 0112391, 0547554, 1227908, and 1400998. I would also like to thank the Center for Gesture Sign and Language at the University of Chicago, particularly my co-directors Susan Goldin-Meadow and Anastasia Giannakidou, for the most stimulating group of colleagues and students one could ever hope for.

I am extremely grateful to Susan Elizabeth Rangel and David Reinhart for being the sign language models for the original photos in this book, and to Andrew Gabel, Rita Mowl, Drucilla Ronchen, and Robin Shay for their help and advice on many issues concerning ASL and the Deaf community. And a big thank you also goes to all of the deaf and hearing people – too numerous to name – who helped with this research over these last twenty years in Nicaragua, Italy, the United Kingdom, Hong Kong, and many other sites. Without your patience and generosity, this work would not be possible.

And, always, thank you to my husband and conversation partner in all things, Arnold I. Davidson, who is a constant reminder of not only how important the life of the mind is but also how important it is to have someone with whom to share it.

1 Introduction

Sign Language versus Gesture; Sign Language versus Speech

Abstract

By working through phonological questions using sign language data we arrive at a new understanding of the very nature of phonology, of the very nature of language. This chapter gives a brief historical look into the field from its inception, lays out the reasons why thinking about sign language phonology opens up new ways to understand the nature of language, broadly construed, and provides enough background on the units of word-level phonology in sign languages to see practical and theoretical connections to parallel issues in spoken language phonology.

1.1 INTRODUCTION TO THE TOPICS OF THIS VOLUME

Most non-linguists take phonology entirely for granted. As native language users we don't have as much metalinguistic awareness of the phonology of our language as we do about morphology and syntax, which are often taught explicitly in school. Children learn about the relationships between sounds and orthography in "phonics" but not about phonology – what the inventory of forms is or how they are combined. Most linguists know that there is a component of the grammar known as phonology, but often they are not sure what should be included there. And many phonologists do not often have to confront the question of what is or is not phonology unless they are doing language documentation and have to construct an inventory and set of constraints for a language that has not been previously studied.

What if those units were in a different modality entirely? How would we use our knowledge of how phonology functions as a system to decide which units are relevant and how they work together? In sign language we don't have as much disciplinary history as spoken language phonology. Our field is only about sixty years old.

Although traditionally based on sound systems, phonology also includes the equivalent component of the grammar in sign languages, because it is tied to the grammatical *organization*, and not to whether the content is auditory-vocal or visual-gestural.

Phonology is the abstract grammatical component where primitive structural units without meaning are combined to create an infinite number of meaningful utterances. These units are also manipulated by language users to communicate their language identity and are implicated in historical change. This definition helps us see that the term "phonology" covers all phenomena organized by constituents such as the syllable, the phonological word, and the higher-level prosodic units, as well as the structural primitives such as features, segments, timing units, and autosegmental tiers, but it does not refer to the vocal or manual medium in which these structures are expressed.

In this volume we will look at sign language phonology from several vantage points, as if looking at it under a microscope from different angles and with different lenses. Often the topic of sign language phonology is introduced by comparing sign language structure to that of spoken languages: "Spoken languages have 'x'; sign languages either do (or do not) have 'x'." In this chapter, we will start out from a different place, based on conversations I have had over the years with those who have doubts about whether sign language has phonology at all. The answer is "yes, it does," but this question lingers because the medium is so unfamiliar.

For the purposes of this volume, a sign language is any one of the more than 200 known manual languages used in the deaf[1] communities of the world. They are produced on the hands, as well as on the face and body. They are shared within a community, they are passed down from one generation to the next, and they serve all of the linguistic and cultural functions that one would expect of a language. If there is a system used for limited purposes, or as a surrogate for speech, it is not included within this designation. An

---

[1] A comment is needed here about the use of "Deaf" versus "deaf" in this book. "Deaf" has been used for several decades when discussing the cultural identity of an individual or community, and "deaf" when discussing the biological definition of hearing loss. I will follow Kusters' (2017) rationale and use "deaf" for all kinds of deaf people in this book. The "D/d" distinction is still important, but as deaf people from an ever wider range of backgrounds are included in academic discourse, the range of terms will become more nuanced, and the binary distinction D/d may not always be appropriate. Instead, groups of signers will therefore be described in prose as they arise.

example of such a surrogate system (not a natural sign language) is the one used in the Walpiri community by hearing women who grew up speaking Walpiri. They use a manually coded version of spoken Walpiri during their rather long period of mourning after they become widows (Kendon, 1980, 1984, 1985, 1987, 1988). Other such systems include manually coded systems of spoken languages throughout the world – e.g., Signed English, Signed French, Signed German, Signed Italian. These systems use signs, sometimes imported from a natural sign language, such as American Sign Language (ASL), but they are used in the service of representing the surrounding spoken language via signs, and they include invented forms to force the grammar to conform more closely to the spoken language. They have sometimes been employed in educational settings to teach the written language of the surrounding hearing communities. These surrogates and invented systems are not considered here.

This first chapter of *Sign Language Phonology* will be divided into two sections – the first addresses differences and similarities in sign and gesture, the second addresses differences and similarities between sign and speech, highlighting some of the historical moments when sign language phonology has had an important role in contemporary debates. The perspective taken in this chapter and in this volume is largely that of generative linguistics. Some of the debates that will be covered in this chapter and in subsequent ones include: Is language handled by a separate network in the brain or by general cognitive abilities? Did language arise in historical time in a gradual way or in an abrupt way? How does the critical period for language affect other areas of competence, such as learning to read?

Even if you are already up to date with the principles of sign language phonology and the history of the field, you still might want to read this first chapter for a fresh perspective of these issues. Consider this short volume as a conversation about sign language phonology. The volume cannot be exhaustive, but it is instead a way to highlight from my perspective those points that make sign language relevant beyond the small group of people in the trenches, people who are specialists. We will cover modality issues, iconicity, interface phenomena, acquisition, processing, language emergence, and variation, all with an eye to what makes them phonologically interesting to linguists, psychologists, anthropologists, historians of science, and child development specialists.

1.2 HISTORICAL PERSPECTIVES ON SIGN LANGUAGE PHONOLOGY

Our disciplinary perspective on sign language phonology has relied heavily on empirical methodology and evidence, because at the start it was important to disprove some naïve pronouncements by some important linguists about sign languages as a simple development from gesture. Sapir wrote, "sign languages are ... in the same category as the gestures of Trappist monks vowed to perpetual silence and the gesture language of the Plains Indians of North America" (Edward Sapir, 1921:21, from Padden & Humphries, 1990). This was incorrect, because we know now that Cistercian and Trappist monks' use of signs is more similar to a surrogate, such as Signed English, since monks follow the word order of the spoken language with which they are most familiar (Barakat, 1975). Bloomfield wrote, "[It] seems certain that these gesture languages are merely developments of ordinary gestures and that any and all complicated or not immediately intelligible gestures are based on the conveniences of speech" (Leonard Bloomfield, 1933:39). This is also incorrect.

Moving to the American Structuralist period in the history of linguistics, Charles Hockett (1960, 1978) held fast to the view that his more "narrow" definition of language should include only those expressed by the vocal/auditory channel. Sapir, Bloomfield, and Hockett needed to be challenged, and challenging such respected voices required sign language researchers to be very careful and convincing in constructing their arguments. These arguments involved system internal evidence, such as distributional patterns, and system external evidence from psycholinguistic experiments, sign errors, variation, the study of language deficits after brain damage, and, eventually, neuroimaging. This volume is, in part, a testament to this strong empirical legacy.

One key moment in changing previously held ideas of sign language phonological structure occurred in the early 1960s–1970s, when Hockett (1960) proposed his design features of language. They were subsequently discussed in the context of sign languages. One topic that has been of ongoing interest in these discussions concerns the design feature *duality of patterning,* which will be defined here as two levels of structure with independent organization, typically phonology and morphology. An English example of this phenomenon is *cans,* which has two morphemes (the stem *can* and the plural morpheme *s*) but one syllable (the vowel *a* is the peak flanked by its onset *c* and the coda cluster *ns*). Sign languages show duality of patterning also.[2] In ASL,

---

[2] The only phonological fact you need to know to understand this example is that movements are syllable nuclei in sign languages.

Figure 1.1 The two ASL stems THINK (left) and SELF (center), which form the compound THINK^SELF (*decide for oneself*, right). The compound (right) has two morphemes but just one syllable, just one movement. (Reprinted from *A Prosodic Model of Sign Language Phonology*, by Brentari, D., Copyright (1998), with permission from MIT Press.)

many compounds retain remnants of two stems but surface as a single syllable. The compound THINK^SELF, meaning *decide for oneself* (Figure 1.1), is composed of the two stems THINK and SELF (two meaning units), but instead of the full forms, each with independent movements, the compound consists of just one syllable (a single movement).

Another discussion associated to Hockett's design features focused on the inclusion of the vocal-auditory channel as a design feature for language, already mentioned in the previous section. The only phonological works on sign language phonology by this time were Stokoe (1960), Stokoe et al. (1965), and Frishberg (1975). Hockett (1978) was reluctant to state publicly that signed and spoken languages were equivalent, most likely because his main interlocutors were concerned primarily with the evolution of language rather than the equivalence between signed and spoken languages. In his oral lectures on the topic, Hockett acknowledged that "for its human users it [Ameslan] is as much like language as it could be given the difference of channel," and he says that there is clear evidence that ASL arose autonomously from English. But Hockett also states that he finds no evidence of duality of patterning in the communication of the chimpanzee, Washoe, or in other apes who had been reported to use a sign language, and Hockett still places a lot of emphasis on the effects of the vocal-auditory and manual-visual channels on the kinds of structures that emerge.[3] At the time, there was a great interest in the

[3] I am profoundly grateful to Robert Ladd for discussing Hockett's writings and lectures of this period with me.

ape-language experiments, and Hockett's caution is understandable to some extent. His mention of the chimpanzee-subject, Washoe, suggests that he was worried that, given the little we knew about sign languages at the time, it would be too easy to conclude that if nonhuman primates, such as Washoe, Nim Chimsky, or Koko, used ASL, and assuming that ASL is a language, then nonhuman primates "have" language. We know much more about sign languages today than we did in 1978, and while nonhuman primates have been taught with great effort to use some limited aspects of language, we are now able to describe the differences between the linguistic competence of humans and higher-order primates with much more precision, both in quantity and quality (Savage-Rumbaugh, 1986).

1.3 SIGN LANGUAGE AND GESTURE

This volume describes the inner workings of the phonology of sign language and how this information has informed other fields of study. But the question that must be addressed first, at least for most non-specialists, is how sign language differs from other types of manual gestures. Duality of patterning is a powerful criterion to separate gesture from sign language, but based on Ladd (2014), phonology displays duality of patterning only in a minority of cases for spoken languages, so it is clear that phonology can be present even without duality of patterning. Following this line of argumentation, duality of patterning might be broken down into component elements. I will argue in Chapter 8 that principles such as MAXIMIZE CONTRASTS (DISPERSION), SYMMETRY within the phonological inventory, and other well-formedness constraints involving ALIGNMENT and FAITH-FULNESS gradually help organize the system in historical time, but they do not emerge all at once, and these eventually lead to duality of patterning and minimal pairs.

Goldin-Meadow and Brentari (2017) have proposed relative properties that distinguish gesture from sign language. The properties converge around the larger point that gesture does not take on the primary burden of communication but is rather parasitic on a given language. Goldin-Meadow and Brentari make the argument that the true comparison between signed and spoken languages is not between speech versus sign alone but rather between speech+gesture versus sign+gesture. Yes, like speakers, signers produced gesture in parallel with the linguistic message. Gestures produced along with speech are "co-speech" gestures, while gestures produced along with sign language are "co-sign" gestures.

"Silent gesture" is another kind of gesture discussed later in this chapter and is what hearing non-signers do when they communicate without their voices – e.g., across a noisy, crowded room or when requested to do so in a laboratory setting. The reason why it is easier to determine what is language and gesture in spoken languages is because they often (not always) appear in very noticeably different modalities (auditory-language for language; visual-gestural for gesture), while sign language and gesture occur in the same (visual-gestural) modality. It is challenging but nevertheless possible to separate gesture from language in each modality.[4]

- Gesture **lacks hierarchical combinatorial structure**. Gestures may have compositional structure, but their combinations are characterized by a flat structure, whereas the combinatorial system that characterizes spoken and signed languages is hierarchical and interfaces many levels of grammar. This applies both broadly across the grammar and specifically to phonology, as we will see later in this chapter.
- Gesture is more **gradient** than language. Gradience per se is not a sufficient marker of gesture. There is a great deal of gradient variation in speech and sign; however, the gradience in language is anchored to a language's phonological and morphophonological categories, while gestures are not so constrained (see Duncan, 2005).
- Gestures are more **variable** than language. Sign languages have an established lexicon, while gestures do not, even though there are many gestural inventories that have been compiled. Popular bookstores are full of compilations of gestural inventories, both culturally specific ones and those that occur in many different cultures. Many such books typically contain emblematic gestures – e.g., the *shush* or *thumbs up* gesture (US emblems), or the *I-don't-care* or *pay-attention* gesture (Italian emblems).
- Co-speech and co-sign gestures are often produced **below the level of awareness** of speakers and signers, and access implicit, non-declarative knowledge. It has been shown, for example, that

---

[4] Even though here we will focus on visual gestures made with the hands and body, it is important to point out that auditory forms can be gestural as well (Haiman, 1980; Okrent, 2002; Shintel, et al., 2006; Grenoble et al., 2015). Both Okrent (2002) and Emmorey and Herzig (2003) argue that all language users (speakers and signers) instinctively know which part of their words can be manipulated to convey analog information. English speakers know that they can say *l-o-o-o-ng*, and not **l-l-l-ong* or **lo-ng-ng-ng*, and ASL signers also know which parts of a handshape can be manipulated to convey the iconic properties of a scene while retaining the phonological characteristics.

co-speech and co-sign gestures are a window into the mind and tell us, for example, that children are in a state of transition within the trajectory of a particular learning process (Church & Goldin-Meadow, 1986; Goldin-Meadow et al., 2012). For example, the gestures of both speaking and signing children are important in identifying the moment when a child is on the brink of learning particular concepts in math.

- A phonological system distributes its contrasts in principled ways to exploit the whole of the articulatory and perceptual space in an organized fashion (for spoken languages, see Boersma, 2003, Downing et al., 2004, van 't Veer, 2015; for sign languages, see Eccarius, 2008, Brentari et al., 2017).

"Silent gestures" produced by hearing people are qualitatively different from co-speech gesture. Silent gesture (as opposed to co-speech gesture) is not parasitic on language and can take on the primary burden of communication for hearing people but primarily in atypical circumstances when speakers cannot speak. Hearing people might communicate this way across a crowded, noisy room. For example, if I want you to meet me at the car, I might gesture – *point-to-you, point-to-me, mimic driving*. Silent gesture is an important laboratory technique frequently employed to encourage hearing people to use their gestural competence to express themselves via gesture alone, when it bears the full burden of communication, in order to better understand how strings of gestures are, or are not, different from signs. Co-speech gestures typically occur at a rate of one gesture per clause; instead, silent gestures can be combined in a sequence, which is helpful when comparing them with a string of signs. In addition, Singleton et al. (1993) and Goldin-Meadow et al. (1996) found that gestures produced without speech by American gesturers were different than co-speech gestures in two ways. As just mentioned, silent gestures occurred in strings, and these strings of gestures were characterized by a consistent (non-English) order. Also in silent gestures, handshapes were more likely to express something about the shape of the object together with a movement, while co-speech gestures do this less often. One important step in becoming a language therefore is when the modality accepts the full burden of communication.

Silent gesture is not a sign language. It has no lexicon – forms are created on the spot – and importantly for this volume, it has no phonology, as determined using several criteria. Brentari et al. (2012, 2017) have shown that gestures concentrate all of their handshape distinctions and complexity in one kind of handshape.

In contrast, sign languages not only have a wider range of contrasts, they also symmetrically divide the distinctions they make in a more balanced fashion across the inventory of handshapes at their disposal (Brentari et al., 2017). Silent gestures, except for emblems, also have no rules of well-formedness (Kendon, 2004). A more in-depth discussion of this will occur in Chapter 5 on the emergence of phonology.

1.3.1 Neuroimaging

An important kind of evidence for a phonological system in a sign language comes from neuroimaging, which will be addressed at length in Chapter 6 on phonological processing. Of course, a fundamental question about the neural organization of sign language is whether it has the same areas of activation as spoken languages. The short answer is that it does; sign languages activate many of the same neural networks as spoken languages. And crucially, gesture and sign language activate the brain in different ways. Here we foreshadow that discussion.

MacSweeney et al. (2001) studied differences in neural activity in fluent signers (hearing and deaf) when they were watching (perceiving) British Sign Language (BSL) sentences versus rapid complex sequences of gestures from a system called TicTac used at racetracks to communicate about betting odds across long distances. The deaf signers (not hearing signers) showed greater activation for BSL than TicTac in the frontal lobe and superior temporal regions—see Figure 6.11 for illustrations. The superior temporal cortex, including the primary auditory cortex and Heschl's gyrus (Areas 41 & 42), is associated with phonological processing for spoken languages and is understood to be recruited to a greater extent when phonological structure is present in spoken languages (Woods et al., 2011). This would therefore explain the native deaf signers' results: BSL sentences are phonologically structured while TicTac is not. In deaf signers, sign language is therefore associated with greater activation in the areas of the brain used for spoken language phonological processing (Petitto et al., 2000; Scott & Johnsrude, 2003).[5]

Neural activation patterns also differ for deaf native signers and hearing non-signers when they are looking at the same meaningful

---

[5] Bavelier et al. (2001) reported significantly greater activation in posterior superior temporal sulcus (STS) in deaf than hearing native signers in response to nonlinguistic motion stimuli as well, so sign language exposure may not be the only factor that determines activation in superior temporal regions.

iconic forms (Newman et al., 2015). This research team used functional magnetic resonance imaging (fMRI) to test deaf native ASL signers and hearing native English-speaking non-signers while they watched video clips containing ASL verbs of motion constructions describing the paths and manners of toy movement (e.g., a toy cow falling off a toy truck) and gestured descriptions of the same events, which look very similar (see Figure 5.1 for examples of similar types of event descriptions in sign and gesture). Among other findings, their results showed that three particular cortical areas – the left, inferior frontal gyrus (IFG, Area 44), the supramarginal gyrus (SMG, Area 40), and the superior temporal sulcus (STS) bilaterally – showed activation in signers and non-signers. This provides some evidence that symbolic communication in both sign language and gesture is capable of activating similar regions. However, there was greater activation in left IFG in signers when viewing linguistic content.

1.3.2 Conventionalization

To summarize this section, let us consider Saussure and the relation between the signified (concept) and the signifier (form; Figure 1.2). This volume encourages us to examine the plane containing options for phonologization *between* concept and form from the point of view of sign languages. This plane concerns how form becomes conventionalized, which can take many different routes. Not all of them are purely arbitrary. A phonological form can (and often does) become conventionalized for nonarbitrary reasons. For example, phonetic motivations can be part of the process of conventionalization – i.e., making forms easy to perceive or produce can be a part of the process. Just because a process is related to ease of articulation does not exclude it from the phonology. Many "weakening" processes in spoken languages (e.g., /p/>/f/>/h/) can be partially explained by ease of

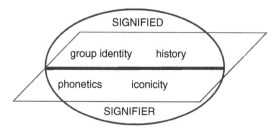

Figure 1.2 Possible mechanisms that can facilitate conventionalization of the signifier-signified relationship

articulation, but it is their distribution that makes them phonological; they often fail to occur where they should.

Sociolinguistic factors may also play a role. A particular demographic might include or exclude a process from their phonological repertoire. Eventually, the same behavior may become part of the phonology of the language as a whole. Likewise, historical relationships or etymology of forms may also play a role in creating new words. And iconicity is also a factor in creating new forms in languages. These conventionalizing forces that lie in the plane between the signifier and signified in Figure 1.2 are not at odds with the phonology because the arbitrariness (a critical property of linguistic form) is in the organization of the system, not in the source of the form. The question is not "why does 'x' occur" but rather "why does 'x' occur precisely *here in this set of forms, and not these other ones*?" In this volume we will explore these phonological motivations in sign languages.

1.4 SIGN LANGUAGE AND SPEECH AT THE WORD LEVEL

Now we turn to some of the similarities and differences between spoken and sign language phonology, and we provide a short introduction to the historical development of the field of sign language phonology. Asking how sign language compares with speech cannot be answered in a theory-neutral way; similarities and differences are bound up with discussions of constraints and constituents that are inevitably defined using specific theories. This section, therefore, is as much about the history of the use of phonological theory in work on sign languages since the 1960s as it is about the differences between signed and spoken language phonology.

Let's start with the observation that phonology does not operate in an identical way across the board throughout the entire lexicon in either spoken or signed languages. All words are not treated alike; they behave differently phonologically according to their morphological structure and historical roots. There have been many approaches to account for the historical relations between morphology and phonology within words, but the one that seems to work best for sign languages has been proposed for Japanese by Itô and Mester (1995a, 1995b).[6] For Japanese, they proposed Foreign, Sino-Japanese (derived

---

[6] Lexical Phonology (Kiparksy, 1982) and a theory of co-phonologies (Inkelas, 2011) are two models that have been developed to handle the relationship between phonology and morphology in the most complex cases of spoken languages.

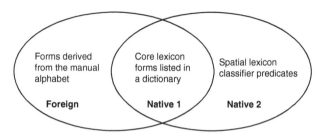

Figure 1.3   The three components of a sign language lexicon (cf. Brentari & Padden, 2001)

from the Chinese ideographic system), and Yamoto (native) components. Yamoto forms obey more phonological constraints than forms in the Sino-Japanese and Foreign components. In several sign languages (Johnston and Schembri, 1999, Brentari and Padden, 2001, Cormier et al., 2012), a similar model has been proposed (Figure 1.3), where forms are divided into Foreign and Native forms, and the Native Lexicon consists of the core and spatial components.

The inventories of handshapes differ across the components in ASL, similar to the differences in Japanese consonants across components. For example, in ASL the E-handshape 🖐 appears only in the Foreign component, which in ASL and BSL contains handshapes drawn from the manual alphabet. The "horns"-handshape 🤟 appears only in the core component, which contains stems and morphological entries that one would find in a dictionary, and the squeezed thumb+index finger handshape 🤏 is a type of size and shape specifier (or SASS) that appears only in the spatial lexicon, which is the most iconic of the components and contains polymorphemic forms known as "classifier predicates" (Supalla, 1982), sometimes called "depicting constructions" or "polycomponential forms." We discuss this portion of the lexicon at the end of the chapter, where we will return to the issues of gesture versus sign, because these forms are especially important for this type of comparison. As we delve further into the details of sign language phonology, we will see that some phonological generalizations do not apply across the whole lexicon but rather to specific parts.

The rest of this chapter will describe the inventories and constituents in sign language phonology, laying the foundation for the rest of the book. The questions one might be able to ask in signed or spoken languages are the same, but they have a different focus. There is an emphasis on the phonetic material of sign languages. As we move through the following sections and address how communication modality influences the abstract representations of phonology, we are really asking about what we believe to be the nature of a phonological system.

1.4.1 The Core Lexicon

Much of the work on sign language phonology pertains to the "core," or "frozen," lexicon of sign languages. The core component consists of stable forms that one might find in a sign language dictionary. Relatively few sign languages have been given deep phonological study, probably about 25 of the more than 200 known sign languages around the world. Most of the findings discussed here come from these sign languages: ASL, BSL, German Sign Language (DGS), Hong Kong Sign Language (HKSL), Israeli Sign Language (ISL), and Sign Language of the Netherlands (NGT). Other sign languages are included as much as possible. Examples from "new" emerging sign languages, such as Nicaraguan Sign Language (NSL), Al-Sayyid Bedouin Sign Language (ABSL), and Central Taurus Sign Language (CTSL), will be important sources of data as well.

In the following sections the hierarchical structure of ASL features will be described incrementally according to historical developments in the field. The criteria that determine whether a system is phonological pertain to issues of well-formedness, contrast, constraints, and constituent structure. Since the refinement of the theoretical work in these areas has been done almost exclusively on spoken languages, it is crucial that we examine data from another modality to confirm or challenge theoretical proposals, so that in some cases constructs can be recognized as the universals they truly are, or as limited to spoken languages if that is the case. One of the contributions that sign languages make to traditions of work in phonology is to reflect on traditionally held views with new kinds of data that can confirm or disprove their theoretical predictions.

1.4.1.1 Well-formedness and Contrast

Well-formedness is a notion that applies to many different phonological constituents – word, syllable, autosegment, timing unit, and feature. At the heart of the question of well-formedness is this: If the form is produced slightly differently with respect to a given structure, what happens to intelligibility? Is the change even noticed? If it is, then we can ask whether the resulting form is judged to be one of several types. Does the change result in a form that is: (i) nonsense (outside the system entirely), (ii) one with a completely different meaning (a minimal pair), (iii) one with a related meaning (a morphological contrast), (iv) one that appears only in a particular context (allophonic), or (v) one that identifies the user as coming from a particular demographic (sociolinguistic)? Here, we discuss a few of these options.

Minimal Pairs. The notion of the minimal pair has become somewhat general, insofar as a minimal change (whatever the linguistic unit) can sometimes be referred to as a minimal pair. Traditionally, however, minimal pairs have been an anchoring point for feature contrasts in words since Trubetzkoy (1939), where a minimal pair is defined as two unrelated stems that differ in a single feature (e.g., English *pete* versus *beet*, where the only difference is the voicing feature on the first segment). Typically, when the number of phonemes for a language is reported, it is based on whether or not there is a minimal pair to justify the inclusion of that segment as a phoneme; therefore, the number of minimal pairs is related to the number of phonemes in a language – saying that a language has "x" minimal pairs makes predictions about the number of units in the inventory. The range of phoneme inventories in spoken languages extends from a low of 6 consonants in Rotokas, a language of New Guinea, to a high of 122 (or more) in !Xóõ, a Southern Khoisan language of Botswana (UCLA Phonological Segment Inventory Database: Maddieson, 1984; Maddieson and Precoda, 1989; Maddieson et al., 2011). The notion of a minimal pair is also related to word shape. A language with a tendency toward monosyllabic, monomorphemic forms, such as Hmong, is more likely to have more minimal pairs of the type just described than a language such as Hawaiian or Mi'kmaq with polysyllabic stems. The number of minimal pairs does not, however, predict the number of words in the language, because languages can create new words in many different ways – by adding syllables, generating reduplicated forms, and performing many other operations without employing minimal pairs (Wedel, 2004). Moreover, the impact of minimal pairs on language acquisition has even been called into question, because even though the discrimination abilities in children are influenced by a child's vocabulary (Swingley, 2009), children can also discriminate among many phonemes before they have minimal pairs for them in their vocabularies (Maye & Gerken, 2000, 2001).

Despite the difficulties in using the minimal pair as a metric for measuring the phonological status of a system, we can say with certainty that sign languages have minimal pairs at the level of word, just as spoken languages do. When William Stokoe (1960) did the first phonological analyses of ASL, he noticed that the three major manual parameters of a sign language – handshape, movement, and location (place of articulation) – had minimal pairs for each. Stokoe called this the Cheremic model, since it could be understood within the Structural Phonemic model (Bloomfield, 1933; Hockett, 1955), but instead of whole sounds, as in the word *phoneme*, Stokoe referred to hands (from Greek *cheír*, cf. *chiro*- [English: *hand*] + -eme). See Figure 1.4 for minimal pairs in ASL and BSL for handshape, place of articulation (POA), movement, plus a fourth parameter – orientation – added by Battison (1978). A fifth parameter, shown for ASL, is non-manual behaviors, first discussed in ASL (Baker-Shenk, 1983) and then more widely (e.g., Boyes Braem, 1990 in Swiss German Sign Language (DSGS); Schermer, 1990, 2001 in NGT; Pendzich, 2017 in DGS).

There are a few things to notice about these minimal pairs in each of the stem pairs in Figure 1.4: (i) the meanings of the two forms are unrelated; (ii) the only thing that changes is the parameter in question; and (iii) none of the forms are iconic (there is little or no resemblance to what they mean). Even though some signs contain iconicity, there is much less iconicity in the core than in the spatial lexicon (Padden, 1988). Crucially, notice that these minimal pairs are different than the typical minimal pairs in English. In the two words in the English minimal pair *pete/beet* there are three timing slots (segments) corresponding to /p/, /i/, and /t/ or /b/, /i/, and /t/, and the difference creating the minimal pair is only on the first slot – the voicing in /p/ versus /b/. If the beginning, middle, and end of the sign were each a timing slot (more on this in the next section), the minimal difference in the handshape, movement, place, or orientation would be present throughout the whole sign.

At first glance this difference in minimal pairs was attributed to the fact that English is spoken and ASL is signed; however, with the wide acceptance of autosegmental phonology (Goldsmith, 1976) it became clear that some spoken languages have "ASL type" minimal pairs too, features that spread throughout the whole word: i.e., vowel harmony (e.g., Turkish, Finnish) and tonal processes (e.g., the Chadic language Margi, the Bantu language Shona). The important point is that a vowel feature [±back] or [±high] has one value that spreads throughout the entire word, just as distinctions in handshapes, orientation, or location do in the signs in Figure 1.4. In addition to being contrastive like the other manual components just mentioned, the movement parameter of sign languages is also associated with syllable structure, which is described later in this chapter.

Figure 1.4 Minimal pairs with handshape, location, movement, and orientation contrasts in ASL and BSL, and in ASL a contrastive non-manual property. (ASL images for APPLE, CANDY, PLEASE, MY, LATE, AND NOT-YET are printed with permission from Valli, C. (2006). *The Gallaudet Dictionary of American Sign Language*. Gallaudet University Press. BSL images are reprinted with permission from Fenlon et al. (2014a). *BSL SignBank: A lexical database of British Sign Language* (First Edition). London: Deafness, Cognition and Language Research Centre, University College London.)

These facts about sign languages have been widely known since Stokoe (1960). What Stokoe did not notice was that it was not the *whole* handshape, movement, or location that created a minimal pair but rather that much smaller differences were responsible for the contrasts. For example, for the handshape contrasts in Figure 1.4 the

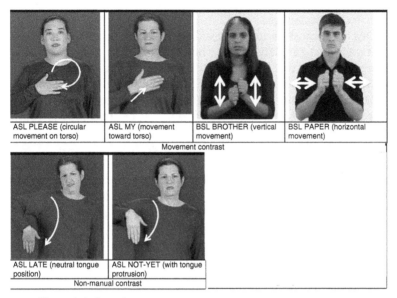

Figure 1.4 (cont.)

joints are responsible (the position of the knuckles and finger joints). All of the fingers are involved in BSL GAY (flexed) and UNSURE (extended), and in ASL just one finger is used in APPLE (bent) and CANDY APPLE (extended). For POA, the chin and fore- head are used in BSL AFTERNOON and NAME, both on the head. For the orientation contrast, the difference concerns only the part of the hand that is facing the location – the fingertips and the radial [index finger side] of the fingers in ASL CHERISH and OLD, and the fronts versus radial side of the fingers in MUM and DANGER. For movement, the contrast resides in the shape of movement in ASL PLEASE and MY (circle versus straight), and the direction of movement in BSL BROTHER and PAPER (vertical versus horizontal).

These smaller units – the features of sign languages – were first noticed by Frishberg (1975), Lane et al. (1976), Friedman (1977) Battison (1978), Mandel (1981), and Poizner (1983), with Liddell and Johnson working on this problem over many years, starting in the early 1980s and continuing until the publication of Liddell and Johnson (1989). These were fundamental discoveries. They demonstrate that each parameter is not in itself a feature but rather an entire class of features.

One of the most common questions in the early years, when Stokoe's work was first circulating, was whether the sign language parameters were features or segments; namely, how did they fit into the Chomsky and Halle (1968) framework outlined in the *Sound Pattern of English* (SPE)? In 20–20 hindsight we can see that the parameters are neither segments nor features but rather autosegmental tiers (Goldsmith, 1976), but the evidence for them was not proposed until almost sixteen years after Stokoe's initial 1960 publication. Moreover, it became clear in work following Stokoe in the 1970s and early 1980s that sign language phonology was not only simultaneous but also included some sequential properties as well. There are some minimal pairs, such as SEND ([flexed] followed by [extended]) versus GRAB ([extended] followed by [flexed]), where the order of handshape features is the only property that creates the contrast, but these are relatively few.

The content of the distinctive features of sign languages came from looking for minimal pairs, but it became increasingly clear that the minimal pair was not going to be a sufficient tool to determine the range of contrasts in sign languages. There simply aren't very many minimal pairs. This in itself is not a problem for languages; Mi'kmaq, an Algonquian language spoken primarily in the Maritime provinces and Newfoundland, has few minimal pairs other than vowel length (Oxford, 2013) and uses other means, such as reduplication, to create new words by adding quantity rather than quality information.

Contrast beyond Minimal Pairs

A few important early studies went beyond minimal pairs to describe phonological structure in sign languages. Lane et al. (1976) and Poizner (1983) used psycholinguistic experiments, while Frishberg (1975), Battison (1978), and Mandel (1981) looked at historical change and morpheme structure constraints to better understand the phoneme inventory in sign languages. Morpheme structural constraints, first proposed in Halle (1959) for Russian, express restrictions on the phonological shape of morphemes in the lexicon, such as the order of consonants in a consonant cluster, or the obligatory agreement in POA in English morpheme-internal nasal+stop clusters (te[m]pest, li[m]bo, le[n]til, ca[n]dy, fi[ŋ]ger, si[ŋ]ger). A few sign language examples are described here.

One versus two hands: One of the most intriguing aspects of sign language phonology is the interaction of the two hands, since there is no parallel to this in spoken languages. The "dominant hand," which will be referred to as H1 throughout this book, is the hand used for one-handed signs, and for fingerspelling in a one-handed alphabet. The other hand is the "nondominant hand," which will be referred to as H2. By analyzing constraints on distribution, it was found that there are a fixed number of types of two-handed signs, and a sign's form can change membership as a result of synchronic variation or historical change. In other words, the way that the two hands interact is phonologically important. Battison (1978) proposed these types:

- Type 0: one-handed forms, such as BSL NAME and AFTERNOON (Figure 1.4);
- Type 1: two-handed forms where the handshapes and movements are the same or mirror images on the two hands, such as BSL BROTHER and PAPER (Figure 1.4);
- Type 2: two-handed forms where the handshapes are the same on both hands, and one hand (the dominant hand) moves while the other (the nondominant hand) is stable, such as BSL UNSURE in Figure 1.4;
- Type 3: two-handed forms where the handshapes are different on both hands, and one hand moves while the other is stable, such as BSL GAY (Figure 1.4).

In Type 3 signs, the nondominant hand is restricted to a small set of unmarked handshapes. These vary a little from language to language, but most are variations of the whole hand (the B-handshape 🖐) or the single index finger (the one-handshape ☝) with different configurations of the joints (see Eccarius and Brentari, 2007). Battison formulated the principles governing two-handed signs as the Symmetry Condition (if both hands move, the handshape and movement should be the same)[7] and Dominance Condition (if there are different handshapes on the two hands, the base hand must be still (not move) and should come from this group of handshapes – B A S C O 1 5 – which happen to be variants of the 🖐 and ☝ handshapes). A few signs violate these constraints in ASL, but not many (e.g., SHOW), and the Symmetry and Dominance Conditions generalize well even to polymorphemic classifier constructions (Eccarius & Brentari, 2007), which are discussed in a subsequent section. The Symmetry Condition is likely to have its roots in ease of articulation (Kita et al., 2014).

---

[7] This physiological use of the term "symmetry" between the two hands is different from the use of symmetry having to do with the symmetry of features across the system as a whole (see Chapter 8).

There are no minimal pairs, to my knowledge, that involve the use of one- versus two-hands (Type 0 versus Type 1), and only one that I know of that is distinguished by the handshape on the nondominant hand (Type 2 versus Type 3), but phenomena on the two hands are a rich source of variation and historical change. Frishberg (1975) analyzed the differences between signs from the 1917 dictionary by Schuyler Long (one of the only historical documents on ASL with photographs)[8] and compared them with ASL from Stokoe, et al. (1965). She found tendencies that were insightful and important, but many of them were very difficult to formalize in spoken language terms. Some of the changes involved the way that the two hands function together as a single articulatory unit, which is unique to sign languages.

Variation studies have observed that a sign can have one- or two-handed variants, and this type of variation is called "Weak Drop" (Battison, 1974; Padden & Perlmutter, 1987; Brentari, 1998). Alternations between one- and two-handed sign variants are important in characterizing Black ASL (McCaskill et al., 2011). Historical changes can also result in a two-handed sign of Type 3 becoming a Type 2 sign, or a Type 2 sign becoming a Type 1.

Features: In sign language phonology the methods of psycholinguistics were exploited relatively quickly and effectively, in addition to working with informants. Psycholinguistic methods seemed adaptable to the situation because no reference grammars of sign languages existed at the time; even now only a few sign languages have been thoroughly described. Moreover, if linguistics is largely about studying I(nternalized)-Language – the knowledge about a language that any individual has who is a native user of that language (Chomsky, 1957) – psycholinguistics can serve well to access this knowledge. For example, to begin to understand the nature of features, Lane et al. (1976) and Boyes Braem (1980) conducted an early confusion matrix study, adapted from Miller and Nicely (1955). The spoken language forms were pseudo-syllables (*ba, da, ga*) presented in noise. Lane et al. (1976) presented ASL pseudo-syllables (handshapes plus a movement) in visual noise. The background was like that of a "snowy" TV screen from the 1970s. First a block of forms was presented in which movement and location were held constant (called a "fixed prime" – a twist of the wrist in the neutral space in front of the signers) and then

---

[8] Now historical materials are more widely available, see Supalla and Clarke (2015), but in the 1970s they were viewable only onsite in the Gallaudet University library.

a second block varied the other parameters in a controlled fashion. Just as Miller and Nicely's study proposed that independent evidence for English distinctive features could be found using this method, Lane et al. proposed that the features [broad] "open," [compact] "closed," [concave] "bent," [spread], [cross], [touch], [ulnar], [radial], [full] "all fingers," [dual] "two fingers," and [index] were distinctive in ASL. The confusion matrix is presented in Figure 1.5. This allowed handshapes to be grouped together into natural classes based on perception. For example, ∜ and ∭ both use [spread] and are therefore a natural class on those grounds, and ⍦ and ∭ are a natural class based on the fact that both handshapes are three-finger handshapes.

Poizner (1983) used a slightly different method to uncover movement features – a similarity measure called "triadic comparison." Triads of movement shapes were generated using point-light displays – movements from stems and from meaningful, morphological affixes that use movement. These were shown to signers and non-signers who were asked to choose the two most similar of the three movements. Repetition (lexical) and cyclicity (morphological) were the two most salient movement types for signers. Plane (midsagittal, vertical, horizontal) and direction (to and from the body) were the most salient for non-signers. Since the results were different for signers and non-signers, the features of movement that were salient for signers were attributed to the phonological system.

The confusion matrix and triadic comparison tasks were novel ways of accessing phonological information. The confusion matrix allowed natural classes to emerge, and potentially rules or constraints could access the features responsible. A bit later in this chapter we will review some constraints that do exactly that. The differences between signers' and non-signers' preferences help us to see which similarities might be due simply to visual, rather than linguistic, similarity. In studies such as these, non-signers are often used as a baseline group with whom signers are compared for precisely this reason. Both groups have access to the salient properties grounded in vision alone, but when there are differences between the groups, we have evidence that signers have access to another system, another strategy. That system is phonology.

By the early 1980s Stokoe's vision of the sign with sub-lexical parameters in a flat structure (Figure 1.6 left) had been elaborated to include a number of features, as shown in Figure 1.6 (right). Even though the parameters were still organized as a flat structure – no parameter dominated any other – the features were dominated by the parameters, and there was also an intermediate set of units between the parameter node and the feature node, where features were placed

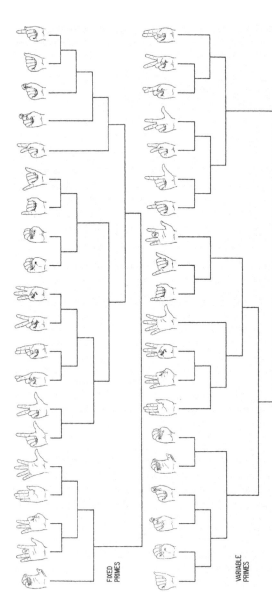

Figure 1.5 Confusion matrix employed in Lane et al. (1976). (Reprinted from Lane, et al., "Preliminaries to a distinctive feature analysis of handshapes in American Sign Language," *Cognitive Psychology*, 8, pp. 263–289, Copyright (1976), with permission from Elsevier.)

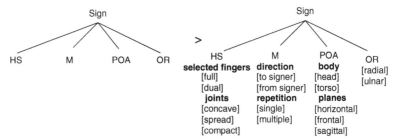

Figure 1.6 The parameters accepted for ASL signs by 1980 (handshape, movement location, and orientation) shown as a flat structure, and how the features that had been proposed for the parameters were organized within those parameters

in subgroups. *Selected fingers* (those that were involved in contact or which could change their joint features during the course of producing a sign) and *joint configurations* are now subgroups of handshape, *direction* and *repetition* were subgroups of movement, and *body* and *neutral space* were subgroups of POA. Figure 1.6 (right) is a schema of that organization. One reason why this structure was never published, in my opinion, is that it appeared quite different from the SPE spoken language phonological representations at the time. Autosegmental phonology had just been launched four years earlier (Goldsmith, 1976) and was unknown in the sign language research community at that time.

1.4.1.2   Hierarchical Structure in Post-Stokoe Phonological Models

The Cheremic model of Stokoe could be understood as part of the Structural Phonemics tradition (Bloomfield, 1933; Hockett, 1955), where the phoneme was the basic phonological unit and with groups of features for place, manner, and voicing having no particular organization. Over the last sixty years in spoken language phonology and thirty-five years in sign language phonology, there have been several proposals for the hierarchical organization of phonological units. Of the models of sign language phonology, we will discuss only four post-Stokoe models here: the Hold-Movement model (Liddell & Johnson, 1989), the Hand Tier model (Sandler, 1989; Sandler & Lillo-Martin, 2006), the Dependency model (van der Hulst, 1993; van der Kooij, 2002; van der Kooij & van der Hulst, 2005), and the Prosodic model (Brentari, 1990a, 1998). These are complete, coherent models accounting for all the manual components, and since no model has proposed

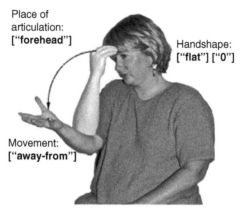

Place of
articulation:
["forehead"]

Handshape:
["flat"] ["O"]

Movement:
["away-from"]

Figure 1.7 ASL INFORM. (From Brentari, D., "Sign Language
Phonology," in G. Gertz & P. Boudreault (eds.), *The SAGE Deaf Studies
Encyclopedia*, (2016) Reprinted with permission from Sage Publishers.)

a phonological account of non-manual features, we leave non-manuals
(i.e., facial expressions and body shifts) aside for now. Each of these
models has added important insights to our understanding of sign
language structure. All acknowledge that

• movements function similarly to vowels;
• the beginnings and ending points have sequential status and are
  important for feature order;
• simultaneous and sequential properties of signs are both very
  important.

In order to discuss these models, the ASL sign INFORM will be used as
a concrete reference (Figure 1.7). This section is not intended to cover
the fine details of each model but rather to give a sense of the way they
work and the similarities and differences among their approaches and
insights. In terms of features, all of the models made some modifications to the set of features in Figure 1.6 in order to make them more
precise, to elaborate on distinctions, or to make the feature set more
complete and cohesive, but all included the four parameters of handshape, movement, place of articulation (location), and orientation,
with subgroups of features within each parameter.

The first model after Stokoe's Cheremic model was the Hold-
Movement model (Liddell, 1984; Liddell and Johnson, 1989; Figure
1.8a). Their analysis divided signs into segments of static Holds and
dynamic Movements, such that signs had timing slots (X-slots). These

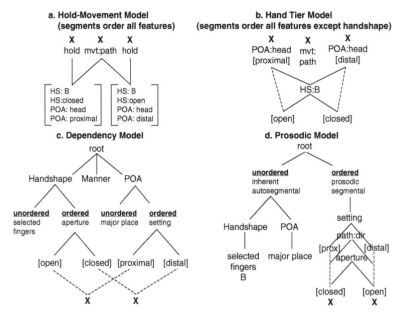

Figure 1.8 Four post-Stokoe models of sign language phonological representation in schematic form: The Hold-Movement model (a); the Hand Tier model (b); the Dependency model (c); and the Prosodic model (d)

segments ordered all features in the sign. Their account was original and captured the generalization that when a sign had two handshapes in a sign such as INFORM – 👌 and 🖖 – they had a stipulated order; INFORM cannot be signed with the handshapes in the reverse order 🖖 followed by 👌 and still be the same sign. In addition, their analysis of compound formation proposed that the last static segment of the first stem in a form such as THINK combined with a single movement and a segment of the second stem SELF to create the compound (see Figure 1.1 for THINK^SELF). They adequately described what was happening in these signs, but there would be further refinements to come, explaining a wider range of phenomena in compound formation.

Liddell and Johnson took a decidedly sequential segmental approach, guided by the generative model laid out in Chomsky and Halle (1968), where segments were the principle unit manipulated in phonological rules. Over time, the segmental units that dominated the SPE approach have been demoted, both in spoken and signed language phonology. The crucial phonological work that is performed by suprasegmental units became clear in spoken languages in auto-segmental phonology (Goldsmith, 1976), feature geometry (Clements, 1985; Sagey, 1986; Clements & Hume, 1995), and Articulatory Phonology (Browman & Goldstein, 1989). These principles were then used in sign languages as well. For example, the Hold-Movement model did not account for assimilation of the two handshapes in a compound, such as the one shown in THINK^SELF in Figure 1.1. Sandler (1989, discussed further below) added the insight that the handshape parameter often spreads across a compound, and if hand-shape spreads, orientation spreads also (notice the thumb regressively assimilates to the beginning of the sign and is not only on the second part SELF). In addition, the Hold-Movement model could not account for why some compounds retained the movements of both stems, while others seemed to reduce to a single movement (THINK^SELF is a member of the latter group). Brentari (1990a, 1990b, discussed further below) found a way to explain this by showing that some movements that appear in stems when they are independent words are epenthetic, and do not appear in compounds because the environ-ment is not favorable for epenthesis.

There were two additional shortcomings of the Hold-Movement model that were noticed soon thereafter. When signs were in a sequence, the Hold-Movement model proposed that Holds were deleted between two movements everywhere, except for cases where there was contact with the POA. It seemed excessive to have to posit contrastive Holds in every sign only to delete them all when signs occurred in a sequence, especially since the presence or absence of a Hold never creates a minimal pair. In addition, for mono-morphemic forms, the features associated within each segment in the Hold-Movement model contained much more redundant information relative to the C and V units of spoken languages. For example, note how both 🖐 and 🖐 are variants of the whole hand, the B handshape 🖐 in INFORM; it occurs in both X-slots in Figure 1.8a. The only features that changed were the joint features – from [closed] to [open]. The Hold-Movement model did not capture this redundancy.

The Hand Tier model would address some of the shortcoming of the Hold-Movement model by representing handshape as an autosegmen-tal tier (Sandler, 1986, 1989; Figure 1.8b), thus re-animating Stokoe's original insights of the simultaneous nature of the sign to some extent. Sandler was the first to recognize that handshape met the phonological criteria established by Goldsmith for an autosegmental tier: stability, morphological status, many-to-one association, and long-distance effects. Evidence for handshape as an autosegment is provided by the SELECTED FINGERS CONSTRAINT (SFC) and the HANDSHAPE SEQUENCE CONSTRAINT (HSC) (Mandel, 1981; Sandler, 1986, 1989; Brentari, 1990b).[9] The SFC captures the fact that when signs are composed of a single stem, they have one set of selected fingers, and when they have more than one handshape, as mentioned above for the B handshape in INFORM, the HSC captures the fact they will be open and closed variants of the same set of selected fingers. In other words, two handshapes change only in joint features – e.g., [open] followed by [closed] or [-spread] followed by [+spread]. A change such as followed by is permitted in compounds because they are polymorphemic, but not in monomorphemic signs. The SFC is seen in other historical contexts as well, addressed in Chapter 8. Selected fingers are therefore unordered, as an autosegmental tier, while aperture (joints) create timing slots that are ordered and segmental.

The Hand Tier model also showed evidence from compounds that handshape dominates the orientation of the hand. In many compounds, if the handshape of the second stem regressively assimilates, so does the orientation of the hand. The orientation alone can assimilate, but the handshape typically does not assimilate alone (without orientation). For example, in Figure 1.9, there are three ways that the first stem of the compound MIND^DROP (*faint*) can be produced: with no assimilation as in Figure 1.9a, with orientation assimilation as in Figure 1.9b, or with both handshape and orientation assimilation as in Figure 1.9c. In Figure 1.9d the second segment of the second stem is shown, which is the same no matter what the first stem looks like, and which is the trigger for both the orientation and handshape assimilation. The first stem does not occur with unassimilated orientation and assimilated handshape, although it is perfectly easy to produce.

Handshape in the Hand Tier model was represented as unordered, and Location and Movement ordered; the unordered Handshape features had to be linked to the Location and Movement features in a separate step. This model also introduced the concept of "Location" instead of "Hold" segments, which eliminated the need for a static period of time at the beginning and end of a movement. Like the Halle-Sagey (1989) model of feature geometry, the feature

[9] The differences between the versions of this constraint have to do with the constituent to which it applies. Sandler (1989) used the morpheme, while Brentari used the syllable and ultimately the prosodic word (Brentari, 1998).

MIND   DROP

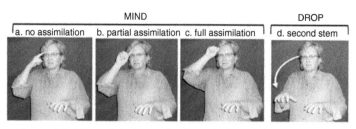

Figure 1.9 Hierarchical organization of selected fingers and
orientation. Three versions of the first part of the compound
MIND^DROP (faint): (a) with no assimilation of handshape or
orientation, (b) with assimilation of orientation alone, and (c) with
assimilation of both orientation and handshape. In (d) the second stem
is shown, which is the same no matter what the first position is like, and
which is the trigger for both the orientation and handshape assimilation

geometry of the Hand Tier model was organized primarily around
articulatory similarity and phonological function. For example, all
features of handshape were grouped together because they were produced on the hands, but orientation was placed lower in the tree based
on the fact that it is dominated by handshape in its phonological
behavior.

The last two models we will discuss here are the Dependency model
(van der Hulst, 1993; van der Kooij, 2002; van der Kooij & van der
Hulst, 2005; Figure 1.8c) and the Prosodic model (Brentari, 1990a,
1998; Figure 1.8d). Although they differ in important details, both of
these models share several properties. First, they use only binary
branching feature class nodes and assign the role of "head" to one
branch and "dependent" to the other, based on which branch has the
greater number of elaborations. For example, in the handshape representation from the Prosodic model shown in Figure 1.10, the top node
branches into *selected fingers$_2$* and *nonselected fingers. Selected fingers$_2$* is
the head because it has a more elaborate structure than nonselected
fingers – i.e., it branches. Likewise, when the *selected fingers$_2$* node
branches further into selected fingers$_1$ and joint configuration, the
selected fingers$_1$ is the head and *joints* is the dependent because
selected fingers$_1$ has the more elaborate structure beneath it.

Second, both the Dependency and Prosodic models agree that handshape and POA have split personalities in sign language phonology –
some features are represented only once in a stem and are unordered
like autosegmental tiers. These comprise the class of inherent features
in the Prosodic model (Figure 1.8d). Other features can change within
a stem and must be ordered and are part of the class of prosodic

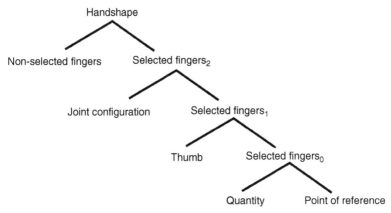

Figure 1.10 Binary branching nodes of the handshape feature structure in the Prosodic model

features. Both the Dependency and Prosodic models ascribe autosegmental status to some features of the parameters of both Handshape and POA because both meet the phonological criteria established by Goldsmith for autosegmental tiers. For example, within Handshape, selected fingers features are unordered and autosegmental in stems, and aperture features are ordered and segmental features of handshape. Likewise, POA consists of unordered autosegmental major places of articulation ± the torso, head, arm, nondominant hand, and neutral space – and ordered setting features such as [top], [bottom], [ipsilateral], or [contralateral], which are segmental and allowed to change within a sign. In spoken languages, we see something similar with features of the larynx. In tone languages, tone is autosegmental and unordered, while voice is segmental and ordered.[10]

Third, in the hierarchy of the Hold-Movement model and the Hand Tier model the segment is placed at the top of the feature tree in the dominant position with other structures beneath the segment in the hierarchy, but the Prosodic model and the Dependency model share a different view. Both the Prosodic and Dependency models propose that an important difference between signed and spoken languages should be represented in the hierarchical, phonological structure; namely, the timing slots are demoted to the bottom of the tree and are predictable from the featural material. The relationship in spoken languages between X-slot, which dominates the feature tree, and

---

[10] Pfau (2016) has proposed that non-manuals may also have ordered and unordered roles.

features, which are dependent, does not serve sign languages well. One reason is that, while contrastive length can be used in distinguishing related forms in the morphology and it is also used extensively in prosodic structure (discussed at length in Chapter 4),[11] it does not generate a minimal pair between two unrelated stems. In spoken languages, length is a commonly used feature for lexical contrast as a difference in quantity, as shown below in Italian (1). Since the number of segments in a stem can be derived from the feature values in sign languages, the segment has been demoted in these two models (van der Hulst, 2000; Brentari, 2002), as shown schematically in (2).

(1) *Spoken language phonology (Italian)*

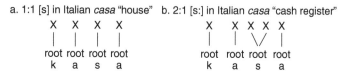

(2) *Organization of phonological material in signed versus spoken languages. Notice the X-slot dominates the feature geometry in (2a) and is demoted to the bottom of the structure in (2b).*

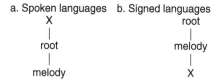

An important difference between the Dependency and Prosodic models, however, is in the organization of features within each parameter. For INFORM, the models' respective representations of this sign would look like those in Figure 1.8c–d. The Dependency model allows physiology to be the major guide in the organization of features; both selected fingers (autosegmental, unordered) and aperture (segmental, ordered) are still located together in the tree, despite their different phonological roles, because they are features of the hand. Major POA and setting features are united using similar reasoning.

The Prosodic model allows the phonological behavior to be the major guide for the organization of the features; all unordered

---

[11] Length is used in the morphology to generate an intensive adjective (Sandler, 1989) – e.g., RED > VERY-RED; GOOD > VERY-GOOD (the hold at the beginning of the sign is longer in VERY-GOOD than in the bare stem) – or to generate a telic verbal form (Wilbur, 2010) FLY > FLY-THERE, READ > READ-THROUGH (the hold at the end of the telic sign is longer than in the bare stem).

features are located together in the tree in the Inherent Features branch (i.e., selected fingers, major place of articulation), while ordered features, such as aperture and setting features, are found in a different place in the structure, called the Prosodic features. As we will see in Chapter 2, this is important for visual sonority and for establishing the basic prosodic unit of the system – the syllable.

We can use the information presented here as a basis to understand experimental evidence concerning phonological processing (Chapter 6), acquisition (Chapter 7), and variation (Chapter 8) since the units proposed in this section are studied and manipulated to investigate how sign language forms are accessed, retrieved, and acquired, and how they vary across time and dialects. This concludes the section on core vocabulary items. We now turn to the other two types of forms in the sign language lexicon.

1.4.2 The Spatial Lexicon

One part of the ASL lexicon consists of signs composed of several morphemes typically packaged around a movement, which functions as a verb; these are verbs of movement and location. They are found in the spatial lexicon (see Figure 1.3), and are called "classifier predicates," "depicting constructions," or "polycomponential forms." Current morpho-syntactic work is largely in agreement that the handshapes are morphemic, and often the linguistic status of a "light" form of the spatial verb is assigned morphological status as well, such as GO or BE-LOCATED (Gruber, 1965; Jackendoff, 1972). In sign languages these forms (unlike classifier forms of spoken languages) are readily augmented by iconic, potentially gestural demonstrations that are borrowed from the environment (Davidson, 2015). In Figure 1.11 we see a classifier predicate that means *two-people–hunched-go forward–carefully*, which is composed of at least three morphemes: (i) the index finger handshapes ($\substack{\text{\o}}$ = *person*); (ii) the path movement (linear path = *go forward*); and (iii) the non-manual expression (pressed together lips and squinted eyes = *carefully*). Other meaningful, potentially morphological, elements in this form may also be involved – e.g., the use of the two hands for the plural (in this case the dual; see Lepic et al., 2016) and the bent distal joint of the index fingers representing individuals that are hunched over. There have been several classification systems for these forms. Some follow the way the predicates behave semantically/syntactically and some have described them more in morphological terms. Here I follow a modified version of Engberg-Pedersen (1993) for handshapes and of Supalla (1982) and Wallin (1992) for movements.

Figure. 1.11   Polymorphemic classifier predicate meaning *two-people-hunched–go forward–carefully*. (Reprinted from *A Prosodic Model of Sign Language Phonology*, by Brentari, D., Copyright (1998), with permission from MIT.)

(3) *Handshape morphemes (affixes to the verbal movements, listed below)*

  a. **(O)bject classifiers:** handshape refers to a whole entity or part of an entity. Examples include:
    • *Semantic classifiers* **(SCLs)** – classes of objects (e.g., vehicles; upright beings);
    • *Whole entity classifiers* **(WECLs)** – whole objects (e.g., book, coin);
    • *Instrumental classifiers* **(ICLs)** – whole instruments (e.g., toothbrush, scissors); and
    • *Descriptive classifiers* **(DCLs)**, sometimes called *size and shape specifiers* **(SASS)** – whole or parts of objects defined primarily by their shape (e.g., bed or paper, which both use the same classifier in ASL to capture their properties of being *flat* and *rectangular*)

  b. **(H)andling classifiers**: handshape refers to the way that objects or instruments are held or manipulated (e.g., *grabbable-object*, such as a cup or bat; *flickable-object*, such as a page). Since objects can be manipulated by body parts other than the hands (tongues, teeth, etc.), we have expanded Engberg-Pedersen's system to include any part of the body that can manipulate objects, such as teeth or legs.

  c. **BodyPart (BP) classifiers**: handshape refers to a part of the body that is connected with the body of an animal or human (e.g., *head*, *legs*, *teeth*).

(4) *Movement Verbs*

  a. **MOTION/ACTIVE VERBS:** movement represents the movement of an object toward or from a specific point (e.g. *move* and *go*).

  b. **POSITION/CONTACT VERBS** (produced by a short downward movement of the hand): movement indicates the specific place where an object exists, but it neither represents the movement of an object nor describes the object (e.g., *be-located*).

c. **EXTENSION/STATIVE/SURFACE VERBS:** movement describes the limits or extension of an object or its location in space, but does not describe the movement of the object itself (e.g., *to be/exist as a flat surface object, to be/exist as individuals in a row, to be/exist as a square-shaped object*).

We will see in Chapter 5 (Figure 5.1) that when asked to produce descriptions of motion and location vignettes, non-signers can produce forms that look a lot like classifier predicates. The big difference between the forms in sign languages and their gestural cousins is their distribution and the role they play in the grammar. For example, these forms can be the only verb in a signed sentence, and they have syntactic features associated with them (Benedicto & Brentari, 2004). Also, the handshapes of these forms are built using the same, limited, phonological handshape inventory of a given language. For example, even if it might be iconically more accurate to allow for width to be expressed by the distinctions allowed by the four fingers (⬧ ⬧ ⬧ ⬧), some sign languages prefer not to use the three-finger form – ASL and DSGS among them (Eccarius, 2008) – and these languages use the three-finger handshape only rarely in the core vocabulary as well.

Recently, it has been proposed that classifier predicates can be both gestural and linguistic, employing a "gestural overlay" (Emmorey & Herzig, 2003). For example, Duncan (2005) describes how signers of Taiwanese Sign Language (TSL) each modified the handshape for the classifier for animals in TSL in a different way (two-finger+thumb handshape ⬧). To capture the fact that the animal under discussion, a cat, was climbing up the inside of a drainpipe, one signer held the three fingers straight while squeezing them together to represent the fact that the cat was squeezed inside the drainpipe. Another signer curved two of the fingers inward in order to show constricted space in the pipe. Duncan argues that the variability in how the signers captured the event is evidence that the modifications are gestural, but the selected fingers are not (i.e., they are morphophonological). These predicates will be central to our discussion in Chapter 4 of the gesture-language interface, and Chapter 5 on the emergence of phonology.

Classifier predicates are not always single prosodic words (Aronoff et al., 2003; more on this in Chapter 4 on Interfaces). For example, the articulation of both hands with aligned beginning and end times may indicate a prosodic word in some two-handed classifiers, as in the HKSL form *person-move-away-from rocket* (Figure 1.12, top), while others seem to be phrases, as seen in HKSL *put-apples-in basket,* where the

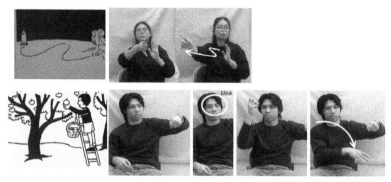

Figure 1.12   The timing of components of classifier constructions hints at constituent structure. From Hong Kong Sign Language: (top) the nondominant hand is stable throughout a two-handed classifier form produced by both hands simultaneously; (bottom) the two hands move in different ways, but the nondominant hand moves first, followed by a blink, and then the dominant hand moves in relation to it. (Reprinted from *Lingua*, 117, Eccarius, P. & Brentari, D., "Symmetry and Dominance: A cross-linguistic study of signs and classifier constructions," pp. 1169–1201, Copyright (2007), with permission from Elsevier.)

beginning and end times of the two hands are not aligned; one hand moves first (the one representing holding the basket's handle) and then remains stable, and then the other hand moves with respect to it (the one putting apples in the basket, Figure 1.12, bottom). There is often a blink between the first and second parts, which suggests that it is a phrase break.

In addition, if the Symmetry and Dominance Conditions discussed earlier in this chapter for two-handed core lexical items are applied to classifier predicates using the handshape features of the specific language, two-handed classifier forms conform to these constraints quite well; that is, when there are complex handshapes involved, one of the hands (the dominant hand) will bear more complexity than the other (nondominant) hand (Eccarius & Brentari, 2007).

Furthermore, despite their superficial similarities with the gestures that hearing people might produce, these forms are difficult for first- and second-language learners to acquire. They also show effects of incomplete acquisition in deaf individuals who are exposed to a sign language as a first language later in life (Newport, 1990; Meier & Newport, 1991).

1.4.3   The Non-native Lexicon: Fingerspelling, Mouthings, and the Foreign Component

The non-native or "foreign" lexicon (see Figure 1.3) includes forms borrowed from other sign languages and forms that include at least one letter of the manual alphabet via fingerspelling.

In this section we focus on fingerspelling, which, at first glance, seems as if it would be easy to describe. There are a limited number of twenty-six units (Figure 1.13 for ASL; Figure 1.14 for BSL), and they are strung together sequentially, one unit after another. Note that the twenty-six letters of the English script are represented in one-handed forms in ASL and in two-handed forms in BSL and the related languages Australian Sign Language (Auslan) and New Zealand Sign Language (NZSL).[12] Since fingerspelling in ASL and BSL is a representation of English orthography, fingerspelling is often thought to be solely a language-contact phenomenon. And as a contact phenomenon, it is noteworthy that all sign languages do not make extensive use of fingerspelling, even within communities of highly literate signers. Signers are bilingual in the ambient signed and written languages in many parts of the world, but not all exploit fingerspelling. While ASL and BSL heavily employ fingerspelling to create new signs and for many other discourse purposes, such as to express a difference in register or tone, many other sign languages – Italian Sign Language (LIS) and NGT among them – do not extensively use a manual alphabet but rather employ (mostly partial) "mouthings" of spoken words (Boyes Braem, 2001; Schermer, 1990, 2001).

Besides being a contact phenomenon, fingerspelling also provides a window into the structure of signs more broadly, as such forms become a part of the core lexicon over time via processes of lexicalization. The letters are not merely beads on a string. Even though ASL and BSL express the letters of the English alphabet in one- versus two-handed systems respectively, in both languages the individual handshapes representing the letters are influenced in systematic ways by the precise timing and configurations of adjacent forms. Battison (1978) proposed general principles about phonological representation based on observed surface forms, particularly lexicalized fingerspelled loan signs. One such general principle is that the number of handshapes and movements in a fingerspelled word is shaped by the preferred word shape of signs more generally. These are signs that originate as sequences of fingerspelled letters but over

---

[12] There is a single one-handed form in BSL fingerspelling, which is -C-.

Figure 1.13   The ASL manual alphabet laid out by Darren Stone and derived from the Gallaudet-TT font. (Distribution details of the font claim that it is copyright (c)1991 by David Rakowski but may be used for any purpose and redistributed freely. Image (cropped here and modified to fit) was created and released into the public domain by Ds13 via en. wikipedia.)

Figure 1.14   The BSL manual alphabet. ("British Sign Language Alphabet" was obtained from Wpclipart.com and is in the public domain. It has been modified to better fit the space.)

time have been modified to become more native-like. One example is the loan sign #BREAD, which changes from the five-letter sequence B-R-E-A-D 🖐️🤏✌️👆✊ to a rapidly repeating change from an open eight handshape to a closed eight ✊🖐️, which deletes the R-E-A and retains the open fingers of the -B- and the closed fingers for the -D-. This conforms to the SFC, discussed earlier, while still maintaining hints of the -B- in the extended nonselected fingers throughout the sign, and of the -D- by repeatedly producing contact between the thumb and middle finger with the index finger fully extended.

In lexicalized fingerspelled forms we also see a reduction in the number of movements as these forms change toward becoming mono-syllabic. In the ASL lexicon 83 percent of forms are monosyllabic and 17 percent are disyllabic (Brentari, 1998; cf. Stokoe et al., 1965), and we see this tendency in both compounds and lexicalized fingerspelled forms as they change over time. The partially nativized forms for #CLUB (BSL) and #SURE (ASL) are shown in Figure 1.15. In both forms the -U- unit has been deleted, and both have fewer movements than their fully fingerspelled forms.

Figure 1.15   Partially lexicalized fingerspelled forms in (top) BSL
C-L-U-B and (bottom) ASL S-U-R-E. (From "One hand or two?
Nativization of fingerspelling in ASL and BANZSL," by Cormier et al. in
Sign Language and Linguistics, 11:1, 2008. Reprinted with kind permission
from John Benjamins Publishing Company, Amsterdam/Philadelphia.
[www.benjamins.com].)

The most widely held view of how fingerspelling functions is captured by the dynamic model of fingerspelling (Wilcox, 1992), which describes the system as composed of not only postures (or holds), which are the typical handshapes (and orientations) that are seen represented on fingerspelling charts, but also of the transitions between postures. The coordination of transitions and postures is regulated at least in part by the signer's biomechanical system of articulator coordination, in a fashion that has been used to describe spoken language production in models such as Articulatory Phonology (Browman & Goldstein, 1992). These claims have been made specifically for one-handed fingerspelling systems, and there are a number of phenomena that have recently been described in these terms (Keane, 2014; Keane et al., 2015; Keane & Brentari, 2016). Two-handed systems, as shown in Figure 1.14 for BSL, appear to be coordinated in similar ways (Cormier et al., 2008).

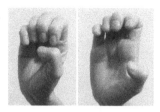

Figure 1.16   Closed -E- (left) and open -E- (right)

Coarticulation is widespread in fingerspelled forms, and the hand-shapes may have several variants, based on letters in the immediate context (Keane, 2014; Keane & Brentari, 2016). Coarticulation occurs in two-handed fingerspelling as well. For example, the letter -B- in BSL, Auslan, and NZSL has two variants: one as shown in Figure 1.14, where both hands have the O-handshape ⌘, and another not shown where both hands have the F-handshape ⌘. Cresdee and Johnston (2014) studied these two variants in Auslan to test a claim made by Auslan teachers that the F-hand variant is preferred by deaf signers while the O-hand variant is preferred by hearing signers. Out of 453 tokens of the fingerspelled letter -B- in the Auslan Corpus, Cresdee and Johnston found that the most common variant (in 74 percent of cases) was actually a combination of the O- and F-hand variants, seen in Figure 1.15 (top right). In many cases this was likely due to coarticulation; note that the nondominant (right) hand of the signer is fully open for the two handshapes prior to -B- in #CLUB, and then in the coarticulated form of -B-, the middle, ring, and pinky fingers remain open.

Sometimes changes in nativized forms enhance movement visibility as it moves from one fingerspelled handshape to another. This process can be understood as a type of phonological dissimilation between the two handshapes, not simply one of phonetic pressure. For example, there are two variants of the letter -E- in ASL fingerspelling: a closed and an open variant (Figure 1.16). Prescriptively, the closed -E- has been thought to be the citation form, but variation is systematic: closed -E- is more frequent at word edges (that is, the more canonical variant is preserved in highly prominent positions), and open -E- is more frequent when it immediately precedes a handshape that is completely closed, such as the sequence E-S. The open -E- serves to enhance the movement between the -E- and the following letter -S- through dissimilation, thereby increasing the visual salience of this change in handshape aperture. Fingerspelling will come up again in Chapter 7 on acquisition.

1.5 NEW THEORETICAL CONTRIBUTIONS TO SIGN LANGUAGE PHONOLOGY

Thus far in this chapter I have laid out how the field has established itself in the field of linguistics. Stepping back a bit to take a broader perspective on this domain of inquiry, we can see that our theories of sign phonology have tried to capture two types of pressures on a phonological system:

(1) The pressures of *efficiency* common to both signed and spoken languages, which include how the units of the system are organized to maximize the information conveyed, as well as ease of production, ease of perception, and the way that the strengths of the particular peripheral systems involved affect it.

(2) The *affordances of iconicity* that all languages exploit, but which sign languages exploit to a greater extent. Our bodies interact with the world in a whole host of interesting ways, and the way that iconicities affect the form-meaning correspondences of units in sign languages is an area that can contribute to our understanding of language more generally.

1.5.1 Optimality Theory

Within the last ten years there have been at least two approaches applied to sign language phonology that grapple with both of these issues mentioned above. Both have grown out of the interest in typological variation in languages, signed and spoken. I will briefly discuss two of these as they are currently being used to analyze sign language phonology: Optimality Theory and Cognitive Phonology. As a working definition for our purposes here, Optimality Theory (Prince & Smolensky, 1993; McCarthy, 2001; McCarthy & Prince, 1994, 1995; Flemming, 1995, 1996, 2017, to name just a few references) is an approach in which constraints are constructed for typologically diffuse processes across languages and applied in a simultaneous fashion, in order to map the ranking for a given language and to obtain patterns across languages. It takes for granted that there is a set of general tendencies against which any given language can be compared. There are four main families of constraints that have been proposed, and these will be taken up again in Chapter 5 on the emergence of phonology.

Edward Flemming (1995, 1996, 2002, 2017) was the first to develop a theory of DISPERSION constraints in spoken languages, and Eccarius (2008) applied this notion to sign languages. Since Dispersion Theory is relatively new, I want to add a few additional remarks that will help

ground our discussion. An explanatory account of phonological patterning must consider the system as a whole, and Dispersion Theory
does this. In its simplest form DISPERSION constraints express the
tendency of languages to increasingly elaborate contrasts of a given
type – "the more the merrier." This elaboration needs some kind of
organization, so naturally other constraints express how these forms
tend to be organized to maximize perception.

SYMMETRY constraints express the tendency for the sets of forms to
arrange themselves in parallel across the phonetic space. For example,
if back vowels have three heights (u,o,a) front vowels tend to have
three heights as well $(i,e,æ)$. For vowels, Trubetzkoy (2001:187) went so
far as to say, "I have never yet run across a system without
a symmetrical vowel system." All systems conform to a small number
of types and can always be represented by symmetrical schemes
(triangles, parallel rows, etc.).[13] An example of a DISPERSION constraint in sign languages is the relation between the joint values for
selected and nonselected fingers in classifiers handshapes. 🖐 represents small round objects, with contact between the thumb and index
finger, and 🖐 represents medium round objects, with a space
between the selected index finger and thumb. In both handshapes
the nonselected fingers assume the opposite value of the selected
fingers, and this relation between open and closed fingers in the
selected and nonselected fingers, respectively, maximizes perception
(Eccarius, 2008).

FAITHFULNESS constraints express the preference for forms to
remain stable across contexts. The pressure to be FAITHFUL can hold
on any phonological unit or property (feature, syllable, morpheme,
and even iconic properties). In ASL, for example, if fingerspelled forms
favored keeping all of the handshapes of the English word in their
canonical form, this would be adherence to FAITHFULNESS. The fact
that fingerspelled words often omit or change the handshapes are
ways that FAITHFULNESS is violated in the service of other types of
constraints, such as MARKEDNESS, discussed next. Moreover, the
degree of FAITHFULNESS to iconicity can vary across different types
of vocabulary items – foreign, core, and spatial. This will be discussed
in Chapter 3 on iconicity.

MARKEDNESS constraints ensure that phonological strings are perceptually intelligible and articulatorily efficient. In ASL, the SFC

---

[13] There are, naturally, exceptions to this, those that have an abundance of sounds
concentrated in one place, requiring secondary places of articulation as Tamil
does, with retroflex ʈ/ɖ, and dental t̪/d̪.

mentioned earlier in this chapter is an example of a MARKEDNESS constraint insofar as it captures a preference of selected fingers to spread across an entire sign. When there are two handshapes in a word (e.g., in a compound), diachronic change favors the SFC. Having one value for selected fingers (rather than many) aids in both ease of articulation and ease of perception.

CORRESPONDENCE or ALIGNMENT constraints describe how different types of units align with one another temporally. For example, in the default case in spoken languages, the edges of morphemes and edges of syllables are aligned. On the left edge of the words *in.#tolerant, dis.#pleasure,* and *un.#characteristic* all prefixes and stems are aligned with syllable boundaries, but on the right edge we see violations: *begi. n#ing, book#s.,* and *tolera.t#ed* all have misalignment of syllables and morphemes. In ASL we can trace a tendency over time toward alignment between a single prosodic word and a single syllable in compounds.

1.5.2 Cognitive and Usage-Based Approaches

Cognitive Phonology is another more recent development in phonological theory, and this approach takes the view that iconic constructions are one way that a lexicon expands its vocabulary (Wilcox & Occhino, 2016; Occhino, 2017). Crosslinguistic studies on spoken languages have suggested that, contrary to the notion that words are purely arbitrary distributions of phonological content, sign languages often exhibit systematic and regular phonological and sub-phonological patterns of form-meaning mappings (Välimaa-Blum, 2005). In an investigation of phoneme distribution in ASL and Brazilian Sign Language (LIBRAS), the claw-5 handshape was analyzed for whether the handshape contributed to the overall meaning of the sign (Occhino, 2017). The results showed that the claw-5 handshape is not randomly distributed across the lexicon but clusters around six form-meaning patterns: convex-concave, unitary elements, non-compact matter, hand-as-hand, touch, and interlocking. These iconic relationships were argued to be at the feature level. In Embodied Cognitive Phonology "arbitrariness" is but one possible outcome from the process of emergence and schematization of phonological content, and arbitrariness exists alongside "motivation" as a legitimate state of linguistic units of all sizes of complexity. Since language is dynamic, these states are not fixed but are in continuous flux, as language users reinvent and reinterpret form and meaning over time.

These approaches of Optimality Theory and Cognitive Phonology need not be in conflict, since they address different dimensions of phonology. Optimality Theory concerns what used to be called the "rule" system of the grammar, elegance in the distribution of form. Cognitive Phonology is more concerned with the clustering of form-meaning mapping in the lexicon. Each can contribute to our understanding of a phonological system.

1.6 SUMMARY

This chapter has provided a glimpse of why sign languages differ from gesture and from speech in terms of their phonological systems. The historical roots and state of the art in the field of sign language phonology have also been described, in part so that it is clear how much has been accomplished cumulatively over the last sixty years. The material covered in this chapter will appear again in future chapters as we address phonological processing, acquisition, the emergence of phonology, and variation.

This book will be a means to describe the current state of the field, but also by looking at the questions addressed here, we will see how sign language evidence has had an impact on the field of phonology as a whole and on the way we view the nature of language. The emergence of phonology also gives a glimpse into how complexity is built up, and where the rupture between nonlinguistic gestural form and sign language phonological structure occurs. Reflections about the ways that mechanisms such as phonetic factors, historical change, and group identity interact with the phonology can have an impact on the study of spoken languages as well. Definitions of constituents and the work on phonological processing and neuroimaging allow us to see how the mind treats phonology as an abstract system, rather than simply as an extension of the networks for the peripheral systems that are engaged. In other words, work on sign languages puts all the work on spoken languages in a new light.

1.7 FURTHER READING

Battison, R. (1978). *Lexical Borrowing in American Sign Language*. Silver Spring, MD: Linstok Press. Reprinted 2003, Burtonsville, MD: Sign Media, Inc.
Brentari, D. (1998). *A Prosodic Model of Sign Language Phonology*. MIT Press.

Fenlon, J., K. Cormier, & D. Brentari. The phonology of sign languages. (2017). In S.J. Hannahs and A. Bosch (eds.), *Routledge Handbook of Phonological Theory* (pp. 453–475). New York: Routledge.

Sandler, W. & Lillo-Martin, D. (2006). *Sign Language and Linguistic Universals.* Cambridge/New York: Cambridge University Press.

Stokoe, W. (1960). *Sign Language Structure: An Outline of the Visual Communication Systems of the American Deaf.* Buffalo, NY: University of Buffalo. (Occasional Papers 8).

van der Hulst, H. & van der Kooij, E. (in press). Phonological structure of signs: Theoretical perspectives. In J. Quer, R. Pfau & A Herrmann (eds.), *The Routledge Handbook of Theoretical and Experimental Sign Language Research.* London: Routledge.

2 Modality Effects

Abstract

There are numerous differences between signed and spoken languages due to the different communication modalities they use, but which ones actually matter for phonology? In this chapter, a range of differences will be laid out: environmental ones, those that depend on the signal, and those related to phonetic and phonological forms. Through the course of this discussion we will see that, despite the major differences between the visual-gestural and auditory-vocal systems used in the two types of languages, many of the same abstract mechanisms are employed by signed and spoken languages.

2.1 WHY IS COMMUNICATION MODALITY SO IMPORTANT?

In Chapter 1, some of the aspects of sign and spoken language phonological structure were described. To be sure, the phonetic content is different between the two modalities even if phonological constituents have similar labels and perform similar functions. The present chapter takes up the question of which differences between signed and spoken languages are potentially due to the communication modality. Communication modality encompasses the signal, articulatory, and perceptual systems, and their potential effects on phonological form. Others have addressed this question previously, notably Newport and Supalla (2000), Brentari (2002), Crasborn (2012), and Meier (2002a, 2012). I draw upon their insights here, as well as add new observations on this theme. Iconicity is a special kind of modality difference, which will have a more detailed treatment in the next chapter.

It will come as no surprise that there are several differences in signal, articulatory systems, and perceptual systems employed by signed and spoken languages. Some, but not all, of these differences have an effect on the phonological systems of these two language types. An important caveat about this discussion (also noted in Crasborn, 2012) is that while the topics in this chapter will be presented as if spoken languages were completely auditory and sign languages completely visual, this is not, strictly speaking, accurate. As emphasized in Chapter 1, the correct comparison between signed and spoken languages ought to be speech + gesture versus sign + gesture (Goldin-Meadow & Brentari, 2017), where speech and sign are both the linguistic aspects of the signal, and gestures are the unconscious additions of *other* aspects of communication on the hands, face, and body in both types of language (Schlenker, 2018).

There is also evidence that spoken languages are perceived visually, as well as auditorily, and in many different ways. Visual cues in spoken languages include emotional states that are visible on the face (Ekman, 1993; Herrmann & Pendzich, 2014), as well as many interactional cues expressed by a wide variety of head movements (McClave, 2000), eyeblinks (Hömke et al., 2017), and torso leans (Wilbur & Patschke, 1998). McGurk and MacDonald (1976) showed that the visible state of the face can influence the auditory perception of consonants; the "McGurk effect" showed irrefutably that listeners who hear /ba/ and see /ga/ (with no lip closure) perceive an intermediate form /da/. Krahmer and Swerts (2007) demonstrated that the degree of prominence in production and perception increases when the accented spoken syllable is accompanied by a beat gesture. More recently, Schlenker (2018) argues that gestures influence the sentential meaning in spoken languages. In other words, manual gestures are known to serve many functions that complement the content of the spoken (and signed) utterances (McNeill, 1992; Emmorey et al., 1999; Kendon, 2004). Nonetheless, for simplicity, the rest of this chapter unfolds as if speech were completely auditory-vocal.

Some differences in the signal, phonetic, and phonological systems are provided in Table 2.1 (cf. Brentari, 2002; Meier, 2002a). The upper portion describes effects related to the signal itself, the middle portion discusses some effects in phonetics (perception and production), and the bottom portion lists some phonological consequences of modality. Terms such as "bandwidth" and "oscillator" will be discussed in the subsequent sections where they are addressed in detail.

Table 2.1 *Differences between signed and spoken languages at the level of the signal, phonetic system, and phonological system (cf. Meier, 2002a)*

Sign languages	Spoken languages
Signal differences	
Light source external to the signer	Sound source internal to the speaker
Sign articulators are directly visible to the "listener"	Speech articulators are largely hidden from the listener
Light travels relatively quickly	Sound travels relatively slowly
High "bandwidth"	Low "bandwidth"
Phonetic/peripheral system differences	
Central vs. peripheral vision	Foregrounded vs. backgrounded sounds
Sign articulators are paired	Speech articulators are not paired
Sign articulation is not coupled to respiration	Speech is coupled to respiration
Sign articulators are large	Speech articulators are small
There is no predominant oscillator	The mandible is the predominant oscillator
Phonological differences	
Morphophonemic interface – feature	Morphophonemic interface – segment, syllable
No Sonority Sequencing Principle	Sonority Sequencing Principle
Word shape – tendency towards monosyllabic/ polymorphemic forms	Word shape – languages differ with regard to their syllable-to-morpheme ratio in words

2.2 SIGNAL DIFFERENCES

Regarding the external, nonlinguistic, communicative context, let us first focus on the source of the signal. The light source in sign languages may come from artificial or natural sources, but it is always external to the body and not entirely under our control. By contrast, the sound source is internal to the speaker and at least in part under the control of the speaker. For example, if the light is dim we cannot change that by changing something expressed by our bodies, while with speech we can control the sound source of speech with our lungs and vocal chords. Of course, loudness also depends on articulatory effort, which will be addressed later in the chapter.

In addition, the articulators in sign languages are directly visible, while the articulators in speech have to be inferred indirectly. For example, when the hands assume a particular shape we can see all moments of the articulatory process, while when the tongue assumes a particular shape we cannot. Listeners have to infer what is happening with the articulators of their interlocutors because they are contained within the body.

How does the visual or auditory signal offer different advantages and disadvantages in constructing phonological units? We consider several relevant factors here. Speed is one factor. Light travels much faster than sound: in a vacuum light travels at 186,000 miles per second (Redd, 2012), while sound travels relatively slowly, 1 mile in approximately 4.7 seconds (or 1,089 feet per second). This affects spatial processing because we can locate objects auditorily by the Doppler effect (Strutt & Williams, 1896), using the time between a sound and its echo (Bregman, 1990), while in vision the location and shape of objects are visible via direct and reflected light at virtually the same time.

On the dimension of complex scene analysis, there are two types of processing: vertical (simultaneous, parallel) processing, when information of different kinds is taken in at the same time, where the advantage goes to vision due to bandwidth; and horizontal (sequential, serial) processing, when information about a scene is presented sequentially, where the advantage goes to audition because of temporal resolution (Bregman, 1990; Meier, 1993, 2002a). However, processing involves detection and identification, and the time required for a subject to *detect* a single auditory or visual stimulus differs from the *identification* of that stimulus. The time required for the higher-order task of recognition, or labeling, of a stimulus, called "threshold of identification," is roughly the same in both vision and audition – approximately 20 ms (Hirsch & Sherrick, 1961). At the level of detection, however, auditory and visual stimuli are processed differently. Humans can detect two individual auditory stimuli, such as chirps (or temporally "resolve" them), when they are separated by an interval of only 2 ms (Green, 1971; Kohlrausch et al., 1992), while it takes closer to a 20-millisecond interval to resolve two visual stimuli, such as light flashes. Moreover, how large a "just noticeable difference" is going to be also depends a great deal on the acoustic region of the frequency of the sound: We discriminate very minimal difference in frequency when the sounds are relatively low, and we discriminate minimal difference in loudness when the sounds are relatively loud.

For signed and spoken language only a portion of the total spectrum of frequencies humans can detect in vision or audition, respectively, is used for language. Rhythmic structure and word/sign comprehension seem to use different frequencies in sign language. For rhythm, studies of "neural entrainment" demonstrate that low frequencies are important for spoken language and for sign language; while they are different in the two types of language, they are at the lower range (<8 Hz). Entrainment studies show that when people listen to connected speech (Giraud & Poeppel, 2012) or watch signs in a narrative (Brookshire et al., 2017), low-frequency oscillations in the cerebral cortex become aligned or "entrained" to quasi-rhythmic fluctuations in speech or sign volume (i.e., loudness). Visual motion in sign language is modulated at lower frequencies than auditory volume in spoken language, and this difference is consistent with the slower movements in the articulators for sign (the hands) vs. the faster movements of the articulators for speech (the vocal tract). Hwang (2011) has demonstrated that signed syllables are slower than spoken syllables but still within the range of cortical entrainment for speech. Entrainment is discussed with regard to syllable structure in Chapter 6.

The total frequency range for sound in humans is 16 Hz to 32 kHz – approximately the lowest to the highest note on a piano. For speech we use only ~100 Hz to 6 kHz, less than 20 percent of the total range. Within that rather broad range, different frequencies are used for different classes of sound and may also be used at different phases of acoustic processing (Poeppel & Idsardi, 2011). Similarly, only a portion of the visual frequencies that humans can perceive is used for sign language; color recognition is not as important as luminance or spatial frequency for sign languages.[1] It is the high spatial frequencies that are important for word recognition in sign languages because discriminating signs requires relatively fine visual details of shape and space. Bosworth et al. (2003) describe the situation as follows:

> The spatial properties of patterns and scenes can be quantified using a Fourier analysis as the amount (or "amplitude") of luminance contrast as a function of spatial frequency contained in the image as a whole. Spatial frequency is defined as the number of cycles of light and dark variations across space. Low spatial frequencies (e.g., 2 cycles per degree of visual angle) make up the large, coarse portions of an object (e.g., the global shape of a tree), whereas high spatial frequencies (e.g., 20 cycles

---

[1] The frequency range for color is 400–800 THz (1 × 1012 hertz = 1 terahertz; Starr, 2005).

per degree) make up the small, detailed portions of an object (like the individual leaves on the tree). When an image of a scene becomes blurry, only low spatial frequencies remain, and the fine detail that is lost is the high spatial frequencies.

Sign recognition was reduced drastically when high spatial frequencies were filtered from the image in an experiment by Riedl and Sperling (1988), and ASL sign comprehension is impaired when a screen that degrades high-frequency information is placed in front of a signer (Naeve et al., 1992) or when high-spatial-frequency spatial noise is introduced (Sperling, 1980). We see therefore that just as in speech where a portion of the auditory information is more useful for discrimination, in sign language, comprehension relies mainly on just a portion of the visual information available, namely the higher-spatial-frequency information.

2.3 PHONETIC DIFFERENCES: PERCEPTION

We now turn to how being deaf, or having general experience with a sign language, interacts with perception and how the body's peripheral systems interact with phonology to affect the shape of signs.

Experimental studies since the late 1980s with native signers (both deaf and hearing children of deaf signing parents or family members) have suggested that daily sign language use, and sometimes deafness itself, may improve or alter visual perception in a variety of ways, both linguistic and nonlinguistic. Neville and Lawson (1987a,1987b, and 1987c) conducted the first event-related potential (ERP) experiments and found that peripheral vision is affected by deafness and sign language experience when they tested three groups: deaf native signers, hearing native signers (CODAs), and hearing non-signers. Dye et al. (2009) followed up on these studies with four groups: deaf and hearing adults divided into signer and non-signer groups. The Dye et al. study refined the type of targeted visual skill to the useful field of vision (UFOV) and required participants to divide attention between central and peripheral locations while also selecting a target from among distractors. It is a demanding task, requiring not only central visual attention but also attention to the periphery and visual selection. Deaf adults required 43–58 ms of display presentation to perform at 79 percent correct, whereas hearing adults required significantly more time – 60–79 ms to achieve the same accuracy. The type of enhancement found for all deaf participants suggests that the effect is the result of early, severe-profound loss of audition rather than use of a sign language, since the effect was seen in both deaf signers and non-signers, with little contribution from signing experience.

Sign language experience is important in other ways. For example, it appears to enhance visual skills that are used grammatically even when they are implicated in nonlinguistic tasks. Deaf and hearing native signers have been shown to possess enhanced or altered perceptual abilities in motion processing (Bosworth & Dobkins, 1999), mental rotation (Emmorey, Kosslyn, & Bellugi, 1993), and processing of properties of facial expression (McCullough & Emmorey, 1997). These abilities are required for sign language comprehension as well as for nonlinguistic activities.

Sign language experience has also been found to alter how linguistically relevant visual stimuli are perceptually categorized, and these issues will be discussed further in Chapter 6 on processing. For example, as was mentioned briefly in Chapter 1 with regard to developing a set of phonological features for ASL, Poizner (1983) found that signers perceive moving patterns in such a way that reflects various phonological categories in ASL. Even though this task did not require any language processing, the signers' judgments were aligned with characteristics of various types of lexical and inflectional movement, while the non-signers' judgments were not. Poizner inferred that these perceptual categories were based upon features of linguistic salience for ASL signers and perceptual salience for non-signers, supporting the notion that language experience can alter perceptual processing more generally.

Categorical perception (CP) studies have also shown a number of differences between signers and non-signers in ASL (Emmorey et al., 2003; Baker, Idsardi, Golinkoff, & Petitto, 2005; Baker, Golinkoff, & Petitto, 2006; Best et al., 2010; Sehyr & Cormier, 2015), in various populations of first- and second-language learners of ASL (Morford et al., 2008; Best et al., 2010), and recently in Hong Kong Sign Language (Zhao et al., 2017). Over recent years, CP for speech has been shown to be unique neither to humans (Kuhl & Miller, 1975) nor to speech sounds (Cutting & Rosner, 1974). CP will be discussed in more detail in Chapter 6 on processing for sign languages, and see Harnad (1987) for a thorough treatment of these issues for speech.

Other types of phonological perception have been studied, which address sensitivity to specific aspects of phonological structure. In a study of long-distance, coarticulatory effects comparing speech and sign language, Grosvald and Corina (2012a, 2012b) investigated the ability of English speakers and ASL signers to perceive "colored" (altered) productions of a neutral value in English and ASL, respectively. In English the neutral vowel [ə] undergoes such coloring, which is perceived more [i]-like or more [a]-like based on preceding vowels (1). *To, at,* and *a* are English words containing a schwa, which can be perceived in these ways.

(1) *English stimuli varying the distance between a full vowel and [ə] coloration*

    a. *It's fun tə* (distance 3) *look up ət* (distance2) *ə* (distance1) **key** (trigger vowel [i])

    b. *It's fun tə* (distance 3) *look up ət* (distance2) *ə* (distance1) **car** (trigger vowel [a]).

In ASL, a parallel case that might be susceptible to "schwa-coloring" is so-called neutral space, which can be perceived [high] or [low] in a differing number of signs preceding HAT [trigger location is high, articulated on the head) vs. PANTS [trigger location is low, articulated near the waist) (2).

(2) *ASL stimuli varying the distance between a high and low POA trigger in ASL*

    Triggering word: **HAT** (high)

    a. (3 signs distance) **WANT** (signed in neutral space) GO FIND **HAT** (trigger on head, high)

    b. (2 signs distance) **WANT** FIND **HAT** (trigger on head, high)

    c. (1 sign distance) **WANT HAT** (trigger on head, high)

    Triggering word: **PANTS** (low)

    d. (3 signs distance) **WANT** (signed in neutral space) GO FIND **PANTS** (trigger at waist, low)

    e. (2 signs distance) **WANT** FIND **PANTS** (trigger at waist, low)

    f. (1 sign distance) **WANT PANTS** (trigger at waist, low)

The experiment with native English speakers showed that they were sensitive to schwa coloring at above-chance levels even when the triggering vowel – /i/ versus /a/ – was two or three syllables away from the trigger. The sign task was more difficult for both signer and non-signer participants watching ASL, even in the condition with a single preceding sign. No single factor could explain this cross-modality difference, and it is clear that more work is needed to tease apart perception of coarticulation in sign languages.

In sign languages, the addressee must look at the person signing to them and the articulators are completely visible; therefore, we might expect that these facts might affect the distribution of features according to how they are organized with respect to the body. Siple (1978) proposed that "central" vision in the signing space is the area of the lower face and neck. This allows for an interlocutor to have the whole face and upper torso within this zone of higher perceptual acuity. The distribution of signs in the central versus peripheral signing space was investigated in both ASL and BSL corpora. Marked and unmarked hand-shapes appear to take this fact into account. (For signs produced on the body; neutral space was excluded.) In both ASL (Battison, 1978) and BSL (Fenlon et al., 2014b) signs with a "marked" handshape (i.e., less frequent handshapes with more complex phonological representations, such as ⛷ or 🖐) were more frequently produced at the head and neck (76 percent; 286/376) – Siple's central areas of visual acuity – than at the trunk and arm. Similarly, 81.7 percent (517/633) of BSL signs produced at the head and neck are one-handed compared to 59.9 percent (169/282) produced at the trunk and arm. And, comparing one-handed and two-handed, Type 1 signs (e.g., BSL NAME and PAPER, see Figure 1.4), one-handed signs are much more likely to occur in the head and neck than two-handed Type 1 signs. Siple (1978) suggested that more redundancy is needed in the signal in areas of lower acuity; therefore, for two-handed Type 1 signs produced on the trunk, having both hands behave in an identical fashion in the periphery of the addressee's vision provides more information to help identify the sign.

These observations suggest that the distribution of some phonological features have their origins in perception. One could imagine a MARKEDNESS constraint within an Optimality Theoretic framework (as discussed at the end of Chapter 1) to address this distribution of form based on ease of perception.

2.4 PHONETIC DIFFERENCES: ARTICULATION

One obvious major difference in articulation between sign and speech is that, as you may already know, some signs utilize a second, identical POA or articulator on the opposite side of the body. That is to say, there are two hands and arms that can move, and many of the passive POAs are in pairs – eyes, cheeks, shoulders, etc. Another major difference between signing and speaking is that unlike speech, signing need not be coordinated with respiration, nor with effects due to the exchange between air pressure and the vocal folds, such as the Bernoulli effect.[2] In sign language, the body recalibrates at the end of phonological constituents, but not necessarily via the breath: the hands and body

---

[2] Positive air pressure from the lungs forces the vocal folds open, but the high velocity air across the vocal folds produces a lowered pressure, which brings them back together.

may relax, or become lower in signing space, but while signing, breathing can continue in a physiological rhythm, not tied to the linguistic string. Anecdotally, one of the hardest habits to break for hearing people who are learning to sign is to stop taking a big breath before starting a signed utterance.

In speech, ease of articulation focuses on issues concerning speed of onset, offset, and of the achievement of desired goals in the active articulators of the tongue, primarily, but also the lips, the velum, and the glottis. Slower transitions in starting or stopping these articulators, or undershoot, are typical effects of ease of articulation. In sign languages, ease of articulation can take many forms as well and operate on similar principles, which we describe in more detail in this section.

The major articulators of sign language are larger and heavier than those of speech. The sheer weight of the articulators might therefore cause a gradual drop of hands and arms through discourse – lower and lower in the signing space. This phenomenon is known as "sign lowering" (Tyrone & Mauk, 2010; Grosvald & Corina, 2012a, 2012b; Mauk &Tyrone, 2012), but it does not seem to be exclusively associated with the pull of gravity. In work by Mauk and Tyrone, they found that during fast signing, signs that were high in the signing space (e.g., FATHER, signed on the forehead) were sometimes lowered in a low-phonetic environment (e.g., RIGHT, signed in neutral space), but there was also the tendency for signs that are produced low in the signing space (e.g., PICTURE, signed in neutral space) to be raised when they were produced in a high-phonetic environment (e.g., SEE, signed at the forehead), and the raising effect was even stronger than the lowering effect. This is unexpected if gravity is the main factor driving this type of coarticulation, and is, in part, the motivation for experiments such as those on "schwa coloring" in ASL by Grosvald & Corina (2012a, 2012b) discussed in the previous section on perception.

Following this line of inquiry further, a recent study of passive articulator movement was conducted on the locations of the forehead, chin, and torso (Tyrone & Mauk, 2016) – namely, the points of contact of signs. Mauk and Tyrone noted that these locations on the body used as points of contact should not be thought of solely as static targets, since even as the hands are the primary articulators in the sign modality, articulatory targets on the head and body can (and do) move around as signs are being produced. As a result, different signs are likely to have different motoric demands, depending on which articulators' movements must be coordinated. The main finding of this study suggests that the forehead and the chin showed larger movement amplitudes during signs with a lexical movement toward these

HARD (elbow movement)   HARD (wrist movement)-distalized

Figure 2.1 (left) Typical production of the ASL sign HARD with elbow movement; (right) the distilized form produced by a signer with Parkinson's disease with wrist movement. (Reprinted from *A Prosodic Model of Sign Language Phonology*, by Brentari, D., Copyright (1998), with permission from MIT.)

locations (e.g., SICK, DISAPPOINTED). By contrast, these articulators moved much less when the chin and forehead were POAs but the lexical movement was not toward the location (e.g., BLACK with the movement across forehead but not directed toward the forehead) or during transitional movements between signs. In addition, the torso did not move to facilitate contact with the hand for torso-located signs, even to a moderate degree, irrespective of the type of manual movement (i.e., lexical or transitional). These findings suggest that all sign locations on the body and head should not be viewed as equally static in models of sign language phonology.

With regard to the issue of articulatory stability of the hands in coordination with the body, two studies by Sanders and Napoli (2016a, b) examined the lexical items in dictionaries of a sample of twenty-four sign languages. They found that movements that allow for more stability of the torso with less effort – e.g., rocking back-and-forth or from side-to-side – were favored in these sign languages' lexicons over signs that would require more effort to retain articulatory stability – e.g., twisting movements.

Coordination of the motor plan has noticeable consequences in signing that is impaired by Parkinson's Disease. Movements are produced by the more distal joints (those further away from the center of the body) instead of the more proximal joints (those closer to the center of the body). The phonetic patterns of signing associated with Parkinson's disease have been shown to favor ease of articulation and simplification of the motor plan (Brentari & Poizner, 1994; Poizner et al., 2000). A sign such as HARD will therefore be produced by the wrist, rather than by the elbow and shoulder (Figure 2.1). One could imagine that the type of coordinated movement of passive and active articulators found in Sanders and Napoli (2016a, 2016b) and Tyrone and Mauk (2016) might be affected by Parkinson's disease as well.

2.5 COMPLEXITY

It is difficult for different branches of research to agree on what complexity means and how it affects phonological form. Articulatory complexity (Taylor & Schwartz, 1955; Ann, 1993, 2006), order of acquisition (Boyes Braem, 1981; Marentette & Mayberry, 2000), and informational complexity (Hara, 2003) are independent measures of complexity. Most of the time these measures converge; that is, there are few instances of frequent handshapes that are articulatorily complex, or vice versa, and infrequent handshapes that are relatively simple. It would be expected that signs with greater articulatory complexity might be more difficult to acquire, either during first- or second-language acquisition, and generally be less frequent across sign languages in much the same way that consonants in spoken language with complex articulation (e.g., /ʎ/ in Italian or retroflex /ɹ /in English) are more difficult to acquire than consonants with simple contact, such as /t/. Studies addressing complexity in sign languages are still quite sparse, and I will discuss them in the following sections.

2.5.1 Articulatory Complexity

Articulatory complexity concerns how much effort is involved in producing phonological forms, but it is extremely difficult to quantify this, particularly for speech or sign articulators, because a number of articulators are involved simultaneously and the relative differences among different levels of complexity would be very small. Impossible gestures are, well, impossible, so they are not on any scale that we could construct. For example, fingers cannot be abducted (spread 🖐) and flexed (closed at the knuckles 🖐) at the same time (Ann, 1993, 2006).

For the articulation of handshape, each finger (index, middle, ring, pinky, and thumb) can be flexed at each of three joints: the metacarpophalangeal (MCP), proximal interphalangeal (PIP), and distal interphalangeal (DIP) joints. Each finger pair can be spread (opened, abduction) or closed (adduction) independently from its neighbor. In addition, the thumb can be independently abducted or adducted at the carpo-metacarpal joint (CM).

Most of the joints can be configured independently by combining muscle activity that extends or flexes each finger, but typically the fingers have the same joint configuration. In their description of the physiology of the hand, physiologists of hand mechanics Taylor and Schwartz (1955) offer several possible reasons why certain handshapes might be infrequent in sign languages, while not specifically addressing sign languages in this work. There is a tendency for the fingers to open or close together, so the B-handshape ⟨image⟩ and S-handshape ⟨image⟩ are easier to produce than handshapes with some fingers flexed and others extended.

This is captured by the Prosodic model as *unified* joint features (for handshapes such as ⟨image⟩) versus *individuated* joint features for handshapes such as ⟨image⟩. In addition, there is a tendency for the DIP and PIP joints to almost always assume the same configuration when the finger is not pressed against a rigid body. Whitworth (2011) showed that PIP flexion alone predicts 85 percent of DIP flexion.

With regard to abduction (spreading), the W-handshape ⟨image⟩ is relatively infrequent in many sign languages (German, British, American, Italian, Swiss German, to name a few), while ⟨image⟩ is relatively frequent in some sign languages (Hong Kong Sign Language is one of them; Eccarius, 2008). This may be because, except for abductors on the thumb and pinky fingers, the intrinsic muscles of the other fingers are specialized for closing (rather than spreading) the fingers, so spreading is more difficult in ⟨image⟩ than in ⟨image⟩.

Moving to the forearm and associated joints of the wrist and elbow, which act together to change the orientation of the hand, there are certain movements of the hand that are associated with certain movements of the forearm. Taylor and Schwartz (1955) note that closing the hand (flexion) facilitates supination of the forearm, as in the ASL sign GRAB-OPPORTUNITY. The opposite is also true of opening the hand (extension), which facilitates pronation of the wrist, as in one of the ASL signs for 'weekend', glossed as SATURDAY-SUNDAY. Other facilitative movements include facilitated wrist extension when there is full flexion of the hand; i.e., the wrist pulls back as the fist closes, as in the emphatic form of ASL Y-E-S (noted by Mandel, 1981). Forward movement of the forearm facilitates flexion (nodding) of the wrist, as in ASL SEND. These tendencies have yet to be studied across various sign language lexicons systematically to determine their utility in constructing a lexicon and in constructing phonological constraints.

2.5.2 Frequency as Complexity

Complexity can be effectively calculated as frequency, determining the amount of information in a particular form (Goldsmith, 2001). The informational complexity score is calculated by taking the negative log of a given probability (E). The higher the resulting number, the higher the information content, or complexity, and the lower the probability or frequency of the form (3).

(3)   Information (X) = –log2 Probability(E)

For example, in spoken Japanese, /t/ is the most frequent consonant, and therefore the least complex, while /u/ is the least frequent vowel and therefore the most complex. Complexity calculated this way is language specific, and it is in accord with work on perception and neighborhood density (see Chapter 5 on processing) because one can access forms containing less frequent units faster than more frequent ones, because more frequent forms reside in a denser phonological neighborhood (Goldinger et al., 1989). Hara (2003) shows that in ASL the B-handshape ✋ is the most frequent and therefore the least complex and a bent H-handshape ✊ the least frequent and therefore the most complex, based on the *Dictionary of American Sign Language* (Stokoe et al., 1965). Hara also performed the same analysis on Japanese Sign Language (JSL), finding the same result regarding the least complex handshape, ✋, and a different result for the most complex handshape, ✊, based on the dictionary of JSL published by Japan Institute for Sign Language Studies (1997). Frequency measures of complexity can be cross-referenced with measures of articulatory complexity with a relatively high degree of correlation; however, there are also a few handshapes that are complex from the point of view of frequency and that are not very complex articulatorily. In ASL the L-handshape 👆 is relatively high in complexity-as-frequency because it appears relatively rarely; likewise, JSL 👆 is relatively high in complexity-as-frequency for the same reason. Neither of these handshapes is highly complex phonetically or phonologically.

2.5.3 Complexity as Expressed by Order of Acquisition

Often, the order of acquisition also is a factor in considering handshape complexity because it is assumed that the earliest acquired handshapes would be the least complex and thus provide an independent measure. Handshape acquisition has been argued to have four stages, shown in Figure 7.3. Stage I includes the index finger ☝, all fingers 🖐, and the thumb alone 👍, along with the joint values for fully open (extended) and fully closed (flexed). Contact is also present at Stage I. Stage II is when young children use the selected versus nonselected fingers correctly in signs: 🖐, which uses the thumb and index fingers as selected fingers and the nonselected fingers are extended, versus 🖐, which uses the same selected fingers and flexed nonselected fingers. Stage III adds the rest of the selected finger groups, and Stage IV adds the rest of the joint configurations. Complexity in acquisition will be discussed further in Chapter 7.

2.5.4 Complexity as Expressed by Phonological Structure

Aristodemo (2013) conducted a study of handshape complexity in Italian Sign Language (LIS) based on phonological structure as proposed in the Prosodic model (Brentari, 1998), whereby the sum of specified nodes and features determines complexity. She found that the model predicts judgments of complexity quite well, and they conclude that the Prosodic model accurately reflects articulatory complexity. Deaf and hearing participants responded differently to curved handshapes, which are quite complex in the Prosodic model: hearing participants judged them to be high complexity, but Deaf participants did not. Thus, in addition to articulatory complexity, other factors may influence complexity judgments, such as frequency.

In summary, one can see that complexity can be understood and measured along different dimensions. Phonetic articulation (joint and muscular involvement), the abstract representation of articulation in phonology (features and association lines), the order of acquisition, and frequency of form are all independent ways of considering complexity. In future work one could imagine teasing apart the contexts in which these different types of complexity most evidently exert their power.

2.6 PROMINENCE: SINGLE VERSUS MULTIPLE OSCILLATORS

A great deal of the work on prominence in the metrical system is available on spoken languages, beginning at the level of the syllable and building into larger and larger prosodic units: see Hyman (1985) and Itô (1986) for the syllable; Halle and Vergnaud (1987) and Idsardi (1992) for the phonological word and the foot; and Beckman 2011 for the phrase.

Iskarous and Goldstein (2018) have studied the consequences of articulator oscillation throughout the metrical system of spoken languages. Rhythmic units such as the syllable may, in both speech and

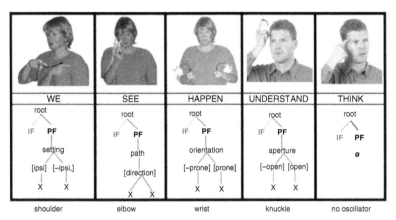

Figure 2.2   The joints of the arm that generate movements in sign
languages, from largest (shoulder) to smallest (hand) with their associated phonological features (Brentari, 1998). If the representation has
no movements specified, a short, straight epenthetic movement is
inserted (far right). Image based on Brentari, 2011

sign, be a way to coordinate the oscillation of articulatory movements;
however, the motor underpinnings of syllables appear to be quite
different in sign and speech. The mandible is the primary oscillator
in speech, and it is associated with peaks in prominence along with
articulatory force (MacNeilage and Davis, 1993; MacNeilage, 2008). In
ASL, the joints of the arm and hand, and movements of the head and
body, can function independently as movement oscillators (Meier
et al., 2008) . None is the "primary articulator" and as a result signed
syllables have a more varied range of oscillators than do spoken
syllables. Consequently, a way to count, organize, and coordinate
them is needed.

The main articulators that can be responsible for movement oscillation in sign language syllables are the body and the arm, each of
which contains smaller articulators that can move alone or in combination with others. The body includes the torso and head, as well as
parts of the face, all of which can move independently, and the arm
contains the shoulder, elbow, wrist/forearm, metacarpal (MCP
"knuckle" joint), and a combination of the proximal and distant interphalangeal joints (PIP, DIP). The articulators of the arm joints are
shown in Figure 2.2. In the Prosodic model, the features of movement
are organized according to their proximity to the center of the body

and the potential size of the movements that can be generated by them. The largest of these used in any signed syllable is the movement oscillator responsible for the syllable nucleus.

2.7 MODALITY EFFECTS ON PHONOLOGY

We now turn specifically to how communication modality affects the phonological structure of sign languages.

2.7.1 Movements, Segments, Features: How Are They Organized?

In this section a few of the major modality effects on phonological form will be described. I will explain first why segments are not the organizational root as they are in spoken language and then describe how they function. Then we will turn to the organization of the oscillators – the articulators of movement.

One rationale for these modality effects is that the signer and perceiver are able to view the articulators directly in signed languages, while in speech they are not. In speech, the articulatory gesture must be inferred based on the links between the acoustic cues or speaker's gesture and the perceiver's knowledge, such that the speaker's words can be re-created in the perceiver. One consequence of this might be that the skeletal tier, containing either segments or moras (abstract units of weight discussed later in this chapter), has more work to do in spoken languages because the perceiver cannot actually see what the speaker is doing. Recall from earlier in the chapter that temporal judgments are also keener in audition than in vision. These two differences – invisible articulators and keen temporal judgment – may be elements of speech that have a powerful and independent organizational role in phonological structure that are realized in X-timing slots. Contrast based on affricates, geminates, long vowels, and diphthongs demonstrates that segmental timing units vary independently from features in spoken languages. In contrast with this, segments are predictable from the featural material in sign languages. The segments – timing slots – have therefore been demoted to the bottom of the feature tree in the Prosodic (Brentari, 1998) and Dependency (van der Hulst, 1993; van der Kooij & van der Hulst, 2005) models of sign language phonology, rather than allowing them to dominate the tree as they do in spoken languages (Figure 1.8 illustrates this).

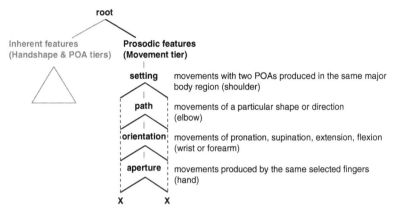

Figure 2.3 The hierarchical organization of movement subtypes in the Prosodic model (Brentari, 1998), with alignment of the segments (X-slots) shown. The largest oscillator (articulator) in any given movement will be the syllable nucleus of the syllable.

Having direct access to the features allows them to be the basis for segments, rather than the other way around, as is the case in spoken languages. An additional reason may be that sign language phonological spaces tend not to be very densely populated phonologically – that is, there are lots of "accidental gaps" in the lexicons of sign languages (van der Kooij & van der Hulst, 2005; van der Hulst & van der Kooij, 2006). This makes distinctions between long and short forms of the same elements less necessary.

Because the number of segments and syllables is predictable from features in signed languages, there are consequences for the hierarchical structure of the system. That is to say, mechanisms must be in place to ultimately align features to timing slots and decide which features or feature classes (tiers) take priority in assigning syllable nuclei. In the Prosodic model, these operations are built into the system, facilitated by the organization of the tiers of the prosodic features node. They are organized so that the segments generated by the features align, and only the segments generated by the largest articulator count as syllable nuclei. This hierarchical organization is shown in Figure 2.3, where the subtypes of movement, illustrated in Figure 2.1, are organized with the most proximal articulator at the top of the tree – capable of larger movements – and those capable of incrementally smaller movements are positioned lower in the structure.

2.7.2 Sonority

The oscillation of several articulators in sign languages (as compared to one primary oscillator in spoken languages) also has an effect on the way that sonority in the sign language syllable operates in the system. Clements (1990:18) defines sonority for spoken languages as

> a composite property of speech sounds which depends on the way they are specified for each of a certain set of features. Plus-specifications for any of these features have the effect of increasing the perceptibility or salience of a sound with respect to otherwise similar sounds having a minus-specification ... We are able to relate the notion "relative sonority" directly to perceptibility, since each of the acoustic attributes associated with a plus-specification for a major class feature enhances the overall perceptibility of the sounds that it characterizes.

Whether one considers sonority to be a phonological construct, a by-product of motoric effort, or based on perceptual saliency, the independence of oscillators/articulators in signed languages has an effect on visual salience. There is not one single articulator that is responsible, as the jaw is in spoken languages.

In spoken languages, evidence for the importance of sonority in phonology comes from the general application of the Sonority Sequencing Principle (SSP), which captures the fact that syllable onsets increase in sonority from one segment to the next and codas decrease in sonority from one segment to the next.[3] The SSP has been shown to be important for determining syllable well-formedness both theoretically (Clements, 1990) and experimentally (Berent et al., 2008; Berent et al., 2013). Berent has shown that there is more likelihood that listeners will perceive a sequence such as _bnif_ with rising sonority in the onset as one syllable and _lbif_ with falling sonority in the onset as two syllables. Falling sonority in the onset (a violation of the SSP) will facilitate the perception of a schwa and hence a second syllable even in languages that have no attested consonant clusters, such as Korean. Data for Korean speakers are shown in Figure 2.4 from Berent et al. (2008).

Similar results exist for English but might be explained by language experience (i.e., onset clusters exist in English and English speakers hear more _bnif_ more often than _nbif_ forms); however, the statistical interpretation cannot be the explanation for the results in Korean because speakers have no experience with onset clusters. Similar results have been obtained with newborns (Gomez et al., 2014).

---

[3] There are some language-specific patterns allowing violations in sonority at word edges – e.g., Polish (Rubach & Booij, 1990).

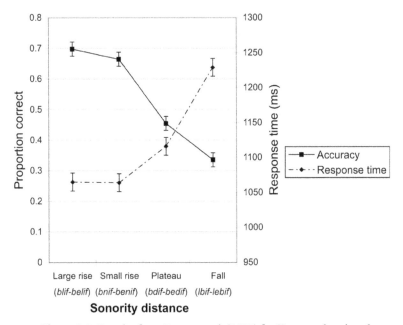

Figure 2.4 Results from Berent et al. (2008) for Korean, showing that a spoken language with no consonant clusters respects the Sonority Sequencing Principle (SSP). (Reprinted with permission from: *PNAS*, 105, Berent, et al., "Language universals in human brains," pp. 5321–5325. Copyright (2008) National Academy of Sciences, U.S.A.)

The SSP is unversal in spoken languages, but sign languages have no SSP not because they lack clusters (many spoken languages lack consonant clusters), but because the reason for not having clusters is fundamentally different. I would argue that because spoken languages depend on a single oscillator, the mandible, sounds must be organized sequentially around this oscillator to be efficiently conveyed. In contrast, sign languages have multiple simultaneous oscillators that can build up sonority within a single unit; therefore, what would potentially count as consonant clusters – segments one after the other – are organized simultaneously (vertically) and realized at the same time, rather than sequentially (horizontally) as in spoken languages. This is a modality-dependent difference in syllable structure. There are constraints on how many movement features can be simultaneously present, and we continue with this discussion in the next section on sonority and movements.

2.7.3 Sonority, Movement, and Syllable Nuclei

How do we know that movements are the syllable nuclei of sign languages? Spoken languages employ a sonority hierarchy, such as the one in (4), which is about how open, how vowel-like, a sound is.

(4) *Sonority hierarchy in spoken languages (Dell & Elmedlaoui, 1985)*
      low V > high V > glide > liquid > nasal > voiced fricative > voiceless
      fricative > voice stop > voiceless stop

In sign languages, movement is the locus of sonority. Movements are the most visually salient part of a sign, just as vowels are the most acoustically salient part of a spoken word. There is now widespread agreement that movement plays a key role in syllable structure with regard to its functional similarity to and suitability as a syllable nucleus (Blevins, 1990; Brentari, 1993; Corina, 1990; Perlmutter, 1992; Sandler, 1993). Sonority hierarchies have been proposed for sign languages (5).

(5) *Sonority hierarchy for sign languages*
      a. Corina (1990)
          movement > handshape change = orientation change > location
          change
      b. Blevins (1993); Sandler (1993)
          path movement > non-static articulator > static articulator >
          location-hold
      c. Brentari (1998)
          path movement > orientation change > handshape change >
          secondary movement

All of the sonority hierarchies in (5) have several features in common: they place movements higher than non-movements and larger movements of the shoulders and elbow (so-called path movements) higher than smaller movements of the wrist or hand. There are four arguments for a sonority hierarchy for sign languages.

The first is that signs with movements (any type) are well formed; without a movement signs are not well formed (Brentari, 1990a, 1990b). There are a few sign languages that have well-formed signs without a movement, such as Hong Kong Sign Language (HKSL; Mak & Tang, 2012), but these forms are rare. Typically, there is a process of epenthesis to repair such ill-formed signs. For example, in ASL when single fingerspelled letters of the manual alphabet and number signs 0–9 (i.e., signs which contain handshape material alone) are produced in isolation as independent words, an epenthetic movement is added (Brentari, 1990; Jantunen, 2007; Geraci, 2009; Jantunen & Takkinen, 2010), similar to schwa epenthesis in spoken languages. Brentari

Figure 2.5 THINK has a movement when produced as a single sign but not in the compound (Brentari, 1993). This alternation is explained by a process of movement epenthesis to insure well-formedness. (Reprinted from *A Prosodic Model of Sign Language Phonology*, by Brentari, D., Copyright (1998), with permission from MIT.)

(1990, 1993) argues that this operation of epenthesis applies in such cases to ensure syllable well-formedness, and a minimal word constraint stating that all signs consist of at least one well-formed syllable. Considering the movement in the compound THINK^SELF (Figure 1.1, reproduced here as Figure 2.5), the first of the component stems THINK has a short movement to contact when produced as a single sign, but not in the compound. Brentari's (1993) explanation is that THINK has no movement at all in its lexical (underlying) form, and a movement is not needed in the compound because one is readily provided by the transition between the two stems. When it occurs as an independent stem, however, it requires a movement to ensure its well-formedness.

The second argument that movements are syllable nuclei is that signs seem "louder" when they are larger. These are typically produced with more "proximal" joints (those closer to the center of the body, those of path movements) than "distal" joints (those produced toward the periphery, those of local movements). Phonetic loudness is not by itself definitive of greater sonority, but just as /a/ is more inherently sonorous than /i/ because /a/ is associated with greater mandible opening (Goldsmith & Larson, 1990), and is higher in intensity than the other vowels (it is louder), a path movement is more sonorous than a local movement because it has greater perceptibility.

Third, the phonological system evaluates which components are more or less sonorous. A diagnostic for which component of a movement is the least sonorous is found in the behavior of [trilled]

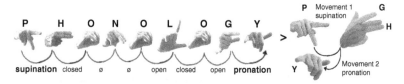

Figure 2.6   The fingerspelled form for P-H-O-N-O-L-O-G-Y (left) and its reduced form (right), which includes only the two wrist movements (cf. Brentari 2011)

movements. Trilled movement features associate to the least sonorant element in the movement if there are two to choose from (Brentari, 1993; Perlmutter, 1992). Specially, if a lexical form has a path movement and an internal movement, the trill associates with the local, less sonorant, internal movement.

Fourth, lexicalization of fingerspelled forms offers another diagnostic of relative sonority in ASL, this time to identify the most sonorous element. In fingerspelled words syllable nuclei are constructed upon the transitional movements between handshapes. These transitions are evaluated for their sonority and the most sonorous ones are selected to be the syllable nuclei of the lexicalized form. For example, #P-H-O-N-O-L-O-G-Y becomes [P-H]σ [G-Y]σ, retaining the orientation changes and deleting many of the other handshapes and the changes between them (Figure 2.6). While these transitions typically involve only finger or hand movements, a few transitional movements between letters involve the wrist and forearm, and these are preferred as syllable peaks over movements of the fingers, precisely because movements of the wrist and forearm are larger than finger or hand movements.

When movements are complex and have two simultaneous movements, the signed syllable nucleus is established based on the larger, more sonorous, component of the movement; therefore, when counting syllables the following principles apply (6).

(6)   *Syllable Counting Criteria (Brentari, 1998):*
   a.   The number of syllables in a sequence of signs equals the number of sequential movements in that string.
   b.   When several shorter (e.g., trilled) movements co-occur with a single (e.g., path) movement of longer duration, the longer movement is the one to which the syllable refers - e.g., ASL

DREAM, which is one syllable containing repeated trilled bending movements.

c. When two or more movements occur at exactly the same time, it counts as one syllable, e.g., ASL INFORM (Figure 1.7) is one syllable containing an aperture change and a path movement.

The idea that movement (rather than handshape or location) conveys the notion of sonority is supported by acquisition and experimentally as well. It has been argued that the repetitive movements in the low-frequency range (around 1.5 Hz) that sign-acquiring infants make when they are going through the syllabic babbling stage is a key milestone in language development (Petitto et al., 2004). There is a more detailed discussion of this work in Chapter 6 on acquisition.

In order to determine whether movement or handshape is the parameter perceived as a "natural" or default syllable nucleus by signers and by non-signers, Berent et al. (2013) conducted a series of experiments – one with signers and three with non-signers. Novel signs were constructed as stimuli with one or two handshapes and with one or two movements as shown in Figure 2.7. Analogous English examples of the ASL stimuli are given in each cell. (These were not part of the experiment and are intended only to be illustrative examples of the analogous syllabic and morphological structure in a familiar spoken language.) Each experiment consisted of two tasks. In one task participants were asked to judge the number of parts *without* meaning and in another to judge the number of parts *with* meaning. Judgments of parts without meaning were taken to be syllabic units, and judgments of parts with meaning were interpreted as morphemes. Those items in the top-right and bottom-left cells with incongruent meaningless and meaningful parts were the most informative, because these items clearly should show differences in the participants' responses if they are making different associations of handshape and movement to morphemes and syllables, respectively.

The results for the incongruent trials of the four experiments (E1–E4) are shown in Figure 2.8a–d. In E1, ASL signers readily associated movement with meaningless units (syllables) and handshape with meaningful ones (morphemes) given only a few training trials and no explicit instruction; this is evident from the interaction seen in Figure 2.8a. In E2, non-signers who had the same instruction and training as the signers in E1 associated movement with both syllables and morphemes, perhaps because it is more visually salient than

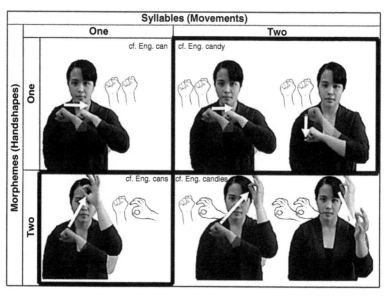

Figure 2.7   Sample stimuli from Berent et al. (2013) with four possible combinations of syllables and morphemes: one syllable/one morpheme (top left); two syllables/one morpheme (top right); one syllable/two morphemes (bottom left) and two syllables/two morphemes (bottom right). The incongruous conditions are outlined in black. (Reprinted from *PLOS ONE*, 8, Berent, et al., "Amodal aspects of linguistic design: Evidence from sign language," 2013. [doi.org/10.1371/journal .pone.0060617] Used and altered under a CC BY 4.0 license.)

handshape (Figure 2.8b). Two additional experiments with non-signers were then conducted to see if they could be taught to pay attention differentially to handshape and movement equally well. In E3 (Figure 2.8c) non-signers were given explicit instruction on the "natural" association of movement with syllables and handshape with morphemes – called "natural" because it corresponded with the judgments of the signers. Non-signers were able to learn the task, and they reliably associated movement syllables and handshape with morphemes with these instructions and training. In a final experiment, E4 (Figure 2.8d), non-signers received explicit instruction and training on an "unnatural" constraint – they were taught to associate handshape with syllables and movement with morphemes – called "unnatural" because it did not correspond with the judgments of the signers. The non-signers were unable to learn the association in the unnatural task;

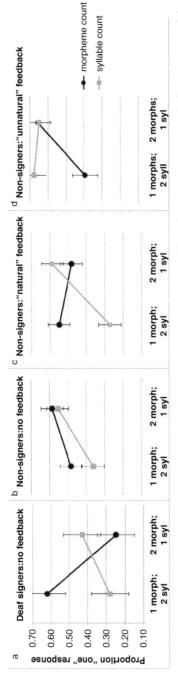

Figure 2.8 Results from the four experiments in Berent et al. (2013). Proportion of "one" responses on the incongruent trials with one morpheme/two syllables and two morphemes/one syllable: (a) Results of signing participants, showing the independent natural association of movement with syllables and handshape with morphemes; (b) results of non-signer participants with no instruction, showing association of movement with both syllables and morphemes; (c) results of non-signer participants with "natural" instruction showing their ability to associate movement with syllables and handshape with morphemes; (d) results of non-signer participants after "unnatural" instruction showing their inability to associate movement with morphemes and handshape with syllables. (Reprinted from *PLOS ONE*, 8, Berent, et al., "Amodal aspects of linguistic design: Evidence from sign language," 2013. [doi.org/10.1371/journal.pone.0060617] Used under a CC BY 4.0 license.)

that is, there is no interaction between morpheme and syllable count in Figure 2.8d.

In prior work (Brentari, 2006; Brentari et al., 2011) it has been shown that non-signers tend to ignore handshape in judging the number of words in a string and to focus heavily on movement, so it was expected that non-signers would not be able to perform this task of Berent et al. (2013) spontaneously, but the fact that they could not even learn to associate handshapes to syllables and movements to morphemes with explicit instruction supports the claim that highly salient properties (in this case, movement) are associated with syllable nuclei, regardless of modality or language experience. Since both signers and non-signers associated meaningless parts with movement much more readily than with handshape, it was concluded that movement is the syllable nucleus of signs.

2.7.4   Syllable Weight

In addition to assigning syllable peaks, sonority can also be important in both signed and spoken languages for assigning syllable weight – heavy syllables versus light syllables. Moraic (or weight) units are employed to assign syllable weight – one mora forms a light syllable, while two or more morae form a heavy syllable – and heavy syllables are more likely to be stressed in many languages (Trubetzkoy, 1939; Hayes, 1989). Syllable weight and sonority are related in important ways, leading Gordon (2006) to propose that both are determined by the amount of energy used to produce the form; they have also been associated with perceptual salience (Ohala & Kawasaki, 1984; Ohala, 1990). In spoken languages duration and information count toward syllable weight. CVV (da:) and CVC syllables (dad) are likely to be "heavy" and CV (da) syllables are likely to be "light"; however, syllable weight is not associated exclusively with length but also with properties that can occur at the same time. Gordon (2006) reports that, in addition to adding moras in time, several tone languages allow a vowel plus high tone to be treated as heavy. In Crow (Kaschube, 1967), Ijo (Williamson, 1989), Kongo (Reh, 1983), Iraqw (Mous, 2007), and Llogoori (Goldsmith, 1992), syllables that would otherwise be treated as light, and not stress-attracting, are allowed to be stressed if they occur with a high tone. The possibility of a combination of simultaneous properties contributing to syllable weight in spoken languages was not widely known until Gordon (2006), which was the first large typological study of these phenomena.

The work by Gordon (2006) shows that the salience of a syllable nucleus can be determined sequentially or simultaneously. The ability of both duration, which is additive across time (and linear), and pitch, which is additive but simultaneous, to contribute to syllable weight in spoken languages leads us to consider the case of syllable weight in sign languages. Discussions on this topic with Goldsmith about Llogoori in the late 1980s led to an analysis of syllable weight in ASL (Brentari, 1990, 1998) that predates Gordon's work on spoken languages and which was extended to other sign languages as well – e.g., Finnish Sign Language (Jantunen & Takkinen, 2010). There is a heavy/light sensitivity that is important for the application of reduplication and which demonstrates that sign syllables are sensitive to the simultaneous layering of movement components as syllable weight. To be concrete, a group of ASL verbs containing one movement element, such as a movement of the elbow *or* movements of the fingers as an aperture change, is permitted to undergo reduplication, resulting in derived nominal forms (e.g., the path movement in ASL SIT can be repeated to derive the nominal form CHAIR (Supalla & Newport, 1978)); in contrast, signs consisting of two or more movements, such as ASL INFORM which contains both a path *and* aperture movement, are much less likely to be reduplicated to obtain a derived nominal form (*INFORMATION via reduplication). This suggests that forms allowing reduplication for nominalization consist of light syllables, while those that disallow reduplication are heavy syllables.

Carstairs-McCarthy (2001) asked whether the syllable, as a unit of phonological description, is modality-neutral (to have the same sense in descriptions of signed and spoken languages) or whether the syllables of signed and spoken languages are really different phenomena. When discussing language evolution, he determined that it was legitimate to appeal to aspects of spoken syllables that are undoubtedly modality-dependent, such as their physiological underpinnings, perhaps in the number and type of oscillators available in the vocal apparatus versus the sign apparatus, which would have an effect on the employment of the SSP. If sign languages used just one oscillator, or one oscillator at a time, we might see evidence of the SSP – e.g., clusters of forms with an increase in sonority for syllable onsets, such as clusters consisting of handshape change, orientation change, then movement (nucleus), and the reverse effects in the syllable offset. This does not occur in sign languages, hence there is no SSP. Instead, the elements are layered simultaneously. This is a modality-dependent difference in syllable structure.

The notion of sonority based on salience is, I would argue, one case of a syllable property that is truly universal and cross-modal. Sonority is readily applied to the perceptually salient elements of form, and even without experience with sign languages individuals associate the same types of meta-properties to syllable sonority in sign languages. Despite the differences between articulators in signed and spoken language, comparative work such as this can ultimately lead to a better understanding of the universality of some of the principles of language organization such as sonority.

2.7.5 Morphophonology and Word Shape

Given all of the differences discussed in this chapter concerning simultaneous versus sequential organization of phonological information, one might expect a modality difference in the preferred shape of words between signed and spoken languages. We now turn to this issue.

Morphemes and syllables are independent levels of structure as we have already seen. Figure 2.9 presents examples of each of the four types of languages that result from crossing these two dimensions (number of syllables, number of morphemes) – a 2 x 2 typological grid. Surveying the languages of the world, some have an abundance of words that contain only one morpheme (e.g., Hmong, English), while others have an abundance of words that are polymorphemic (e.g., ASL, Hopi). Some languages have many words that contain only one syllable (e.g., Hmong, ASL); others have many words that are polysyllabic (e.g., English, Hopi).

English (Figure 2.9, top right) tends to have words composed of several syllables (polysyllabic) and one morpheme (monomorphemic); e.g., *character* [kæ.ɹək.tɚ], with three syllables and one morpheme, is such a word. Hmong (Figure 2.9, top left) tends to have words composed of a single syllable and a single morpheme (Ratliff, 1992; Golston & Yang, 2001). Each of the meaningful units in the Hmong sentence *Kuv. noj. mov. lawm.* (English: "I ate rice") is a separate monomorphemic word, even the perfective marker *lawm*, and each word contains a single syllable (each marked here by a period). Hopi (Figure 2.9, bottom right) tends to have words composed of many morphemes, each composed of more than one syllable; the verb phrase *pa.kiw.–maq.to.–ni.* (English: "will go fish-hunting") is a single word with three morphemes, and the first two of these morphemes each contains two syllables (Mithun, 1984). Finally, ASL (Figure 2.9, bottom left) has many words/signs composed of several morphemes packaged into a single syllable (i.e., one movement). Here we see a classifier form that means *people–go forward–carefully*, which is composed of three morphemes expressed in an additive way by features: (i) the index

	Monosyllabic	Polysyllabic
Monomorphemic	*Hmong*	*English*
# of morphemes # of syllables	1 #noj# 1 .noj.	1 #character# 3 .kæ.ɹǝk. t3˞.
translation	"eat"	"character"
Polymorphemic	*ASL*	*Hopi*
# of morphemes # of syllables	3 #people–go forward–carefully# 1 .go forward	3 #pakiw–maqto–ni# 5 .pa.kiw.maq.to.ni.
translation	"people go forward carefully"	"will go fish-hunting"

Figure 2.9 (top) Examples of word structure in the four types of languages that result from crossing number of syllables with number of morphemes. A period indicates a syllable boundary; a dash indicates a morpheme boundary; and a hash mark (#) indicates a word boundary; (bottom) a depiction of the polymorphemic, monosyllabic ASL form meaning *people-go forward-carefully*. (Reprinted from *A Prosodic Model of Sign Language Phonology*, by Brentari, D., Copyright (1998), with permission from MIT.)

finger handshapes (⌖ = *person*); (ii) the path movement (linear path = *go forward*); and (iii) the non-manual expression (pressed together lips and squinted eyes = *carefully*). All of these forms are morphemes because they are productive and discrete.[4]

---

[4] Note that the ASL sign in Figure 2.9 (bottom) contains three additional meaningful elements: (i) the two hands indicating that two people are moving; (ii) the bent knuckle indicating that the people are hunched-over; (iii) the orientation of the hands with respect to one another indicating that the two people are side by side. These form-meaning associations require further grammatical diagnostics to determine if they are truly morphemic (see Brentari, 1995, 2002). The bent finger may be a restricted morpheme, often used with the *person* and *vehicle* classifiers, and as for the two hands representing two people side by side, this may just be one of many analog types of orientation to one another that can be represented. The use of the two hands to represent the plural may not be discrete enough or productive enough to be a morpheme (Lepic et al., 2016).

Spoken languages have been identified that fall into three of the four cells in this typology. No spoken language has been found that falls into the fourth cell; that is, no spoken language has been found that is polymorphemic and monosyllabic; however, the signed languages analyzed to date fall into the fourth cell. Although sign languages are different in kind from spoken languages, they fit neatly into the grid displayed in Figure 2.9 and, in this sense, can be characterized by general linguistic tools.

2.8 SUMMARY

In this chapter we have discussed the structural impact of the visual modality on sign languages and how their structure adapts to their visual medium while adhering to the functions of a phonological system. We have focused on the effects of the visual-gestural modality on sign languages, but there is an effect of the auditory-vocal modality on spoken languages, too – an effect that is assumed and is an implicit question in most work on spoken language phonology and phonetics.

2.9 FURTHER READING

Berent, I., Dupuis, A., & Brentari, D. (2013). Amodal aspects of linguistic design: Evidence from sign language. *PLOS ONE*, 8, 1–17.
Bosworth, R., Wright, C., Bartlett, M., Corina, D., & Dobkins, K. (2003). Characterization of the visual properties of signs in ASL. In A. Baker, B. van den Bogaerde, & O. Crasborn (eds.), *Cross-Linguistic Perspectives in Sign Language Research* (pp. 265–82). Hamburg: Signum.
Brentari, D. (2002). Modality differences in sign language phonology and morphophonemics. In R. Meier, D. Quinto, & K Cormier (eds.), *Modality in Language and Linguistic Theory* (pp. 35–64). Cambridge: Cambridge University Press.
Fowler, C. A. (2004). Speech as a supramodal or amodal phenomenon. In G. Calvert, C. Spence, & B. E. Stein (eds.), *Handbook of Multisensory Processes* (pp. 189–201). Cambridge, MA: MIT.
Meier, R. (2012). Language and modality. In R. Pfau, M. Steinbach, & B. Woll (eds.), *Sign Language: An International Handbook* (pp. 574–601). Berlin: Mouton de Gruyter.

3 Iconicity

Abstract

In this chapter, the ways that iconicity and phonological constraints work together in sign languages will be described. Different types of iconicity will be delineated, and then a number of examples will be provided of how the phonetic pressures of ease of articulation, ease of perception, and iconicity conspire in sign language phonology. Iconicity is pervasive in sign languages, which makes these languages fertile ground for research on the topic, and it offers a way for work on sign languages to make a contribution to linguistic theory more broadly.

3.1 INTRODUCTION TO CENTRAL ISSUES OF ICONICITY IN SIGN LANGUAGES

In the last chapter, issues were addressed concerning the impact of modality on phonological structure – auditory-vocal versus visual-gestural. Here we address a particular type of modality effect – iconicity. The topic of iconicity in language, and particularly in signed languages, is vast, covering all linguistic areas – e.g., phonetics, phonology, morphology, pragmatics, lexical organization, acquisition, and the evolution of language. See, for example, the fourteen-volume series on iconicity by Nänny and Fischer (2002) in which Grote and Linz (2003) address sign language iconicity. The current chapter discusses only those aspects of iconicity that are specifically relevant for the phonological and morphophonemic representation of sign languages.

Iconicity has been a serious topic of study in cognitivist, semiotic, and functionalist linguistic perspectives, particularly when dealing with productive, metaphoric, and metonymic phenomena (Taub, 2001; P. Wilcox, 2001, 2005; S. Wilcox, 2004; Russo, 2005; Cuxac & Sallandre, 2007). Much of this work addressed how our experience as human beings, with a particular type of body and ways of interacting with the world, shape language. By contrast, with some notable exceptions, such as Wilcox and Occhino (2016) and Occhino et al. (2017), until quite recently phonology has been studied within a formal approach, using tools that make as little reference to meaning or iconicity as possible (exceptions include Eccarius, 2008; Brentari & Eccarius, 2010; Wilcox et al., 2010). This tendency is derived from the sense that iconicity is antithetical to phonology. I will argue in this chapter that this is not the case.

In this chapter we argue that there need not be competition between phonology and iconicity, although teasing apart the effects of both is important. Iconicity and phonology are separate enterprises; iconicity is a particular kind of relation with meaning, and phonology is about the formal organization of the expression of that meaning. A form can be highly iconic and fit perfectly into the phonology at the same time. Waugh (2000) argues that it is time to "slay the dragon of arbitrariness" and embrace the link between form and meaning in spoken language. According to Waugh, linguistic structure at many levels (lexicon, grammar, texts) is shaped by the balance between two dynamic forces between form and meaning – one force pushing structures toward iconicity and the other pushing them toward non-iconicity. Under this view, iconicity is a natural pressure on all languages (spoken or signed). The visual modality offers a wider range of possibilities for iconicity, and sign languages make extensive use of it, but there is no denying that the auditory modality employs it as well. It is now clearer than ever that the resolution of Plato's famous debate between Cratylus and Hermogenes about whether language is "natural" or "conventional" is that it is neither one nor the other, but both. Because of the sheer size and scope of a language in all of its components, its organization must be conventional, but it also embraces the natural and the iconic whenever it can and in a variety of ways. We have the opportunity to study iconicity in sign languages in an in-depth way because there seem to be many more types of visual, motor, and proprioceptive iconicity that can be incorporated into a sign language than types of auditory or vocal iconicity that can be incorporated into a spoken language. The ability to retain iconicity can be seen as an advantage for sign language. Spoken languages are a bit "iconicity-impaired."

"Iconicity" refers to the mapping of a concrete source domain to the linguistic form (Taub, 2001); it is one of three Peircean classifications: iconicity, indexicality, and symbolism (Peirce, 1958). From the very beginning, iconicity has been a major topic of study of sign language research, despite the fact that the phonological inventory and its distributional properties can be constructed without it. As shown in Chapter 1, ASL has a phonological level of representation constructed using exclusively linguistic evidence, i.e., based on the distribution of forms – minimal pairs, phonological operations, and processes of word formation. Yet iconicity is always there, it is useful on many levels, and it is a pressure on the system just like ease of perception and ease of articulation (Eccarius & Brentari, 2010).

Iconicity has been best dealt with in relative, rather than absolute, terms and in ways that are specific to each of the parameters. Frishberg (1975) and Klima and Bellugi (1979) have established that signed languages become less iconic over time, but iconicity never reduces to zero, and it continues to be an active pressure on sign languages in both word creation and grammar; however, there is no means to quantitatively and absolutely measure just how much iconicity there is in a sign language's lexicon or grammar. The question "Iconic to whom, and under what conditions?" is always relevant, so we need to acknowledge that iconicity is generation-specific (signs for TELEPHONE have changed over time, yet both are iconic), context-specific (the sign for PERIPH-ERAL is different for a part of a city and for a part of a computer system, yet both are iconic), and language-specific (signs for TREE are different in Danish, Hong Kong, and American Sign Languages, yet all are iconic). Iconicity resides primarily in the sub-lexical units – parameters or features as described in Chapter 1 – and there may be several layers or types of resemblance, and not all are appropriately called "iconicity" (Taub, 2001; Russo, 2005).

After all of the work showing indisputably that signed languages have phonology and duality of patterning over the last several decades, one can only conclude that it is the *distribution* (and not necessarily the substance) at each constituent level that must be arbitrary and systematic in order for phonology to exist. Iconicity should not be thought of as either a hindrance or opposition to a phonological grammar but rather as another independent dimension, on par with ease of production or ease of perception, that helps to shape a phonological inventory.

The Saussurean notion of arbitrariness has been misunderstood and does not prohibit iconic sign formation (here I mean the term in its semiotic sense). Arbitrariness refers to both parts of the sign relation separately – the signified piece and signifier piece – and each is carved up in an arbitrary fashion. In other words, in the domain of the signified, it is arbitrary that French has one word, *mutton,* for animal/food while English has two – *sheep* as animal, and *lamb* as food – or that Italian Sign Language has multiple signs for cheese, while ASL has just one. It is also arbitrary that French has contrastive nasal vowels and English does not (Grote & Linz, 2003) or that Hong Kong Sign Language has five 3-finger handshapes – ✋, ✋, ✋, ✋, ✋ – while ASL has four – ✋, ✋, ✋, ✋. Linguistic signs are the conventionalized (not necessarily arbitrary) pairings between the signifier and the signified.

Iconicity contributes to the phonological shape of forms more in signed than in spoken languages, so much so that we cannot afford to ignore it. Iconicity is a strong initial factor in building signed words, but it can also restrict outputs, and it can ultimately engage with arbitrary distributions in the morphology and phonology of sign languages. In the following sections I will describe the issues that surround this notion generally and how sign languages contribute to understanding them, followed by some well-known examples of how iconicity effects interact with the phonology and morphophonology of sign languages. I will conclude with a brief description of some new work that is investigating iconic modification in gesture and sign language. Iconicity is also relevant in first- and second-language acquisition, and this will be addressed in Chapter 7 on acquisition.[1]

3.1.1 Types of Iconicity

The resemblance between phonological form and iconicity can take any of the following routes, and in many psycholinguistic studies discussed in Chapter 6 on processing and in Chapter 7 on acquisition it is not always clear what definition of "iconic" is being used. In the following paragraphs, some of these definitions are made more precise; they are based on Taub (2001).

First-order resemblance is one type of iconicity, which tends to be sensory. For example, in both ASL and English, temporal iconicity can be used to utter a phrase slowly when the event happened slowly – *she ... fell ... asleep*. Proprioception can be used in signed and spoken

---

[1] Other types of nonarbitrary relationships between form and meaning, such as synesthesia, will not be addressed. Sensory synesthesia is based on a kind of crosstalk between adjacent processing areas or hypersensitivity, which may or may not have to do with literal resemblance in the world; therefore, it might have nothing to do with iconicity. For example, certain colors may be associated with numbers, which is clearly not iconic; however, many of us have the experience of associating high-pitched /i/ with small objects, which is an example of crosstalk between motor (size of the cavity) and auditory neural networks that is iconic. "Higher-order synesthesia" might also be iconic and synesthetic, such as seeing "V" as a letter, or as the Roman numeral "5," based on context or the cultural constructs to which one is exposed. Like iconicity, synesthesia can be "bottom-up" (sensory) or "top-down" (higher cognition, sometimes metaphor, or mediated by other cultural constructs), as described in Ramachandran and Hubbard (2001).

languages as well. In English a large oral cavity can represent a large object or even the relative size of objects, as when the Romantic poet John Keats in "Ode to Psyche" uses the linear order of vowels to represent how a flower blossoms, from more closed to more open (/ʊ >ɛ>a/ with b**u**ds and b**e**lls and st**a**rs without a name (cf. Grigely, 1996). In sign languages proprioception can be used to represent alternating action with alternating movements (e.g., ASL RIDE-A-BIKE) or by producing the ASL sign LONG by running your finger down your arm (in ASL) or your interlocutor's arm (in protactile ASL) to represent the degree of length. Modality-specific examples of iconicity are also possible: auditory ones in speech, as in onomatopoetic sounds *buzzzz, meow,* etc., and visual ones in sign languages (and in manual gestures generally); many size-and-shape specifiers (see Chapter 1) have first-order resemblance.

Metaphorical resemblance is a different type of iconicity that involves associations at a higher level of cognition: e.g., a round shape in handshape or a tracing movement can represent a unified entity, such as the ASL sign GROUP. Other iconic metaphors in English might be used to represent making an entity complete, as in *Let's round out the group*; or speed used to convey the notion of "skilled," as in ASL TAKE-OFF or in English *he's very quick,* meaning smart.

Affective iconicity is less discussed in the literature, but it is important as well. It involves copying the speaker's affective state in style tone or intonation. These phenomena are widespread in spoken and sign language, particularly but not exclusively in quotations (Davidson et al., 2015, for sign languages; Dingemanse et al., 2016, for spoken languages); for example, a roll of the eyes can communicate boredom on the part of the quoted person rather than the speaker herself. In this chapter sensory and affective iconicity will be kept distinct.

3.1.2 Avoiding the "Gesture-Is-Iconic/Language-Is-Not" Trap: Clarifying the Relevant Terms

The distribution of iconic forms will become increasingly important throughout this chapter in gesture versus sign, and across the three types of vocabulary in a sign language lexicon (foreign, core, and spatial). I therefore want to define some terms before proceeding because they are relevant in dealing with iconic and non-iconic forms in sign language phonology.

Categorical: Iconicity can be distributed in a continuous or categorical fashion. Psycholinguistic evidence can be helpful in determining phonological status. Both place of articulation (POA) and handshape were targeted in a series of studies by Emmorey and Herzig (2003). They had ASL signers and gesturers perform a production task and a perception task involving various meaning–form relationships that are iconic. In the production and perception tasks both signers and hearing non-signers treat space in an analogue fashion. The handshape results, however, showed more notable differences between signers and non-signers. On the perception task, participants were asked to view ASL clips describing ten different sizes of medallion and then select a disc matching the size of the medallion. Overall, signers were more sensitive than gesturers to small differences in the handshape moving from a squeezed thumb + index finger handshape ⟨image⟩ to a more open but very similar handshape ⟨image⟩, or between various sizes of opening in a handshape such as this one ⟨image⟩. Signers showed an analogue sensitivity to the ten disc sizes when dealing with all discs at once to show relative sizes, while non-signers were less sensitive to handshape as an indication of size. On the production task with signers only, the ten different disc sizes were shown to participants one at a time, and the signers produced the corresponding handshapes. The handshapes signers produced were categorical forms. For the ten sizes of medallion, signers used three types of handshapes: all were curved handshapes, and all used the index finger, but they differed in three structural ways to indicate size: ⟨image⟩ for small medallions they used contact; ⟨image⟩ for medium ones they used a curved index finger without contact; and for large medallions they used a two-handed ⟨image⟩ form.

Emmorey and Herzig's results suggest that iconcity involves morphophonological categories for size and shape represented via handshape, but there is also a gestural overlay that can be employed to add gradient information. Signers are sensitive to this gradient information when making comparisons. In all cases the thumb and index are the fingers selected indicating "thin," the bent joints indicating "round," and three categories for size take care of the rest.

Hybrid Linguistic-Gestural Forms: The results of the Emmorey and Herzig (2003) studies suggest that the iconic handshapes that signers use are both linguistic and gestural. The selected fingers representing "thin" and the curved fingers representing "round" are categorical properties of handshape, but the space between the thumb and fingers is gestural. This analogue gestural system is employed if precise, comparative judgments are needed among the ten categories of medallions – joints are particularly susceptible to this type of gestural use.

Contrast: Iconic forms can be categorical morphologically, phonologically, or both. In the cases that follow, three types of contrast as set forth by Clements (2001) for features are used as theoretical grounding. Note that none of the criteria in (1) depend on the source of the material being non-iconic. These criteria were applied to features at first, but they might be applied to other phonological constituents as well.

(1) *Type of contrasts as outlined in Clements (1993):*
   a. Distinctive: creates a minimal pair
   b. Active: used in a phonological rule or constraint
   c. Prominent: used as a morpheme

If a unit meets even one of these criteria, then it merits inclusion in the phonological system. Consider as an example the /s/-/z/ contrast in English, for which [voice] is both distinctive and active. The [voice] contrast participates in minimal pairs in English so it is distinctive (*[s]ing* versus *[z]ing*) and participates in a rule of neutralization in three specific morphological contexts – plural (*mouse pad[z]* versus *pat[s]* of butter), third singular (*she pad[z]* around the house in her socks; she always *pat[s]* me on the head), and possessive (*Carl'[z]* versus *Pat'[s]*) – so it is active. In ASL, the feature [flexed] is distinctive (APPLE ⟨⟩/CANDY ⟨⟩ in ASL; GAY ⟨⟩/UNSURE ⟨⟩ in BSL, see Chapter 1) and prominent in ASL as well (e.g., upright being ⟨⟩ versus bent upright being ⟨⟩). The [direction] of movement is distinctive because it is contrastive – see TEND and BE-MOVED/TOUCHED-BY (Figure 3.1) – and [direction] is also prominent (morphological) in the system of verb agreement. The [stacked] feature is contrastive in all three ways – distinctive, active,

Figure 3.1 The distinctive use of the [direction] feature showing values away from and toward the body in the ASL minimal pair TEND (left) and BE-MOVED/TOUCHED-BY (right)

and prominent. The distribution of both [direction] and [stacked] are discussed at length later in this chapter.

3.2 ICONICITY ACROSS THE LEXICON

What problems can be confronted or insights gained from considering iconicity in sign language phonology? It would be odd, even counter-productive, not to use iconicity when it is so readily available. It has been said that signed languages use iconicity "because they can," since the physical properties of entities, as well as their positions and movements, can be quite well represented using a visual-gestural communication modality. For this reason, Brennan (2005) proposed that spoken languages use iconicity in a limited way in their lexical items, not because there is a linguistic restriction against it to which sound symbolism and onomatopoetic forms are the exception, but simply because the sound-speech modality is not very well suited to it. A lexicon simply cannot be easily constructed based on how entities in the world sound.[2]

Other reasons why iconicity may be so prevalent in sign languages may be because of how they arise and their relatively young age. Let us consider the contexts in which signed languages arise. In inventing a homesign system, isolated individuals live within a hearing family or community and devise a method for communicating through gestures that become systematic (Goldin-Meadow, 2001). Initially, before there is a community, per se, signs begin to be used through interactions among individuals, and these systems develop at first within a context where being transparent is important in making oneself understood to those around you with whom you do not share a system.

In most signing communities of the Deaf-World, signed languages are passed down from generation to generation not through families but through schools, athletic associations, and social clubs. This group of sign languages includes many with which we are familiar (ASL, BSL, HKSL, DGS, etc.) and the emerging language Nicaraguan Sign Language (NSL), which also belongs to this "community" class of sign languages. Another way that sign languages develop is in stable communities in which there is a high incidence of deafness; these are

---

[2] Iconicity does exist in spoken languages in reduplication (e.g., Haiman, 1980b) as well as expressives and ideophones. See, for example, Bodomo (2006), Grenoble et al. (2015), and Dingemanse et al. (2016). See also Okrent (2002) and Shintel et al. (2006) for the use of vocal quality, such as length and pitch, in an iconic manner in spoken languages.

sometimes called "village" sign languages (Meir et al., 2010). These sign languages develop in communities with a high incidence of deafness due to genetic factors, such as what happened on the island of Martha's Vineyard in the seventeenth century (Groce, 1985), in the case of Al-Sayyid Bedouin Sign Language (ABSL; Sandler et al., 2005; Meir et al., 2007; Padden et al., 2010), and several others (see Zeshan & de Vos, 2012), including Central Taurus Sign Language (CTSL; Ergin & Brentari, 2017). The contribution of these systems to our understanding of the emergence of phonology will be addressed in depth in Chapter 5, but here I simply point to the fact that the strongest form of iconicity, which is transparency, is crucial at the early stages of the emergence of a sign language.

Confusion between the concepts of "transparency" and "iconicity" can often cloud this discussion. Homesigners must be transparent to be understood, but signed languages are rarely transparent; that is, non-signers cannot guess the meaning of current ASL signs from their forms. In one of the first studies of transparency (Klima & Bellugi, 1979: 22), ten hearing participants were shown ninety signs of abstract and concrete nominals, and they were able to make reasonable guesses about meaning for only nine of the ninety signs (10 percent). Even when the task was multiple-choice, the participants could not provide correct answers at a level above chance; therefore, ASL is not transparent. Let us now turn to iconicity.

How is iconicity distributed across the lexicon? One general way to think about this might be what Hwang et al. (2017) call "patterned iconicity." This captures the common ways in which certain entities in the world evoke specific ways of representing them on the body; in other words, all dimensions of the body are not equally exploited by the grammar across all types of vocabulary. This group of researchers found that in several populations, including a group of American non-signers and three groups of signers (Japanese Sign Language, CTSL and ASL), *tool* vocabulary tended to use "manipulation" as a strategy whereby the head and body represent the agent using the tool. *Animal* vocabulary tended to use a "personification" strategy, whereby the animal body parts are mapped onto the human signer or gesturer. *Fruit* and *vegetable* vocabulary had a split pattern: forms might be represented either by manipulation (e.g., how they are handled in food preparation) or by using an "object" strategy that represents the size and shape of the object. These patterns are not claimed to be universal; however, they were prevalent across these groups, even if they can be modified by the social context in which people live. The iconic affordances suggested by the way humans interact with or relate to entities in the world are important. This work suggests, in keeping with cognitive phonology, that the manner in which meaning is mapped onto the body (the morphophonological patterns, if you will) is not arbitrary, nor is it affected exclusively by MARKEDNESS pressures of ease of articulation and ease of perception. One could imagine that these iconic affordances are the raw material that comes to be shaped and categorized by the phonology in sign languages.

3.2.1   Iconicity in Word Building: Movement and Event Structure

Can movement iconically express event structure? Wilbur argues that it can, and that by using the features and feature geometry proposed in Brentari (1998), the morphophonology of sign language predicates iconically reflects the temporal components of Pustejovsky's (1995) event types – states, processes, achievements, and accomplishments. Wilbur has been involved in research on the relationship between movement and meaning in signed languages since the 1980s (Wilbur et al., 1983, 1999, 2008). Her work has analyzed the prosodic uses of movement for stress, accent, and emphasis as well as the use of movement in aspectual morphology. She recently developed the Event Visibility Hypothesis (EVH; Wilbur, 2010), which is a proposal for how the structure of predicates in sign languages adheres to a type of mapping between event structure and phonological form in core lexical verbs.

In English, event structures are inaccessible via the phonology although these structures are recoverable through syntactic tests. The semantic and syntactic tests cannot be reiterated in the space allotted here, but evidence is provided in Wilbur (2010) that these distinctions are part of the semantic *Aktionsart* of the event. Wilbur argues that in signed languages (she has investigated several of them), event structure is overtly expressed in the phonology of verbs: States (Ss) are [-dynamic] and have no movement; processes (Ps) are [+dynamic] and have a movement; telic events transition between a process and a state (P ->S); and achievements are transitions between two nonidentical states (S->S). Furthermore, processes are homogenous and exhibit no changes other than the passage of time, while telic and inchoative events are heterogeneous (telic events slow to a stop; inchoative events initiate from a static state). Brentari's phonological movement inventory (1998) is correlated with the event structure of categories of predicate signs, which are grouped into those that are atelic (states and processes), telic punctual transitions, and telic non-punctual transitions. Wilcox (2004, 2010) has discussed the use of movement for temporal aspect across sign languages, more broadly, as an area of sign language morphology where temporal iconicity plays an important role, and Wilbur has delved into acceleration and deceleration of movement via the EVH to highlight the relationship of iconicity to formal semantics.

Telic and atelic predicates exploit changes in the movement features and the associated segmental structure of the form. The features of movement are employed; telic predicates exploit the transitions between the two different specifications for handshape, orientation, setting, or directional path movements (examples of telic verbs are given in Figure 3.2).

Crucially for the phonology, the segmental structure of telic and atelic verbs is different. In the telic predicates SEND, HAPPEN, POSTPONE, and HIT the two segments are not identical (indicated by the "Fa" and "Fb" in the two segmental slots), while the two segments of atelic predicates are identical and contain a [trilled] movement that is expressed on both segments in RUN, PLAY, and READ (indicated by the "Fa" in both segmental slots). Another critical difference is that the telic form has an endpoint, measured as a rapid deceleration of the movement, and the atelic form does not. While deceleration, per se, has not been among the phonological features proposed for any sign language for word-level phonology (see Chapter 1), this type of movement with rapid deceleration may be a part of prosodic morphology, since there are

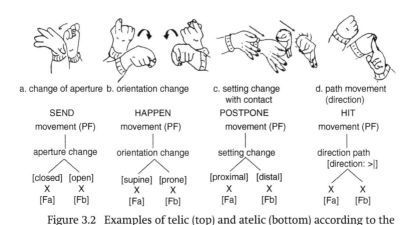

Figure 3.2 Examples of telic (top) and atelic (bottom) according to the Event Visibility Hypothesis along with the phonological representation of trilled movements. (Reprinted with permission from Wilbur, R. (2010). "The semantics–phonology interface." In D. Brentari (ed.), *Sign Languages* (Cambridge Language Surveys, pp. 355–380) © Cambridge University Press.)

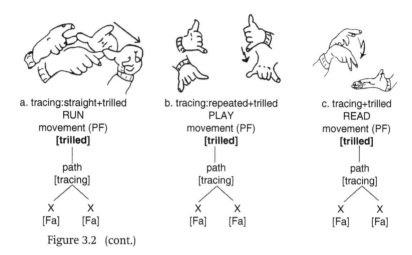

a. tracing:straight+trilled
RUN
movement (PF)
[trilled]
|
path
[tracing]
X   X
[Fa]   [Fa]

b. tracing:repeated+trilled
PLAY
movement (PF)
[trilled]
|
path
[tracing]
X   X
[Fa]   [Fa]

c. tracing+trilled
READ
movement (PF)
[trilled]
|
path
[tracing]
X   X
[Fa]   [Fa]

Figure 3.2 (cont.)

numerous verbs for which there are telic and atelic variants, such as
READ versus READ-THROUGH, WRITE versus WRITE-UP, DRIVE versus
DRIVE-THERE. This indicates that a morpheme that is still very productive can also be "baked into" some core lexical forms, as shown in Figure
3.2.

This analysis has been able to establish that there is a relationship
between event structure and phonology (meaning and form) that is
both iconically motivated and phonologically constrained, and Wilbur
has argued that these structural components of predicates help to
explain why sign languages look so similar to one another in this
regard. Interestingly, when given a forced choice task, even non-signers
are sensitive to this distinction (Strickland et al., 2015). Forms with and
without deceleration were shown to non-signers, and the results
showed that non-signers were able to reliably associate the atelic and
telic verbs with their predicted movement in forced-choice tasks,
including items having lexically unrelated meanings and signs from
three different sign languages (Italian Sign Language, Turkish Sign
Language, and Sign Language of the Netherlands).

Another way that iconic properties found in gesture play a role in
building a lexicon involves the use of two hands. In a study by Lepic
et al. (2016) the use of two-handed signs was analyzed in Swedish Sign
Language (SSL), Israeli Sign Language (ISL), and ASL. They found that
72 of 256 in these three sign languages overlap in their use of the two
hands. They suggest that this may be related to the constellation of

meanings associated with two-handed signs in which the two hands represent multiple component parts or the boundaries of an overall, typically symmetrical, shape which they call lexical plurality, figure/ ground relationships, or the application of a process over a large area, such as RAIN.

To summarize the section on the lexicon and iconicity, we see that indeed iconicity plays an important – we might even call it a central – role in motivating form–meaning relationships within a sign language lexicon. The idea of being faithful to the iconic structure is modulated by the phonological principles – predicting where the iconic forms occur and where they do not. It is not sufficient to merely notice iconic mappings, but rather it is necessary to include their distribution across the lexical and morphological classes of a sign language lexicon. These interactions are still understudied and we look to the future for more work in this area.

3.2.2 Arbitrary Distribution of Orientation in Iconic Classifier Constructions

The parameter of orientation in classifier handshapes also interacts with iconicity in classifier constructions. This involves whole entity classifiers, descriptive classifiers, body part classifiers, and handling classifiers (see Chapter 1 (3)–(4) for definitions of classifiers).

Benedicto and Brentari (2004) and Brentari (2005) argued that, while all types of classifier constructions use handshape morphologically, the phonological features involved in the larger articulatory structure can vary from type to type. Handling and limb/ body part classifier constructions use orientation in a morphological way, while whole entity and descriptive classifiers do not. This is shown in Figure 3.3, which illustrates the variation of the forms using orientation phonologically versus morphologically. The whole entity classifier in Figure 3.3a *person-upside-down* and the descriptive classifier in Figure 3.3b *flat-table-upside-down* are not grammatical – i.e., the orientation cannot be altered in the ways indicated to show a different relation of the body or table top to the ground (shown by an "x" through the ungrammatical forms). In contrast, the corresponding body part classifier in Figure 3.3c *by-legs-be-located-upside-down* and the handling classifier in Figure 3.3d *grasp-gear shift-from-below* are grammatical when articulated with the two differing orientations.

a. whole entity (1-HS: person)   *b. surface extension* (B-B-HS:flat surface)
phonological use of orientation

c. body part (V-HS: person)   *d. handling* (S-HS: grasp)
morphological use of orientation

Figure 3.3   Examples of the distribution of phonological and morphological uses of orientation in classifier predicates. (top – a,b) Whole entity and descriptive/extension classifier handshapes do not allow morphological use of orientation, while (bottom – c,d) body part and handling classifier handshapes do allow orientation to be used morphologically. (From Brentari, D., "Sign language phonology: ASL," In J. Goldsmith, (ed.), *The Handbook of Phonological Theory*, published by Blackwell. © 2011 Blackwell Publishing Ltd. Publishing Ltd. Reprinted with permission from John Wiley and Sons.)

3.2.3   The Feature [Stacked] and Iconicity

An example of iconicity that we will discuss in some depth concerns a single handshape-specific feature in the system of ASL – [stacked] shown in Figure 3.4 – that behaves differently across the different lexical components and exhibits all three types of contrast: distinctive, active, and prominent (see (1)). This feature allows each of the fingers to have increasing flexion at one or more joints, and the effect is that an interlocutor can see the fingers spread when the palm is facing the midline. The relevant distinction is between "plain" spread fingers ⚫ and "stacked" spread fingers ⚫ when the selected fingers are held constant. The analysis presented here from Eccarius (2008) and Brentari and Eccarius (2010) addresses the degree to which this handshape feature interacts with the iconic elements of sign language in the core, spatial, and foreign components (see Figure 1.3 and surrounding text in Chapter 1 for a description of these lexical components). A comparable example from a spoken language comes from

[±labial] in the Japanese. In foreign vocabulary it is contrastive, but in native vocabulary it is not (2).

(2) *Distribution of [h] and [f] in Japanese (Ito & Mester, 1995a):*
   a. core distribution (native vocabulary: Yamoto, Sino-Japanese, and Mimetic components)

*[fa],	*[fe],	*[fi],	*[fo],	[fu]
[ha],	[he],	[hi],	[ho]	ø

   b. foreign distribution (borrowings)

[fa],	[fe],	[fi],	[fo],	[fu]
[ha],	[he],	[hi],	[ho]	ø

The difference between plain and stacked handshapes (e.g., ✌ versus ⊰) produces a minimal pair in the foreign lexicon – the fingerspelled letters -V- versus -K-, as seen in Figure 3.4 (top); it is therefore *distinctive* in this context. In the core lexicon [stacked] has no minimal pairs but is implicated in a rule which changes a plain handshape, such as ✌, to a stacked handshape ⊰ in signs where the fingertips are supposed to be apart ([spread]) in the body's vertical plane but the palm faces inward toward the midsagittal plane. Brentari (1998) has argued that palms facing the midline is the default signing position, so ease of articulation is the phonetic motivation for this change. The result is a stacked handshape, which we see in SEE, VERB, and FALL (Figure 3.4, middle, for SEE and FALL). **[Stacked] is therefore** *active* (allophonic) **in the core**.

In the spatial lexicon, [stacked] is meaningful in different ways in whole entity and in body part classifiers. In whole entity classifiers (Figure 3.4, bottom left), such as vehicle, [stacked] means "on its side" and refers to the palm, but it does not iconically refer to the fingers. The parts of the vehicle do not have to be splayed in the way indicated. In body part classifiers (Figure 3.4, bottom right), where the fingers represent legs, the plain handshape represents a person "on her back," and the stacked handshape is an iconic representation of a person on her side, representing the legs as someone does when performing leg extensions, for example, in exercise class. The differences among the different components can be expressed as a set of ranked constraints in Optimality Theory (see Eccarius & Brentari, 2010, for details).

This analysis shows that contrasts and constraints on individual features engage with principles of iconicity, and they are distributed throughout the different components of a sign language's phonological system in arbitrary ways.

foreign: the letter-V-   the letter-K-

core: SEE "plain"   SEE [stacked]   FALL "plain"   FALL [stacked]

"upright"   "on its side"   "on her back"   "on her side, leg bent back"
spatial: semantic CLvehicle   person(legs) BPCL

Figure 3.4   Examples of [stacked] handshapes in the three components
of the ASL lexicon: (top) plain 🖐 versus [stacked] 🖐 handshapes in the
foreign component of the ASL lexicon where there is a minimal pair
(V̲ANILLA versus K̲ITCHEN; (middle) [stacked] 🖐 handshapes in **core**
lexical items before and after the allophonic rule has applied – SEE and
FALL; (bottom) meaningful differences in the **spatial** lexicon where
classifier constructions reside: whole entity (vehicle) classifiers (*vehicle-
standing-upright* versus *vehicle-on-its-side*) and body part classifiers *person-
lying-on-her-back* versus *person-on-her-side-doing-backwards-leg-extensions*.
(Comprised in part using images from "A formal analysis of phonological
contrast and iconicity in sign language handshapes," by Eccarius, P. &
Brentari, D. In *Sign Language and Linguistics*, 13, 2010, pp. 156–181.
Reprinted with kind permission from John Benjamins Publishing
Company, Amsterdam/Philadelphia. [www.benjamins.com].)

3.3 ICONICITY IN THE GRAMMAR: AGREEMENT

One area in sign language grammars where iconicity has been studied
extensively and plays an important role in sign language grammar is
verb agreement. The phenomenon of verb agreement appears to be
hybrid, both linguistic and gestural in nature. For the moment let's
focus on ASL. The ASL verb ASK (with an opening index finger), when

Figure 3.5 Examples of morphological use of the [direction] feature: verb agreement in ASK (ASL). When the verb is moved away from the signer (a), it means *I ask you*; when it is moved toward the signer (b), it means *you ask me*.

moved in a straight path away from the signer (with the palm facing out), means *I ask you*; when the same verb is directed toward the signer (with the palm facing in), it means *you ask me* (see Figure 3.5). This phenomenon is found in many sign languages (see Mathur & Rathmann, 2010a, 2010b; Rathmann & Mathur, 2012) and is comparable to verb agreement in spoken language, insofar as the difference between the two sign forms corresponds to the difference in meaning marked in spoken language by person agreement with the subject and/or object.

Agreement verbs in sign languages typically manifest the transfer of entities, either abstract or concrete. The locational-loci of sign language verb agreement are regarded as visual manifestations, overt indices of the locations of the pronominal elements in question, rather than of grammatical categories, such as gender or number (cf. Meir, 2002, and references cited therein). Referents in a signed discourse may be tracked both syntactically and iconically. And the syntactic function may be expressed by means of a phonological feature, which is constrained by both the morphology and the phonology. Crucially, Meir argues for an abstract construct used in a transfer (or directional) verb, "DIR," which is the iconic representation of the semantic notion "path" used in theoretical frameworks such as Jackendoff (1996: 320). DIR denotes spatial relations of objects (e.g., *Mary put the book on the shelf* is represented [Mary cause [[book move] to shelf]]).[3]

Transfer verbs with the morphological DIR feature may or may not also have a phonological [direction] feature, indicating a "to" or "from" direction. When it is present DIR may be realized by path movement, be

---

[3] DIR can appear as an independent verb or as an affix to other verbs. In German Sign Language it can appear as an auxiliary.

morph. DIR	no	no	yes	yes
a. APOLOGIZE	b. ADMIT	c. SAY-YES	d. HELP	
phono [dir] path	no	yes	no	yes
phono [dir] orientation	no	no	yes	no

Figure 3.6   Examples of the phonological expression of verb agreement in ASL. In APOLOGIZE (a) there is no phonological [direction] feature or [DIR] (morphological agreement). In ADMIT (b) there is phonological [direction] but not morphological [DIR]. In SAY-YES (c) morphological agreement [DIR] is marked on the orientation of the hand. In HELP (d) morphological agreement [DIR] is marked on the path movement (cf. Brentari, 2011)

realized by the orientation of the hand, or be null phonologically (Brentari, 1988, 1990b, 1998). Crucially, the abstract morpheme DIR and phonological [direction] are arbitrarily assigned language specifically and cross-linguistically (Mathur & Rathmann, 2010a, 2010b). We can see the language-specific arbitrary distribution of DIR in the signs in Figure 3.6 from ASL.

APOLOGIZE (Figure 3.6a) takes both a subject and indirect object argument, but it has neither a morphological DIR nor a phonological [direction] feature. It is always expressed in the same way and the movement is on the body. ADMIT (Figure 3.6b) has a phonological [direction] feature but no morphological DIR; the verb is expressed the same way regardless of the argument structure (who is admitting [something] to whom); the arguments are not expressed in the verb. SAY-YES (Figure 3.6c) has both a morphological DIR and a phonological feature [direction] expressed only on the orientation of the hand. HELP (Figure 3.6d) also has both a morphological DIR and phonological feature [direction], and the phonological feature is expressed only on the path movement.

There are three types of verbs attested in ASL (Padden, 1983): those that do not manifest agreement ("plain" verbs) and those that do, which divide further into those known as "spatial" verbs, which take only source-goal agreement grounded in topographical space (e.g., *bicycle+rider moves from a-to-b*), and "agreement" verbs, which take not only source-goal agreement but also object and potentially subject agreement (e.g., *he helps her*; Meir, 2002; Meir et al., 2010). Meir argues that the main difference between verb agreement in spoken languages and signed languages is that verb agreement in signed languages seems to be determined thematically in semantics, rather than syntactically by formal organization. Agreement typically involves the representation of phi features of the NP arguments, and functionally it is a part of the referential system of a given language. And, typically in spoken languages, there is a closer relationship between agreement markers and structural positions in the syntax than between agreement markers and semantic roles. However, sign language verbs can agree not only with themes and agents, they can also agree with their source and goal arguments (Kegl (1985) was the first to notice this). The combination of syntactic and semantic motivations for agreement in signed languages was formalized as the "direction of transfer principle" (Brentari, 1988), but the analysis of verb agreement as having an iconic source in verb agreement was first proposed in Meir (2002).

   This analysis of the expression of agreement shows that the iconic, semantic, and phonological elements of verb agreement are distributed in an arbitrary way, and that despite the iconicity in content, this organization can be captured only by an account that employs the grammar in the explanation. Iconicity alone will not suffice.

   There is growing consensus that the particular values for the points of reference used in verb agreement (those at the beginning and end of the movement) may be gestural in nature; in other words, the distribution of DIR is arbitrary, but the specific values for the references in space that are assigned may either be default, in which case there will be general direction and no specific ending locus, or iconic and drawn from interaction with the world (see Lillo-Martin & Meier, 2011a, 2011b). Thus, these agreeing verbs in sign differ from their counterparts in spoken languages in that the absolute number of locations toward which the verbs can be directed is not a discrete (finite or listable) set, as are agreement morphemes in spoken languages. They are "shifters" in the Jakobsonian sense (Jakobson, 1971). Liddell (2003) prefers to call verbs of this sort "indicating" verbs (rather than "agreeing" verbs), because they indicate, or point to, referents just as a speaker might gesture toward a person when saying *I asked him*. In addition to the fact that it is not possible to list all of the loci that could serve as possible morphemes for these verb signs, the signs differ from spoken words in another respect. Verb movements encoding specific details (such as height) may also carry other meanings, such as specific (high) versus general (low) – see Barbera (2012) – social status (boss/worker), or may indeed be gestural and indicate the actual height of the individuals involved (Fischer & Gough, 1978; Liddell & Metzger, 1998; Liddell, 2003). This is why these forms are thought to be hybrids.

Liddell (2003), Liddell and Metzger (1998), and Dudis (2004) argue that the analog and gradient components of these signs endow them with gestural properties. Meir (2002) and Lillo-Martin and Meier (2011a, 2011b) argue that one part of the form is linguistic – namely, the [direction] feature of the movement to or from the signer.

To sum up this section, iconicity is an important aspect of building a sign language grammar; however, iconicity plus phonetic pressures are not enough to explain the distribution of form. We therefore have evidence that iconicity is constrained by the phonological and morphological systems in the cases that have just been described.

3.4 ICONICITY IN SIGN LANGUAGE PROCESSING

Until recently, iconicity was thought to play little role in first-language acquisition of a sign language (Bonvillian et al., 1990) or in language processing in native signers; for example, Poizner, Bellugi and Tweeney (1981) proposed that iconicity has no reliable effect on short-term recall of signs. Emmorey et al. (2004) showed specifically that motor-iconicity of signed languages (involving movement) does not alter the neural systems underlying tool and action naming. Thompson et al. (2005) have also shown that the meaning and form of signs are accessed independently, just as they are in spoken languages. More recent work has taken up this question again (Vigliocco et al., 2005; Perniss et al., 2010; Thompson et al., 2009, 2010; Bosworth & Emmorey, 2010), and we review the current debate here.

One of the first studies to look at iconicity and language processing was Grote and Linz (2003). They did a picture verification task with signers of German Sign Language (DGS), non-signing speakers of German, and DGS/German bilingual hearing individuals. Words or signs were presented auditorily or visually, respectively, and then pictures were shown. In the case of DGS, pairings of sign and picture were controlled for iconicity. Reaction times (RTs) were significantly faster for iconic pairings in DGS than non-iconic ones, and for hearing non-signers there was no difference for the same German words, none of which were iconic. Interestingly, the bimodal, bilingual DGS/German hearing participants had a weaker but still significant difference for the German words, suggesting cross-modal activation in the bilingual case. In Chapter 6 on processing and Chapter 7 on acquisition we discuss bilingual effects in more depth.

In Vigliocco et al. (2005), signers and non-signers were asked to do a triadic comparison whereby three semantic classes – tools (e.g., scissors, broom); tool-actions (e.g., drilling, drawing), and body-actions (e.g., slapping, punching) – were presented in either signs (for the BSL participants) or printed words. Paired tools and tool-use forms were not presented in the same trial (SCREWDRIVER, USE-A-SCREWDRI-VER). Signers were more likely to group the tools and tool-use forms together, while non-signers were more likely to group the tool actions and body actions together (showing a preference for distinguishing actions from tools). The researchers concluded that shared iconic properties of the signs was the explanation of this difference, and they suggested that BSL signers pay attention to iconicity as part of their language processing strategy. This result may have also been due to a more general sense of relatedness of form, since many of these forms share stems in the verbal and nominal forms, which are very similar phonologically.

Thompson et al. (2009) performed a lexical decision task addressing visual relatedness on native signers, non-signers, and late second-language (L2) learners. They studied whether native ASL signers had faster RTs when recognizing signs for which corresponding pictures were of objects in which the iconic properties of the signs were made salient. Native ASL signers were faster to respond to whether the sign matched the picture after seeing an iconically salient picture than after a non-salient one, while English speakers had no response advantage for the same pictures. The non-signers were aware of the iconicity, since they were able to provide iconicity ratings for signs in the study that were correlated with those of the native signers. The authors attribute the faster RT for native signers to automatic processing of iconicity.

Bosworth and Emmorey (2010) refuted Thompson's findings, however. In their priming task, deaf signers made lexical decisions to the second item of a prime target pair. Iconic target signs were preceded by signs that were (a) iconic and semantically related, (b) non-iconic and semantically related, or (c) semantically unrelated. In addition, a set of non-iconic target signs was preceded by semantically unrelated primes as fillers (see Figure 3.7). Significant facilitation was observed for target signs when they were preceded by semantically related primes. However, iconicity did not increase the priming effect. The target sign (e.g., PIANO) was primed equally by the iconic sign GUITAR or the non-iconic sign MUSIC. In addition, iconic signs were not recognized faster or more accurately than non-iconic signs.

Thompson et al. (2010) then tried another experimental method. Native signers and non-signers were asked simply to judge if the handshape of the signs presented was straight or curved (a phonological question unrelated to iconicity), but what they were really

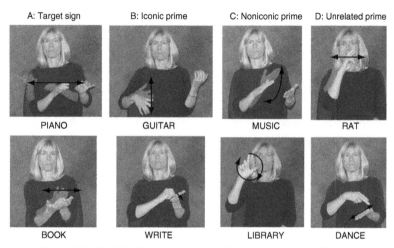

A: Target sign   B: Iconic prime   C: Noniconic prime   D: Unrelated prime

PIANO   GUITAR   MUSIC   RAT

BOOK   WRITE   LIBRARY   DANCE

Figure 3.7   (far left) Target signs and three types of preceding signs in a priming task assessing iconicity: semantically related iconic, and semantically related non-iconic, and unrelated non-iconic signs. (Reprinted with permission from *Journal of Experimental Psychology: Learning, Memory, and Cognition*, 36, Bosworth, R. & Emmorey, K., "Effects of iconicity and semantic relatedness on lexical access in American Sign Language," pp. 1573–1581, 2010.)

interested in was if there would be faster RTs for iconic signs. The team found that iconicity, particularly handshape and movement iconicity, inhibited RTs and accuracy in BSL signers. Because their results show a difference between the processing of iconic and non-iconic signs, the researchers conclude that at some level above phonology, the lexicon should include a specification for when a particular parameter of a sign is iconic; this has also been suggested by Friedman (1976) and Boyes Braem (1981).

3.5 CONCLUSION

Returning to the image from Chapter 1, we can see that iconicity is a mechanism ready to be exploited in sign languages for conventionalization. A form of language can become conventional for nonarbitrary reasons. Iconicity and phonology are not in conflict with each other because the arbitrariness is in the organization of the system, not in the source of the form.

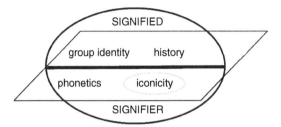

Figure 3.8 Possible mechanisms that can facilitate conventionalization of the signifier–signified relationships

I would agree with Perniss et al. (2010) that iconicity, in addition to arbitrariness, is a general feature of language as she has proposed. As mentioned throughout this chapter, the Saussurean notion of arbitrariness has sometimes been misunderstood. This relationship does not prohibit iconic forms to be genuine linguistic signs. Arbitrariness refers to both parts of the semiotic sign's relation separately – the signified piece and signifier piece – and linguistic signs are the conventionalized pairings between the two that are shared by a whole community. So when we consider these pairings, as shown in Figure 3.8, we see that iconicity is one way that the relationship between signified and signifier can be mediated, even as the phonological spaces (distributions of elements) are carved up arbitrarily. The research attention paid to iconicity in signed languages allows a wider range of iconic forms in a wide range of grammatical components to be taken into consideration, as this chapter has shown.

3.6 FURTHER READING

Demey, E. & van der Kooij, E. (2008). Phonological patterns in a dependency model: Allophonic relations grounded in phonetic and iconic motivation. *Lingua*, 118, 1109–1138.

Emmorey, K., Grabowski, T., McCullough, S., Damasio, H., Ponto, L., Hichwa, R., & Bellugi, U. (2004). Motor-iconicity of sign language does not alter the neural systems underlying tool and action naming. *Brain and Language*, 89, 27–37.

Meir, I. (2010). Iconicity and metaphor: Constraints on metaphoric extension of iconic forms. *Language*, 86. 865–986.

Perniss, P., Lu, J. C., Morgan, G., & Vigliocco, G. (2017). Mapping language to the world: The role of iconicity in the sign language input. *Developmental Science*, *21*(2), e12551.

Taub, S. (2001). *Language from the Body: Iconicity and Metaphor in American Sign Language*. Cambridge: Cambridge University Press.

4 Interfaces

Abstract

In this chapter, the ways that sign language phonology and prosodic structure interface with the other components of the grammar will be described, including how the nondominant hand interacts with morpho-syntactic and prosodic constituency. The most novel of the interfaces that will be discussed in this chapter will be the gesture–language interface, but the phonetics–phonology, morphology–phonology, and syntax/semantics–phonology interfaces will be discussed as well. This chapter also describes the details of higher-order prosodic structure not defined in earlier chapters – the phonological word (P-word; also referred to as the prosodic word), phonological phrase (P-phrase), and intonational phrase (I-phrase) – and provides evidence for prosody as independent from the rest of the grammar. This is of paramount importance because, in addition to showing how various components are interconnected, mismatches among different autonomous components of the grammar are one way we know that those components exist.

4.1 INTRODUCTION TO INTERFACE PHENOMENA IN SIGN LANGUAGES

In this chapter, we will address many different types of interface phenomena in sign languages. First of all, we will describe those aspects that are gestural-linguistic – "hybrid" – forms in sign languages, mindful of the fact that sign languages express both language and gesture in one modality more often than spoken languages do (see Chapter 3 on iconicity); therefore, the sign + gesture and speech + gesture comparison presents some challenges.

The gestural interface typically does not employ an entire word as a gesture, although this can occur, as it does in Wolof when speakers use clicks and other sounds expressively (Grenoble et al., 2015). It also occurs in sign languages, as when signers of Italian Sign Language (LIS) incorporate Italian emblematic gestures into their utterances, e.g., the gesture for *perfetto* and the sign for it are the same; Wilcox et al. (2010) have discussed this type of gestural incorporation in historical time in LIS. These gestures might function in a way that is similar to emojis used in texting; they cannot be placed just anywhere in the string. In all cases, but particularly the cases of incorporating features, rather than whole gestures, linguistic knowledge is required about where feature-based, iconic, idiosyncratic, gestural modifications can occur; specifically, they occur where the phonology allows them to be, where contrasts in form, meaning, or rule application are not relevant.

Throughout this chapter, it will be important to keep the notions of "comprehensibility" (or "accessibility") and "gestural" distinct from one another. Obviously, many aspects of iconic, linguistic modifications such as UNDERSTAND-A-LITTLE (Figure 4.1) are not universally accessible, but not every gestural property is universally accessible either. There are many emblematic gestures that are culturally specific yet still gestural, such as the Italian emblematic gesture for *be careful*, in which an index finger touches beneath one's eye. The reverse is also true, not everything that is accessible is gestural, and some accessible properties of signs are absolutely linguistic. Changes in the speed of movement such as acceleration and deceleration are linguistic, and yet also accessible to non-signers (Strickland et al., 2015), as are many non-manual properties of expressive facial expressions (Brentari et al., 2018). Zeshan (2006) and Quer (2012) discuss headshake for negation across sign languages. The negative headshake is accessible to non-signers, but it also has L-specific distributions with differing crosslinguistic patterns in sign languages representing grammatical negation. Its accessibility does not interfere with it also having linguistic status.

After describing several phonology–gesture interface phenomena, we will then turn to the more typical interface phenomena found in abundance in signed and spoken languages: phonetics–phonology, morphology–phonology, and syntax/semantics–phonology. In this chapter it is more important than ever to keep in mind the criteria for a unit to be phonological or morphological. To be phonological, a unit has at least one of these three roles in the system: (i) it participates in a minimal pair and is *distinctive*, or (ii) it is productive and discrete in terms of meaning (i.e., it has morphological status and is *prominent*), or (iii) it is implicated in a phonological rule and is *active*. These criteria and terms are drawn from Clements (2001); they are not mutually exclusive, and at least one of these has to be true for a unit to be phonological. Because a unit's morphological status is mentioned in these criteria, the diagnostics for a morpheme should be refreshed here as well. In order to be morphological, a form must have one or more of these properties: must be (i) discrete (i.e., contain a limited number of consistent features), (ii) productive (i.e., it affixes to a wide range of hosts), and (iii) related to a single meaning (i.e., the meaning should be relatively narrow and identifiable). We assume that these diagnostics are statistically rather than absolutely true, as in an optimality theoretic framework.

4.2 THE LANGUAGE–GESTURE INTERFACE

When is a signer gesturing, and when is she signing? It is becoming increasingly clear that to know a language, signed or spoken, includes knowledge about where, when, and how a gesture can be introduced; that is, native language users intuitively know where to find the spaces – the gaps – in the system where additional, idiosyncratic gestural forms can enhance the linguistic form. We might call this the gesture–language interface. Brentari (2018) has proposed two different types of gesture–language interfaces. One is the *inter*-modality interface, where the language and gesture are in different modalities, as they are most of the time in spoken languages, and the other is the *intra*-modality interface, where the language and gesture appear in the same modality.[1]

4.2.1 The *Inter*-modality Gestural Interface

The *inter*-modality gestural interface (aural-oral speech along with visual-manual gestures) will be mentioned here only briefly since it is not our focus, but it is worth noting that there are interface constraints that determine the location of gestures in relation to speech. Nobe (2000) and Loehr (2007) have discovered important generalizations about the close alignment of co-speech gestures and the pitch-accented syllables of a spoken phonological phrase. In addition, Krahmer and Swerts (2007) have discovered that the use of a beat gesture enhances the production and the perception of prominent syllables in spoken Dutch. In addition, Brentari et al. (2013) have discovered that the use of gesture enhances the formant production of pitch-accented vowels, particularly in stress-timed languages, such

---

[1] The term "paralinguistic" is sometimes used as a synonym for "gestural" by some researchers. Emmorey and Herzig (2003) describe these phenomena for sign languages as the "gestural overlay."

as English, as opposed to syllable-timed languages, such as Italian. At the sentence level some types of prosody can also be paralinguistic, expressing mental states (Bolinger, 1983). This can be witnessed in the case of facial expressions: for example, eyebrow wiggles, a facial expression that may be a type of emblematic gesture that is not affective, per se, but is more expressive in nature, carrying the meaning "Tom foolery."

4.2.2 The *Intra*-modality Gestural Interface

We turn now to the *intra*-modality gestural interface, the use of gesture and language in the same modality, which can occur at the feature, word, or phrasal levels in signed and spoken languages. In her paper on spoken and sign language gestures, Okrent (2002) points out that adding extra time to the vocal element in the word *long* to mean "excessively long" – *long* > *looooonnng* – is gestural. Similarly, in ASL adding extra time and distance by moving the index finger farther up the arm than normal to mean *very long* is also gestural.[2] This is an example in both languages of the intra-modality interface at the featural level. There are not very many ways that spoken languages can exploit gesture in this way at the word level in the speech signal: intensity for quantity, pitch for size (small versus large), or duration of vowel for duration of the event (long versus short).

Sign languages, on the other hand, have a number of ways that gesture can be overlaid onto sign structure. Emmorey (1999) and Liddell (2003) were two of the first researchers to recognize gesture in sign languages.

4.2.2.1 Distinctive Features

Some types of featural modification directly engage with the distinctive features of a lexical form. This type of word play is a way of exploiting the potential, sometimes linguistically inaccessible, iconicity in the distinctive features of the language. Two examples of this are shown in Figure 4.1. In ASL, UNDERSTAND can be modified to mean UNDERSTAND-A-LITTLE or UNDO-UNDERSTANDING. UNDERSTAND-A-LITTLE takes the typical form of the word (Figure 4.1, left) and modifies the selected finger; it is signed with the pinky finger (Figure 4.1, middle), which is smaller than the index finger. The index and pinky fingers independently create a distinctive contrast in ASL – IDEA and PENNY is a minimal pair. A third form (Figure 4.1, right) involves the reversal of the movement and can mean UNDO-UNDERSTANDING,

---

[2] ASL also has a morpheme that means "intensive."

Figure 4.1 Three forms of UNDERSTAND in ASL: (left) the citation form, (middle) UNDERSTAND-A-LITTLE, and (right) UNDO-UNDERSTANDING

where the location, handshape, and type of movement are all the same, but the aperture change is reversed from opening to closing. The modifications to UNDERSTAND can be understood as gestural because, while they employ distinctive features and are meaningful, their use is not productive or discrete.

4.2.2.2 Phonetic, Gestural Properties

Another sort of iconic, featural modification exploits more accessible and more variable types of iconicity, as seen in Lu and Goldin-Meadow (2017). They studied the addition of non-manual featural modifications that are added to classifier forms in ASL. In their study, signers and gesturers were asked to describe the differences between two forms. The more similar the two forms were, the more likely it was that native (but not non-native) signers used a type of iconic gesture to describe the difference. These forms are gestural *not* because they are iconic, such as sucked in cheeks to mean *narrow* or puffed cheeks (one cheek or both) to indicate *large* or *larger,* but because they vary from signer to signer in the same way that Duncan (2005) describes how Taiwanese signers varied in their description of the confined space of a drainpipe (described in more detail in Chapter 1). In Lu and Goldin-Meadow (2017), Duncan (2005), and Sandler (2009), the selected fingers of the handshape did not vary but other aspects of production did, including non-manual properties of the face. Schlenker (2018) also discusses manual properties used in this way, for example the speed with which a movement is produced in a verb, such as ASL's form for GET-LARGER or EXPAND, which can indicate gesturally how fast a group is growing: slowly using slower movements, faster using faster movements.

The types of phonetic gestural modification discussed above require that we first reflect on the criteria for minimal pairs, phonological rules, and iconicity. We see that in the process of applying the criteria for phonology and morphology rigorously across the parameters of sign languages, we can determine independently what is linguistic and what is gestural in form. Here are some examples.[3]

Words + gestural features: At the word level, pointing gestures or pointing signs contain gestural and linguistic elements in one mixed form (Fenlon et al., 2019). In sign languages, points can function grammatically as pronouns, but the specific locative values associated to the reference in space for the point may be added by gesture, just as they are for the points produced in co-speech gesture. In studying naturally occurring conversational dyads in BSL and a set from the Tavis Smiley television series, Fenlon et al. (2019) found that there were a number of structural differences shown between gesture and signed points: signed points are shorter than gestural points, and signed points appear most often with the 1-handshape ⚡, while gestural points appear most often with the B-handshape ⚡. From their distribution, it is clear that signed points are also functioning as pronouns, determiners, or locative predicates.

Morphology + gestural features: Many researchers are now arguing that there are some parts of a verb's structure that are linguistic and some parts that are gestural (see Brentari, 2011; Lillo-Martin & Meier, 2011a, 2011b). For example, in classifier predicates, as discussed in Chapter 1, there is no dispute that many properties of handshapes are morphological, but for movement there is likely a linguistically "light" verb such as BE-AT or MOVE, which is expressed by some movement features. These are coupled with a gestural layer to show a special arrangement of the object(s) in a particular location or specific loci at the beginning and end of the path movement. The evidence that the movements of classifier forms function as predicates is that they can function as the only predicate in a sentence; however, some of the *content* of the predicate itself may be gestural. Also, as discussed for agreement verbs in Chapter 3, they will or will not have a morphological DIR and/or a phonological [direction] feature (Meir, 2002), but the specific values of the loci in space will be gestural.

Since the forms we have discussed in this section do not meet the criteria for morphemes, I believe it makes more sense to appeal to the gestural nature of these forms and call them "hybrids," which include

---

[3] This is by no means an exhaustive set of examples.

properties that are linguistic and properties that are gestural. Some researchers have continued to think of these nonproductive meaningful forms as morphemic. Van der Hulst and van der Kooij (in press) have argued that phonology and morphology are "conflated" in these forms. Mufwene (2013) has made a similar suggestion, although he does not confine himself to these forms but asserts that the phonological and morphological components are generally conflated in sign languages; this sweeping statement is clearly incorrect as we have seen from the duality of patterning in forms, such as compounds, as illustrated in Figure 1.1, and in the results discussed in Berent et al. (2013) for monosyllabic-polymorphemic and disyllabic-monomorphemic forms. Usage-based approaches (Bybee, 1994) to morphology would probably not want to enter this debate at all, since their goal is to identify statistical patterns from marginal to extremely regular using the same linguistic terms.

Clauses + gesture: In this section, examples of the phonology–gesture interface that count as mental states, demonstrations, and speaker attitudes will be addressed. The grammatical ones will be addressed in the next section. At the clausal level all facial expressions in sign languages can be considered "prosodic" in the broadest sense, in that facial expressions of all types enhance sentence meaning in a variety of ways – grammatical and paralinguistic. Is there a way to distinguish paralinguistic gestures from grammatical ones? Dachkovsky (2007) compared well-known affective and grammatical facial expressions in Israeli Sign Language (ISL) that look similar, such as brow raise and brow furrow. Brow raise signals both surprise and yes/no questions, and brow furrow can convey both displeasure/anger and also wh-questions. She found the differences listed in Table 4.1.

Table 4.1 *Differences between affective and grammatical facial expressions*

	Grammatical facial expressions	**Affective facial expressions**
Scope	Consistent	Not consistent
Timing	Rapid onset and offset	Gradual onset and offset
Obligatoriness	Relatively obligatory	Optional
Musculature of the face	Higher number of facial action units	Lower number of facial action units

(cf. Dachkovsky, 2007)

The distributional properties of scope, timing, and obligatoriness of the two types of facial expressions were found to be quite different. Grammatical non-manuals are more constrained in their scope and timing and are relatively more obligatory than affective non-manuals; they have better defined domains and more rapid onsets and offsets. Grammatical non-manuals also have more individuated muscle movements than affective expressions, particularly those of the eyes.

Some findings suggest, however, that differences between affective and grammatical non-manuals in sign languages in onset and offset are observed in only some of the possible non-manual articulators or some types of expressions. For example, Dachkovsky's results pertained to the eyes and brows, but in a study of Finnish Sign Language (FinSL) the structural distinctions between affective and grammatical head tilts could not replicate the ISL result. The FinSL study used motion capture, which carefully annotated the onset and offset of four head movements – single and continuous nods, thrusts (head forward), and pulls (head back; Puupponen et al., 2015). The semantic and pragmatic functions and "affective" (or "expressive") functions of these head movements could not be distinguished from one another on the basis of their onset and offset.

4.3 INTERFACES OF PHONOLOGY AND OTHER GRAMMATICAL COMPONENTS

We now turn to how the phonetic, morphological, and semantic/syntactic components interface with phonology. In many ways, the issues that arise in these sections are not so different from the ones that are discussed in the spoken language literature, but we will see how the visual nature of sign languages plays a role here as well. The distribution and reorganization of gestural form seems to be one of the first indications of grammar, for both manual elements, such as points, and non-manual elements, such as non-manual facial expressions. The seeds of phonology may serve to work with these meaning–form combinations to become systematic in their distribution. This topic will be taken up again in Chapter 5 on the emergence of phonology in homesign and sign languages, where we will discuss how forms that are iconic in their source come to be distributed over time within the phonological space and according to the principles of dispersion, symmetry, and correspondence (Flemming, 1995, 2002, 2017).

Table 4.2 *Morpho-syntactic and corresponding prosodic units*

Morphological unit	Phonological units
Morpheme, stem	(Feature), mora, syllable
Morphological word	Phonological word
Syntactic phrase: XP	Phonological phrase
Clause	Intonational phrase

(cf. Nespor & Vogel, 1986)

Our anchor for this discussion will be the prosodic hierarchy of Nespor and Vogel (1986), which we will refer to as it becomes relevant for particular morpho-syntactic units (Table 4.2). These two types of units are by no means isomorphic, but they are the units most often paired together.

4.3.1   Phonetics–Phonology Interface: Constrained Flexibility

In this section we address variability in phonological form with respect to phonological features, allowing for forms to have a certain level of flexibility without slipping out of their phonological category. A good example of this in spoken languages is English voicing. Adults produce variation with respect to voice onset time (VOT), but this occurs *within the linguistically relevant categories* (i.e., within the delineation for each voicing category in a given language). In English there is variation in the expression of voicing by position, insofar as the onset versus coda of syllables have a different voicing threshold to be perceived as voiced or voiceless (Jakobson et al., 1952). There is also variability in the articulatory gesture of the lips interacting with that of the jaw to achieve closure in the bilabial sounds *p* and *b*, as well as inter- and intra-speaker variation of both voicing and closure (Smith et al., 2000; Goffman et al., 2007). Nonetheless, a voiced /b/ and voiceless /p/ are perceived as distinct from one another. We also see effects of categorical perception demonstrated by the fact that native speakers fail to hear the small differences within-category, e.g., within the /b/ category or the /p/ category. This happens for handshape in ASL as well; in categorical perception experiments of handshape, native signers show a loss of within-category distinctions (Emmorey et al., 2003; Morford et al., 2007). Morford et al. (2007) write, "the earlier in life participants were exposed to ASL, the more their perception skills are optimized to the *linguistically relevant variation* in the signed language signal"

"C" HANDSHAPES
curved-open to extended

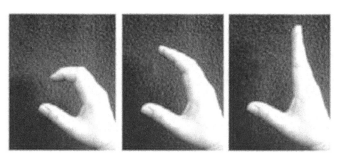

Figure 4.2   Handshapes in core, foreign, and spatial vocabulary
employed to investigate phonetic preferences for the same phonological handshape in different parts of the lexicon. (Reprinted with permission from "Contrast differences across lexical substrata: Evidence
from the ASL handshape," by Eccarius, P. & Brentari, D., in Adams, et al.
(eds.), *Proceedings from the 44th Annual meeting of the Chicago Linguistic
Society, Vol. 2*, pp. 187–201, 2008.)

(italics mine). Morford found that non-signers and non-native
signers do not behave in the same way as native
signers. Categorical perception is discussed in more depth in
Chapter 6.

"Goodness-of-fit" judgments for handshape from the work of Eccarius
(2008) also demonstrate systematic variability in ASL. Eccarius analyzed
the handshape preferences of native signers when they occur in different parts of the lexicon: core, spatial, and foreign (see Figure 1.3). In the
forms that had neither a minimal pair nor an associated meaning – e.g.,
in core lexical items such as in the ASL sign SEARCH (see Figure 4.2) –
native signers preferred the middle form, where the fingers were mid-
way between "flexed" and "extended." In the forms where there was
a minimal pair, such as the initialized foreign form CHICAGO (which
uses the handshape on the left in Figure 4.2) versus the core form NEVER
(which uses the handshape on the right in Figure 4.2), signers preferred
these two handshapes, respectively. When the pair of handshapes were
associated with specific morphology in classifier handshapes, such as
round-pipe (which uses the handshape on the left in Figure 4.2) versus
square-plank (which uses the handshape on the right in Figure 4.2),
signers also had strong preferences for forms that associate with one
of each of the two meanings. Eccarius's work shows that signers are

flexible to a certain degree, particularly for the joint features, but *within the linguistically relevant categories.*

The type of work just discussed shows that when meaningful differences are not involved – when there are no minimal pairs or morphological differences – native signers employ a certain type of phonetic flexibility. The differences indicate that the signers were employing linguistically relevant categories in their preferences concerning the quality and quantity of the flexibility allowed. There are thus structural points of reference to determine the amount and type of variation or gradience that is allowed, and these factors are affected by the linguistic units, by context, and by language experience.

There are two other important types of phonetics–phonology interface phenomena. One is the addition of features that enhance ease of articulation. One case of feature addition occurs with the [stacked] feature, which has a minimal pair in the foreign lexicon – -V- versus -K- – but not in the core lexicon. In the core lexicon [stacked] is optionally added by a rule. When the palm is facing the midsagittal plane but the fingers are [spread] in the vertical plane (Figure 4.3) the handshape becomes [stacked]. This feature would be in the phonological inventory because it is implicated in this rule as an *active* feature. This

Figure 4.3 The [stacked] feature used allophonically in ASL: (left) Citation form of SEE; (right) SEE [stacked], which is an alternative surface form used when the palm is facing toward the midsagittal plane (rightmost image from "A formal analysis of phonological contrast and iconicity in sign language handshapes," by Eccarius, P. & Brentari, D. In *Sign Language and Linguistics*, 13, 2010, pp. 156-181. Reprinted with kind permission from John Benjamins Publishing Company, Amsterdam/ Philadelphia. [www.benjamins.com].)

Figure 4.4   Flexion of the metacarpal joint used allophonically: (left) Citation form of *person-move-from-"a"-to-"b"*; (right), *person-come towards* (cf. Crasborn et al. 2000).

feature was discussed in more depth in Chapter 3 for its selective iconicity across the lexicon.

A case of feature addition involves the feature [flexed] at the metacarpophalangeal knuckle joint (MCP) under certain conditions (Crasborn, 2001). For example, note that the knuckle is straight in Figure 4.4 (left), which is the citation form of *person-move-from-"a"-to-"b,"* when the palm is facing away from the signer's chest, but the knuckle is bent in Figure 4.4 (right) when the palm is facing the signer's chest. According to the criteria outlined for phonological features in Clements (2001), this [flexed] feature would be included in the phonological system because it is implicated in this rule, even though in Sign Language of the Netherlands (NGT) there are no minimal pairs using this feature. In the foreign component of ASL the two handshapes for -U- and -N- are a minimal pair in ASL based on this feature.

The last type of interface phenomenon we will address in this chapter is a prohibition against combinations of features that are difficult to produce (Mathur & Rathman, 2010a., 2010b; Sanders & Napoli, 2016a, 2016b). Such prohibitions create gaps in the morphological and lexical space due to difficulty of production. In Mathur and Rathman (2010a, 2010b), they describe a prohibition against a combination involving a flexed wrist, a movement of the elbow toward the chest, and the ipsilateral side of the body (e.g., *each of them-gives-me; each of them-watches-me*). There are no stems with this combination of features, and there is a gap in the agreement paradigm of some ASL verbs due to this prohibition.

These phonetic facts grounded in the physicality of production result in enhancements and prohibitions that affect the phonological and morphological systems, and they appear crosslinguistically in many sign languages.

4.3.2 Morphology–Phonology Interface

This section concerns how morphological units come to be conventionalized. Although many of these forms may also contain various amounts of iconicity, once such forms are regular and productive, they behave just like any other (non-iconic) morpheme, since at that stage they are discrete, productive, and, as suggested by Brentari et al. (2012a) and van der Hulst and van der Kooij (in press), tend to utilize elements of the phonology that are already independently motivated phonologically.

We have already discussed in Chapter 3 the joint feature [stacked] and the path feature [direction], and their ability to be both morphemic and iconic. Quantity features of handshape (how many fingers are selected - 𝄞 𝄞 𝄞) are examples of forms that are morphemic and iconic as well - they express width iconically and are also constrained (Eccarius, 2008). In other words, there is abundant evidence of the feature–morpheme association. Aronoff et al. (2005) argue that this is a modality effect, as we have discussed at length in Chapters 2 and 3.

Lexical and morphological conventionalization involve reducing the variation in form–meaning association in two ways: On the form side, it means stabilizing the form to one that obeys the phonotactics of syllables and prosodic words to a large extent, and on the meaning side, it means reducing the range of meanings to a predictably small number, ideally to just one meaning. In the next section concerning the morphology–phonology interface, we see how the phonological units of the mora, segment, syllable, word, and phrase organize meaningful forms in morphology and syntax into phonological units.

4.3.2.1 Morphology and the Syllable

The syllable, mora, and segment are the units that are primarily involved in the morphology–phonology phonotactics, so their definitions are reviewed here, along with their participation in interface phenomena. The *syllable* in sign languages is defined with reference to sequential units of movement. Movements are syllable nuclei, as discussed in detail in Chapters 1 and 2. The criteria for counting syllables are repeated here for convenience (1). One path movement produced at the shoulder or elbow is equivalent to a syllable in sign language (Brentari, 1998), and in the absence of a path movement, a local movement produced by a movement of the forearm, wrist, or finger joints may serve as a syllable nucleus as well.

(1)   *Syllable Counting Criteria (Brentari, 1998):*
   a. The number of syllables in a sequence of signs equals the number of sequential movements in that string.
   b. When several shorter (e.g., secondary) movements co-occur with a single (e.g., path) movement of longer duration, the longer movement is the one to which the syllable refers.
   c. When two or more movements occur at exactly the same time, it counts as one syllable, e.g., ASL INFORM (Figure 1.7) is one syllable containing an aperture change and a path movement.

There are a few morphological forms that are syllabic. Aronoff et al. (2005) discuss several of these in ISL, such as "adjective" + *not exist*, as in IMPORTANT+ *not exist* (*not important*), or SURPRISE + *not exist* (*not surprising*). Another is the "verb" + zero morpheme, as in UNDERSTAND + *zero* (*understand nothing*) or SEE + *zero* (*see nothing*). What they argue is that simultaneous morphology at the sub-syllabic level is more common. This brings us to the mora.

4.3.2.2   Morphology and the Mora

The *mora* is a sub-syllabic unit of syllable weight in signed and spoken languages, and mora assignment is also related to sonority. The more sonorant features are, the more likely they are to contribute to moraic structure. Vowels, which are high sonority, receive a mora, and if they are long they are bimoraic. Consonants that are low sonority are not typically moraic, but if they are geminates (CC) sometimes they can be (Gordon, 2006). The modality difference between signed and spoken languages is that morae are added simultaneously in signed languages, not sequentially as they typically are in spoken languages; that is, simultaneous movement units are used for counting morae. Brentari (1998) has demonstrated that morae are organized simultaneously in ASL morphophonology. There are two relevant cases that serve as evidence. One is a well-known derivational process that derives nominal forms and was discussed in depth in Chapter 2 via reduplication. Monomoraic stems (light syllables with one movement component) allow reduplication, while stems that are bimoraic or heavier (heavy syllables with two or more simultaneous movement components) disallow reduplication. The forms referred to in (1c) with a path and local movement would be heavy and bimoraic: INFORM (Figure 1.7) disallows * INFORMATION. A second case are verbs that are repeated in their plural forms. One such stem is ASK (see Figure 3.5, from Corina,

Table 4.3 *The distribution of the number of morae in core lexical stems of FinSL*

Syllable type	N	%
1 mora	131	57
2 morae	80	35
3 morae	19	8
4 morae	1	–
Total	231	100

1990). When the form becomes ASK multiple people, the path movement is lost and a repeated handshape change remains.

The distribution of morae in a sign language lexicon typically follows a cline, as shown in Table 4.3 for monomorphemic forms in FinSL (Jantunen, 2006; Jantunen & Takkinen, 2010). The majority of forms have just one mora, with the proportion reduced further and further as morae are added until there is just a single form found with four simultaneous morae. While this is just a representative sample, a similar cline occurs in ASL, with 82 percent of the signs in the *Dictionary of American Sign Language* (DASL) containing simple movements (mono-moraic forms), and 18 percent containing more complex movements (Brentari, 1998). A recent study of a portion of Valli's (2006) *The Gallaudet Dictionary of American Sign Language* found a slightly higher number of 24 percent (Martinez del Rio, 2018).

4.3.2.3 Morphology and the Segment

Segmental structure (timing slots) has been argued to be a locus of the phonology–morphology interface as well. Wilbur has been involved in research on the relationship between movement and meaning in signed languages since the 1980s (Wilbur et al., 1983, 1999). She has developed the Event Visibility Hypothesis (Wilbur, 2008, 2010), which is a proposal for how the structure of predicates of signed languages adheres to a type of mapping between event structure and phonological form (discussed in detail in Chapter 3; and see also Figure 3.2). Wilbur argues that by using the segmental structure proposed in Brentari (1998) we see that the morphophonology of sign language captures the forms of telic and atelic predicates directly. This analysis has been able to establish that there is a relationship between event structure and segmental structure (meaning and form) that is both iconically motivated and phonologically constrained, and Wilbur has argued that these structural components of predicates are one reason why sign languages look so similar to one another.

Importantly, and pertinent to our current discussion, even though the telic and atelic forms are recognizable to non-signers in a fixed choice task (Strickland et al., 2015), these forms would count as morphological, since they are productive, discrete, and constrained in meaning in sign language (and therefore *prominent* in Clements' 2001 terminology). This contrasts with the forms discussed in the gesture–phonology interface that are idiosyncratic, not discrete, and not constrained in meaning.

4.3.2.4 Morphology and the Prosodic Word

Recall also from Chapter 1 that each of the parameters has a set of features that does not change during the execution of a monomorphemic sign. These are, for example, selected fingers for handshape and major place of articulation (POA). There is also a set that does change, such as aperture for handshape and setting for POA. Putting these all together, we can characterize these preferences at work in the word, syllable, and moraic structure of words in ASL (2), although not all of these necessarily can be generalized across sign languages. These could also be considered MARKEDNESS constraints as described in Chapter 1.

(2) *Word-morae-syllable preferences in sign language stems*
   a. Mono syllabicity (Coulter, 1980): one sequential movement per word/sign.[4]
   b. Mono-moraicity forms (Jantunen, 2006): one movement component per word/sign. In other words, there is a tendency toward mono-valency of the inherent features of handshape, major POA, and some non-manuals (Brentari, 1998).
   c. Mono-valency of handshape: whenever possible reduce the number of parameter values to "one."

We can see the syllable and moraic preferences in (2) at work in several sign languages at the next highest unit in the prosodic hierarchy, the *prosodic word* (P-word); none of these is satisfied 100 percent of the time, indicating the violability of these constraints. In future work we might be able to determine if the triggering units referred to in (2) are solely responsible for the realization of these preferences or if frequency also plays an important role.

---

[4] There are disyllabic monomorphemic signs, such as ASL DESTROY, which show that the syllable and morpheme not isomorphic (Brentari, 1998).

SCHOOL   THERE
(ASL, independent signs)

SCHOOL-THERE
(coalescence)

I (1-handshape)   COOK
(ASL, independent signs

I (assimilated B-handshape)   COOK
(cliticization with handshsape assimilation)

FEMALE   SAME
(independent ASL signs)

FEMALE^SAME *sister*
(ASL compound with spread of mouthing
across the compound)

Figure 4.5   Examples of the prosodic word in ASL: (top) as Coalescence; (middle) as a combination of pronoun+verb form from ASL where handshape assimilation has occurred; (bottom) where non-manual spreading has occurred. (The bottom images are printed with permission from Valli, C. (2006). *The Gallaudet Dictionary of American Sign Language.* Gallaudet University Press.)

The tendency toward monosyllabicity is seen in coalescence (Sandler, 1999a, 2012a), demonstrating the phonotactic in (2a), shown in Figure 4.5 (top) – SCHOOL THERE. In such cases a disyllabic two-sign phrasal form is reduced to a monosyllabic P-word. In this case, the prosodically weak pointing sign THERE is signed by the dominant hand while the nondominant hand spreads from the Type 1, two-handed sign SCHOOL (in these signs both hands have the same handshape and movement). The resulting prosodic word retains the handshape and movement of the sign for SCHOOL. This type of coalescence can occur only when a two-handed sign is involved.

A second case of the prosodic word unit at work involves combinations of a sequentially cliticized pronoun form and a verb. These examples consist of two 1-handed signs, such as in Figure 4.5 (middle), 1sg+COOK, where the handshape of the verb regressively assimilates to the pronoun. The two movements (syllables) are retained, but the selected fingers of handshape become monovalent.

Compounds are considered single prosodic words, and the one in Figure 4.5 (bottom), FEMALE^SAME (*sister*) shows that the output achieves all of the phonotactic constraints in (2) – mono-syllabicity (2a), mono-moraicity (2b), plus mono-valency (2c). First, the movements of both of the stems are deleted in favor of using a single movement that transitions between the two locations; this is a strategy for adhering to mono-syllabicity (2a). Second, the change from the first to the second of the two input stems' handshapes of the compound would result in a handshape change and a path movement (a bimoraic form), but the resulting compound eliminates the handshape change and keeps only the path movement; this is a strategy for adhering to mono-moraicity (2b). Third, the handshapes of the two stems merge to contain features of the two handshapes (the thumb of FEMALE and the index of SAME); this is a strategy for adhering to the constraint in mono-valency (2c).

Patterns of non-manuals are also important in many prosodic words, particularly those of the mouth (Brentari and Crossley, 2002; Boyes Braem, 2001). Notice that non-manual mouthing in the compound FEMALE^SAME "sister" (Figure 4.5 (bottom right), extends across the whole compound moving from an "s" to an "r" mouth shape. In some cases this non-manual spreading can also be seen across a stem+affix as well, as in DOCTOR (stem)+PERSON (affix) "doctor" in Swiss German Sign Language (DSGS; Boyes Braem, 2001). Similar phenomena have been reported in NGT, BSL, and Swedish Sign Language (SSL; Pfau & Quer, 2010). The direction of spreading may differ crosslinguistically, and all of these tendencies have some exceptions; none is valid absolutely.

4.3.2.5 Morphology and Phrases

The notion that phrasal prosody has meaning is not new; we've known for a long time that a rising phrase-final tone signals a question: *You're coming (H)?* versus a statement *You're coming (L)*. Fortunately, the domain of inquiry has expanded dramatically in recent years, thanks to a large body of work on this topic (see Pierrehumbert & Hirschberg, 1990; Beckman and Venditti, 2011, and references therein). Even so, it has been difficult to determine which specific tunes are morphological in spoken language prosody. An example of this from spoken language (English) is seen in work by Kuramada et al. (2014), who demonstrated that the timing of a pitch accent on the verb changes the truth value of the sentence (*It* **looks** *(H) like a zebra*) or noun (*It looks like a* **zebra** *(H)*). The sentence with the pitch-accented verb has the interpretation "It is not a zebra it just looks like one," while the sentence with the pitch-accented noun has the interpretation "It is a zebra." In another recent example on the use of prosodic prominence as pitch accent in both production and perception, Etxeberria and Irurtzun (2014) argued that the word *ere* in Basque has two meanings that are distinguished by prosody alone (3). One means English *too* (carrying an additive meaning, where the background assumes "x" and *ere* means "also y"), and the other means English *even* (carrying a scalar meaning, where the background assumes "not x"). *Ere* is always the pitch-accented syllable, but it has a significantly higher than normal pitch accent for scalar cases. In these cases, we see that even the degree to which the pitch is raised can make a big difference for the sentence's meaning and can carry morphological status.

(3) *ere in Basque (Etxeberria and Irurtzun, 2014)*

    a. Jon **ere** etorri da (normal pitch accented **ere**)
       John even come AUX
       John came too. (background, x=John would come)
    b. Jon **ere** etorri da (raised pitch **ere**)
       John even come AUX
       Even John came. (background, x=John would not come)

We focus here on non-manual elements of sign language intonation.[5] Determining which non-manual markers in sign languages are morphological is as difficult as determining the role of pitch in spoken languages. Some facial expressions are affective/expressive or are comprehensible across a culture for other reasons. For example, negative headshake is an accessible, gestural form that has linguistic status in sign languages because it has scope over particular manual constituents in many sign languages (4; Neidle et al., 2000; Quer, 2012). In ASL the negative headshake must spread across the whole VP in the sentence in (4) if there is no negative manual sign NOT (4c–d), but if NOT is present, the negative headshake can occur over NOT alone or over the whole VP (4a–b). Headshake is therefore considered morpho-syntactic in sign languages.

---

[5] Intonational cues in sign languages may be both manual and non-manual (Brentari et al., 2011), but we focus on the non-manual cues here.

(4) *Scope of negative headshake in ASL (Neidle et al., 2000)*

		neg		
a.	JOHN	NOT	BUY	HOUSE

		neg		
b.	JOHN	NOT	BUY	HOUSE

		neg		
c.	*JOHN	BUY	HOUSE	

		neg		
d.	JOHN	BUY	HOUSE	

John did not buy a house.

"Constructed action" may be another quintessential example of the marriage of language and paralinguistic prosody (Quer, 2005), because it concerns non-manual components that can be gestural, as "demonstration" (Clark & Gerrig, 1990; Davidson, 2015), but they function in a linguistic way because of their alignment with the elements of the clause. In a sentence with constructed action during quoted speech, the *shift* (of the body position and accompanying non-manuals) is linguistic. This shift signals that constructed action or constructed dialogue is occurring, but the values on the face and body during the quoted portion of the utterance are gestural (Figure 4.6).

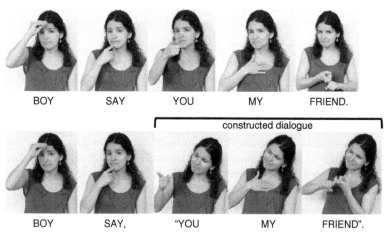

Figure 4.6 (top) The ASL sentence translated into English as *The boy said you are my friend* without a point of view predicate (third-person, non-quoted discourse), and (bottom) the ASL sentence translated into English as *The boy said, "You are my friend!"* with a constructed dialogue form (i.e., quoted discourse) representing the first person, boy's point of view.

Paralinguistic facial expressions concerning mental states and speaker attitudes can also assume grammatical status in imperatives speech acts expressed via I-phrases. To explore this question further, Brentari et al. (2018) analyzed the set of temporal and non-manual prosodic cues that accompany four types of sign language (ASL) imperatives in production and comprehension to investigate how such facial expressions in ASL might function as indicators of sentence meaning. They were also interested in determining how accessible this prosody is to non-signers. All sentences had two signs and were controlled for syllable count: verbs with a single path movement executed by the elbow (PICK, TAKE, THROW-AWAY, KEEP) and a reduplicated noun (BOOK, HAT, PAPER, WATCH). Each verb+noun sentence was produced in four different imperative contexts (commands, explanations, advice, and permission) and in a neutral context, by a single, third-generation, ASL signer. The production results showed that, among the non-manuals annotated, the cue eyes wide was predictive of commands, head nod was predictive of sentences with permission, and neutral sentences showed fewer mouth movements overall. The temporal cues were also informative in determining sentence type, which emphasizes the fact that a constellation of cues rather than a single cue may be responsible for sentence interpretation. Sentence durations, sign duration (particularly the verbs), and hold durations were consistently shortest in commands and longest in neutral sentences. These ASL sentences were shown to four groups: ASL signers, signers of German Sign Language (DGS), hearing American non-signers, and hearing German non-signers, with the hypotheses that culture (American versus German) or language experience would make a difference in performance (signer versus non-signer, or ASL versus all other groups). In all groups, neutral sentences were easily discriminated from imperatives, and among the imperatives, commands were the most accurately identified, suggesting that commands are a kind of prototypical imperative across groups. Even though all groups performed above chance overall, the ASL signers were significantly more accurate than the other three groups on this task, particularly for imperatives that are not commands, suggesting that the particular distributions of facial cues and timing have been grammaticized, and experience with them improves the ability to interpret them. However, since the DGS and two non-signing groups were also able to interpret the cues to a large extent, this result also indicates that these constellations of cues are accessible to non-signers. From this study we can see how visual prosody can participate in the semantic/pragmatic components of language and at the same time have meanings that are also comprehensible to individuals without language-specific experience.

To sum up this section on morphology and how it interfaces with the prosodic units of Nespor and Vogel's 1986 hierarchy, we see that sign languages have well-defined morphemes at all of these levels – feature, segment, mora, syllable, word, and phrase. We have discussed the intonational phrase so far, and the phonological phrase will be discussed in the separate section later in this chapter on the nondominant hand (H2). It would be interesting to have quantitative evidence for distributional differences of these units as compared with spoken languages. We have come to accept as canon that sign languages have more simultaneously layered morphology due to the use of the visual modality; however, it would be extremely helpful to have studies of signed and spoken language corpora when making these claims.

4.3.3   Prosodic Units and Sentence/Discourse Meaning

Beyond morphology, the phonological word, phonological phrase, and intonational phrase are also important in terms of delineating constituents and packaging meaning for sentences and discourse. This section is concerned with parsing constituents and assigning clausal meanings and dependencies. We first address two key theoretical questions. First, "Do prosodic domains reflect syntactic constituents or semantic generalizations?"; that is, does prosody interact directly with the syntax or only indirectly via the semantics? We will see in Section 5.3.1 that there is some evidence that prosody interacts directly with the semantics, not the syntax. Second we ask, "To what extent are prosody and syntax independent?" Sandler (2010) has proposed that grammatical complexity in prosody and syntax develop together and gradually become distinct from one another, and this will be discussed in more detail in Chapter 5 on the emergence of phonology (see Section 5.3.1). In brief, she analyzed the structure of narratives of four signers of Al-Sayyid Bedouin Sign Language (ABSL), an emerging sign language in Israel: two older signers and two younger signers. They found that younger signers, who have had the language model of the older generation of signers, produce prosodic cues to indicate dependency between semantically related constituents, such as the two clauses of a conditional, revealing a type and degree of complexity in their language that is not frequent in that of the older pair of signers. In addition, in the younger signers several rhythmic and (facial) intonational cues are aligned at constituent boundaries, indicating the emergence of a grammatical system. Prosodic cues are typically the only cues to structure, and the complexity of prosodic structure is matched by syntactic complexity in the younger signers in other ways too, independent of non-manuals. Younger signers are more likely to use pronouns as abstract grammatical markers of arguments and to combine predicates with their arguments within a constituent. In the older signers, indications of relations across clauses that would correspond to complex sentences are almost nonexistent. Both manual and non-manual cues are important throughout the prosodic hierarchy, and the examples provided here involve phenomena of timing, non-manual behaviors, and manual markers, particularly those of nondominant hand spread.

The prosodic units of the I-phrase and utterance have been analyzed in several sign languages – ASL (Wilbur, 1999a, 1999b; Brentari & Crossley, 2002), ISL (Nespor & Sandler, 1999; Sandler, 2012a), NGT (Crasborn & van der Kooij, 2005), and HKSL (Sze, 2008), among them. There are also a few papers that discuss higher-order prosodic structure crosslinguistically (Tang et al., 2010; Dachkovsky & Sandler, 2013; Sáfár & Kimmelman, 2015; Kimmelman et al., 2016). Such crosslinguistic studies are very important if we are to establish the range of possible forms and the fact that conventionalization involves not only differences in form but also differences in distribution.

In terms of chunking portions of the sign stream into constituents, there is clear autonomy between prosody and syntax in adults (in other words, there is some non-isomorphy), but frank non-isomorphy is relatively rare; most cases of non-isomorphy occur when collapsing two smaller units into one larger unit, so differences are because units are combined and omitted, rather than reorganized into different units (Brentari et al., 2015b). For example, two smaller potentially independent I-phrases are uttered as a single I-phrase – e. g., [CAROL VISIT GRANDMOTHER]$_{IP1}$[GO EVERY-WEEK]$_{IP2}$ > [CAROL VISIT GRANDMOTHER GO EVERY-WEEK]$_{IP1}$. Without going into the details of the theoretical implications for this claim, this would suggest that isomorphy is a kind of default setting, with non-isomorphy expressing specific structures or appearing only in special circumstances (Truckenbrodt, 1999, see debates between Truckenbrodt, 2012, and Selkirk, 2011, on this issue). I-phrases in spoken and signed languages typically correspond to the root sentence or clause. Constructions that are structurally external to the sentence (such as parentheticals, nonrestrictive relative clauses, and topicalizations) often form I-phrases on their own in spoken and signed languages (see Figure 4.6 for an example of this with quotation; Nespor and Vogel, 1986; Nespor & Sandler, 1999; Sandler and Lillo-Martin, 2006).

4.3.3.1 Parsing Prosodic Constituents

Several manual and non-manual markers have been identified that mark the boundaries of an I-phrase, such as lengthening the final sign (Grosjean & Lane, 1976), eye blinks (Wilbur, 1994), brow raise (Wilbur & Patschke, 1999), brow furrow (Sandler & Lillo Martin, 2006), body leans (Boyes Braem, 1999), and squint eyes (Sandler, 1999a). These prosodic markers do not always occur independently but combine with one another sequentially and simultaneously (i.e., prosodic layering, see Wilbur, 2000). Some of these are "edge" phenomena, which happen at the edges of this constituent (e.g., lengthening, eye blinks), and some are "domain" phenomena, which extend across the whole constituent, and their change in value marks the edges of the constituent (e.g., body leans, squint, brow raise). At the I-phrase and utterance levels, Sandler and Lillo-Martin (2006) have proposed that temporal cues (sign duration and pause duration) are used primarily for finding the boundaries of phrasal constituents and non-manual cues are primarily for intonation and meaning.

A quantitative study of phrasal prosodic cues of native ASL signers who were younger children, older children, and adults largely confirms this division of labor for ASL (Brentari et al., 2015), but this generalization is not absolute. Exceptions to this dichotomy are eye blinks and head nods (non-manual cues) that often can be used to chunk constituents as a replacement for or in addition to temporal cues, such as lengthening (Tang et al., 2010), and the acceleration of movement (a temporal cue) that can be used to make a sign more prominent or give it emphasis (Wilbur, 1999a). The cues for the utterance and phonological phrase (P-Phrase) use many of the same cues as I-phrases, but for an utterance there is a total recalibration of manual and non-manual cues. The cues for the P-phrase are, for the most part, weaker versions of patterns seen at the I-phrase, discussed in detail in the next section, such as less frequent eye blinks, or lengthening of the final sign that is less dramatic at the end of a P-phrase than in an I-phrase.

Timing markers associated with the I-phrase include lengthening of the phrase-final sign (Nespor & Sandler, 1999; Wilbur, 1997, 1999b; Wilbur & Zelaznik, 1997; Brentari et al., 2011) and lengthened pauses (Grosjean and Lane, 1977). In contrast to languages like English where stress can be shifted to the lexical item in focus in situ, sign languages prefer prominence in I-phrase-final position (Nespor & Sandler, 1999; Wilbur, 1997), and they shift prominent forms to this position in order to allow them to more easily express prominence features. Phrase-final lengthening involves the whole syllable – movement and final hold.[6] In addition, signs that are stressed are produced higher in the signing space and display increased muscle tension and sharp transition boundaries (Wilbur, 1999b). The length of a pause can also be correlated with the strength of a boundary (Grosjean & Lane, 1977). In an examination of pauses produced by five native signers of ASL, the mean pause duration was higher between sentences (229 ms) and lower at lower-level boundaries (e.g., 134 ms between conjoined clauses), with durations shorter than in spoken languages (> 445 ms between sentences; 245–445 ms between conjoined clauses).

To summarize, manual cues are more reliable than non-manual markers in dividing up strings of signing into I-phrases and utterances in ASL (Brentari et al., 2015a, 2015b), and a similar claim has been made for ISL (Sandler & Lillo-Martin, 2006); however, non-manual cues are important for parsing constituents, as well as for determining meaning as we have seen in the previous section. We have discussed paralinguistic non-manual behaviors at the beginning of this chapter and described how negative head shake or mental state non-manuals can still function grammatically due to their systematic alignment with constituents of a sentence, even when they are comprehensible to non-signers. Next, we discuss the specific non-manuals that have a clear grammatical status and that are used prosodically to mark constituency as well as in the syntax/semantics to add grammatical meaning.

4.3.3.2   Attribution of Sentence Meaning

In this section let us first address two of the most important structural criteria for a non-manual marker to be considered grammatical: componentiality and crosslinguistic differences. Grammatical facial expressions are componential in ways the emotional expressions used in imperatives (discussed in the previous section) are not; that is, each component of the facial expression provides a specific contribution to the overall meaning of the sentence. An example of this is seen in counterfactual conditionals in ISL, which involves both raised eyebrows and eye squint. When these two markers are combined, they

---

[6] Perlmutter (1992) proposed the mora (the final hold) to account for this phenomenon, but phonetic evidence from Tyrone et al. (2010) from motion capture measurements indicates that the whole syllable is lengthened.

Figure 4.7   Example of changes in the non-manual markers between the two I-phrases in a conditional phrase of ISL, including eyebrow changes (raised > neutral), eye changes (squint to neutral), and head position changes (forward to back). (From Sandler, W., "Prosody and syntax in sign languages," *Transactions of the Philological Society*, 108. Published by Blackwell. © Transactions of the Philological Society © The Philological Society 2011. Reprinted with permission from John Wiley and Sons.)

typically characterize counterfactual conditionals as in (5); see Figure 4.7. These markers can be broadly interpreted when viewed independently, yet they gain specificity when produced in combination with other features with which they are co-articulated and in particular lexical or phrasal constituents.

(5)   *Componentiality of non-manual markers in Israeli Sign Language (ISL, Dachkovsky and Sandler, 2009: 306)*

<u>   br + sq   </u>
IF GOALKEEPER HE CATCH BALL, WIN GAME WIN
If the goalkeeper had caught the ball, they would have won the game.

Some non-manual markers in ASL and ISL, such as brow raise, are used for multiple functions – topics, yes/no questions, and conditionals all use brow raise – which raises the question as to whether these non-manuals may point to a deeper semantic or pragmatic generalization. Sandler (2010, 2012a) has proposed that in ISL brow raise "signals continuation and forward directionality" indicating that the phrase that it spans is linked to the following phrase in some way, and this forward directionality links these three functions of brow raise. The eye squint is said to designate shared information between the speaker and the addressee, and when combined with brow raise results in a counterfactual.

To strengthen an analysis unifying brow raise functions, we turn to work on spoken languages. Haiman (1978) has observed that conditionals are like topics; that is, a consequence is evaluated against a background state of affairs. And conditionals are similar to polar questions in the sense that two alternatives are in play. Evidence for Haiman's observations comes from spoken Turkish, where the conditional marker *–se* can be replaced by the marker for polar questions *–mi* in colloquial speech, and the typical conditional marker *–se* is often used for contrastive topics (Croft, 1990). This generalization across polar questions, conditionals, and topics in sign languages can also be compared with the crosslinguistic tendency in spoken languages to mark both nonfinal clauses and interrogatives with high phrasal tones, which also signal forward directionality (see, for example, Venditti & Beckman, 2011). Sandler also builds on Bartels's (1999) analysis of high boundary tones. Bartels explains that there is a general implicature of continuation of a final high tone in one unit with the next unit that can have different, relatively more concrete semantic or pragmatic interpretations, depending on other properties of the utterance, and Sandler argues that the same is true of brow raise. This lends support to the argument that these markers perform a similar function to intonational tunes in spoken languages (Pierrehumbert & Hirschberg, 1990). This has led Truckenbrodt (2012), for spoken languages, and Sandler (2012a), for sign languages, to argue that intonation interfaces with semantics directly and with syntax only indirectly.

The second criterion for grammatical non-manuals, besides componentiality, is that there are observable crosslinguistic differences in their behavior and structure, similar to the way that the same vowel (e.g., /o/) can be phonetically different across spoken languages. Dachkovsky et al. (2013) showed that ISL and ASL signers produced squints differently phonetically – ISL signers tighten their lower eyelids to produce a narrowed eye aperture, while ASL signers raise the cheeks to accomplish the same result. In addition, ASL signers use squint to mark given information only when that information is very low in "givenness" (low accessibility), while ISL uses it at both low and mid degrees of accessibility.

Eyeblinks at I-phrase boundaries have been attested for many sign languages (Baker & Padden, 1978; Wilbur, 1994, for ASL; Nespor and Sandler, 1999, for ISL), and this cue also exhibits crosslinguistic differences. Tang et al. (2010) demonstrated that, although blinks in ASL, DSGS, Hong Kong Sign Language (HKSL), and Japanese Sign Language (JSL) consistently occur at I-phrase boundaries, they combine with different cues in I-phrase final position, and blinks in HKSL occur frequently at lower-level prosodic boundaries as well.

To the extent that there are differences among intonational systems of different sign languages, we have strong confirmation of both the importance of their role and the claim that they are conventionalized.

4.3.4 Nondominant Hand (H2)-Spread

We end this chapter with a discussion of the interaction of the two hands with regard to prosodic and morpho-syntactic structure. The spread of the nondominant hand, which has also been referred to as Weak Hand Holds (Safar & Kimmelman, 2015), or H2-spread (Brentari, 1998; Nespor & Sandler, 1999) occurs in a wide range of contexts and has been used as an argument for the units of the P-word and the P-phrase, as well as for linking elements across clauses (Liddell & Johnson, 1986; Nespor & Sandler, 1999; Brentari & Crossley, 2002; Safar & Kimmelman, 2015). This interaction can be quite complex, and it involves several levels of lexical and prosodic structure that we have discussed thus far in this chapter; therefore, we are discussing these issues all together in one section here.

Sometimes an independent meaning is not associated with the nondominant hand (H2), called "phonological" (or prosodic) spreading, and sometimes H2 has meaning and is a mechanism for maintaining the relevance of that meaning across a domain. The interaction of the two hands is especially interesting, in part because the phonology takes advantage of physically symmetrical, independent articulators on the two sides of the human body, which is unique to sign languages.

Compounds, which are P-words in ASL, exhibit H2-spread, as seen in the form FEMALE^SAME *sister* in Figure 4.5; in this form the trigger is the nondominant hand of the second sign, which assimilates regressively (Liddell & Johnson, 1986). Nespor and Sandler (1999) have argued for another specific type of H2-spread in ISL P-phrases, which is also true in ASL to a large extent as seen in (6) and Figure 4.8, where H2 can spread progressively. PASTA (the first sign) is a two-handed sign in ASL and the nondominant hand (the signer's left hand in Figure 4.8) progressively assimilates over the production of the sign ITALIAN, a one-handed sign, and not over the next sign in the sentence (DELICIOUS) since this would extend across a P-phrase boundary. In both the compound and P-phrase examples, H2-spread does not carry an independent meaning, and the function of spreading is to mark a prosodic constituent.

Figure 4.8   The progressive spread of the nondominant hand in
a P-phrase of the trigger sign PASTA to the target sign ITALIAN

(6)   *Nondominant hand spread with the domain of a phonological (inter-mediate) phrase (ASL)*

H1:   <u>PASTA   ITALIAN]_{PP}</u>   DELICIOUS
H2:   PASTA
Italian pasta is delicious.

In the sentence in (7) and Figure 4.9 there are two instances of spreading at the third level of structure – the I-phrase – linking two parentheticals with the main clause [SHE] MISUNDERSTOOD (Brentari & Crossley, 2002). The first parenthetical shows H2-spread of the sign MISUNDERSTOOD on the dominant hand (H1) throughout the parenthetical *I sent the 20th*. The second parenthetical shows H2-spread of the sign TWENTY from the phrase *I sent the 20th*, which is signed on the nondominant hand and held throughout the parenthetical *She misunderstood … she thought the 28th*. The second parenthetical is embedded in the first, and the instances of spreading are ways of keeping track of how their constituents' meanings relate to the meaning of the sentence as a whole.

(7)   *Parenthetical: (Brentari & Crossley, 2002, ASL)*
H1: [SHE] <u>MISUNDERSTOOD</u>   [SHE]   THINK   28
H2:   MISUNDERSTOOD POINT-1SG SEND 20
(She) misunderstood. I sent the 20th. (She) thought [I meant] the 28th.

Sáfár and Kimmelman (2015) did a comprehensive study of the use of H2-spread in NGT and Russian Sign Language (RSL). They analyzed all of the instances of H2-spread in a data set of narratives and in conversations, which were about 3 percent of the total corpus of over 20,000 annotations. They divided instances of H2-spread into four types (8): phonetic, when adjacent signs use the same

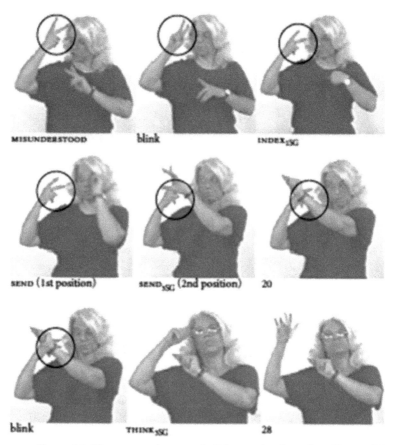

Figure 4.9 The progressive spread of the nondominant hand in two ASL parenthetical phrases of the trigger signs MISUNDERSTOOD and TWENTY (circled). (From "Prosody on the Hands and Face: Evidence from American Sign Language," by Brentari, D. & Crossley, L. In *Sign Language and Linguistics*, 5, 2002, pp. 105–130. Reprinted with kind permission from John Benjamins Publishing Company, Amsterdam/Philadelphia. [www.benjamins.com])

nondominant handshape; syntactic, when spreading corresponds to a syntactic domain such as an XP (those addressed in Nespor & Sandler,1999, are called "syntactic" in this classification system); iconic, when they involve classifiers; and discourse, when the nondominant hand carries a topic of conversation across two clauses ((7) and Figure 4.9). In the Cognitive Linguistics literature such forms are also referred to as "buoys" because "they maintain a physical presence that helps guide the discourse as it proceeds" (Liddell, 2003: 223).

(8) *Types of H2-spread (Safar & Kimmelman, 2015)*
  a. phonetic: ease of articulation because two adjacent signs use the same nondominant handshape
  b. syntactic: corresponding to a syntactic domain, such as the XP or clause
  c. iconic: those involving classifier constructions, particularly spatial relations
  d. discourse: H2 is used to refer to the topic of conversation over two or more clauses

The proportions of types of H2-spread in NGT are shown in Figure 4.10 for narrative and conversation contexts (Sáfár & Kimmelman, 2015); iconic and syntactic uses are the most prevalent. Iconic use of H2-spread is most prevalent in narratives, while syntactic uses dominate in conversation.

In terms of their relationship to clausal boundaries, a little more than one-third (36 percent) of all instances of H2-spread occur within a single clause, at the P- or I-phrase level. Slightly more, 38 percent,

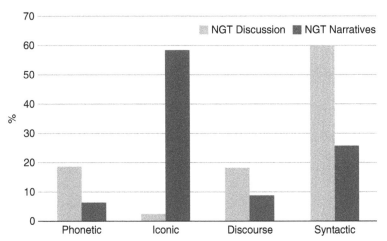

Figure 4.10   The proportion of H2-spread of different types in NGT conversation (gray bars) and in narratives (black bars). (From "Weak hand holds in two sign languages and two genres," by Sáfár, A. & Kimmelman, V. In *Sign Language and Linguistics*, 18, 2015, pp. 205–237. Reprinted with kind permission from John Benjamins Publishing Company, Amsterdam/Philadelphia. [www.benjamins.com])

crossed a clause boundary – i.e., they have a domain of two clauses – and 26 percent of holds were maintained over more than two clause boundaries. These were not broken down by type. Both one-handed and two-handed signs were the "source" or trigger sign of the spreading. Importantly, Sáfár and Kimmelman analyzed the right edges of H2-spread to see whether articulatory factors dominated (whether the nondominant hand was needed to articulate the next sign) or constituent factors (the right edge of a P-phrase or I-phrase). Eighty-one percent of cases were articulatory, but in cases where the right boundary did not coincide with a new sign, there was no consistent relationship to other constituent boundaries. In some cases, loss of the H2 corresponded to a prosodic or syntactic boundary, but in other cases it did not.

In the Sáfár and Kimmelman data, there are cases where the nondominant hand spreads beyond a phonological phrase boundary or failed to spread to a phonological phrase boundary when expected. These findings suggest that H2-spread may have one-way predictability as a marker. In other words, when you can independently identify a compound or phonological phrase that includes a two-handed sign, it is likely to exhibit spreading; however, when any single instance of H2-spread is observed, its use is not predictable, since it functions in so many different ways. Nonetheless, H2-spreading is an important factor in sign languages that binds constituents together.

4.4 CONCLUSION

To conclude this chapter, we have seen that the language–gesture interface in sign languages forces us to confront how grammars constrain the placement and types of gestures that can appear in a given language. Sign languages offer many opportunities to observe gesture and language in the same modality (intra-modality gesture) – probably more than spoken languages – but without corpus studies one cannot be sure. Spoken languages make widespread use of gesture in the manual modality and speech in the vocal one (inter-modality gesture), and it would be interesting in future work to better understand the roles of these gestures in all aspects of grammar and prosody.

In addition, units of sign language phonology and prosody interface with many aspects of the grammar – phonetics, morphology, semantics, discourse, and syntax. There are phonotactics that describe the preferred structures for morphemes, stems, and words. At higher levels of prosodic structure, the timing of prosodic features interacts with the semantics and syntax of sentence meaning. Nespor and Vogel's (1986) prosodic hierarchy for spoken languages is valid for sign languages as well, demonstrating that prosodic and morpho-syntactic domains are non-isomorphic and therefore autonomous in signed and spoken languages.

4.5 FURTHER READING

Brentari, D, Falk, J., Giannakidou, A, Herrmann, A., Volk, E. & Steinbach, M. (2018). Production and comprehension of prosodic markers in sign language imperatives. *Frontiers in Psychology, Special issue on Visual Language* (W. Sandler & C. Padden, eds.). DOI: 10.3389/fpsyg.2018.00770

Dachkovsky, S., Healy, C., & Sandler, W. (2013). Visual intonation in two sign languages. *Phonology, 30*, 211–252.

Liddell, S. (2003). *Grammar, Gesture, and Meaning in American Sign Language.* Cambridge: Cambridge University Press.

Sandler, W. (2010). Prosody and syntax in sign languages. *Transactions of the Philological Society*, 108, 298–328

Wilbur, R. B. (2010). The semantics-phonology interface. In D. Brentari (ed.), *Sign languages: A Cambridge Language Survey* (pp. 357–82). Cambridge University Press.

5 The Emergence of Phonology

Abstract

In this chapter, issues concerning the emergence of phonology will be addressed by tracing the paths of phonology
and morphophonology as they move from gesture, to
homesign, and across multiple stages in cohorts (or generations) of young sign languages. The material covered in
the first four chapters of this volume will provide theoretical context for the emergence of phonology. Relevant
work on spoken languages, which has observed and mod-
eled processes of emergence or mapped them typologically, will be discussed, and some of the principles of
phonological systems will be articulated, such as paradigm
uniformity, conventionalization, symmetry of the phonological inventory, and well-formedness constraints on phonological constituents. Based on ongoing work we can also
address some of the social factors that may be important in
different rates of emergence in different social contexts or
"language ecologies."

5.1 INTRODUCTION TO THE ISSUES

What does it mean to have phonological structure when we are looking at two very similar productions, such as those in Figure 5.1, where
the form produced by an American gesturer with no sign language
experience and the one produced by a deaf signer of American Sign
Language (ASL) look so similar? The gesture and sign language descriptions in Figure 5.1 are descriptions in response to the same scenes: on
the left, they are descriptions of a pen standing upright (Figure 5.1a, b)
and, on the right, of someone using a pen to write a letter (Figure 5.1c,
d). On the conceptual level, the iconic relations between form and
meaning are often the same in the sign and gesture cases. All four
productions in Figure 5.1 are two-handed forms, and the hands representing the pen and the writing surface have the same kind of handshape and a similar relationship between the two hands.

Figure 5.1 A pen standing upright on a table (a,b) and a pen being used to write (c,d) produced by an American gesturer (a,c) and by a signer of ASL (b, d)

When does a system that does not have phonology (silent gesture) become a system that does have phonology? One proposal for how this process might unfold more generally is that the raw material of iconic gestures used by hearing people, who are typically the initial communication partners of deaf people, becomes conventionalized, phonologized, and grammaticalized in homesigners (Morford & Kegl, 2000; Zeshan, 2003; Pfau & Steinbach, 2004; Marshall & Morgan, 2015). But how do we unpack the notion of conventionalization in phonological terms? Some differences between gesture and sign language outlined in Goldin-Meadow and Brentari (2017) and in Chapter 1 are repeated here for convenience.

(1)   *Criteria for distinguishing gesture from language (cf. Goldin-Meadow & Brentari, 2017)*
   • Gesture lacks **hierarchical combinatorial structure**, as we have seen in Chapter 1 for class nodes and features.
   • Gesture is more **gradient** than language, insofar as the gradience in language is anchored to the language's phonological categories, while gestures are not so constrained (see Duncan, 2005).
   • Gesture is more **variable** than language. Sign languages have an established lexicon and morphological categories, while gestures do not.
   • Co-speech and co-sign gestures are often produced **below the level of awareness** of speakers and signers, and access implicit, non-declarative knowledge.
   • A phonological and morphological system (not gesture) distributes its contrasts in a **symmetrical** fashion within the articulatory and perceptual space using principles of paradigm uniformity (Boersma,

2003; Downing et al., 2004; van 't Veer, 2015; for sign languages, see Brentari et al., 2017).

Mapping the path from gesture to homesign to sign language has become an important research topic since it allows linguists the opportunity to follow the historical path of a sign language *al vivo* in a way that is not possible for spoken languages. Homesign systems are developed by deaf individuals who grow up without the benefit of traditional language input – spoken or signed. To be sure, homesigners have input, but it is in the form of the incomplete set of co-speech gestures of hearing people rather than a traditional language model. Goldin-Meadow's work over the last decades has shown that the gestures of hearing people, even in families with a deaf child, are qualitatively different and do not demonstrate the linguistic properties of a single deaf homesigner's system (Goldin-Meadow & Mylander, 1983; Goldin-Meadow et al., 1996; Goldin-Meadow, 2003).

Fischer (1978) and Schembri et al. (2005) have also suggested that the atypical patterns of language transmission in deaf communities may also contribute to this process, since few deaf signers acquire sign language from deaf signing parents and most are born into hearing families; even among the small minority of deaf families the generational depth of deafness greater than two generations is extremely small. This means that each generation may partly "re-creolize" the grammar, since with each new generation it is based primarily on transmission across a single prior generation. In addition, the greater capacity of the visual-gestural modality for iconic representation might mean that some aspects of sign languages do not move far from their gestural origins.

Much of what will be described in the rest of this chapter addresses the reorganization of iconic properties of signs in the earliest linguistic systems, among homesigners and the first groups (or cohorts) of signers in emerging signing communities. The main thrust of the argument is actually pretty simple: even though much of the raw material of sign languages draws upon the emblematic, iconic, and deictic gestures of the surrounding hearing community, it is the *distribution* of the subcomponents of these forms that makes them arbitrary, that makes them part of the phonological or prosodic system.

In order to follow the path of a single form–meaning unit from gesture to sign language, samples of data from a number of populations are important. Adult homesigners are extremely important in these investigations. They are deaf individuals who have had a lifetime of using a visual/gestural system as their primary means of communication but (i) have not acquired a spoken or written language and (ii) have not acquired a conventional manual language. Because of their lack of typical language input in either of these modalities, they are in the initial stage of language creation. Despite their impoverished language-learning conditions, the communication systems of homesigners contain many, but not all, of the properties of natural language.

Much of what we know about sign language emergence comes from careful analysis of properties that vary in their distribution across cohorts. Sometimes, homesigners have the opportunity to come together and communicate with one another, which results in a second population that comprises the second stage in the development of a sign language. In 1978, the existing center for special education in Nicaragua's capital Managua was expanded and a vocational center for adolescents was established, creating an opportunity for deaf people of different ages to communicate freely and interact continuously over time. This in turn created a community from which Nicaraguan Sign Language (NSL) could emerge (Senghas et al., 2005). The first cohort[1] of signers gathered in 1978 and in the next ten subsequent years during the 1980s ushered in the "initial contact" period that launched the emergence of NSL (NSL1). New members were continually entering the community, and subsequently there were a relatively large number of younger students who received this initial signing as their language model in the second decade of the community's existence. The decade of the 1990s introduced a new variety of NSL that benefited from the language model of NSL1. The 1990s is therefore referred to as the "sustained contact" period that allowed cohort 2 (NSL2) to emerge. NSL2 was further stabilized and modified with respect to NSL1. NSL then continued to develop as new waves of children joined the community and learned the system developed by their older peers (NSL3, NSL4, etc.).

The pathway from homesign to sign languages just described in Nicaragua with the locus of the community in a school – called a "community" sign language – is one of two social situations that can give rise to sign language. The second way a sign language can be created is in the context of a stable community of hearing and deaf

---

[1] The division into cohorts of Nicaraguan signers is somewhat arbitrary. Those in the first ten years in the 1980s are considered Cohort 1 and those in second ten years are referred to as Cohort 2.

people in which there is a relatively high incidence of deafness, typically due to consanguineous marriage. These are referred to as "village" sign languages (Meir, 2010). In village sign languages, deaf individuals not only find and interact with each other regularly but also use the sign language frequently with their extended hearing family. The hearing individuals in these communities exhibit varying degrees of sign language proficiency. The incidence of deafness in many village sign language communities is considered substantially higher than what is found in the general population. Such cases have been studied in a wide range of locations throughout the world. In Israel this is the situation with Al-Sayyid Bedouin Sign Language (ABSL; Sandler et al., 2005, 2011a, 2011b). Wendy Sandler and her team have been studying ABSL for the past several years. The language is found in a Bedouin village in the south of Israel in the Negev desert, where the presence of a gene for deafness and marriage patterns within the community has resulted in the birth of a relatively large population of deaf people over the past seventy-five years – about fifty times more than the proportion of signers in the United States. The language originated with the five sons of the patriarch, who migrated from Egypt with their father and set up tents in the Negev; the language is approximately 75 years old.

Other village sign languages include Central Taurus Sign Language (CTSL; Ergin, 2017; Ergin & Brentari, 2017), Adamarobe Sign Language (AdSL; Nyst, 2010), and those of India and Pakistan (Zeshan, 2006). Martha's Vineyard in the United States also had a village sign language in use in the seventeenth century (Groce, 1985). At its height, the proportion of deaf users of Martha's Vineyard Sign Language relative to the total hearing population was between 2 percent and 4 percent — much higher than half of 1 percent (.5 percent), which is the incidence of deafness in the United States.

In the case of village sign languages, the initial contact stage may be protracted because the ratio of deaf to hearing members of the community is quite small, as the number of deaf people is small overall and the number of new deaf child learners is limited to the actual number of deaf babies born. In addition, the high degree of shared context in the village social environment may exert less communicative pressure on an emerging language because discourse centers around familiar themes and topics, which could potentially also slow the development of complex linguistic devices (Senghas et al., 2005). These social factors may influence the time course and quality of the linguistic properties that appear.

It is difficult to say which is the more typical case of sign language emergence – a community sign language or a village sign language. In the community sign language case, the number of deaf people using the system as their primary language is greater than in the village sign language case, but transmission is not via families, as it typically is for spoken languages and for village sign languages. The community sign language model has been replicated many times in the history of deaf communities, where a school draws deaf people together and ulti-mately creates a community that lasts into adulthood, and so for Europe and the United States it is the more familiar way for sign languages to develop. In the case of village sign languages, sign lan-guages emerge within preexisting, stable social groups and transmis-sion is more likely to occur within extended families, but the number of deaf individuals using the system as their primary mode of commu-nication is small, and if the gene pool undergoes significant changes, the community is likely to disappear, as it did on Martha's Vineyard. Moreover, even if hearing people learn and use the system, they may be less likely to produce language innovations because they do not use the system as their primary means of communication.

While it might be tempting to call the initial contact varieties created as homesigners come into contact with one another "pid-gins," it is more accurate to call them "initial contact varieties" because they differ in one very important respect from spoken pidgins. Examples of spoken pidgins include Tok Pisin, from Papua New Guinea (Wurm & Mühlhäuslen, 1985), and Nigerian Pidgin (Holm, 2000) – both predominantly based on an English vocabulary – and Chinook Jargon (Lang, 2008), a contact variety based on several Native American languages from the Pacific Northwest. In contrast to the creators of the emerging sign lan-guages discussed here, all users of spoken pidgins possess a native language. That language is simply not very useful in the situation where they find themselves, and so pidgins are created to bridge the gap. The effect of the contributing languages can take two forms, which may have distinct effects: the effect of having *any* native language and the effect of having a *particular* native lan-guage, whose structures may or may not be compatible with those of the languages contributing to the pidgin. The emerging sign languages that we are discussing here are developed without the scaffolding of any base language, and they are based on individual homesign systems. This reduces or excludes the influence of pre-existing linguistic structures. Likewise, the term "sustained con-tact varieties" will be used instead of the term "creole" because of their origin. Emerging languages may be transmitted across real generations (as in village sign languages) or across generations as defined in terms of when an individual comes in contact with the community (as in community sign languages).[2]

In all of this work gesture is also an important source of information – both co-speech and silent gesture. Thus, hearing non-signers are a population important as a baseline group to see what gestural competence looks like. Data from what we will call "standard" sign languages, such as ASL, Italian Sign Language (LIS), German Sign Language (DGS), and many others, are also very important in order to understand the range of possibilities for sign language grammars. We know where emerging sign languages are headed, but we want to be sure to consider multiple possible solutions for a grammatical expression.

One question in the background of work on language emergence is, "which aspects of language appear more quickly in one type of language ecology than another – community or village – and how large does a community have to be to count as a community?" This chapter will expand on this point a bit as we move to a new context for studying homesign, where we consider the three distinct social contexts – or ecologies – of language emergence (Horton, 2018): that of individual homesigners surrounded only by hearing people, community homesigners who are in contact with other peer homesigners at school, and family homesigners who have at least one or two family members who are also homesigners.

5.2 WHERE DO PHONOLOGICAL FEATURES AND PHONOLOGICAL PATTERNS COME FROM?

We now turn to the main focus of this chapter – where do phonological features and phonological patterns come from? Returning to the forms in Figure 5.1, which look very similar in gesture and ASL, how do we know that the ASL forms have a phonological system while the silent gesture forms do not? The answer to this question takes us to the very core of what we believe phonology to be. As was discussed in Chapter 1, duality of patterning is a powerful criterion to separate gesture from sign language, but in accord with Ladd's (2014) recent arguments,

---

[2] It is interesting here to mention Supalla's comments concerning his own experience growing up in an ASL household (Supalla, 2009): He commented on the fact that he was aware of signing differently at home and at school, and so it appears that deaf families can maintain an idiosyncratic manner of signing, even in a relatively well-established community, such as the one that sustains ASL. This is a different use of the term "homesign".

phonology displays duality of patterning only in a minority of cases even in spoken languages (for example, the syllable and the morpheme can be perfectly isochronous), and so it is clear that phonology can be present in the absence of duality of patterning.

We will see that it is only by understanding how a particular form relates to other forms within a signer's (or sign language community's) repertoire that we can discern whether a property is phonological. Coppola and Brentari (2014) propose three stages toward using a feature or set of features within a morphophonemic system (2). These stages have to do with developing *oppositions,* in the sense of Trubetzkoy (1939), because otherwise, if one looks at a single token, it is impossible to know if mapping a particular meaning to a form is part of a system or a device created on the spot.

(2)   *Stages toward becoming phonological*
- **Stage 1: Increase Contrasts:** Recognize the particular feature(s) as a form that can be manipulated to create different meanings or used for grammatical purposes.
- **Stage 2: Create the Opposition:** Distinguish the distribution of two features or feature values in one's system, associating one feature with one meaning and the other to another meaning to some degree. This association does not have to be complete or absolute.
- **Stage 3: Apply the Opposition Productively:** Apply the feature or class of features productively to new situations where the same opposition is needed.

Delving more deeply into this question of where phonological features come from, I would argue that the factors that contribute to the process of phonological emergence concern "internal" phonological pressures, involving the system's self-organization as a whole, as well as "external" pressures of phonetics, social factors, culture, frequency, and embodiment. I would further argue that evidence of internal pressures that organize the system appears early in language creation, and only when several phonological principles (discussed in this chapter) emerge do we eventually see phonological rules and minimal pairs. In other words, minimal pairs and allophonic rules are at the end of the timeline of creating phonology, not at the beginning.

The kinds of pressures internal to the system that are relevant here are common in spoken language phonological systems, but they are discussed in terms of naturalness and typological frequency (Flemming, 1995/2002; Mielke, 2005). There are several means by which systems achieve a phonological status, all with the general motivation of creating a system that can do the work of transmitting information efficiently, and theories of sign language phonology have tried to capture two types of pressures on a phonological system:

- The pressures of *efficiency*, common to both signed and spoken languages, include how the units of the system are organized to maximize the information conveyed, as well as ease of production, ease of perception, and the way that the strengths of the particular peripheral systems involved affect it.
- The *affordances of iconicity*, which all languages exploit, but which sign languages exploit to a greater extent, acknowledge that our bodies interact with the world in a whole host of interesting ways. The way that iconicities affect the form–meaning correspondences of units in sign languages is an area that can contribute to our understanding of language more generally.

Recall from Chapter 1, Section 1.5.1 that in Optimality Theory (Prince & Smolensky, 1993) there are four important main families of phonological constraints (McCarthy, 2001), and these are listed in (3) with examples provided from the spoken language literature. The most common phenomena across languages are elevated to the level of constraints, yet all constraints are violable since there are exceptions across the world's languages to varying degrees (see Chapter 1 for additional comments).

(3) *Families of constraints on a phonological system and spoken language examples*

a. **CORRESPONDENCE** or **ALIGNMENT** constraints describe how constituents from different components of the grammar organize themselves with respect to one another. For example, the left edge of a word should line up with the left edge of a stem. The word *un#.just* does this, because both the stem and the second syllable start in the same place; *u.n#a.ligned* does not do this, because the beginning of the stem is not in the same place as the beginning of the syllable to which it belongs. This will be taken up in Section 5.3.1 in the discussion of prosody and syntax (Sandler et al., 2011b).

b. **DISPERSION** constraints refer to how phonological units (features, syllables, segments) are organized throughout the system, using principles such as *feature economy* and *symmetry*. Feature economy is the preference to utilize features in a dense way to fill the articulatory and perceptual space. For example, if there are three members for one set of segments – e.g., *p,t,k* – there will be three members across other classes too – *b,d,g* – not just one or two members – *b,d*. Symmetry also organizes features so that they use the entire articulatory space *in a regular pattern*. For example, if *p,t,k* exists as a pattern for voiceless stops, voiced stops *b,d,g* may follow this pattern as well. This will be taken up in Section 5.3.2 in the discussion of the phonemic space of handshape (Brentari et al., 2011; Coppola & Brentari, 2014; Brentari et al., 2015, 2017).

c. **FAITHFULNESS** constraints express the preference for forms to want to be stable across contexts. This constraint was discussed in Chapter 3 on use of iconicity and the [stacked] feature (Eccarius & Brentari, 2010).

d. **MARKEDNESS** constraints ensure that phonological strings are perceptually intelligible and articulatorily efficient to produce. For example, nasals tend to be voiced, as are the following stops: *nd* is preferred over *nt* because of articulatory ease. These will be taken up in Section 5.4 in the discussion of the emergence of form in ABSL compounds and the use of the Handshape Sequence Constraint (see Chapter 1 for more comments on this constraint).

Work on "patterned iconicity" may also play a role in this process (Hwang et al., 2017; Lepic et al., 2016; Occhino, 2017; Horton, 2018; Abner et al., 2019). Because of the extensive use of visual and proprioceptive iconicity in sign languages, certain phonological properties may come to have specific sets of form–meaning correspondences, such as curved fingers for round objects, spread fingers to represent individuation, or repeated movement to represent iterativity.

5.3 APPLYING INTERNAL PHONOLOGICAL PRINCIPLES IN EMERGING SIGN LANGUAGES

In this section I illustrate how the constraints described in (3) come to manifest themselves in emerging sign languages using three case studies. In Section 5.3.1 we discuss the development of the prosodic system as a vehicle for grammatical dependencies (Sandler et al., 2011b) in ABSL. In Section 5.3.2 we will describe changes in handshape moving toward greater symmetry (Dunbar & Dupoux, 2016), creating a balance between selected fingers and joints in two types of classifier handshapes in silent gesture, homesign, and well-established sign languages (Brentari et al., 2012a, 2015a, 2017; Coppola & Brentari, 2014). In Section 5.3.3 we will trace the loss of iconicity and move toward more abstract use of morphophonemic forms, particular to the property of repetition in the noun–verb contrasts in adult homesign and across successive cohorts of NSL (Abner et al., 2019).

5.3.1 The Development of Grammatical Non-manuals and Their Alignment

This first case study involves ALIGNMENT constraints in ABSL (Sandler et al., 2011b), using a set of one minute of narratives from four second-generation signers – two aged 40–50 and two about twenty years younger. The analysis also included a previously recorded story of one of the first-generation ABSL signers, now deceased. Sandler and colleagues traced the development of prosody and its relation to the development of syntax. The research team found that older signers have shorter units and used facial expression primarily for affect, while the younger signers used facial expression and head position not only for affect but also to show syntactic dependencies between clauses.

The narratives were broken into prosodic phrases based on the cues outlined in Chapter 4. By using the Facial Action Coding System (FACS, Ekman & Friesen, 1978), the non-manual cues were coded and analyzed for their content, context, and alignment with the accompanying manual signs and their prosodic cues.

In Table 5.1 we see an excerpt of one of the first ABSL signers talking to a group of hearing young men about an event in the history of the Al-Sayyid tribe. Each prosodic phrase is an utterance, typically separated from the next utterance by salient pauses. Many of the utterances in the example are a single sign, sometimes accompanied by affective non-manuals. Notice that many of the arguments and other

Table 5.1 *Narrative by one of the first users of ABSL*

GLOSS	TRANSLATION
RUN-AWAY	They each took off (on horseback) and galloped.
RUN	
RUN	
SWORD	(The man with) the sword hit (the Al-Sayyid man).
GUN	
HIT	
GUN BLOCK	(He) blocked it with his gun.
HIT	
SHOOT	(He) shot back (at his attacker).
SHOOT	
HORSE FALL	The horse fell.
EYE FALL-OUT	(The rider's) eye fell out.
KAFFIYEH TWIRL	(The Al-Sayyid man) waved (his) *keffiyeh* (to summon people).

(cf. Sandler et al., 2011b)

Table 5.2 *Narrative by one of the two older users of ABSL*

GLOSS	TRANSLATION
WOMAN BABY THERE TENT CRA-DLE THERE WOOD SIDES	The woman puts the baby down in the tent there in a wooden cradle.
CRADLE THERE PUT LEAVE	She puts the baby there and leaves it.
PICK-UP BABY NURSE ABOUT TIME ONE TWO	She breast-feeds the baby and leaves it for an hour or two.
LEAVE THERE FINISH	

(cf. Sandler et al., 2011b)

kinds of information are in parentheses, indicating that they had to be inferred from context.

An excerpt of one of the two older, second-generation signer's stories is provided in Table 5.2 about a folk immunization treatment against scorpion bites that was once administered to babies. The utterances are longer and references clearer than those in the narrative in Table 5.1. There is alignment of the ends of units, marked by the hands, with head movement and sometimes with affective facial expression to mark constituents; however, there are no linguistic facial expressions to mark dependencies between clauses. The relationship between adjacent clauses is one of coordination; e.g., "x" happens *and* "y" happens.

The final example is from a younger signer recounting a dream (Table 5.3). The sentences are longer than those of the older signer's in Table 5.2. The younger signers increased the ratio of nouns to verbs, as well as their use of pronouns, which made their narratives more cohesive and comprehensible. Moreover, clause dependencies were indicated by the non-manual cues of facial expression, which the authors analyze as linguistic intonation in the younger signers, such as brow raise, indicated by "≫"; e.g., "x" happens *why?* "y."

The alignment of the ends of phrasal units with a cluster of cues marking constituents is also more consistent in this younger signer's passage than in either of the two passages in Tables 5.1 and 5.2. (As in Tables 5.1 and 5.2, the signed prosodic phrases are on separate lines in the GLOSS column.)

Sandler and colleagues clearly demonstrate that prosody becomes less affective and more grammatical across the generations of ABSL signers. The emerging syntax develops, as indicated by the presence of

Table 5.3 *Narrative by one of the two younger users of ABSL*

GLOSS	TRANSLATION
SHE DREAM	She dreamed. (in the dream)
FATHER YOU(R)	
HE LOOK AT-HER ≫	Your father, he looked at her. Your
FATHER SAY WHY YOU	father said, "Why haven't we seen
LONG-TIME SEE NONE	you for such a long time – Why?"
WHY	
SHE MORNING REMEMBER	In the morning she remembered.
MORNING≫	In the morning she woke up
SHE MORNING GET-UP SIT THINK	and sat thinking
[PREGNANT SHE≫	She was pregnant. The short wife
SHORT WIFE PREGNANT≫	was pregnant. She came to you
SHE COME-TO-YOU PREGNANT]≫	when she was pregnant. She'd
GIVE BIRTH	give birth (soon), she reckoned
SHE RECKON . . .	

Note: Square brackets indicate prosodically marked parenthetical material. I-phrases marked for dependency are followed by "≫". Material in parentheses in the translation was filled in by the translator and is not found in the gloss (cf. Sandler et al., 2011b)

argument structure, in a way that is intertwined with the use of prosody to mark constituency and with grammatical uses of the face employed to mark dependencies among clauses. Thus, even these few short samples indicate that there is a fundamental change in the function of non-manuals in the emerging ABSL prosodic system and that the specific type and alignment between the manual and non-manual components of signing convey increasingly complex sentential meaning.

5.3.2 Dispersion and Handshape Morphology within the Phonemic Space

In this second case study we investigate the possible phonemic space in sign language handshapes and ask, "To what extent can we see changes in the 'handshape space' (equivalent to a consonant or vowel space in spoken languages) in the emerging phonological system of NSL?" This pertains to the principles of DISPERSION in (3b). A series of experiments was conducted to understand the processes by which handshapes such as those illustrated in Figure 5.1 become phonological (Brentari et al., 2011; Coppola & Brentari, 2014; Brentari et al., 2015a, 2017). We have found that signers of emerging and standard sign languages, such as ASL and LIS, exhibit different distribution of handshape features – namely, in the selected fingers and joints features – than silent gesturers do.

The hypothesis is that as sign languages develop phonology, they would (i) use the entire articulatory space rather than localize contrasts within one set of features; (ii) organize the features in a symmetrical way across the two types of features; and (iii) possibly associate different sets of features with different meanings. This would mean balancing the use of these joints and selected fingers across different functions to create meaning-form correspondences.

This hypothesis relates to the notion of symmetrical inventories in spoken languages. For example, Oxford (2014) describes phonological change in Algonquian vowel systems, where two of the changes move toward more symmetrical systems in the Proto-Eastern-Algonquian (PEA) vowel system as it changed from the Proto-Algonquian (PA) system. One involves a new [high] contrast that was added in PEA that was not in the PA system. The extra high vowel created an asymmetry in which the high vowels contrasted for [labial] while the non-high vowels contrasted for [coronal]. In two of the daughter languages – Unami Delaware and Mi'kmaq – the pressure to re-balance the vowel inventory resulted in a new non-high [labial] vowel sequence. In the next section we see how sign languages also create symmetrical functional divisions of labor in their use of joint and selected finger features in their morphophonology.

Two types of iconic handshapes that have been shown to be morphemic are targeted (the types shown in Figure 5.1): those that represent the shape of objects (called *entity classifiers* in sign languages, but *object handshapes* here so as not to ascribe morphological status prematurely; Figure 5.1a,b) and those that represent how objects are handled or manipulated (called *handling* handshapes; Figure 5.1c,d). Additional examples are given in Figure 5.2.

A series of studies focusing on the phonological shape of these two types of handshapes is at the heart of this work (Brentari et al., 2011, 2013, 2015a, 2017). These two types of handshapes were targeted because they are morphological and syntactic in sign languages (Benedicto & Brentari, 2004), and they are ubiquitous in gesture, sign language, and in emerging sign languages. Figure 5.3 shows the current feature organization for handshape in the Prosodic model. The joint features are organized around those that change for the entire hand, called "unified" joint features, such as [spread] and [flexed],

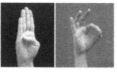

Object handshapes   Handling handshapes

Figure 5.2 Examples of (left) object handshapes and (right) handling handshapes. (From "Handshape complexity as a pre-cursor to phonology: Variation, emergence, and acquisition," Brentari, et al. *Language Acquisition*, 24, 2017, reprinted by permission of the publisher, Taylor & Francis Ltd, www.tandfonline.com.)

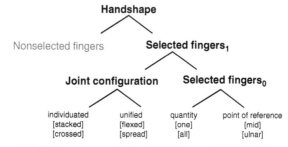

Figure 5.3 Feature organization for joints and selected fingers within handshape (cf. Brentari, 1998, modified based on Aristodemo, 2013)

versus those that allow for different values for each individual finger, called "individuated," such as [crossed] or [stacked] features, where the joint configuration of each finger is different articulatorily.[3] The selected fingers node is composed of "quantity" features that indicate how many fingers are selected – one [one], all fingers [all], two fingers [one]>[all], or three fingers [all]>[one] – and "point of reference" features, which are only used when the fingers do not reference the index [radial] side of the hand but rather the middle finger or fingers on the pinky finger [ulnar] side of the hand.

We study this phenomenon of handshape dispersion in terms of complexity, which can be studied in a variety of ways (see Section 2.5). We placed selected fingers and joints on a complexity scale in terms of

[3] The joints node has minor modifications from Brentari (1998) due to Aristodemo (2013), who conducted perceptual experiments investigating complexity.

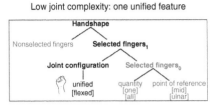

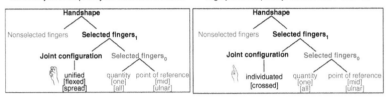

Figure 5.4 Handshapes with low, medium, and high joint complexity (cf. Brentari, 1998, modified based on Aristodemo, 2013)

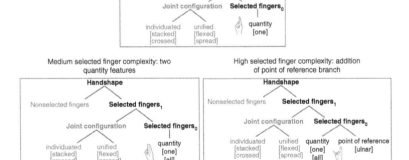

Figure 5.5 Handshapes with low, medium, and high selected finger complexity (cf. Brentari, 1998), modified based on Aristodemo (2013)

acquisition (Boyes Braem, 1990b), frequency (Hara, 2003), and phonological structure (Brentari, 1998). In terms of phonological structure, each successive level of complexity adds more features or adds more hierarchical structure, as we see in Figures 5.4 and 5.5.

First let's turn our attention to joint features. Handshapes with low joint complexity (assigned "1") have no more than one unified feature (either flexed or spread, not both) under joint configuration. Handshapes with medium joint complexity (assigned "2") may have two such unified features. Handshapes with high joint complexity (assigned "3") are those with individuated features [crossed] or [stacked] (Figure 5.4).

We turn next to selected finger complexity (Figure 5.5). Handshapes with low selected finger complexity (assigned "1") have no more than one quantity feature (either [one] or [all], not both) under the selected fingers$_0$ node. Handshapes with medium selected finger complexity (assigned "2") may have one additional structure, either an additional quantity feature [one] > [all] (no point of reference features) or a branching structure with one feature each under quantity and one under point of reference. Handshapes with high selected fingers complexity (assigned "3") are those containing two quantity features and a feature under point of reference, and the three-fingered handshapes feature fingers ([all] > [one]) because they are so infrequent with respect to the other finger groups.

More examples of low-, medium-, and high-complexity handshapes are shown in Figure 5.6

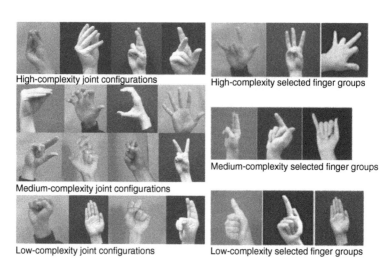

Figure 5.6   Examples of low-, medium-, and high-complexity hand-shapes for joints (left) and selected fingers (right). (From "Handshape complexity as a pre-cursor to phonology: Variation, emergence, and acquisition," Brentari, et al., *Language Acquisition*, 24, 2017, reprinted and order of forms modified by permission of the publisher, Taylor & Francis Ltd, www.tandfonline.com.)

Scenes without an agent (Non-agentive events)	Scenes with an agent (Agentive events)
1. [object] on table	6. Put [object] on table
2. [object] on table upside down	7. Put [object] on table upside down
3. *Multiple [objects] on table (regular arrangement in row/s)*	8. *Put multiple [objects] on table (regular arrangement in row/s)*
4. Multiple [objects] on table (random arrangement)	9. Put multiple [objects] on table (random arrangement)
5. [object] moving without an agent (typically falling)	10. Demonstrate function of [object]

Figure 5.7 Examples of vignettes used to elicit object handshapes (left) and handling handshapes (right) for a form with potentially high-complexity selected finger group ☝ (Reprinted by permission from Springer Nature: Springer, *Natural Language & Linguistic Theory*, "When does a system become phonological? Handshape production in gesturers, signers, and homesigners," Brentari, et al., 2012a.)

We now turn to studies comparing handshape complexity – analyzing both overall complexity (joints and selected fingers) and joint and selected finger complexity separately – across hearing non-signers using silent gesture, homesigners, and signers, in a range of ages, countries, and contexts. All of the data, consisting of descriptions of ten vignettes, balanced for scenes with and without an agent to address whether these descriptions would map onto handling and object handshapes, were gathered from signers, homesigners, and silent gesturers in adults and children across several sign language and gesture communities. Crucially, these vignettes (Figure 5.7) were balanced to elicit equal numbers of low-, medium-, and high-complexity handshapes across objects. For example, book was chosen to elicit a low-complexity finger group 🤏, string to elicit a medium-complexity group 🤙, and airplane to elicit a high-complexity finger group ☝. We hypothesized that the range of contrasts across the handshape phonemic "space" will be evenly distributed in sign language systems but not necessarily in gesture.

5.3.2.1   Overall Handshape Complexity

The first analysis considers the overall handshape complexity – nouns and verbs together, summed across selected finger and joint complexity for all ten object descriptions and across the four study groups in Nicaragua: silent gesturers, homesigners, NSL cohort 1, and NSL cohort 2 (Figure 5.8). We find that homesigners have the highest handshape complexity, and the gesture group has the lowest handshape complexity, among the four groups studied.

This basic result can be interpreted as follows. An individual homesigner does not have limits on the complexity used in her forms, while the NSL1 signers experience a community with whom negotiation and efficiency of communication become higher priorities. Homesign is a system that has not been passed down from one generation to the next. The structural regularities that homesigners exhibit in their own signing are often not appreciated by homesigners' communication partners, who are typically hearing family members (Carrigan & Coppola, 2017). Thus, homesigners are the producers but not receivers of their system. Thus, it may be that DISPERSION (adding contrasts) is at work in the homesign group, generating an ample set of contrasts, but none of the principles to trim and organize the system have a chance to work because they require interaction with others within

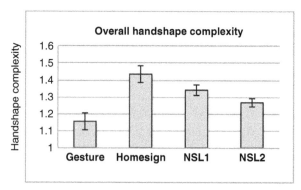

Figure 5.8   Average overall complexity across adult study groups in Nicaragua

a community of users (NSL1) and across subsequent cohorts who also have a language model (NSL2). A homesigner is able to expand the inventory but perhaps not reorganize it efficiently or show the effects of feature economy.

The gesture result (relatively low complexity) can be interpreted as lacking DISPERSION to the point that the system does not have enough raw material with which to work. Returning to Coppola and Brentari's (2014) stages of morphophonological creation (2) – (i) increase contrasts, (ii) create an opposition, and (iii) apply the contrast productively – one might say that the gesture group has not even recognized the potential for contrast that the hand has to offer.

5.3.2.2 Differential Morphological Function for Joints and Selected Fingers

How does the complexity of handshape form get organized with regard to meaning? The distribution of finger groups and joints creates both phonological and morphological contrasts in sign languages. We now turn to how the two interact with one another in the system. As we saw in Figure 5.1a,b, the gesturer and the signer both use the B-handshape 🖐 as a base hand to represent a flat surface and the 1-handshape ☝ to represent a pen, but we must ask how these handshapes fit into the system as a whole. In ASL ☝ contrasts with several other selected finger groups 🖐 🖐 🖐 ✌ 👌 and 🤙, while in gesture there is contrast only with the 🖐 finger group. We can also ask how the joint configuration of ☝ fits into the set of joint contrasts in the language. ☝ contrasts with several other selected joint groups in ASL – 👆 👆 👆 👆. Notice that the handshapes have different joints that are flexed: ☝ is fully extended, 👆 is flexed at the knuckle joint only, 👆 is flexed at the interphalangeal joint only, and 👆 is flexed at both the knuckle and interphalangeal joint. Sign languages vary across these two dimensions independently in both phonological structure (as we see here) and morphology. As we will see, silent gesture does not.

Gesturers – both adults and children – do not display independent componentiality of joints and selected fingers in handshape. We find that gesturers channel their high-complexity forms for both selected fingers and joints into handling handshapes. In contrast, adult and child signers split up their complexity in a systematic way, namely, higher selected finger complexity is concentrated in object hand-shapes and higher joint complexity is concentrated in handling

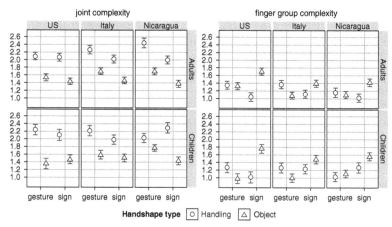

Figure 5.9 Joint and selected finger complexity across signers and gesturers: (top) adults from the United States, China, Italy, and Nicaragua; (bottom) children and adult comparisons from the United States, Italy and Nicaragua. (From "Handshape complexity as a precursor to phonology: Variation, emergence, and acquisition," Brentari, et al., *Language Acquisition*, 24, 2017, reprinted by permission of the publisher, Taylor & Francis Ltd, www.tandfonline.com.)

handshapes (Eccarius, 2008; Brentari et al., 2017). We see this in Figure 5.9 for three adult groups and three child groups – from the United States, Nicaragua, and Italy.[4] While all gesture and sign groups show higher joint complexity in handling handshapes, only the adult and child signers (including those of the emerging language NSL) show high selected finger complexity in object handshapes, indicating a form–meaning contrast for both of these handshape feature classes (joints and selected fingers). In a related analysis, we found that signers often show lower joint complexity in handling handshapes compared to their gesture-producing counterparts from the same countries. In other words, in the process of phonologization, some of the joint complexity of handling handshapes is reduced (Brentari et al., 2017). The sign language system is thus more symmetrical, and it reflects a division of labor between these feature classes to express meaning.

---

[4] There are no native signers in Nicaragua. The NSL2 adults were all early learners, and the child NSL2 signers had at least six years' signing experience.

This is not a simple matter of "hand-as-hand" iconicity being recognized earlier than "hand-as-object" iconicity. Rather, it represents the protracted acquisition of the systematic mapping of phonological forms to morphological structures. For example, until age 7, ASL-signing children do not systematically use handling handshapes to express agentive, transitive events. This morphological mismapping continues even after the children have begun making a distinction between object handshapes and handling handshapes in terms of finger complexity. This time course of acquisition suggests that the analysis of elements into multiple, distinct phonological forms precedes the mapping of these forms to another level of structure.

A similar analysis was done on selected finger complexity with four adult homesigners along with gesturers and signers from the United States and Italy (Brentari et al., 2012a; Figure 5.10), and, longitudinally, with one child homesigner from Nicaragua (Coppola & Brentari, 2014; Figure 5.11). And here we see some of the missing steps between DISPERSION and SYMMETRY – how a system transitions from being one without phonology to one that has phonology. Three of four adult homesigners patterned like signers, with higher selected finger complexity in the object handshapes and lower selected finger complexity in handling handshapes. The homesigners also showed lower joint complexity in handling handshapes than that of gesturers, but higher than that of signers. The hints of the phonologization of these forms are thus seen when selected finger complexity in object handshapes increases, and some of the full phonetic range of joint complexity of the handling handshapes is lost, demonstrating feature economy.

A longitudinal study of one homesigning Nicaraguan child, Julio (Coppola & Brentari, 2014), showed that this pattern is not a given in a homesigner from the start. Julio exhibited the gesturers' pattern at age 7, where object and handling handshapes show no statistical difference from one another, but his system transformed itself to the signers' pattern at age 12, where the selected finger complexity is higher in object handshapes, even if the complexity of the handling handshapes has not yet significantly lowered when compared with previous samples (Figure 5.11).

These results suggest that a homesign system is capable of changing throughout a lifespan, even if it happens at a slower rate, and some patterns that appear quite early in acquisition when there is a language model may require more time to emerge in a homesign system.

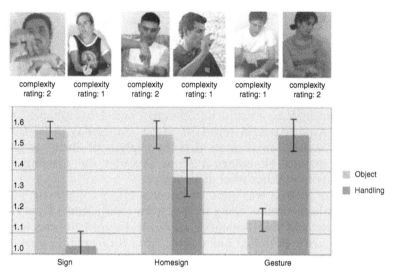

Figure 5.10   Selected finger complexity in adult signers, homesigners, and gesturers. Adult signers and homesigners used higher complexity in selected finger groups in object handshapes and lower in handling handshapes. Gesturers used the opposite pattern – i.e., higher complexity finger groups in handling handshapes and lower in object handshapes (cf. Brentari et al., 2012a).

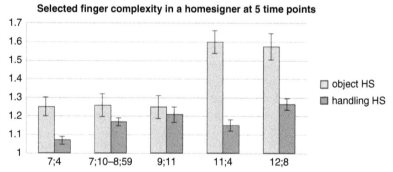

Figure 5.11   Average finger group complexity for a single Nicaraguan child at five time points. (Reprinted from *Frontiers in Psychology*, 5, Coppola, M. & Brentari, D., "From iconic handshapes to grammatical contrasts: Longitudinal evidence from a child homesigner," 2014. [doi .org/10.3389/fpsyg.2014.00830] Used under a CC BY 3.0 license.)

We can now summarize these findings. Gesturers show neither DIS-
PERSION nor SYMMETRY in their system, while signers exhibit both
DISPERSION and SYMMETRY in theirs. Signers produce object handshapes with a higher finger complexity than handling handshapes,
a pattern not observed among gesturers, and lower joint complexity in
handling handshapes than gestures. These structural differences correspond to two types of morphological handshape types – object handshapes, which exhibit "hand-as-object" iconicity, where selected finger
groups correspond to different classes of objects as they are located or
move in space without an agent, and handling handshapes, which
exhibit "hand-as-hand" iconicity to represent handling and manipula-
tions by agents. At the heart of these linguistic constraints may also be
phonetic and general cognitive mechanisms, which aid in making language production, processing, and retrieval more efficient (Johnson &
Hume, 2003).

These generalizations can be formalized in an Optimality
Theoretic account of how phonology might emerge in a sign language. At all stages of this process, the pressures of iconicity, ease
of articulation, and ease of perception are at work, both in gesturers and signers, but none of them alone is sufficient to account
for these changes. The first step involves the notion of DISPERSION
(Flemming, 2002), which stipulates that inventories of phonological elements will seek to have many distinctions and that while
systems with few distinctions will include only simple forms,
systems with more distinctions will additionally include more
complex forms. The use of DISPERSION must precede the appearance of any other phonological patterns, because a wide range of
forms needs to be present before a complex pattern of
organization can emerge.

Next we find CORRESPONDENCE, which requires that each form
be matched with a meaning, such that form-meaning mappings
are unambiguous (Xu, 2007; Brentari et al., 2012a). This corresponds to Stage 2 of Coppola and Brentari (2014); namely, to
create the opposition in the form–meaning correspondence. This
implies association (even if incompletely at first) of joints features
with handling handshapes to mean "agentive, transitive" and
selected finger features with object handshapes to mean "non-
agentive, intransitive."

The final step involves the organizational notions of global
SYMMETRY and FEATURE ECONOMY ultimately maximizing the feature possibilities of joints and selected fingers so that there is
a greater distinction between the two handshapes that is

manifested in the balanced use of the two dimensions available within handshape – selected fingers and joints. These patterns are available to apply to novel contexts at this stage. This corresponds to Stage 3 of Coppola and Brentari (2014), which is to make the opposition productive.

Our work has shown that in mapping the handshape space phonologically, both in national sign languages and adult homesigners (but not in gesture), there is a disassociation of joints and selected fingers as feature classes. We have found that while gesturers and signers both use complex handshapes in describing vignettes, signers systematically balance finger and joint complexity across handshape classes, object versus handling: higher finger complexity in object handshapes and higher joint complexity in handling handshapes. Homesigners are part of the way there – they raise selected finger complexity without lowering handshape complexity. What appears to be simple iconic mapping at first blush is in fact an intricate interaction between iconicity, morphology, and phonology.

5.3.3   Repetition: Loss and Reorganization of Iconicity in Distinguishing Nouns and Verbs

This final example of an emerging phonology concerns how forms gradually lose iconicity and move toward more arbitrary forms in creating a structural distinction between nouns and verbs. This study also employed scenes or "vignettes" to elicit noun and verb forms, and it was constructed with paired object-action items used commonly in Nicaragua. The vignettes also included iterative and non-iterative events, since iterativity is one possible iconic use of reduplication or repetition in verbs – i.e., to represent an action performed repeatedly by a movement produced repeatedly.

There are at least three ways that the task could have elicited structures that are iconic. First, verbs might be more likely than nouns to elicit larger movements in order to allow for clearer expression of the manner of the verb. Differential use of proximal versus distal joints is also commonly used to mark this distinction crosslinguistically (Brentari et al., 2015a). Second, the base hand is more likely to be used in verbs because the base hand often represents the affected object in sentences such as SCISSORS-CUT-PAPER. Third, iterative events might be more likely to elicit repeated movements than non-iterative ones. Reduplication is a very common structural modification seen in spoken and sign language morphology (Supalla & Newport, 1978; Berent et al., 2014, 2017). In this section we will see how this strategy emerges as one of several ways that the linguistic form expresses the noun–verb contrast (Abner et al., 2019).

The task was performed by ASL signers and four groups of adults in Nicaragua: homesigners, and groups of signers of NSL from cohorts 1, 2, and 3. Only the Nicaraguan groups will be discussed here. After analyzing their productions, several strategies for marking noun versus verb forms across the groups were observed. The first is not a phonological one at all but rather based on word order: NSL and homesign utterances are typically verb-final. The three phonological strategies included (i) the use of more proximal joints for verbs and distal joints for nouns (see Chapter 2 and the glossary), (ii) the use of repetition in nouns and single movements for verbs, and (iii) the use of the base hand in verbal forms (versus no base hand in nominals).

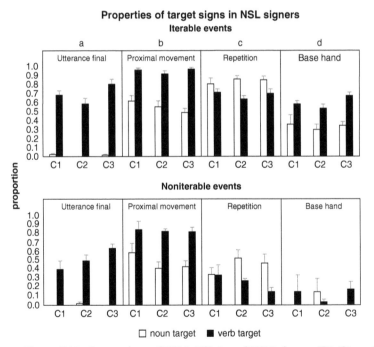

Figure 5.12 Comparison of NSL1, NSL 2, and NSL3 signers (C1, C2, and C3 in the figure) on the four types of devices used to express the noun–verb distinction: (a) utterance position; (b) joints; (c) repetition; and (d) base (nondominant) hand. (From Abner et al., 2019.)

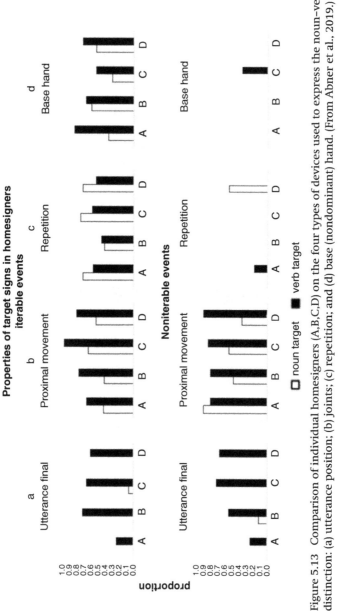

Figure 5.13 Comparison of individual homesigners (A,B,C,D) on the four types of devices used to express the noun–verb distinction: (a) utterance position; (b) joints; (c) repetition; and (d) base (nondominant) hand. (From Abner et al., 2019.)

Two of the devices that are iconic – proximal movements for verbs and the use of the base hand – are used in all cohorts. Focusing on repetition across cohorts, however, we see that it is only in signers of NSL2 and NSL3 that repetition is used to consistently mark nouns across both iterative and non-iterative events.

When we look closely at the homesigners we see how this shift might have occurred. The use of repetition in nouns is already present in three of the four homesigners, but only when the verb is iterative. Hence for them it is an iconic strategy, perhaps to represent the object as it is used iteratively.

Repetition starts out being used iconically in homesigners for nouns, but only in NSL2 and NSL3 is repetition generalized within the system to consistently mark the difference between nouns and verbs across both iterative and non-iterative events. It is the distribution of the phonological property of repetition that makes it morphophonemic, not its appearance per se.

5.4 EXTERNAL PRESSURES ON A PHONOLOGICAL SYSTEM

External factors are those that have to do with our anatomy and physiology as human beings, as discussed in the embodiment literature (Wilson, 2002), both alone and in a particular social or cultural community, as well as the affordances of the specific articulatory and perceptual systems used in the language. These relate to factors external to the system. Bottom-up pressures that affect conventionalization are shown in (4).

(4) *External pressures that affect conventionalization (pressures from outside the system):*
  (i)   naturalness, iconicity of the referent
  (ii) phonetic pressures: ease of articulation and ease of perception
  (iii) language ecology
  (iv) cultural associations
  (v)   frequency of type and token

Regarding naturalness and iconic affordances, Hwang et al. (2017) studied the iconic strategies of handshape (object and handling), as well as personification (the signer becomes the object). Gesturers and signers in three countries – Japan, the United States, and Turkey – were analyzed and in all countries there was a tendency to use personification for animals and handling handshapes for tools. For food, however, strategies were split between object and manipulation strategies; the sign for CABBAGE would be as likely to be represented as a round object as something to be chopped. This suggests that at least some classes of objects and events prioritize certain iconic affordances cross-culturally, while others show cross-cultural variation.

Regarding phonetic pressures, there is a preference for domain cues across entire constituents and a preference for simultaneous structure. Outcomes of this pressure include the manifestation of visual sonority. In this context it might mean that forms are more likely to contain a single handshape across an entire word, as the SELECTED FINGER CONSTRAINT (SFC) suggests (see Chapter 1). These are aspects of phonological structure that have been linked to the way that visual information is efficiently conveyed via the body and hands.

Language ecology (physical, social and cultural circumstances) may also play a role – namely whether a homesigner is the only deaf person in her circle of acquaintance, has other deaf homesigners as family members, or has deaf friends at school who are homesigners. Horton (2018) explored these factors in her study of homesigners in Guatemala and found that indeed the language ecology does seem to affect the rate at which different aspects of language emerge – such as stable words, morphological forms, and phonological complexity.

With regard to cultural associations, a sign's form may be based on the iconicities embedded in different cultures due to different experiences with the objects in question. Whether one eats with chopsticks or with a knife and fork will affect the instrument's handshape, and the way tomatoes might be commonly used – squeezed for their juice or cut for salad – might also affect the sign's form.

Finally, frequency of use may also play a role in how quickly a feature becomes part of the phonology. By studying corpora, we can investigate exactly how type- and token-frequent a property is and how that correlates with the use of that feature in minimal pairs.

5.4.1 Applying Principles External to the Phonological System in Emerging Sign Languages

Sandler et al. (2011a) have argued that the creation of wholistic words and the prosodic organization of semantically related words are the first grammatical elements to emerge in a new language, while syntax, phonology, and morphology come later (Sandler, 2014; Sandler, 2016). The phonetic and social pressures such as those mentioned above have been argued to be factors in the emergence of phonology in ABSL, even though Sandler et al. (2011a) argue that a phonological

Figure 5.14 (left) Two variants of DOG; (right) one family's form of EGG showing assimilation of handshape (from Sandler et al., 2011a)

system per se does not exist in ABSL because no duality of patterning has been observed. They were, however, able to identify the kernels of phonological structuring among lexical forms, which show more regularity in family groups than is evident across the community as a whole, and which Sandler et al. (2011a) termed "familylects."

In ABSL there is higher variation among signs for the same concept than there is in ASL (Israel & Sandler, 2011). For example, in the sign for DOG we see the iconic strategy of barking influencing both of the forms in Figure 5.14a,b (left), but the place of articulation (POA) is different.

Despite this variation, as signs become more conventionalized with more use, internal formational elements begin to undergo alternation, irrespective of (or even in contradiction to) the meaning of the sign, as we see in the compound for EGG. As seen in Figure 5.14 (right) this compound is comprised of BIRD (shape of beak) + a handling handshape (medium-sized round object). As you see in Figure 5.14 (bottom right), the handling handshape in the compound of this familylect has regressively assimilated to the first part of the compound, and the first handshape is no longer iconic for the beak of the bird. Sandler et al. (2011a) argue that the frequency and conventionalization of a lexical form allow for the meaning to be detached from the form enough that a phonetic pressure, such as ease of articulation, can emerge. This is consistent with a usage-based approach to the emergence of phonology (Bybee, 1994). The loss of iconicity within this familylect that we see in Figure 5.14 via handshape assimilation conforms to the SELECTED FINGERS CONSTRAINT (SFC) seen across many standard sign languages. In Chapters 1 and 4 we discussed how

P-words typically have just one set of selected fingers, which favors ease of articulation.

Sandler (2014) has also argued that phonetic features can give rise to phonology at its early stages, where minor variation in a handshape that would not create a phonemic distinction marks out a particular new sign language as unique – e.g., one language might use the closed -E- exclusively and another language the open -E- exclusively (see Figure 1.16). While phonology must eventually demonstrate minimal pairs and phonological rules, and be shared across a language community, perhaps all properties that are hallmarks of a fully formed phonological grammar are not present at the beginning stages of phonological emergence. Moreover, we would argue that iconicity need not be lost in order for phonology to appear, but rather it may simply be reorganized.

5.4.2 Are Internal or External Factors More Important in Emerging Phonologies?

In order to compare the internal and external factors involved in emerging phonologies, it might be worthwhile to consider the finger complexity case as discussed earlier in this chapter.

Consider that even standard sign languages, such as ASL, have a majority of forms composed of low-complexity forms. In the elicited task with ten objects in NSL, we found six selected finger groups: (symbols), (74 percent, level 1 complexity), (symbols) (22 percent, level 2 complexity), (symbol) (4 percent, level 3 complexity). This is comparable to the ASL lexicon. In a set of core vocabulary from a reliable ASL dictionary (Stokoe et al., 1965), Hara (2003) found that 74 percent of ASL forms consist of handshapes in low-complexity selected finger groups – (symbols), or (symbol) – and 26 percent are in medium- and higher-complexity groups. In contrast, Sandler et al. (2011a) reported that, on a task of naming 128 lexical items, 96 percent of ABSL forms contained a (symbol) or (symbol), leaving only 4 percent to be formed from other, more complex handshapes from the medium- and high-complexity groups.

We are not proposing that selected finger complexity can definitively serve as a criterion to establish whether a particular language or a particular individual has or does not have a phonological system. Rather, finger complexity may be one among a set of first indications of phonological reorganization. We suggest that the language ecology may be a crucial difference between NSL and ABSL due to the ways in which the language is transmitted among members (Meir et al., 2010; Kisch, 2012). As we mentioned at the beginning of this chapter, ABSL is a *village sign language*, with a very small number of deaf users (currently 120–150), a high proportion of hearing users, and a relatively slow rate of acquiring new members, because new members enter the community only by being born into it. NSL, in contrast, is a *deaf community sign language*, which has a robust number of deaf users (currently 1,300–1,400), has relatively few hearing users, and more opportunities to admit new members, with twenty-five new members entering annually when they enroll in school (Senghas, 2005). These factors are likely to have an impact on the number of opportunities for the analysis and reanalysis of forms, which can then yield to reorganization.

A crucial question appears to be, "How many individuals create a community, and what type of contact facilitates conventionalization?" Horton (2018) in her work in Nebaj, Guatemala, has been investigating handshape complexity as described in Section 5.3.2 in children in several types of language ecologies. Using a measure called a *dispersion index* (the ratio between the number of sign tokens a participant produces on a lexical naming task and the number of unique handshape types within the set of signs) Horton has found evidence that "individual" homesigners have the highest dispersion index. These are homesigners who lack any typical language input. The group with the next highest dispersion index is the "peer" homesigner group. These are homesigners who go to school with other homesigners, and they could be considered similar to the community sign language case, NSL. The group with the lowest dispersion index is the "family" homesigner group. These are homesigners who have at least one deaf family member who also uses homesign, and they could be considered similar to the village sign language case, ABSL. These results concur with those offered independently throughout this chapter. There are two reasons for a low dispersion index. One reason might be reorganization strategies, such as SYMMETRY and FEATURE ECONOMY; NSL2 signers exhibit this motivation, and we know this because the language has undergone stages with higher dispersion. Another might be because the phonology has not yet been sparked to emerge. This is what happens in gesturers and the early cohorts of a village sign language.

A higher number of unique handshapes corresponds to an inventory with higher complexity. Recall in Section 5.3.2 that homesigning adults had the highest handshape complexity of all of the Nicaraguan groups studied (see Figure 5.8). NSL1 and NSL2 have lower dispersion indices and lower handshape complexity. We interpreted the lower handshape complexity in NSL1 and NSL2 signers to be due to reorganization strategies, such as SYMMETRY and FEATURE ECONOMY but the ABSL signers also appear to have lower handshape complexity than NSL. This is in line with Horton's findings as well, because the spark to begin phonologization may not yet have occurred. Horton's work adds an empirical comparison between peer and family homesigners, which shows that peer homesigners (similar to NSL) have higher handshape complexity than family homesigners (similar to ABSL).

5.5 CONCLUSIONS

To summarize, every phonological contrast in a sign language can be traced back to origins in raw, undifferentiated gestures of many different types – emblematic, deictic, and, particularly, iconic gestures; however, crucially, none of the re-organizational patterns described in this chapter were found in the gestures from which the signs originated. DISPERSION is evident in homesign as it builds on the group of contrastive forms, and SYMMETRY and FEATURE ECONOMY are found in young sign languages. As more distinctions arise, new mappings can be realized, paving the way for more complex patterns to appear. And as each new cohort learns the language, the patterns of phonological reorganization become stronger.

Sign languages do not merely echo or exaggerate the patterns present in gesture systems. In sign languages, the gestural roots of signs are often evident in their form. We see this in the iconic influences that underlie "hand-as-object" representations and "hand-as-hand" representations, and in the iconic repetition of movement for iterative events in the origins of the noun–verb distinction. But the iconic raw material is then reshaped and reorganized into a system of signs over time using abstract, linguistic categories involving phonological features and meaning (in this case, meaning associated with morphology). Consequently, the organizational principles of sign languages grow to be qualitatively different from those of gesture.

I would argue that iconicity is one important factor, along with other pressures, such as ease of articulation, ease of perception, and DISPERSION, SYMMETRY, and FEATURE ECONOMY, that influence the shape of the system. Sign languages exploit iconicity, but ultimately iconicity in signs assumes a distribution that takes on arbitrary dimensions. In other words, phonology and iconicity are not mutually exclusive (see also Meir, 2002; van der Kooij, 2002; Eccarius, 2008; Padden et al., 2010). In this way, iconicity is organized, conventionalized, and systematized in sign language grammar, but it is not eliminated. There are rare cases of a sign form going completely against iconicity; however, more often the form is simply more rigidly constrained than would be predicted by iconicity, as we have seen in this chapter.

Processes of morphophonology appear to be more important early on in emergence than the need to create minimal pairs in stems. In other words, it may be more important to distinguish nouns from verbs, or to distinguish transitive and intransitive verbal forms; minimal pairs may be epiphenomenal, and appear only when enough different motivations for them are in play. In addition, the relatively large number of degrees of freedom offered by the range of articulators available in sign language may indeed reduce the likelihood of minimal pairs for brand new words in the lexicon, as van der Hulst and van der Kooij (2006) have argued. These facts make it likely that minimal pairs and allophonic rules will appear later in this process.

Language learners are key to this process of reorganization. In order to learn language, children must be able to identify the basic elements within a complex structure. This analytical eye, focused on an arbitrary arrangement, can detect categories, boundaries, and seams in the system, where previously there were none. Thus, learners create new elements as they learn.

5.6 FURTHER READING

Brentari, D. & Goldin-Meadow S. (2017). Language emergence. *Annual Review of Linguistics 3*, 363–88.

Carrigan, E. & Coppola, M. (2017). Successful communication does not drive language development: Evidence from adult homesign. *Cognition*, 158, 10–27.

Goldin-Meadow, S. & Brentari D. (2017). Gesture, sign and language: The coming of age of sign language and gesture studies. *Brain and Behavioral Sciences*, 39 doi:10.1017/S0140525X15001247.

Sandler, W. (2016). What comes first in language emergence? In N. Enfield (ed.), *Dependency in Language: On the Causal Ontology of Language Systems. Studies in Diversity in Linguistics 99* (pp. 67–86). Berlin: Language Science Press.

Senghas, R., Senghas, A., & Pyers, J. (2005).The emergence of Nicaraguan Sign Language: Questions of development, acquisition, and evolution. In J. Langer, C. Milbrath, & S. Parker (eds.), *Biology and Knowledge Revisited: From Neurogenesis to Psychogenesis* (pp. 287–306). Mahwah, NJ: Lawrence Erlbaum Associates.

6   Sign Language Phonological Processing

Abstract

Is phonological form perceived, understood, stored, and accessed in the same way and with the same neural mapping in signed and spoken languages? This is the complex and multifaceted question that the work on sign language processing has addressed since the beginning. The methodologies and technologies used to address this question have become more sophisticated over the last sixty years. Since the beginning, a psycholinguistic tradition was at the center of the work on sign languages, and we trace the trajectory of this work in this chapter.

6.1 INTRODUCTION

While there may be some small differences of the neural mapping among first-acquired spoken languages, we know that the neural network across spoken language is sufficiently similar that we easily generalize across the results from laboratories working on spoken German, Chinese, Russian, Spanish, French, etc. (see Xiang et al., 2015, for an example of crosslinguistic ERP work on English and Chinese).

A remaining important question is whether the processing, retrieval, and neural mapping of spoken languages and signed languages are fundamentally the same, which is a much bigger leap. We might expect much larger differences comparing signed and spoken languages in processing and neural mapping since they engage different peripheral systems, and perhaps especially in phonology this might be true because of the different modalities involved.

In this chapter we address these questions considering sign language phonological processing. The two major questions concern what phonological units are involved and whether the neural networks are the same for signed and spoken languages. We start with a review of processing studies that address the units of sign language phonology, many of which use behavioral techniques. In general, linguists depend a great deal on distributional properties to identify sub-lexical phonological units, as was mentioned in Chapter 1, but such methods do not always obtain completely satisfying results. For example, minimal pairs have not been found for all phonological features in American Sign Language (ASL), and so it has been very useful to examine external evidence from phonological processing (discussed here) and language acquisition (addressed in Chapter 7) to independently support distributional facts about phonological units and operations. Next, we turn to questions of neural mapping itself, starting from the beginning using classical methods of studying brain-damaged patients to more current methods – fMRI, ERP, PET, and other imaging techniques.

6.2 LANGUAGE PROCESSING OF PHONOLOGICAL UNITS

In this section we will see evidence from psycholinguistic experiments that help us answer the question, "Which phonological units are important for sign language phonological processing?" We will explore several different ways that the literature has addressed this question from behavior studies and neural mapping.

6.2.1 Production Evidence: Slips of the Hand

One widely accepted psycholinguistic method of accessing phonological units is to observe how and where "slips" occur – slips of the tongue in spoken languages or slips of the hand in sign languages. Fromkin (1973) did extensive work on slips of the tongue and demonstrated the utility of these errors; her database on types of slips of the tongue continues to grow even after forty years. Such spoken slips of the tongue include the sort where two words form a blend (e.g., *break bun* > **brun**) or featural errors such as a *fifty pound bag* > *fifty-pound* **p**ag (assimilation of voice) and *left hemisphere* > **h**eft **l**emisphere (metathesis of segments). Do signers experience slips of the hand (the equivalent of slips of the tongue) or tip-of-the-finger phenomena (equivalent to tip of the tongue), making phonological units apparent? In previous chapters we have addressed how the parameters of handshape, movement, place of articulation (POA), and non-manuals have been shown to be compositional, using a wide range of distributional evidence, such as assimilation, reduction, and enhancement operations. Similar findings have come from slips of the hand for sign languages.

In sign languages, Klima and Bellugi (1979) studied a wide variety of slips of the hand, which were subsequently also studied systematically in German Sign Language (DGS; Hohenberger et al., 2002). In Table 6.1 we see a comparison of DGS slips of a hand (left) and German slips of the tongue (right). As noted by Hohenberger et al. (2002), the types and distribution of slips are quite similar in DGS and German, suggesting a common set of processing mechanisms. The only type of slip that seems to occur in German but not in DGS is the phrasal type, where a morpheme is either misplaced or stranded at the end of the phrase in German but not in DGS – e.g., *mein malay-**isch-er** Kolleg-e* might be produced as *mein malay-**er-isch** Kolleg-e* or *mein malay-**isch** Kolleg-**er***. Hohenberger et al. (2002) suggest that this lack of stranding or exchanging slips in DGS might be due to the relatively greater degree of simultaneous affixation of morphological material in signed languages as compared to spoken languages (see Chapter 2 on modality effects in signed and spoken language phonology).

A typical DGS phonological slip of the hand can be seen in Figure 6.1, showing an anticipation slip involving handshape: the target handshape in SEINE (*your*) is typically signed with the B-handshape ⟨🤚⟩, but the signer produced the same handshape as in the subsequent sign for ELTERN (*parents*), the Y-handshape ⟨🤙⟩. Note that this might be explained by the same SELECTED FINGER CONSTRAINT as discussed in Chapter 1 and the constraints on the phonological word mentioned in Chapter 4.

Another type of phonological slip that demonstrates that handshape is compositional, rather than a single unit, appears in Figure 6.2 from Klima and Bellugi (1979), showing another instance of anticipation. The selected finger group of the second sign in SEE regressively assimilates to the first sign, but the joint configuration does not (the joint configuration is the same as in the original handshape in MUST).

6.2.2   Production Evidence: Tip-of-the-Finger Phenomena

Besides slips of the tongue or hand, another type of phonological error that is useful in revealing phonological structure is the "tip-of-the-tongue" (TOT) or "tip-of-the-finger" (TOF) phenomenon, which typically involves proper names (e.g., if the target word is a city name, such as Evanston, and you might remember that the name starts with "E"). Word onsets appear to be especially important in recalling such forms for ASL also. Thompson et al. (2005) analyzed TOFs of thirty-three deaf

Table 6.1 *Comparison of signed and spoken language "slips" in German Sign Language (left) and German (right)*

	DGS					German					
	n	%	word	phon.	morph.	n	%	word	phon.	morph.	phrase
Anticipation	44	21.7	9	32	3	1027	20.7	143	704	177	
Perseveration	45	22.1	12	31	2	906	18.3	155	644	107	
Harmony	13	6.4		13							
Substitution	5	2.5	4		1						
-Semantic	38	18.7	35		3	1094	22.1	783	147	164	
-Formal	1	0.5			1						
-Both	1	0.5	1								
Blend	32	16.7	30		1	923	18.6	658	13	242	10
Fusion	18	8.8	18			13	0.3	10	2	1	
Exchange	2	1	1		1	774	16.6	200	439	135	
Deletion	4	2	2	2		182	3.7	46	78	58	
Addition						35	0.7	8	17	10	
Total	203		112	78	12	4951	100	2003	2043	894	10
Total %	100		56.2	38.4	6			40.5	41.3	18.1	0.2

Figure 6.1 A slip of the hand in German Sign Language involving regressive assimilation of the whole handshape (cf. Hohenberger et al., 2002)

Figure 6.2 A slip of the hand in ASL involving regressive assimilation of the selected fingers (cf. Klima & Bellugi, 1979)

signers – native, early, and late(er) learners of ASL (mean 10.5 years) – who were asked to produce names for famous people, place names, and low-frequency words, all of which tend to be (but are not always) fingerspelled. Of the seventy-nine TOFs produced, the majority (55) were for fingerspelled words and fewer (24) were for lexical signs. The fingerspelled forms involved the first or last letters, or both. For lexical signs, participants were equally likely to recall handshape, location, and orientation, which are simultaneously present at the beginning of a sign, and least likely to recall movement, which unfolds across the duration of the entire sign. In more than half (10/19, or 53 percent) of the TOFs, participants reported more than one phonological parameter – i.e., no single parameter was clearly dominant in facilitating sign recall, but rather it was the initial segment at the left edge of the word that was important. This provides some evidence for a timing unit, such as the segment in ASL (see Chapter 1 for further discussion).

Work on TOT phenomena has also contributed to general theoretical debates about the processing mechanisms that underlie these phenomena more generally. Spoken language bilinguals have been shown to experience TOT phenomena more frequently than monolinguals (Gollan & Acenas, 2004). Work on TOTs and TOFs in bimodal bilinguals (i.e., those who are proficient in a signed and a spoken language) provided a tool for determining whether bilingual processing costs should be attributed to modality-independent factors related to bilingualism, such as dual lexical representations at the lemma level, or to modality-sensitive factors, such as shared phonological representations, competition for linguistic articulators, or perceptual conflicts. Pyers et al. (2009) followed up on the Thompson et al. (2005) study and investigated monolinguals (English speakers), unimodal bilinguals (English-Spanish), and bimodal bilinguals (English-ASL). They found that both bilingual groups had more frequent TOTs or TOFs than the monolingual group. The results still favor the left edge of the word for both TOTs and TOFs, and these results also add more to the explanation of bilingual TOTs/TOFs, in general. Since TOTs/TOFs are more frequent in bimodal and unimodal bilinguals than in monolinguals, they must be related to the lemma level, rather than one that involves overlapping or competing phonological content between the two languages, since ASL and English share no overlapping phonology.

What we might take away from the results discussed thus far is that both the segmental unit (combination of handshape and POA features that appear simultaneously at the beginning of a sign) and autosegmental units, such as selected fingers, are important for processing and retrieval. From some of the slips of the fingers we learn that an autosegmental analysis of form is needed: MUST SEE spreads only the selected finger group from SEE to MUST, which is evidence of decomposition of the handshape. From the TOF results we also learn that sequential units are important for recall, and it is the timing slots at the left edge of words and signs that persist in memory in the TO(T)ongue or TO(F)inger phenomena in both modalities.

6.2.3 Perceptual Evidence: Movement

How do signers perceive or comprehend various aspects of sign language phonology? This question has been addressed using a variety of corpus and behavioral methods. To foreshadow the general conclusion, all of these studies lead to the conclusion that phonological perceptual processes are quite similar in signed and spoken languages. We first address aspects of phonological processing of movement at the word and syllable levels and then move on to the other four parameters.

In this section we address the roles of movement in terms of word building, rhyming, and reduplication, as it has been studied perceptually. The arguments for movement functioning as a syllable nucleus were described in detail in Chapter 2 and will only be mentioned here briefly: movements (not handshapes) are associated with meaningless parts of words, and individual movement components exhibit differential properties of sonority for morphophonological rules and prosodic constituency as morae.

In many of the studies that follow, several populations of signers are recruited, and sometimes non-signers as well, in order to address how language experience influences processing. Typically, data from the differing signing groups address issues of age of acquisition. Data from the non-signers serve (i) as a type of baseline for comparison on a comparable task in spoken language (when comparable spoken language items are used as stimuli), (ii) to help us understand what happens when sign language is not processed as language but rather as a nonlinguistic set of complex visuospatial representations, and (iii) to help us understand cross-modal or amodal properties of language.

6.2.3.1   Segmentation

Where do signers naturally put word breaks? Brentari (2006) and Brentari et al. (2011) conducted a segmentation experiments with signing and non-signing groups to see which changes of values in the three manual parameters were more likely to be perceived as a word break – first in ASL (Brentari, 2006) and later in Austrian Sign language (ÖGS) and Croatian Sign Language (HZJ; Brentari et al., 2011). Some of the major word-level phonotactics employed in this study have already been discussed in Chapter 1. Within a word, the SELECTED FINGERS CONSTRAINT and the HANDSHAPE SEQUENCING CONSTRAINT stipulate that only aperture features can change within a stem (not selected fingers). In place of articulation (POA), setting features can change within a stem, but not major POA features. Within movement, repetition or alternations of the same movement are possible within a stem, but not combinations of different movements. In the experiment, both signers and non-signers depended the most on the movement parameter to count words (signs): items with two movements were likely to be judged as two signs. However, signers were also sensitive to phonemic changes in handshape as well, while the non-signers were not.

The technique of "word spotting" (McQueen, 1996; McQueen & Cutler, 1998) has also been used to ask where word breaks naturally occur in sign languages. This design in spoken languages correctly captures the generalization that listeners find it harder to detect English *apple*, for example, in *fapple* (where *[f]* alone would be an impossible word in English), than in *vuffapple* (where *vuff* could be a word). The authors refer to this as the PROSODIC WORD CONSTRAINT (Norris et al., 1997), because strings tend to be divided into the most well-formed prosodic words possible. Orfanidou et al. (2010) employed this design in British Sign Language (BSL) to determine whether the modality differences between sign and speech would give rise to different strategies for segmenting phonological strings. Signed and spoken languages pose the same computational problem for phonology in the sense of Marr (1982),[1] so both types of languages might segment forms in the same way; however, since signs use simultaneous structures more extensively (e.g., handshape and location features extend across a whole word) and forms tend to be monosyllabic, different strategies for segmentation might be used. Orfanidou et al. (2009) did this by testing the applicability of the PROSODIC WORD CONSTRAINT on BSL. The word-spotting experiment employed sign pairs in which an attested BSL sign was preceded by either a possible or impossible monosyllabic BSL pseudo-sign. The impossible pseudo-signs were forms that had more than three movement components in a single syllable (e.g., a handshape change, an orientation change, and a movement with a particular shape), which are rare or unattested in many sign languages (Jantunen & Takkinen, 2010). The authors found that deaf signers of BSL were faster and more accurate in spotting the BSL signs when the preceding pseudo-signs were possible BSL signs than when they were impossible BSL signs. The authors conclude that regardless of the modality, the PROSODIC WORD CONSTRAINT influences segmentation of phonological strings.

6.2.3.2 Similarity Judgments

Since movement is crucial for sign syllabification, and for various types of morphological meaning, as we have discussed in previous chapters, we will now ask how sign language movement is perceived by signers and non-signers. Poizner et al. (1983) were the first to examine movement. They used point-light displays, a technique which isolates the movement from the other parameters of the sign in a task of triadic comparison (Figure 6.3).

A set of fifteen movement shapes used in ASL lexical items and fifteen used productively in the ASL morphological system of aspect were shown to signers and non-signers; participants were instructed to

---

[1] Marr treated vision as an information-processing system and proposed that any type of information-processing systems takes place at three distinct levels of analysis – computational, algorithmic, and physical. This idea is known in cognitive science as Marr's Tri-Level Hypothesis.

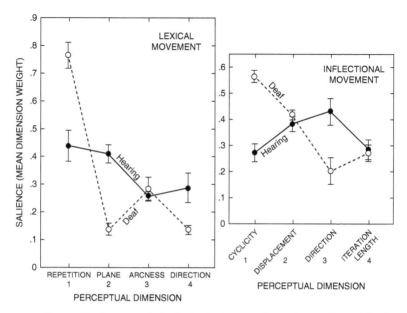

Figure 6.3 Perceptual similarity judgments from signers (dotted line) and non-signers (black line) for lexical and morphological movements, showing different patterns for the two groups. (Reprinted by permission from Springer Nature: Springer, *Perception & Psychophysics*, "Perception of movement in American Sign Language: Effects of linguistic structure and linguistic experience" (Poizner, H., 1983).)

choose the item in the triad that did not look like the other two. Results showed that signers and non-signers exhibit different patterns of similarity judgments; therefore, the different types of movements are perceived differently in the two groups (see Figure 6.3). Deaf signing participants found cyclicity and repetition to be very salient for making similarity judgments, while hearing participants found direction to be very salient. Equally important was the finding that signers found repetition in lexical movements and cyclicity in morphological movements (a type of repetition) to have the highest level of salience in stem and morphological movements. Repetition is a movement feature commonly used in plural formation (Horton et al., 2015), and in nominalization (Supalla & Newport, 1978; Abner et al., 2019), as we have discussed in the last chapter on phonological emergence (Abner et al., 2019). We will see that when non-signers are clued into the linguistic role that movement might be playing, both signers and non-signers appear to have a preference for repetition as a morphological strategy (Berent et al., 2014, 2016).

6.2.3.3 Rhyming

What counts as a "rhyme" in sign languages? Hildebrandt and Corina (2002) investigated the natural perceptual groupings of sign similarity in three populations: native signers of ASL, non-native signers of ASL, and hearing non-signers. In the first experiment a central target and alternatives sharing two parameters with the target sign were shown to participants, along with a filler ((M)ovement+POA, M+handshape (HS), POA+HS, filler). Participants were asked to choose from the alternatives surrounding the central target the one that was the most similar to it. All groups chose forms that shared M+POA most frequently, followed by the other two combinations, M+HS and POA +HS. The hearing subjects and late learners also showed a significant difference between M+HS and POA+HS choices. A second, related experiment was conducted with the same groups, where a target sign was shown with three alternative choices sharing just one parameter. The native group's pattern of results suggests that they may prefer movement when making similarity judgments, but this was not supported statistically. For both native signer and non-signer groups, movement was the preferred parameter for similarity; however, POA and M were not statistically different in either the native signer group or the non-signer group. Non-native signers were more likely to base similarity on handshape. These results show that POA and movement are important in choosing sign language "rhymes."

6.2.3.4 Reduplication

Given that the phonetic systems are quite different, we might ask if signed and spoken language users have the same preferences for ways to build new words. A series of studies attempted to answer this question using a variety of lexical decision tasks. They were conducted to investigate the salience of syllable repetition based on movement (Berent et al., 2014, 2016) and to investigate the role of reduplication in sign language phonology and morphology in signers and non-signers. In particular, they investigated whether syllable repetition is preferred as a phonological strategy to create minimal pairs (creating different lexical stems) or as a morphological strategy (creating words related in meaning).

In the first study (Berent et al., 2014), deaf ASL signers were presented with XX and XY pseudo-signs one at a time (where "X" and "Y" are syllable types) and asked to make a lexical decision. The stimuli were ASL pseudo-signs, generated with an XX form, in which the syllables (HS+MOV+POA combinations) were the same in the two syllables, or an XY form, in which the two syllables were different. They found that when pseudo-sign syllables are XX forms, deaf ASL signers took significantly longer to reject the non-sign than XY forms, even when the handshapes used in the XX pseudo-signs did not occur in ASL, and were therefore obviously not native forms. In other words, syllable reduplication was found to be a robust form of word formation, so robust that it interferes with rejecting a form as a non-ASL sign. This type of result occurs in spoken languages as well. Speakers take longer to reject spoken forms that conform to a recognizable word pattern, such as reduplication, even if they include non-native segments (Berent et al., 2002). In agreement with the Poizner (1983) study, this study demonstrates that repeated movement is an important grammatical device in the grammar of sign languages.

The next set of studies took this paradigm further to ask if repetition (or "doubling" as a neutral term) is a device used preferentially in phonological or morphological representation (Berent et al., 2016). They hypothesized that doubling would be (i) dispreferred as a phonological device in creating completely new stems (due to "identity," or the OBLIGATORY CONTOUR PRINCIPLE (OCP), Yip, 1988) and (ii) preferred as a morphological device in generating morphologically related forms (reduplication). Two populations were tested in twelve total experiments: four with English speakers judging English pseudo-words; four with English speakers judging ASL pseudo-signs; and four with English and Hebrew speakers judging ASL pseudo-signs.

The first set of experiments, abbreviated "E," with English speakers and English stimuli (E1–4), showed that participants dispreferred reduplication as a mechanism for creating minimal pairs when there was no meaning involved (E1) but preferred it as a strategy for creating morphologically related forms that could be interpreted as plural formation (E2 and E4b), as shown in Figure 6.4 (top). The next four experiments (English speakers and ASL stimuli) showed the same results, even though the English speakers had no prior experience with ASL (Figure 6.4, middle; E5–8). Participants showed a dispreference for creating new signs with reduplication in the absence of meaning (E5) but a preference for reduplicated forms under the same conditions as before – when a base form was given and the word created could be interpreted as a plural (E6a and E8b). These results show that the morphological preference for reduplication is cross-modal or amodal. Finally, Hebrew speakers and a new set of English speakers responded to ASL forms that were paired morphologically but in two different

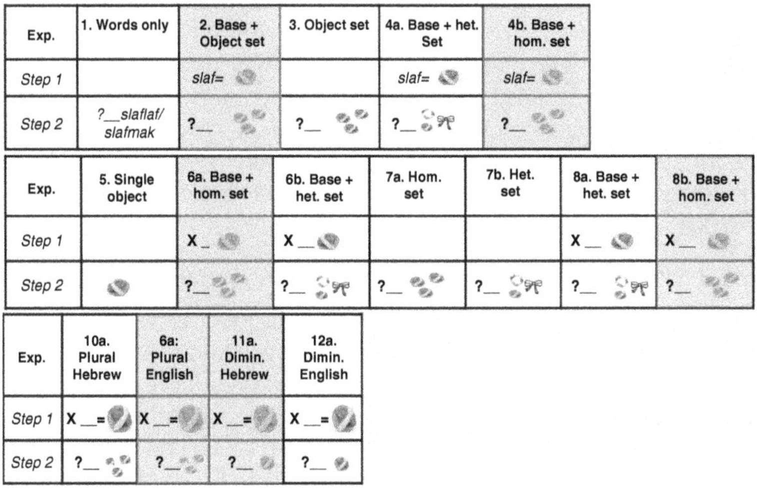

Exp.	1. Words only	2. Base + Object set	3. Object set	4a. Base + het. Set	4b. Base + hom. set
Step 1		slaf=		slaf=	slaf=
Step 2	?__slaflaf/ slafmak	?__	?__	?__	?__

Exp.	5. Single object	6a. Base + hom. set	6b. Base + het. set	7a. Hom. set	7b. Het. set	8a. Base + het. set	8b. Base + hom. set
Step 1		X_	X_			X_	X_
Step 2		?_	?_	?_	?_	?_	?_

Exp.	10a. Plural Hebrew	6a: Plural English	11a. Dimin. Hebrew	12a. Dimin. English
Step 1	X__=	X_=	X__=	X_=
Step 2	?_	?_	?_	?_

Figure 6.4 Example stimuli of Berent et al. (2016): (top) English speakers responding to English stimuli; (middle) English speakers responding to ASL stimuli; (bottom) English and Hebrew speakers responding to ASL stimuli. The experiments where a morphological preference for reduplicated forms was obtained are highlighted in gray.

ways – as plurals and as diminutives (Figure 6.4, bottom; stimuli from 6a, plus three new stimulus sets: E10a, 11a, and 12a). English speakers had a preference only for reduplicated ASL forms that were related to plural meanings as before (E6a), while Hebrew speakers had a preference only for reduplicated ASL forms that were related to diminutive meanings (E11a). While English marks plurals (not with reduplication), and has no productive diminutive, in Hebrew reduplicative nouns often denote diminution and attenuation but never augmentation or plurality. These results show that even as the morphological preference applies, it does so in a way that is modified by specific language experience.

It is clear from the results just presented here, and in Chapter 2, that movement plays an important role in syllabification, word building via reduplication, and in rhyming. All of these functions follow well from the formal arguments in previous chapters about movement's role as the backbone of signs, as the "vowel-like" element, and as the syllable nucleus. Poizner and colleagues' (1983) results were just the beginning of this work in showing that signers and non-signers process movement forms differently – linguistically and non-linguistically, respectively. But as we see in the Berent et al. studies, movement can be presented in a way that encourages its interpretation to be linguistic even in non-signers; namely when repetition is associated with word meaning. These studies also showed that the morphological association with reduplication is tempered by specific language experience. Finally, we see that syllable repetition itself is a universal word-building device, and that this device is accessible cross-modally and particularly in morphological word building.

6.2.4   Perceptual Evidence: Handshape

In this section we address the phonological processing of the other parameters. Because so much work has focused on the phonological processing of handshape, much of the discussion here will focus on handshape features. Handshape has been the parameter for which there is a good deal of consensus that there is hierarchical representation of features and autosegmental status for classes of selected fingers and joint features. As such, it is a good testing ground to understand the psychological reality of these phonological elements.

6.2.4.1   Categorical Perception

The classic categorical perception (CP) paradigm includes both an identification task and a discrimination task, and typically (in speech) it is aimed at the level of feature processing. A series of forms at equidistant intervals are used as stimuli. For the identification task a form at one interval is shown to participants who judge it to be more like one or the other of the two extremes. The CP effect is the resulting S-shaped distribution in Figure 6.5, where forms in the middle of the continuum have more varied responses. The discrimination task involves showing pairs of forms that are two intervals apart and asking participants whether they are the same or different. The discrimination peak is typically where participants can see the difference between the two forms most easily, and for the classic CP result, this peak of discrimination should appear in the same place as the category break of the identification task, as shown in Figure 6.5 (i.e., the ABX task; see Harnad, 1987, for a comprehensive overview).

CP does not apply solely to linguistic material and may be accounted for by natural sensitivities to specific types of auditory or visual stimuli, rather than by mechanisms that have evolved specifically for language; for example, CP has been shown to apply to plucking and bowing sounds in music (Jusczyk et al., 1977; Roberson & Davidoff,

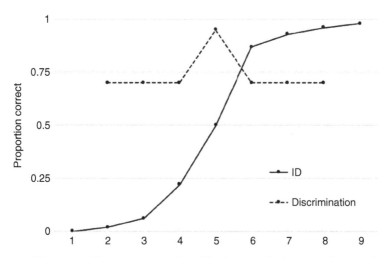

Figure 6.5 The two parts of an ideal categorical perception result: (i) an S-curve for identification indicating two categories, and (ii) a discrimination peak that occurs at the point where the two categories on the S-curve become evident

2000). Neither is CP restricted to human behavior; it is found in chinchillas and Japanese quail (Diehl et al., 2004; Kluender & Kiefte, 2006). Lexical effects play a role as well, so CP is not entirely phonological (Whalen, Best, & Irwin, 1997), and linguistic experience also influences categorization and discrimination, at least for some units that have been studied – e.g., plosive consonants in spoken languages (Aslin & Pisoni, 1980) and handshapes in sign languages (Morford et al., 2008; Best et al., 2010). Nevertheless, CP is one kind of evidence that can assist in determining whether a property is phonological or not, because it aligns to a large extent with a property's phonemic status in spoken language (Liberman et al., 1957, 1967; Eimas, 1963). In addition, even in the absence of a classical CP effect, differences in performance on this task can be informative.

Most of the work on CP in sign languages has focused on the processing of handshape features and feature classes (Newport, 1982; Emmorey et al., 2003a; Baker et al., 2005, 2006; Boutora & Karypidis, 2007; Morford et al., 2008; Best et al., 2010; and Sevcikova, 2014). CP effects have also been found in the non-manual component (McCullough & Emmorey, 2009), but no CP effects have been found for POA and the paradigm has not been attempted with movement.

A variety of stimulus types have been used in these experiments: video stimuli; static photographs, attested signs; pseudo-signs; stimuli produced by signers; stimuli produced by animation software. Some stimuli show the whole signer from the head to the hips (the typical signing space), and some show only the POA and the handshape. Most studies control for phonemic versus allophonic status.

Some studies have targeted individual features, such as [±spread] fingers, or [±contact] between the thumb and other fingers. Some studies have targeted feature classes, such as selected fingers or joint configuration, and some have targeted the whole parameter of hand-shape, POA, or facial expression. I mention this range in stimuli because, as controlled and well known as the CP paradigm is, there is still quite a bit of room for variation in the way the experiment is conducted, and the way the stimuli are constructed may have an effect on the results. Figures 6.6–6.9 show a sample of some of the stimuli used in these studies. Figure 6.6 shows the static stimuli used in Emmorey et al. (2003), targeting phonemic and allophonic hand-shapes using attested signs built with Poser™ software. Figure 6.7 shows still images from the pseudo-sign video clips used in the Best et al. (2010) study, addressing the individual [spread] feature of the fingers of handshape. Figure 6.8 shows sample images from the ani-mated movie clips used in Morford et al. (2008). Figure 6.9 shows sample stimuli from McCullough and Emmorey's work on CP effects in facial expressions.

A survey of CP investigations shows that the results have been quite mixed. Sometimes CP effects are found only for clusters of features that represent phonemic forms (not allophonic forms), and only in signers (not in non-signers; Emmorey et al., 2003a; Baker et al., 2005). When specific features are used, however, such as [±spread] (Best et al., 2010) or [±contact] (Morford et al., 2008), no classical CP effects were found. In a recent CP study of Hong Kong Sign Language (HKSL), Zhao et al. (2017) found a CP effect for selected fingers but not for joints (where minimal pairs were attested in both feature classes). This finding supports the head-dependent relation for handshape proposed in the Hand Tier (Sandler, 1989), Prosodic (Brentari, 1998), and Dependency (van der Hulst, 1993) models of sign language phonology, all of which agree that of the two classes of handshape features (selected fingers and joints), selected fingers dominates joints. Recall from Chapter 1, the selected fingers$_1$ node is the head and nonselected fingers the dependent, and lower down in the tree, selected fingers$_0$ is the head and joint configuration the dependent.

A)

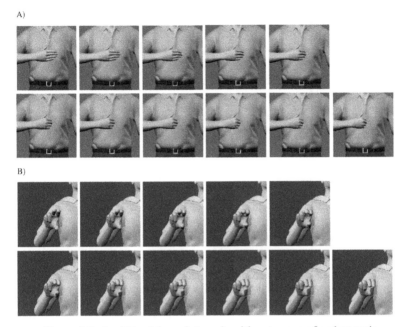

B)

Figure 6.6 (top) Handshape intervals with extremes of a phonemic minimal pair: fully extended 🤚 PLEASE/fully closed ✊ SORRY; (bottom) handshape intervals with extremes of an allophonic pair: flat-open, first position NO 🫳 /flat-closed, second position NO 🫴. (From "Categorical perception in American Sign Language," by Emmorey, et al., *Language and Cognitive Processes*, 18, 2003, reprinted by permission of the publisher, Taylor & Francis Ltd, www.tandfonline.com.)

The CP paradigm has also been employed to address cases where sub-lexical elements of sign languages are known to be meaningful (Sehyr & Cormier, 2015). They found that for handshapes that represent how objects are grasped and manipulated and can indirectly indicate the size and shape of the object both hearing non-signers and deaf signers exhibited CP effects, but signers showed faster reaction times (RTs) and less variability overall on the task. It might be surprising that non-signers show a CP effect, but remember, CP effects can be seen in a nonlinguistic signal (Jusczyk et al., 1977; Roberson & Davidoff, 2000) and even by nonhumans (Diehl et al., 2004; Kluender & Kiefte, 2006).

Likewise, age of acquisition is an important factor that influences phonological processing, and differences in performance between

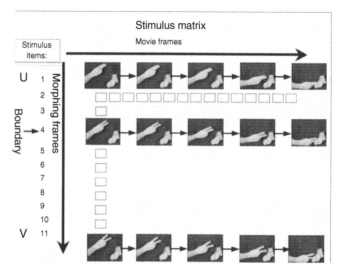

Figure 6.7 Example stimuli from Best et al. (2010): (x axis) frames in a clip showing a pseudoform utilizing a continuum of two-finger hand-shape intervals ranging from unspread to spread . (Reprinted by permission from Springer Nature: Springer, *Attention, Perception, & Psychophysics*, "Effects of sign language experience on categorical per-ception of dynamic ASL pseudosigns," Best, et al. (2010).)

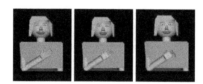

Figure 6.8 Sample stimuli from the animated video stimuli used in Morford et al. (2008). (Reprinted from *Cognition*, 109, Morford, et al., "Effects of language experience on the perception of American Sign Language," pp. 41–53, Copyright (2008), with permission from Elsevier.)

early learners, late learners, and adult L2 learners of ASL were found to be similar in CP performance (Morford et al., 2008). All three groups performed similarly across the category boundary. The difference lies in the native signers' loss of fine phonetic distinctions *within* category, particularly around the handshape prototype. For example, between native and adult L2 signers, there was a difference of only 6 percent in

Figure 6.9 Sample stimuli from McCullough and Emmorey (2009): (top) grammatical intervals for the continuum of grammatical facial expressions "th" (meaning *awkwardly*) to "mm" (meaning *with ease*); (bottom) affective intervals for the continuum of facial expression from happy to sad. (Reprinted from *Cognition*, 110, McCullough, S. & Emmorey, K., "Categorical perception of affective and linguistic facial expressions," pp. 208–221, Copyright (2009), with permission from Elsevier.)

accuracy on the least similar handshapes, but for the most similar handshapes, a difference of 16 percent accuracy was found. In other words, the boundary of handshape categories and the ability to perceive handshape differences well at these boundaries were the same for all three groups. From these results, Morford et al. (2008) conclude that the categorical nature of forms is stronger in native signers.

McCullough and Emmorey (2009) also used the CP paradigm for non-manual facial expressions. They used as endpoints two adverbial non-manuals in ASL – the tongue-thrust "th"-non-manual (*awkwardly*), which was morphed into a "mm"-non-manual (*easily* (Figure 6.9, top)). They compared responses from this continuum of grammatical facial expressions to one of emotional facial expressions, with endpoints of anger and disgust (see Figure 6.9, bottom). Both signers and non-signers showed CP effects for the linguistic non-manuals, and non-signers (but not the signers) showed CP effects for affective non-manual as well. These results indicate that non-signers treat all facial expressions the same, while signers treat those facial expressions that are used in the grammar of their language differently than those used for emotions and mental states. They, like Morford et al. (2008) and Sehyr and Cormier (2015), showed that CP effects do not appear in response to exclusively linguistic phenomena.

All of these studies suggest that the CP methodology should not be interpreted as an "all-or-nothing" determination of whether a parameter or feature is phonological or not, but rather as a means to show differences in aspects of performance and to isolate aspects of phonological structure: the whole face or hand, the class of features or autosegment, or specific features. These differences can also give us useful information about language experience and about age of acquisition effects.

6.2.4.2   Goodness-of-Fit Tasks

An alternative to the CP paradigm is a meaning identification task combined with a goodness-of-fit task, which can give information about not only category boundaries but also about best exemplars (i.e., prototypical examples) of structures. Knowing best exemplars is particularly useful in cases where no minimal pair exists (as is often the case in sign languages), since the location of category boundaries can shift depending on the lexical (word versus non-word) status of the stimuli used, but the best exemplar tends to remain stable (Allen & Miller, 2001). Eccarius (2008) used a smaller scale version of this paradigm to try to determine whether hand-shape features induce consistent or different perceptual categories across the three lexical components – foreign, core, and spatial (i.e., classifiers) (see Chapter 1). She wanted to know whether features known to be prominently (morphologically) contrastive in one part of the lexicon – e.g., HS1 versus HS3 in the spatial component for classifiers   LONG-THIN-ROUND-OBJECT   versus   LONG-THIN-FLAT-OBJECT (Figure 6.10, bottom) – retain those category boundaries in other parts of the lexicon. The answer to this question is not straightforward, since no known minimal pairs exist across this particular set of handshapes for foreign (e.g., the initialized form OPINION, Figure 6.10, top) or core (e.g., TEACH, Figure 6.10, middle) signs. The results of this goodness-of-fit task suggested that best

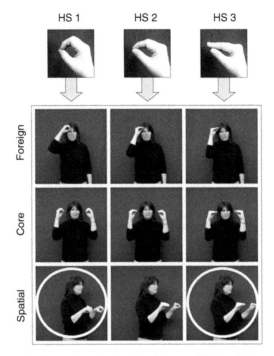

Figure 6.10 Example stimulus handshapes (HSs) and signs used in Eccarius (2008). An identification task verified a meaningful contrast in the spatial component (bottom) between the handshape endpoints, (HS1 and HS3, indicated with circles), but best exemplars suggested that the contrast was not consistent across all three components of the ASL lexicon. (Images used with permission.)

exemplars (and therefore category boundaries) can indeed vary across lexical type. Future research using full-scale goodness-of-fit tasks to test contrasts in sign languages, especially in the absence of minimal pairs, may yield important information about phonological categorization.

To sum up this section, we see that phonological processing of units in sign languages is very similar to that of spoken languages in terms of utilizing features, classes of features, and syllables. We also see that engaging signing and non-signing participants in psycholinguistics experiments can be informative in different ways, because non-signers may show inherent cognitive biases in certain types of sign language stimuli, while signers show preferences for the forms used in their phonological and morphological systems. However, we cannot assume that non-signers have no sensitivity at all to sign language structure. We see a sensitivity to movement and location in both signers and non-signers for rhyming (Hildebrandt & Corina, 2002) and sensitivity to movement in segmentation (Brentari, 2006) and to movement repetition (Berent et al., 2013, 2016). Moreover, when it is possible to do so, speakers bring their spoken language intuitions from their native phonology and morphology to bear on their decisions regarding forms from sign language (Berent et al., 2016). In other words, not all shared judgments from non-signers should be assumed to be "purely" cognitive in nature; they may be colored by their spoken language linguistic experience, even in a different modality, and potentially indicate cross-modal or amodal principles of language.

6.3 PHONOLOGICAL PROCESSING AND NEIGHBORHOOD DENSITY

Increasingly in spoken language phonology, questions about how the frequency of form interacts with lexical access, complexity, markedness, and phonological processing have been investigated with usage-based approaches (Bybee, 1994, 2003), exemplar phonology (Pierrehumbert, 2001), and with models where frequency is equal to "information" (Goldsmith, 2001). In these "information"-based models, the idea is that the higher the frequency, the lower the amount of information, and the lower the frequency, the higher the amount of information. This method has been important in understanding which factors affect lexical access and retrieval in spoken languages for a variety of phenomena (Andrews, 1992; Goldinger et al., 1992), and it is now widely accepted that babies use statistical principles as they acquire language (Aslin et al., 1998). Exemplar theories of phonology and usage-based theories have been very helpful in explaining the common, but complex, process of French liaison (Bybee, 2001; Laks et al., 2018). Yang (2017) has further developed this idea to propose a critical threshold for token-for-word learning and for learning lexical exceptions, which decreases as the tokens affected increase. Called the Tolerance Principle, it uses corpus-based evidence to support the idea that word learning works better with small quantities of data, so that lexical exceptions are learned best when the total vocabulary is small. This provides an empirical explanation for how children easily acquire a grammar with minimal input, a grammar containing rules that might be very difficult for adult learners.

Neighborhood density is another way of thinking about frequency. Scholars target a particular unit – feature, segment, syllable, or word – showing that a unit with a large number of neighbors inhibits retrieval (slows it down); the idea is that there is more competition while accessing the target word. In contrast, a unit with a small number of neighbors facilitates retrieval (speeds it up). The effects of neighborhood density on language processing in sign languages have been investigated as well; however, one drawback is that large, reliable tagged corpora of sign languages are rare (but see the BSL Sign Bank, the BSL Corpus Project, the Auslan corpus, and the Asian Sign Bank[2]). One way to circumvent this lack of frequency data is to get judgments from signers about sign familiarity. High-familiarity forms are assumed to be more frequent and low-familiarity signs less frequent.

One of the most typical designs for a study addressing phonological neighborhoods is a lexical decision task. Attested and unattested, but possible, words or signs are presented to participants. Participants then decide as quickly as they can if the target form is or is not a word. Carreiras et al. (2008) used this type of design to study the effect of handshape and location (POA) in Spanish Sign Language (LSE) in conditions of high and low familiarity, and high and low frequency. Familiarity ratings were obtained by signers' judgments, and frequency was calculated based on token frequency from an LSE dictionary (Pinedo Peydró, 2000). Native signers had faster RTs than non-natives, and sign familiarity and neighborhood density were both significant factors in predicting how quickly participants responded, although not in a uniform way for handshape and POA. For POA there was an inhibitory effect for neighborhood (slower RTs in larger neighborhoods, such as neutral space) but shorter RTs for signs with highly familiar POAs. There was also an interaction between familiarity and neighborhood: low-familiarity signs were recognized more rapidly when the POA came from a small neighborhood, but there was no effect of neighborhood density for highly familiar signs.

For handshape, there was an effect of facilitation (faster RTs in smaller neighborhood). Signs with low neighborhood densities had shorter RTs than the mean, but these results were affected also by age of acquisition (they were significant only in non-native signers) and by

---

[2] http://bslsignbank.ucl.ac.uk/, www.bslcorpusproject.org/, https://researchdata .ands.org.au/auslan-australian-sign-language-corpus/125009, http://cslds.org /asiansignbank/

whether the form was or was not an attested sign (the effect was significant only for pseudo-signs). The authors suggest that the results may have to do with the size of the disparity for high- and low-density neighborhoods: one sign in twenty is likely to be in a low-density neighborhood sign for POA, because only one POA (neutral space) is high density; all other POAs are considered low density. Meanwhile, one sign in six is likely to be a low-density neighborhood sign for handshape, because four handshapes (B, 1, A, & 5) are high density, and all other handshapes are considered low density.

Caselli and Pyers (2017) investigated the effects of lexical frequency, neighborhood density, and iconicity in the signs of deaf children from parental reports using a set of signs from the MacArthur communicative development inventory (Anderson & Reilly, 2002). They found that neighborhood density and lexical frequency, as well as iconicity, independently facilitated vocabulary acquisition. Despite differences in iconicity and phonological structure, signing children, like children learning a spoken language, track statistical information about lexical items and their phonological properties and leverage these factors to expand their vocabulary.

6.4 NEUROLOGICAL MAPPING OF SIGN LANGUAGE PHONOLOGY

We now turn to the neural mapping of sign language phonology in the brain. This section provides a survey of neuroimaging studies that address which areas of the brain are involved in the processing of sign language phonology. An important question since the beginning of work on sign languages has been whether signed and spoken languages use different neural mappings. Before the advent of neuroimaging technology, such as EEG (ERP), fMRI, and PET,[3] which allow researchers to study the live brains of healthy individuals, the only way to address this question was to study cadaver brains or to study brain-damaged patients – speakers and signers – and infer that the specific, damaged regions in the brain in such patients were responsible for different types of observed language breakdown. These studies also inferred that the connection between impaired language and

---

[3] Abbreviations: EEG is an electroencephalogram, yielding ERP event-related potentials. An fMRI is a functional magnetic resonance image, and a PET image is positron emission tomography. These will be discussed further in subsequent sections.

locus of brain damage gave an indication of where specific language processes took place in healthy individuals. There is no doubt that studies of brain-damaged patients have taught us a great deal about the organization of spoken and sign languages, starting from the nineteenth century (Broca, 1861) and continuing until the 1980s, particularly after World War II where data from a large number of patients with traumatic brain injury were gathered in one place (Dronkers et al., 1995, 2000). From early work on the brains of cadavers (Broca, 1861/1960; Wernicke, 1874) and on individuals with damaged and disordered brains, it was discovered that many (but not all) language functions occur in the left hemisphere – morphology, phonology, etc. – and many (but not all) nonlinguistic functions occur in the right hemisphere – spatial relations, facial recognition, art, music, but also prosody and discourse reference.

Hickok et al. (1996) proposed that this division of labor is not based on the characteristics of the sensory or motor systems involved in language but on the very nature of linguistic versus nonlinguistic forms. Work on sign language aphasia did a great deal to validate this result and also demonstrated that much of the neural mapping for language is similar across modalities. We will be referring to Figure 6.11 as we discuss the neural networks implicated in sign language phonological processing: *gyri* refer to bumps on the cortical surface, and *sulci* refer to creases or depressions on the cortical surface.

The volume published by Poizner et al. (1987) was a groundbreaking set of studies on brain-damaged signers, which described six cases of ASL signers who had experienced strokes – three with left-hemisphere damage (LHD) and three with right-hemisphere damage (RHD). In that work, they demonstrated that damage to Areas BA 42/22, Wernicke's area, in signer Paul D., resulted in semantically empty but fluent signing similar to the speech of aphasic speakers with damage in this area. Damage to Areas BA 44/45, Broca's area, in signer Gail D., resulted in halted, more telegraphic signing, similar to the speech of aphasic speakers with damage in this area (see Figure 6.11). They also observed the surprising result that movements toward locations produced in a motorically similar way could be affected very differently by different lesion sites. Signers with RHD exhibited impaired use of movements referring to actual spatial layouts. In contrast, signers with LHD exhibited frank language aphasias, so pronouns and agreement verbs were affected.

With regard to work on healthy brains, ERP was one of the first techniques used for speech (Hillyard et al., 1979), and this method, which measures electrical activity on the scalp, was also used to address sentence processing in sign languages. Neville et al. (1997)

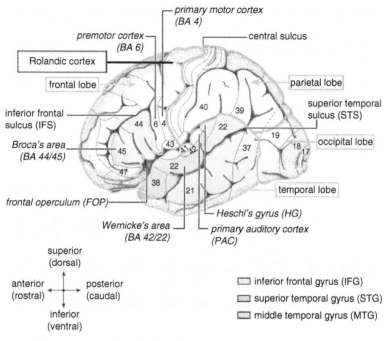

Figure 6.11   Regions in the left hemisphere attributed to language processing. (Reprinted from [http://operativeneurosurgery.com/doku .php?id=heschl_s_gyrus] and used under a CC BY-SA 4.0 license.)

used this method to analyze the responses of four groups to sentences with semantic and syntactic anomalies – native deaf, native hearing, later learners of ASL (after age 17), and non-signing participants. Neville's studies reported several surprising results: (i) in processing sentences in their native language all participants showed activation in the typical language areas for speech in the left hemisphere; and (ii) in the native ASL signers (hearing and deaf) the corresponding areas were activated in the right hemisphere to some extent as well. This type of analysis was also performed using fMRI (Neville et al., 1998), which measures blood flow in the brain (see Hillis et al., 2000, for a survey of some of the first papers using this technique for spoken language aphasia). The results of both of these papers indicated that similar areas of the brain were used to process sign or speech anomalies and that the early acquisition of a fully grammatical, natural language (signed or spoken) is important for neural mapping.

Since the corresponding right-hemisphere areas were activated when hearing and deaf native signers processed sentences in ASL, but not when native speakers process English, the authors inferred that the specific nature and structure of ASL result in the recruitment of the right hemisphere into the language system. These studies suggested that the right hemisphere might be more involved in signed than in spoken languages, and this result has been tested a number of times since, which will be addressed later on in this chapter. Phonology was not the primary focus of these early neuroimaging studies of sign languages – they targeted morphology, semantics, and syntax. Since this chapter is about the neural mapping of phonology, from now on we will focus on studies directly addressing the areas of the brain associated with phonological processing.

Is there a specialized area for processing sign language phonology? In the early studies from brain-damaged signers, Poizner et al. (1987) pointed out a few observations concerning phonological substitution errors by LHD signing aphasics, which tended toward less marked forms, as occurred in the patient referred to as Karen L. (Figure 6.12). In several subsequent papers, the phonological errors of sign aphasics were compared with signers with Parkinson's disease (Brentari & Poizner, 1994; Brentari et al., 1995; Tyrone et al., 1999; Poizner et al., 2000). The main findings of this work showed that aphasic signers exhibited selection errors, while Parkinsonian signers exhibit an intact feature system but disrupted motor plan, resulting in hyper-alignment of handshape and movement and more generalized oversimplification of handshapes. To be specific, Brentari and Poizner (1994) analyzed the alignment of changes in handshape along with their corresponding movements, both within signs and in transitional movements. They found that in typical signing, the start and end of the handshape change and the start and end of the movement are aligned within signs, but not during transitional movements between signs. In signers with Parkinson's disease, however, this alignment occurred both within signs and during transitional movements, demonstrating that they have a disrupted, in this case simplified, motor plan. In other words, the damage caused by phonemic aphasia versus Parkinson's Disease creates phonological versus phonetic impairment of handshape, respectively.

One of the earliest studies specifically reporting on sign language phonology as it is represented in a neurologically impaired, awake signer is Corina et al. (1999). These authors were able to study a non-aphasic signer, deafened at eighteen months due to meningitis, who produced names during cortical stimulation. This was a rare opportunity to access the cortex as the signer was preparing for epilepsy surgery. Broca's area (BA 44/45 in Figure 6.11) is anatomically quite

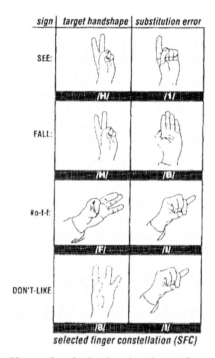

sign | target handshape | substitution error

SEE:

/H/   /1/

FALL:

/H/   /B/

#o-f-f:

/F/   /1/

DON'T-LIKE

/B/   /1/

selected finger constellation (SFC)

Figure 6.12   Phonemic substitutions in selected finger specifications for handshape. (Reprinted from *Brain and Language*, 48, Brentari, et al. "Aphasic and Parkinsonian signing: Differences in phonological disruption," pp. 69–105, Copyright (1995), with permission from Elsevier.)

near to the motor areas of the cortex controlling the mouth (lower regions of areas 4 and 6). The motor area controlling the hand is anatomically more distant in the Rolandic cortex (see Figure 6.11). Yet under stimulation to supramarginal gyrus (SMG, see Figure 6.11, area 40), the signer showed great difficulties producing handshapes and movements associated with individual signs. Thus, the authors concluded that the SMG and the regions nearby may be participating in aspects of motor control that underlie the complex movements of the articulators used in the service of phonology, both spoken and signed.

Petitto et al. (2000) addressed neural activation for sign language phonology and for lexical tasks using PET, which measures metabolic activity in the brain. They analyzed the neural activity of signers and non-signers of ASL and the sign language of Quebec (Langue des Signes Quebecoise, LSQ). Stimuli in four conditions were employed: in perception signers watched pseudo-signs and attested signs, and in production signers imitated signs, and generated verbs from nouns. Deaf signers revealed bilateral activity in the superior temporal gyrus (STG, Area 22; see Figure 6.11), when they were responding to stimulus items in the first two tasks; no such activity was found among the hearing group when they viewed the identical non-signs or signs. The STG is a much larger area than what is typically considered the "primary auditory cortex" (PAC, see Figure 6.11), but the areas are overlapping. These authors concluded that portions of the STG are involved in phonology in spoken and signed language. There was also activation in the left inferior frontal gyrus (IFG, including Broca's Area; Area 44/45 in Figure 6.11) during lexical (semantic) processing across in the deaf groups (ASL and LSQ). The pattern of IFG activation in the deaf participants was very similar to that previously associated with the search and retrieval of spoken words. These results were also supported by a study by Corina (1999) showing that there is left-hemisphere dominance for language, irrespective of handedness.

A team at the Center for Deafness Cognition and Language at University College London has also been investigating the neural mapping of BSL phonology using fMRI. MacSweeney et al. (2004) compared the neural activity in sequences of BSL signs versus sequences of gestures from a system used by bookies in Great Britain at the horse races, called Tic Tac. Sample stimulus items are shown in Figure 6.13. The regions activated in three groups were compared: native deaf signers, native hearing signers, and hearing non-signers. In both signing groups, activation was more extensive for BSL than Tic Tac in the left hemisphere, predominantly SMG, the area implicated in the Corina et al. (1999) study, and STG, the area implicated in the Petitto et al. (2000) study. Tic Tac also engaged the right hemisphere occipital region (Area 19, see Figure 6.11). Native deaf signers showed more extensive activation than the hearing signers, but the pattern of activation was the same. The non-signers showed a very different pattern, with more activation associated with Tic Tac than BSL, and this activation was primarily in the occipital area.

The authors conclude that in the absence of a phonological system, participants analyze these sequences as complex dynamic visuospatial displays. The authors were also interested in possible activation in Heschl's gyrus and PAC (see Figure 6.11) but concluded that sign phonology specificity in this region is secondary to the much more extensive activation in response to

Figure 6.13   Example stimuli from MacSweeney et al. (2004): (top) examples of Tic Tac stimuli and (bottom) BSL stimuli. (Reprinted from *Neuroimage*, 22, MacSweeney, et al., "Dissociating linguistic and nonlinguistic gestural communication in the brain," pp. 1605–1618, Copyright (2004), with permission from Elsevier.)

visual gesture. The authors do not argue that the STG is dedicated to phonological processing but rather that it acts together as a network to support phonological similarity judgments (Hildebrandt & Corina, 2002) and other linguistic and nonlinguistic processes. They concluded that modality has little effect on the neural processing in signed or spoken language phonology.

MacSweeney et al. (2008) also studied the impact of age of first-language acquisition on rhyming in deaf BSL signers. Participants were asked to perform three tasks, and their neural activity was measured using fMRI. The three tasks were: an English rhyme task (Figure 6.14a), a BSL rhyme task (participants were asked if two signs were produced in the same location; Figure 6.14b), and a lexical same/different task (Figure 6.14c). In deaf signers, the superior parietal lobe (see Figure 6.11) was more active during the BSL rhyming task and the inferior and superior frontal gyri (IFG and SFG, Area 44 and the area just above it; see Figure 6.11) were more active during the English rhyming task, which are the areas used by speakers on similar tasks. Since the neural network used by deaf BSL signers was the same as the one used by speakers (Fowler et al., 2004), MacSweeney and colleagues, in this study and a related one using ERP (MacSweeney et al., 2013), concluded that these areas are "supramodal" (the terms

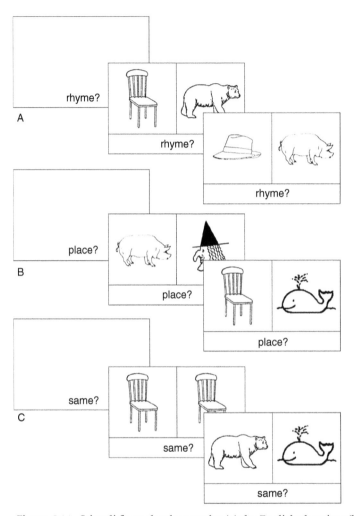

Figure 6.14   Stimuli from the three tasks: (a) the English rhyming; (b) the BSL rhyming; and (c) the same/different task. (Reprinted from *Neuroimage*, 40, MacSweeney, et al., "Phonological processing in deaf signers and the impact of age of first language acquisition," 2008. [doi .org/10.1016/j.neuroimage.2007.12.047] Used under a CC BY 3.0 license.)

"supramodal," "amodal," and "cross-modal" are used interchangeably). Because it has been argued that different parts of the left IFG may show preferential engagement in different aspects of language processing, the posterior portion of the IFG was analyzed separately.

This region was found to be engaged to a greater extent by deaf than hearing participants performing the same English rhyming task, even when behavioral performance was taken into account (see also Aparicio et al., 2007). The authors suggest that when the auditory component of speech is absent, the articulatory/motoric component makes a greater contribution to speech-based phonological processes.

Emmorey et al. (2011) conducted an independent fMRI study in order to identify neural regions that automatically respond to linguistically structured but meaningless manual gestures. Deaf native ASL signers and hearing non-signers passively viewed ASL pseudo-signs and non-iconic signs, in addition to a fixation baseline. For the contrast between pseudo-signs and baseline, greater activation was observed in the left posterior superior temporal sulcus (STS, which is between areas 22 and 37 in Figure 6.11) for deaf signers compared to hearing non-signers. There was increased activation for pseudo-signs over attested signs in the left posterior STG and in the left inferior frontal sulcus (IFS, just above Area 44 in Figure 6.11), but no regions were more active for attested signs than for pseudo-signs. For hearing non-signers there were no significant differences in activation in the relevant areas. The authors concluded that the left STS is involved in recognizing linguistic phonetic/phonological units within a dynamic visual or auditory signal, and that less familiar structural combinations (i.e., pseudo-signs) produce increased neural activation in this region, just as it does for pseudo-(spoken) words in speakers. The authors conclude that the left STS is more engaged for signers because this region becomes attuned to the phonological elements of a sign language. MacSweeney and Cardin (2015) expand on this discussion and suggest that activation in deaf individuals in STG may be due to a number of factors, such as greater cross-modal activation as a result of reduced auditory experience, or it could be due to late and insecure language acquisition that triggers compensatory mechanisms for cognitive processing, including the recruitment of the STG for visual working memory processing.

Cardin et al. (2015) also used fMRI to ask if handshape and location activated the same phonological neural network, and if so, is it activated to the same degree. The groups studied were hearing non-signers, deaf non-signers, and native, deaf BSL signers. The stimuli consisted of four types: sets 1 and 2 were BSL and Swedish Sign Language (SSL) signs that were non-cognates, set 3 were BSL and SSL signs that were cognates, and set 4 were impossible signs for either language. Handshape and location were studied independently, and participants were asked to judge on a scale of 0 (simple) to 4 (complex) how complex they thought the signs were. Compared to both deaf signers and deaf non-signers, hearing non-signers recruited occipital and superior parietal regions across tasks and stimulus types when compared to baseline. This result thus demonstrates that at least some of this effect is driven by the difference in hearing status between the groups and not by sign language knowledge. Moreover, in all groups the handshape task activated the ventral (front) area of the IFG more strongly and location in the dorsal (back) area of the IFG, suggesting that this differentiation is not due to language experience; however, pseudo-signs were associated with a stronger activation in deaf signers. Just as in the Emmorey et al. (2011) study, these results suggest that the neural demands for linguistic processing are higher when stimuli are less coherent or have a less familiar structure with respect to a given phonological system.

Emmorey et al. (2016) also investigated the phonological neural activation in the production of four different types of signs using PET: one-handed signs articulated in neutral space, one-handed body-anchored signs, two-handed signs in neutral space, and fingerspelled (one-handed) printed English words. Compared to the baseline task, there was common activation in the SMG bilaterally, which was interpreted as reflecting phonological retrieval and encoding processes, possibly related to both word-internal phonology (left hemisphere) and prosodic structure (right hemisphere). Fingerspelling engaged ipsilateral motor cortex and cerebellar cortex, in contrast to both types of one-handed signs, as well as greater activation in the visual word form area (the area engaged for written language), which may reflect greater timing demands and complexity of handshape sequences required for fingerspelling. Body-anchored signs engaged bilateral superior parietal cortex to a greater extent than the baseline task and neutral space signs, reflecting the motor control and proprioceptive monitoring required to direct the hand toward a specific location on the body. Less activation in parts of the motor circuit was observed for two-handed signs compared to one-handed signs, possibly because, for half of the signs, handshape and movement goals were spread across the two limbs. An additional explanation might be that two-handed symmetrical signs have a simpler motor plan than one-handed signs, as indicated by a process known as "shadowing," whereby the nondominant hand produces the same handshape as on the dominant hand. This occurs in signers with Parkinson's disease (Poizner et al., 2000) and in unimpaired signers when the nondominant hand is not actively engaged (Sáfár & Crasborn, 2013; Kimmelman et al., 2016).

6.5 CONCLUSIONS

Signed and spoken language phonological processing and neural mapping are remarkably similar, and based on the accumulated evidence
thus far. Phonological processing in each modality appears to be
independent from the sensorimotor characteristics of the language
signal. There is still a possibility that bilateral activation of the SMG
may be stronger in native deaf signers (for sign language phonology)
than in speakers (for spoken language phonology); this debate continues. These studies also suggest a cross-modal or amodal increase in
processing demands when stimuli are less coherent or obey fewer of
the phonotactics both at a perceptual and at a linguistic level. Unusual
combinations of phonological parameters or violations of phonological rules result in higher demands on the system, independently of
previous knowledge of the language, and it may be that the phonological characteristics of a language may arise as a consequence of more
efficient neural processing for the perception and production of the
language components.

Another major finding is that signers and non-signers look alike on
some tasks, although we see that non-signers do not, by and large,
process sign language phonological material in the same way that
signers do (e.g., Hildebrandt & Corina, 2002; Berent et al., 2013;
Cardin et al., 2015). This suggests two possible explanations that
complement one another; they are not mutually exclusive. One
comes from the results showing similarities between deaf native signers and hearing speakers processing their respective languages; some
linguistic units – features, syllables, etc. – are processed similarly, and
also some phonological and morphological operations – e.g., reduplication – are similarly preferred or dispreferred across modalities. Such
findings point to similar hierarchical compositionality for phonology
and to the possibility that some core aspects of phonological and
morphological operations may be cross-modal, amodal, or
supramodal.

A second explanation can be extracted from similar processing of the
same input; namely, similarities in performance of signers and non-
signers have to do with the fact that even non-signing participants can
be encouraged to process sign language as language, even when it is not
a familiar language or even in a familiar modality. There is some
evidence that hearing babies recognize sign language as linguistic
input even when it is not the ambient language (Baker et al., 2005;
Brentari et al., 2011), so later in life non-signers still may show some

residual effects of this skill, especially given their continued use of co-speech gesture, facial expressions as visual prosody, and emblematic gestures. A stronger version of this claim is that at least some aspects of gestural competence are part of the locutionary and illocutionary aspects of language (Schlenker, 2018b), and when presented with sign language, speakers recruit this knowledge when asked to process sign language structure.

6.6 FURTHER READING

Emmorey, K., McCullough, S., & Brentari, D. (2003). Categorical perception in American sign language. *Language and Cognitive Processes, 18,* 21–46.

MacSweeney, M., Campbell, R., Woll, B., Giampietro, V., David, A., McGuire, P.K., Calvert, G.A., & Brammer, M.J. (2004). Dissociating linguistic and nonlinguistic gestural communication in the brain. *NeuroImage* 22, 1605–18.

MacSweeney, M., Waters, D., Brammer, M.J., Woll, B., & Goswami, U. (2008). Phonological processing in deaf signers and the impact of age of first language acquisition. *Neuroimage, 40,* 1369–79.

McCullough, S., & Emmorey, K. (2009). Categorical perception of affective and linguistic facial expressions. *Cognition,* 110, 208–21.

Petitto, L. A., Zatorre, R.J., Gauna, K., Nikelski, E.J., Dostie, D., & Evans, A. C. (2000). Speech-like cerebral activity in profoundly deaf people processing signed languages: Implications for the neural basis of human language. *Proceedings of the National Academy of Sciences,* 97, 13961–6.

7 Sign Language Acquisition

Abstract

Phonological acquisition and the milestones associated with it have been an important testing ground for theoretical claims since the inception of generative phonology, and the theme of this chapter builds on those from previous chapters. We have described how a sign language phonological system is influenced by the visual modality and by iconicity, how it is processed and how it emerges. We now add data from sign language acquisition to this picture, asking what evidence there is for the units proposed so far in the phonological system of a child or infant.

Typical first-language (L1) phonological acquisition is a critical piece in any child's development as she makes contact with the world, and as we will see, it is also an important stepping-stone for reading. We also address acquisition in several other circumstances where sign language is acquired, as it pertains to second-language (L2) learners, late learners of an L1, and bilingual development. These populations are unique in ways that will become clear as they are introduced throughout the chapter.

7.1 INTRODUCTION

This chapter has both theoretical and practical implications. From the outset, it is impossible to write a chapter on sign language acquisition without first addressing how deaf children are exposed to language in the first place. A large proportion of deaf children show a wide range of atypical circumstances for acquisition. Let me explain why. The deaf population is very small; in a typical, genetically diverse population, the proportion of deaf people is about 0.5 of 1 percent – approximately 1 out of 200 people; however, this includes hearing loss that is acquired late in life and well into adulthood, thus not all of these individuals were deaf from early in life, and not all are signers. There are estimated to be about 350,000–500,000 signers in the

United States. Add to this the fact that, since most hearing loss is not genetic, more than 90 percent of deaf children are born to hearing families (Schein, 1989). Of the 350,000–500,000 just mentioned, probably closer to 30,000–40,000 are lucky enough to be born into an American Sign Language (ASL)-signing family that can provide the conditions for "typical" language acquisition – that is, households where infants have full and easy access to a language used fluently by their parents from birth, and where that language is used by the extended community with whom the children come into contact. For a typical hearing infant, her spoken linguistic environment plays a clear role in both speech perception and later language development. Children's spoken language development has been longitudinally tied to several characteristics of the input provided by primary caregivers, such as feedback, language emphasis, and responsiveness (e.g., Hart & Risley, 1995). Similarly, speech perception skills relate to caregivers' articulation of phones (Cristia, 2011). The impact of input quality on early sign development in a number of linguistic domains is also clear, and deaf signing parents surpass their hearing counterparts in input quality – including, not surprisingly, the phonological dimension – by providing a higher number of phonological contrasts (Lu et al., 2016). So even though some linguistic properties are present in the most extreme case of homesign, where typical linguistic input is lacking for one's whole lifetime as we have discussed in Chapter 5, "typical" acquisition implies signing parents, and we call individuals who have the advantage of deaf signing parents "native" signers.

At best, hearing families start to learn about the deaf community and to learn to sign themselves when a deaf child comes into their home. Many hearing families do not sign with their children at all, or do not sign fluently, and some even prevent their deaf children from being exposed to sign language based on advice from the medical establishment. While many families are opting to rear their children as bilinguals whenever possible because of the advantages of bilingualism – both deaf and hearing (Marschark, 2009) – many professionals still do not advocate strongly enough for bilingualism for deaf children. Due to the lack of support by the medical establishment, the small size of the deaf community, and their relatively weak political impact on policy, many deaf children are often not exposed to sign language until they are old enough to make the choice for themselves, or until other monolingual attempts to teach the spoken language have not achieved the desired result.[1]

---

[1] This chapter is not going to enter into the cochlear implant (CI) debate. The Food and Drug Administration (FDA) approved the use of cochlear implants CIs in

Regarding L1 acquisition, the research presented in this chapter will help answer the question of whether the acquisition of a sign language, particularly sign language phonology, contributes to building a linguistic scaffold for a deaf child to become a balanced bilingual – i.e., to be comfortable and proficient enough in ASL and English to succeed in higher education, in society, and in life as a whole, and particularly for acquiring literacy. All deaf people in the United States are bilingual to a large degree and use English in their everyday lives – often written, but sometimes spoken English too. Deaf people have access to the spoken and written language across a broad range of communicative behaviors – through augmented hearing devices, lipreading, subtitles, co-speech gesture and nonverbal communication, as well as reading and writing.

In this chapter the typical case of L1 acquisition in a signing environment will be covered first, followed by other populations within the deaf community. These individuals help us understand the *critical period for language acquisition* (Lennenberg, 1967) in a more in-depth way, a concept that increasingly is understood as a set of critical windows that open and then later close during childhood and early adulthood.

Besides deaf children born in signing environments, hearing children born in signing environments are exposed to sign language in a typical fashion as well, in addition to learning the spoken language of the surrounding hearing community. Many of these individuals grow up using a signed and a spoken language fluently. As adults these "bimodal bilinguals" are referred to as Children of Deaf Adults (CODAs) and as children they are referred to as KODAs (cf. "kids"). This population has become important in studying bilingualism in order to test theories in several areas: about how the brain develops, how two languages are stored and retrieved, and whether linguistic interference is based on competition at the phonological or the lexico-semantic level.

children aged 12 months and above in 2000. Having a cochlear implant does not preclude learning a sign language. Sign language serves a deaf child easily and naturally, whatever speech quality a cochlear implant can eventually provide. As this book has clearly laid out, sign language is inherently organized around the visual modality that is best adapted to the primarily visual world in which deaf people live (Humphries et al., 2014). To hear what speech and music through a cochlear implant sound like, I invite you to visit www.youtube.com/watch?v=SpKKYBkJ9Hw and consider what it would be like to receive all language input in this manner – educational content, good news, bad news, poetry, jokes, and intimate conversations.

A wide range of non-native signers[2] will be described in this chapter as well. For example, there is a large group of hearing people who learn ASL as a second language (L2) as adolescents or adults and have various levels of proficiency – either balanced bimodal bilinguals or bilinguals in various stages where a first spoken and second signed language are imbalanced. This group of individuals is also a very important study population for bilingualism, in order to compare them with individuals who learn sign language as an L1 (but at a wide range of ages), and subsequently a spoken/written language as an L2 later in life.

Deaf individuals who are not exposed to any language until later in childhood or even adolescence, referred to as "late L1" signers, are an additional, unique group described in this chapter. These are individuals who, for a variety of reasons, have not been exposed to a sign language or spoken language until much of the critical period of language acquisition has passed. In the hearing community such cases of language deprivation are extremely rare – cases such as Genie and the Wild Boy of Avignon – and in the spoken language cases the individuals were isolated not only from language input but also from social interaction. In the case of late L1 deaf signers, parents may provide a nurturing social environment, but a number of factors may contribute to depriving these individuals of a nurturing *language* environment at a young age. The range of ages of sign language acquisition within the deaf community allows us to study the effects of the critical period of language acquisition without confounds from other factors.

This chapter discusses evidence from observational studies, as well as behavioral and neuroimaging studies. Naturally, studies involving children are mainly behavioral (but for imaging studies on infants, see Petitto et al., 2004, 2016; Stone, 2017; Stone et al., 2017), but acquisition studies can also involve adults in order to investigate the outcomes of different linguistic experience, and so behavioral and neuroimaging studies of adult populations who use a sign language can be extremely informative as well.

7.2 TYPICAL FIRST-LANGUAGE (L1) ACQUISITION

The motivating factor for first-language research on sign language phonology revolves around two questions. The first is whether the

---

[2] In the literature "non-native" is a cover term that can refer to many different groups of signers: L2 signers, deaf and hearing, are non-native, as are late L1 signers.

time course of acquisition is the same for children acquiring a signed or a spoken language. The second major question is related, but more specific: What kinds of acquisition evidence is there for the phonological constituents discussed in Chapter 1 – features, autosegmental tiers, syllables, etc? Substitution errors and the differential time course for these constituents provide evidence for the psychological reality of such constituents.

7.2.1   Iconicity in L1 Acquisition

Before addressing the acquisition of sign language phonology per se I want to mention a few words about the role of iconicity in phonological acquisition. This question has been around since the beginning of the field (Klima & Bellugi, 1979). Until recently, iconicity was believed to not play an important role in the acquisition of first signs (Launer, 1982; Orlansky & Bonvillian, 1984; Newport, 1990; Meier & Newport, 1991; Meier et al., 2008), but more recent work has revisited this question (Thompson et al., 2012; Caselli & Pyers, 2017). An early Orlansky and Bonvillian (1984) diary study reported that iconic signs were not overrepresented in the child's first signs. Also, Launer (1982) studied early sign production in two deaf children of deaf parents, ages 1;0 and 2;0, and reported that children did not produce iconic enhancements in their signs as much as they reduced the iconicity of a sign by various types of substitution errors. Meier et al. (2008) confirmed these results with four deaf children, systematically analyzing how often children made iconic enhancements to signs. Whether or not iconicity plays a role in child L1 sign language acquisition is still under debate; however, iconicity appears to be important in infant-directed signing (IDS), also called signed "motherese," to which we turn next.[3]

7.2.2   IDS and Iconicity

Infant-directed interaction is multimodal even in circumstances when a child is learning a spoken language from hearing parents. It involves touch, nonverbal gestural enhancements, as well as exaggerated pitch contours. In hearing mother–infant interaction, the use of touch and speech together may be important for early word learning of body

---

[3] See Thompson et al. (2012) for an alternative view. They asked parents of deaf children in the United Kingdom to fill out Communication Development Inventories every month for their children between 8 and 36 months. These parents reported an advantage for iconic signs in production and comprehension. See also Caselli & Pyers (2017).

parts in 4- and 5-month-olds (Abu-Zhaya et al., 2017). Mothers also modify their actions more frequently when demonstrating objects to infants versus adults, and such modifications have been called infant-directed action (IDA) or "motionese" (Brand et al., 2002, 2007). When caregivers demonstrate an object to a one-year-old child acquiring a spoken language, their movements are produced in closer proximity, at a higher level of interactivity, and tend to be larger, simpler, and to involve more repetitive actions for the child's benefit. In infants 6–8 months and 11–13 months, increased eye gaze, more object exchanges, and fewer action types per turn were found in demonstrations to infants relative to adults. Since gestural factors are important in spoken motherese, it is not surprising that there are modifications of the face and body in IDS as well.

Deaf caregivers make their signed communications to infants more salient in a number of ways that have been found across many sign languages, and infants attend better to IDS than to adult-directed signing (ADS) (Masataka, 1992). Caregivers use larger movements, hold the signed forms longer than usual, increase the repetitiveness of signing, produce the forms slowly, sign directly on the infant's face or body, and displace the production of the form away from its normal position to facilitate the infant's visual attention. This work has been done in ASL (Erting et al., 1990; Spencer et al., 1992; Holzrochter & Meier, 2000), Auslan (Mohay et al., 1998), British Sign Language (BSL; Harris et al., 1989), Japanese Sign Language (Masataka, 1992), and Sign Language of the Netherlands (NGT; van den Bogaerde, 2000).

Researchers have begun to ask about the specific nature of the modifications parents make in child-directed signing. With regard to iconicity, Ortega, et al. (2014) found out that, in addition to prosodic and phonological modifications of signing input, deaf parents favor using iconic forms in child-directed signing more than in adult-directed signing. Perniss et al. (2017) reported that when deaf mothers in a laboratory were asked to imagine they were playing with their children using BSL, the mothers employed more iconic modifications, particularly when toys were not present than when the toys were present. The researchers suggested that iconicity plays a role in child-directed signing, particularly in contexts where the topic of conversation – in this case, toys – is not present.

In terms of the timing of prosodic and iconic modifications during development, a study of mothers who used Israeli Sign Language (ISL) with their infants (10 months to 3 years, 4 months) found that purely phonetic-phonological-prosodic modifications taper off during the course of this 2.5-year developmental time period, but iconic modifications spike at the 1-word stage (Fuks, submitted). This suggests for a small data set that caregivers may have a sensitivity – either conscious or unconscious – to when iconic modification might be most beneficial to their babies.

To sum up, the similarities between sign language "motherese" and spoken language "motionese" are remarkable, and they show that hearing and deaf caregivers are sensitive to how to use their whole bodies to enhance general communication and language with their young children. Focusing on sign language, more research is needed to understand whether a child's sign production is weighted toward iconic signs, but it is clear that caregivers may use both prosodic and iconic modifications in IDS in systematic ways to introduce signs and their meaning to their infants.

7.2.3   Time Course of L1 Acquisition in ASL Phonology

How does sign language phonological production unfold in a child in the most favorable of conditions with fluent signers at home? We know from decades of work on signed and spoken languages that mistakes made by children acquiring language often are not mistakes but rather clues to the structure of language – how it is componentialized, how its constituents are constructed, which elements are acquired together, and which are acquired at distinct points in time. One point to take away from the previous discussion of signed motherese is that movement plays a large role in attracting the attention of infants, and in sign languages, as we have seen in earlier chapters, properties of movement are an important way that strings of signs are broken into constituents. We might therefore understand this to mean that for sign languages, prosodic bootstrapping, whereby strings are broken into smaller pieces for further analyses and statistical learning of phrasal and word meaning, is associated with properties of movement of the hands, face, and body.

7.2.3.1   Syllabic Babbling in Sign Languages

As discussed in Chapters 1 and 2, sign language movements constitute syllable nuclei. In two classic studies of movements made by infants between 10 and 14 months, Petitto and Marentette (1991) and Petitto et al. (2004) found that babies exposed to sign language produce syllabic babbling in the manual modality. They argue that that manual babbling integrates linguistic and motoric principles. The first study was observational, and it characterized babbling as: (i) being produced

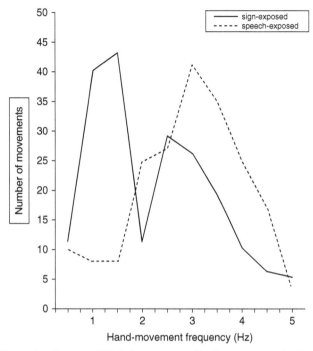

Figure 7.1 Low- and high-frequency cyclical movements in sign- and speech-exposed infants. Note the additional, low-frequency repetitive movements in sign-exposed infants. (Reprinted from *Cognition*, 93, Petitto, et al., "Baby hands that move to the rhythm of language: Hearing babies acquiring sign languages babble silently on the hands," pp. 43–73, Copyright (2004), with permission from Elsevier.)

with a reduced subset of combinatorial units that are members of the phonetic inventory of sign languages, most notably ⊘ and ⊕ hand-shapes; (ii) involving reduplication, produced without meaning or reference; and (iii) being an important point on a continuum from syllabic babbling to first words.

The second of these studies used motion-capture to study sign babbling, and Petitto et al. (2004) showed that sign-exposed babies produce a low-frequency type of cyclic repeated movement (between 1 and 2 Hz) that is not seen in the speech-exposed babies (see Figure 7.1). These were the movements that were characterized as babbling, not only because they differed from the higher-frequency, repetitive movements seen generally, but also because they showed the same behaviors that were characterized as babbling in the observational study. Syllabic babbling makes possible the baby's discovery and production of the syllable as a core structure of their language (Vihman, 1996), and signing babies show evidence that they use this structure in their early productions. In terms of perceiving well-formed syllabic movements in early acquisition, Stone et al. (2017) conducted a study whereby more sonorant and less sonorant lexicalized fingerspelled forms were shown to 6- versus 12-month-old sign-naïve infants, adult signers, and adult non-signers. We have also seen in Chapters 1, 2, and 4 that sonority is relevant for syllable structure and well-formedness, and mediates fingerspelling lexicalization; the final lexicalized form that has its roots in fingerspelling is determined by sonority differences in the letter-to-letter transitions in the original serially fingerspelled form. Younger infants and signing adults were sensitive to sonority while older sign-naïve infants and non-signing adults were not. Hence, there is an early sensitivity to visual sonority that is present in hearing infants even prior to the moment when syllabic babbling begins. Berent et al. (2013) refer to sonority as an important, amodal feature of human language learning and perception.

7.2.3.2   Milestones Associated with Children's First Signs

What feature classes (or parameters) are the easiest for an L1 signing child to produce? A child acquiring a sign language typically, in the home as an L1, starts using her first words at around 1;0 (years; months) to 1;5, and these are core vocabulary items, typically nouns and verbs (Baker & Woll, 2009). McIntire (1977), Boyes Braem (1990b), and Bonvillian and Siedlecki (1993) asked parents to keep diaries of their signing children's first signs, and this provided a first look at the acquisition of the three primary manual parameters. They reported that place of articulation (POA; also called "location") was the first parameter over which children gain mastery, then movement, and finally handshape. The results of Conlin et al. (2000) and Cheek et al. (2001) for ASL, Morgan et al. (2007) for BSL, do Carmo et al. (2013) for Portuguese Sign Language, and Takkinen (1995) for Finnish Sign Language corroborated the early results from diary studies with studies following signing children from signing homes longitudinally, annotating and quantifying their correct productions. The results for substitution errors across four children and parameters are given in Figure 7.2 (ages 7–17mos.; Meier, 2006). The Cheek et al. (2001) study found that the most frequent handshapes, palm orientations, hand-internal movements, and hand arrangements (one- and two-handed) observed in deaf and hearing babies' pre-linguistic

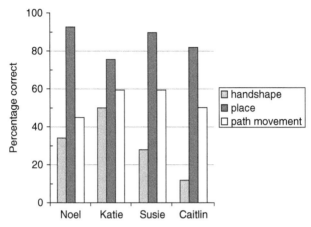

Figure 7.2   Error rates on the three manual parameters of signs in four deaf children of deaf parents. (Reprinted from Meier, R., "The form of early signs; Explaining signing children's articulatory development," in Schick, et al. (eds.), *Advances in the Sign Language Development of Deaf Children*, 2006, pp. 202-230, by permission of Oxford University Press.)

gestures were also observed in the earliest signs of deaf children or as substitutions in their signs.

The "errors" in these studies were substitution errors, and we focus on these in the next section for movement and handshape since this is where most of these substitutions occur.

Movement: Regarding movement, three trends are found in the errors of young children: proximalization, repetition, and simplification. When children substituted a more proximal joint for a more distal one in the production of a sign – e.g., a shoulder movement for an elbow movement, or an elbow movement substituted for wrist movement – this was called "proximalization" (Meier, 2006). The modifications toward proximalizations align with predictions that follow from the representation of movement as proposed in the Prosodic model (Brentari, 1998). As discussed in Chapters 1 and 2, the Prosodic model has a hierarchical structure of movement, with movements produced by the most proximal joint at the top (shoulder), then elbow, wrist, and finger joints in successively lower positions in the feature hierarchy. The children who proximalize movement and who move movement up in the hierarchy, and the signers with Parkinson's disease, discussed in Chapter 2, who distalize movement and move movement down in the hierarchy, both support the representation of movement as a set of hierarchically coordinated elements, and the two processes have been captured by the more general term of "movement migration" (Brentari, 1998). The Prosodic model facilitates representations for both of these processes.

Repetition was a notable feature of Gemma, the BSL child studied in Morgan et al. (2007), who produced almost half of her signs with additional repetition. Morgan also reported that Gemma simplified movements that were internally complex – e.g., if they had both hand-internal "local" movement and a "path" movement produced at the elbow, Gemma omitted one element of the movement. A sign, such as ASL's INFORMATION (see Chapter 1, Figure 1.7), with this type of omission might be produced with the path movement at the elbow but not the aperture movement of the hand. Meier (2006) attributes proximalization and repetition, at least to some degree, to motor control, since repetition is difficult to control in very young children (Thelan, 1991). Moreover, the finding concerning repetition could be linked to those of Berent et al. (2014), discussed in Chapter 2, who have argued that reduplication is a core mechanism of word building in both signed and spoken languages. This cross-linguistic, cross-modal tendency toward repetition in morphology may be linked to this early propensity for reduplication in children, demonstrating how certain motoric patterns come to be reinforced phonetically, phonologically, and morphophonologically in a grammar.

Handshape: With regard to handshape, Boyes Braem (1990) proposed four stages of handshape development, as shown in Figure 7.3. Marentette and Mayberry (2000) elaborated on Boyes Braem's developmental trajectory with supporting evidence for Stage I and II handshapes, both in terms of timing and for substitutions of handshapes from an earlier stage for target handshapes belonging to later stages. For example, the handshapes of Stage I, produced with more than 50 percent accuracy at 1;9 (McIntire, 1977), are also those that the pre-linguistic infant is capable of producing in reaching, grasping, and pointing (Fogel, 1981). A subset of these also appears in the syllabic babbling produced by the children in the Petitto studies discussed earlier in this chapter. Stage II handshapes are variants of those already mastered in Stage I but show the child's ability to differentiate between selected and nonselected fingers and show increased mastery over joint control.

Pola, the child in Boyes Braem's diary study, was at Stage III by 2;7. This is in accord with the other observational studies mentioned above. Stage III and IV handshapes are distinguished from those

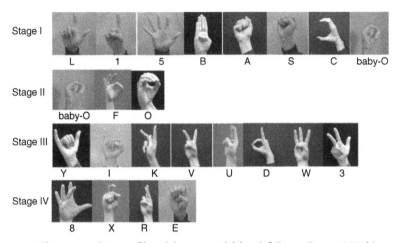

Figure 7.3   Stages of handshape acquisition (cf. Boyes Braem 1990b)

acquired earlier because they require inhibition and extension of the middle, ring, and pinkie fingers, as well as control of nonadjacent fingers, predicted to be difficult due to the "serial finger order" factor; namely, handshapes are more difficult to produce when the selected fingers are out of serial order. The distinction between Stage I and II handshapes compared to those of Stage III and IV is supported by the work of Ann (1993), based on a study of ASL and Taiwan Sign Language and the anatomy and physiology of the hand.

Furthermore, in longitudinal data for two deaf children born to deaf parents acquiring Hong Kong Sign Language (Pan & Tang, 2017), they found that a new handshape was acquired first with the selected fingers of the given handshape in its extended form (the default joint configuration), and subsequently more complex joint configurations for that selected finger group were acquired.

These findings support the head-dependency relationship proposed by the Prosodic and Dependency models of sign language phonological representation. If you recall from Chapter 1 (Figure 1.10), in the Prosodic model the selected fingers$_2$ node is the head and nonselected fingers the dependent, and lower down in the tree selected fingers$_1$ is the head and joint configuration the dependent.

Overall Complexity: If children simplify their motor plan at younger stages of development, one could ask how this changes over the course of acquisition. Mann et al. (2010) investigated this question systematically with a repetition test of movement and handshape complexity using pseudo-signs. Handshapes in Stage I were considered simple and all others complex. Movements were either "local" (internal) movements of the hand or lower arm, or "path" movements of the elbow or shoulder. The movements were simple if they contained one component and complex if they had both an internal and a path movement. There were seven levels of complexity balanced across items with different types of path movement and internal movement. Three age groups of children acquiring BSL and three corresponding non-signer control groups were tested (3–5, 6–8, and 9–11 years old). Participants were asked to reproduce the form they saw in the stimulus video clips. Results demonstrated that knowledge of sign language phonology was important because deaf signers were able to complete this task at a younger age than hearing non-signing children; the youngest group of non-signing children could not perform the task and had to be left out of the study altogether. The signers also repeated the pseudo-signs significantly more accurately than non-signers at each age, despite no difference in general fine motor skills between the signing and non-signing groups. The three groups of deaf signing and two groups of non-signing children made fewest errors on path movement and most errors on handshape and internal movement (mostly omissions), with no advantage for orientation over handshape. This study provides evidence that the ability to reproduce signs is independent from general fine motor skills and corroborates the order of acquisition found for L1 acquisition of movement prior to handshape.

7.2.4 Acquisition of Classifier Handshapes

One way to ask whether sign language development is exclusively motoric is to ask whether the acquisition of form is uniform across all three parts of a sign language lexicon – core, spatial, and foreign (see Chapter 1 for an explanation of these lexical components). So far we have been discussing the acquisition of core vocabulary, but children acquiring a sign language as an L1 in the home from their parents start using classifier constructions at around 2;6–2;11 (Supalla, 1982). Despite their superficial similarities with some of the gestures that hearing people might produce, classifier predicates are difficult for L1 and L2 learners to acquire. An important study that demonstrated the difference between the handshapes acquired by children in core vocabulary and classifier predicates is Kantor (1980). She analyzed the productions of children acquiring ASL at the earliest stages of L1 development as they use the same handshapes in core lexical and spatial descriptions using classifier predicates. She found that producing a handshape correctly in a core lexical item does not guarantee correct use in a classifier context. For example, a three-year-old child learning ASL routinely used the V-handshape in the lexical verbs FALL or SEE, and the three-handshape in the sign for THREE, but the child could not reliably produce these handshapes in the classifier predicates *by-legs* or *vehicle*, which use the same handshapes. This finding reinforces the tripartite division of the lexicon described in Chapter 1, and the fact that the acquisition of these handshapes cannot be character-ized by motor constraints alone, but rather, just as in spoken lan-guages, the linguistic structure and function of the form also plays a critical role.

The acquisition of handshape in classifier predicates also addresses the role of iconicity in language acquisition discussed earlier. The morphologically simpler forms (the core vocabulary) are acquired first and mastery of the classifier system is not achieved until age 7–9 (Schick, 1990; Brentari et al., 2013). As we will discuss shortly, classifier predicates also show effects of incom-plete acquisition in deaf individuals who are exposed to sign lan-guage later in life (Newport, 1990; Meier & Newport, 1991). Moreover, at the earliest stage when they appear, these forms are typically not used in an adult manner but as whole words rather than productive morphological forms, and there are often hand-shape substitutions in these forms – e.g., simpler substitutions for the more complex or for the "airplane" classifier (Baker & Woll, 2009).

7.2.5 Prosodic Acquisition

Chapter 4 described the basic properties of the manual and non-manual cues used in the prosodic hierarchy of constituents in ASL, from mora to utterance. We now ask how the prosodic system is acquired. This is especially important because of the interface between facial expressions for affect, mental states, and grammatical expressions. In some ways this recalls the recent discussion of classi-fier handshapes: some non-manuals, just like some handshapes, look very similar to the ones gesturers might use, but, like classifier hand-shapes, mastery of the prosodic system extends in later development (7–9 years). What is the order of prosodic and grammatical use of these cues? This is a question about both prosodic structure and the way that prosody and syntax interact.

In early perception and comprehension, IDS may be important, and there is evidence that in early acquisition (9 months) even hearing babies from hearing households are attuned to well-formed sign language prosodic phrases (Brentari et al., 2011); this is a period in acquisition when prosodic bootstrapping assists babies in segmenting the linguistic stream for further statistical analysis (Jusczyk, 1999).

In child sign language production Reilly et al. (1990, 1994) and McIntire and Reilly (1996) propose three principles with regard to non-manuals and ASL grammar. First, the system of non-manuals is acquired compositionally; that is, each non-manual is acquired on its own time course according to its role in the grammar, and not surprisingly, affective uses precede grammatical uses. Second, when a particular grammatical structure has both a manual component and a non-manual to express the same meaning, the manual component appears first. Third, first-language acquisition of ASL exhibits a U-shaped curve composed of three stages of non-manual acquisition: appearance, reanalysis/reorganization, and mastery. For example, Reilly et al. (1991) noted that deaf children start using eyebrows grammatically in the first half of their third year for yes/no questions, but then this cue disappears when a new structure requires it - i.e., conditionals. At first, three- and four-year-olds produce conditionals exclusively with the manual sign IF, even if they have previously used raised eyebrows for asking questions, and only at 7;0 and later do they imitate and produce conditionals with both manual and non-manual components with the correct timing.

Brentari et al. (2015b) investigated the use of prosodic cues (manual and non-manual, grammatical and purely prosodic) across three age groups - younger children (4-6), older children (8-10), and adults. Their results showed that there is clearly a division of labor between the cues that are produced to mark constituents and those that contribute to semantic and pragmatic meaning, as Sandler has also argued (Sandler & Lillo-Martin, 2006). In all groups the manual cues are more predictive of prosodic boundaries than non-manual markers, and in the older children it is not even clear that the non-manuals help a great deal in chunking constituents. Annotations were statistically analyzed without cues, then with non-manual cues alone, then manual cues alone, and then both non-manual and manual cues. Comparing statistical models with Akaike Information Criterion (AIC) measures, the model with manual cues alone was significantly better than with non-manual cues alone, and the model with both types of cues was just slightly better than the one with manual cues alone, but not reliably so. It was also clear that younger children acquire manual cues first – e.g., phrase-final lengthening – and there are fewer nonmanual cues overall. This work is in accord with the proposal that non-manuals might be considered more like the tunes of spoken intonation (Sandler, 2012a). Brentari et al. (2015b) also found that adults are more likely than children to spread non-manual cues to the edges of syntactic constituents.

This sign language pattern of prosodic acquisition is very similar to the acquisition of prosody in children acquiring a spoken language. Prosodic acquisition continues into the middle school years (Patel & Brayton, 2009), so the time course of prosodic acquisition in both signed and spoken languages might be best seen through the lens of McIntire and Reilly's three stages – appearance, reorganization, and mastery – not once, but several times as these cues are integrated with increasingly complex morphological, syntactic, and discourse structures. In spoken language acquisition, Shport and Redford (2014) found, for example, that children aged 6;2–7;3 could maintain duration and intensity for number words in a straight list (thirteen, fourteen), but had difficulty integrating word-stress patterns with phrasal-prominence patterns for both duration and alignment of high tones in order to achieve distinctions such as [chocolate milk] [and bananas] versus [chocolate] [milk] [and bananas]. In other words, children between 6;2 and 7;3 use both duration and intonational cues correctly in single words but have not mastered their integration into larger prosodic units. The progression from appearance to reorganization to mastery is borne out in the ASL results as well.

7.2.6 Acquisition of Fingerspelling

Padden (2006) has argued that the acquisition of fingerspelling involves two different kinds of skills: first, acquiring fingerspelling as a part of ASL, which is important for one's competence in the language, and second, acquiring fingerspelling as a link with English, which is an important skill in a deaf child's pathway to reading.

Regarding the first skill, anecdotal reports show the first uses of fingerspelling occurring early in development, long before deaf children learn to read. At 24 months, Padden (2006) reported a deaf child who fingerspelled c-h-p for *chip* with the orientation and movements correct but the -i- missing. Another example involves a different 24-month-old deaf child capturing a difference in movement between i-c-e (with an open-closed internal movement) and r-i-c-e (with a circular path movement). A third example comes from a third child fingerspelling the name d-e-e mistakenly as l-e-e –

there was an error in the first letter (-L- ✌ and -D- ☝ look similar because both have the single index finger extended), but the child's form retained the bouncing movement used when fingerspelling doubles letters. In all three cases, there were mistakes in the hand-shapes but not in the movements.

Examples of the second type of fingerspelling skill – associating it with English spelling – come from Kelly (1995), who describes a deaf mother practicing spelling with her child using words on index cards. She asked her child to fingerspell them, but the child was unable to do so and didn't understand what the words meant until the mom finger-spelled them to the child. The relationship between fingerspelling and print has been studied for at least twenty years. Padden and Ramsey (1998) had children watch videos of signed sentences, each containing one fingerspelled word, and asked the children to write them down. They argued that the task could be broken into two parts: the ASL skill of recognizing the fingerspelled word, but then the ASL-English skill associated with writing the word in English. This skill of writing the words down was significantly correlated with the Stanford Achievement Test for Reading. Stone et al. (2015) also found that fingerspelling abilities predict reading abilities above and beyond correlation with general proficiency in ASL.

Another example comes from deaf teachers' awareness of this con-nection between English terms and fingerspelling. Humphries and MacDougal (2000) described the pedagogical device known as "chain-ing" (i.e., fingerspelling a word, then signing the same word, then fingerspelling the word again), which is used in elementary school and almost exclusively by deaf teachers to introduce new concepts to deaf pupils in the classroom. This practice capitalizes on the link between fingerspelling, English, and reading, and by fingerspelling and using the ASL sign for the word in close proximity to one another, the connection between ASL and English is reinforced.

In a more recent study of adults, Sehyr et al. (2016) investigated the link between fingerspelling and spoken phonology in matched hearing and deaf readers in a recall task. They asked if speech-based or manually based phonological similarity would affect recall of fingerspelled words. The stimuli were controlled for sound-to-print, orthographic similarity (e.g., *blue, chew, due, Jew, shoe, two, who, you* versus *king, farm, tax, bug, some, with, cry, that*). Speech-based phonological similarity effects were observed even in deaf readers – lists with dissimilar phonological words were recalled with more accuracy than similar words (Figure 7.4).

Manual similarity based on the fingerspelled forms themselves did not affect recall for deaf signers. These findings suggest that

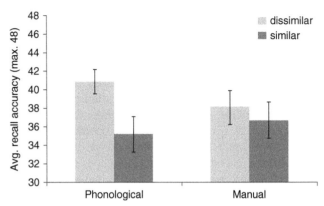

Figure 7.4   Recall of fingerspelled English words in deaf readers when similarity/dissimilarity was based on spoken English (left) and when it was based on the manual form. (Reprinted from Sehyr, et al., "Fingerspelled and printed words are recoded into a speech-based code in short-term memory," *The Journal of Deaf Studies and Deaf Education*, 2017, 22 (1), pp. 72-87, by permission of Oxford University Press.)

fingerspelling is strongly linked to English phonology for deaf adult signers, and the fingerspelled words are automatically recoded into a speech-based code in short-term memory. Words presented via print also showed a spoken speech-based similarity effect for both hearing and deaf groups. The relationship of fingerspelling and literacy will be taken up again later in this chapter.

To sum up, in L1 acquisition motoric and linguistic factors are at work, just as in spoken languages; however, to understand these two types of factors, knowledge is needed of both the specific anatomy and physiology of sign languages (bottom-up) and the linguistic constraints and constituents involved (top-down). Motor constraints can be seen in the order of acquisition of the major manual parameters. POA requires less fine motor coordination, and deaf children acquiring the language in a typical fashion at home show more errors in handshape and movement than in POA. In most cases, the types of handshape substitution errors favor less motorically complex forms. With regard to movement, a lack of motor control appears in the over-repetition of forms and in the proximalization of movements.

Linguistic structure is also very important. All of these findings from L1 acquisition attest not only to the compositional nature of the five parameters of handshape, movement, place of articulation, orientation, and non-manuals, but also to a more sophisticated hierarchy as proposed in more recent phonological models. First, the Dependency and Prosodic models of phonological representation established selected fingers as the head and joints as the dependent, and indeed more complex finger groups are acquired first in their most simple form with extended fingers and subsequently using more complex joint configurations. Second, the movement migration patterns of proximalization in children (and distalization in signers with Parkinson's disease, as discussed in Chapter 2) follow a coordinated hierarchy of movement types as predicated by the Prosodic model. Third, the correct use of a handshape in a core vocabulary item does not mean that it will also be correctly used in classifier predicates, supporting the proposal for the separate components of the lexicon.

7.3 SECOND-LANGUAGE (L2) ACQUISITION

The number of hearing adults learning ASL has been growing. The *New York Times* has reported that more than 90,000 students were enrolled in sign language classes in 2009 in the United States, compared with only 4,304 in 1995 (Lewin, 2010). This has increased research interest in understanding how hearing adults learn a sign language and in improving curricula for pedagogical purposes. Moreover, this group is an important comparison group for other populations learning a language in typical and atypical circumstances – first-language child learners, deaf people learning a first or second sign language later in life, and unimodal bilinguals. We therefore turn to L2 acquisition in this section.

7.3.1 L2 Acquisition of Sign Parameters

Does L2 acquisition of sign parameters follow the same time course as L1 acquisition? The answer is mixed. We will see that POA is still the easiest of the three parameters to learn as an L2, just as it is in L1, but movement errors are more frequent than handshape errors in L2, while handshape errors are more frequent than movement errors in L1. Mirus et al. (2001) studied the type of movement migration known as proximalization in adults, the same process that was also found in the spontaneous productions of young children (Conlin et al., 2000). In a single sign repetition/imitation task, Mirus et al. (2001) analyzed the productions of deaf and hearing L2 sign language learners in Germany and in the United States, both hearing and deaf – American deaf ASL signers learning German Sign Language (DGS), German deaf DGS signers learning ASL, hearing Germans learning DGS, and hearing Americans learning ASL. They found that, like young children acquiring ASL in early childhood, adults learning a sign language as an L2 also produce a great deal of proximalized forms and some distalized forms as well. Comparing the four groups, the two hearing L2 groups made more errors than the two deaf L2 groups producing signs with one movement component (i.e., single joint, monomoraic forms, such as ADMIT, see Figure 3.4b) or two movement components (i.e., multiple-joint, bimoraic forms, such as INFORM, Figure 1.7); results are shown in Figure 7.5.

Bochner et al. (2011) conducted a large study (137 participants) of a paired-comparison discrimination task in native, beginner L2, and in more advanced L2 signers. The highest proportion of errors in the L2 groups occurred in movement contrasts, followed by handshape and orientation, followed by place of articulation, which had the lowest proportion of error, similar to young deaf children acquiring ASL as an L1. Schlehofer and Tyler (2016) replicated Boechner et al.'s results. Sample stimuli are given in Table 7.1. Williams and Newman (2016a) showed that even when varying the proficiency in the model (a native versus an L2 sign language model) processing mistakes were more prevalent in movement (63.6 percent) than in handshape (31.6 percent) or POA (4 percent).

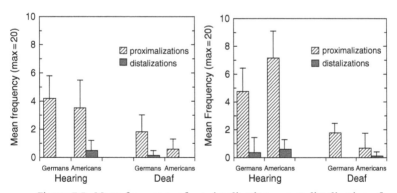

Figure 7.5 Mean frequency of proximalization versus distalization of movement in the imitation of (left) single-jointed and (right) multiple-jointed ASL signs in deaf and hearing L2 learners. (Reprinted from Mirus, et al., "Proximalization and distalization of sign movement in adult learners," in Dively, et al. (eds.), *Signed Languages: Discoveries from International Research*, 2001, pp. 103–119, with permission from Gallaudet University Press.).

Table 7.1 *Sentence pairs for the discrimination task in Boechner et al. (2011)*

Orientation	IMPORTANT TIME, BALANCE/MAYBE *It is important to balance your time.* *Your time may be important.*
Handshape	FEEL HORSE WIN, MAN BET/AGREE *The man bet that the horse would win.* *The man agreed that the horse would win.*
Location	MY MOTHER/FATHER BLONDE *My mother has blonde hair.* *My father has blonde hair.*
Movement	YOUR APPOINTMENT/HABIT NEED CHANGE *You should change your appointment.* *You should change your habit.*
Complex morphology	THOSE THREE/THOSE FOUR NEED BUY TICKETS *The three of them need to buy tickets.* *The four of them need to buy tickets.*
Same	SPAGHETTI, WE ORDER TOO-MUCH *We ordered too much spaghetti.*

In addition, Williams and Newman (2016b) found that sonority (associated with movement) affected learning in L2 signers. They rated a set of signs according to a sonority scale, as described in Chapter 2, where ratings were shoulder [5] > elbow [4] > wrist [3] > knuckle joint [2] > finger joint [1]. Participants performed a picture-matching task, and then a second task where they had to learn the associations between pictures and matched non-signs. They found that high-sonority signs were more quickly matched and more accurately learned. These researchers speculate, therefore, that since L2 learners have the most difficulty with movement it may be argued that the acquisition of the movement parameter may be the key to greater sign language proficiency. This type of study has not been tried with young L1 signers, but Stone et al. (2017) found deaf infants watch fingerspelling with more sonorous movements (larger movements) between letters for longer periods than when the fingerspelling has reduced transitions. This hints at the role that movement may play in learning sign language as an L1 or an L2.

7.3.2   L2 Acquisition and Iconicity

Previous work has shown that, generally, iconicity plays more of a role in L2 learning than L1 acquisition (Campbell et al., 1992; Baus et al.,

2013). There is a notable difference between L1 and L2 learners with respect to their experience interacting with the world, which in turn affords adults more access to iconicity as a helpful device for sign recall and recognition.

Ortega and Morgan (2015) address the issue of iconicity in L2 learning in a recent production study while controlling for phonological complexity in BSL. They used a set of stimuli that consisted of video clips of 300 individual BSL signs that were controlled for familiarity, age of acquisition (AoA), and iconicity, along with six levels of complexity. Iconic and non-iconic signs showed different patterns in accuracy. There was interaction between iconicity and complexity (Figure 7.6); at lower levels of complexity, signs that were iconic were more accurately produced by L2 signers than arbitrary signs, but with greater complexity the pattern was reversed and signs that were iconic were articulated less accurately than arbitrary signs. This suggests that iconicity may aid in production primarily when signs are not very complex phonologically, and may contribute to the impression (but only the impression!) by some students required to take a language in high school or college that sign languages may be easy

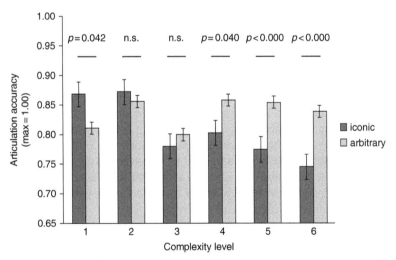

Figure 7.6 The interaction between iconicity and complexity in L2 BSL production. (Reprinted from Ortega, G. & Morgan, G., "Phonological development in hearing learners of a sign language: The influence of phonological parameters, sign complexity, and iconicity," *Language Learning*, 65. © 2015 *Language Learning* Research Club, University of Michigan. Reprinted with permission from John Wiley and Sons.)

to learn because in the beginning iconicity assists accurate L2 sign production.

7.3.3   Acquisition of Classifier Constructions in L2 Signers

Iconicity is important for L2 learners of signed languages when learning core lexical signs (Lieberth & Gamble, 1991; Campbell et al., 1992; Baus et al., 2013), and POA is the most iconic component of many types of classifier constructions because there may be a direct mapping between the relative locations of objects in the real world and the relative locations of the hands in signing space. Handshape is somewhat less iconic, because the mapping between the shapes of real objects and the shape adopted by the hands is less direct and more conventionalized. Classifier handshapes would therefore be expected to be least accurately produced by L2 learners and classifier POAs most accurately if classifier learning is related to iconicity. Marshall and Morgan (2015) investigated the accuracy of L2 BSL signers on these two parameters using an ingenious task asking signers to describe the difference between two static images that referenced handshape or POA and found that, as expected, the L2 signers aligned better with native BSL signers' classifier production for POA than handshape. Thus, iconicity does at least partially predict classifier production accuracy in L2 learners.

7.3.4   Acquisition of Prosody in L2 Signers

The acquisition of prosody in L1 signers continues into the middle school years, and prosody is difficult for L2 adult sign language learners as well. It is also difficult to compare deaf and hearing signers with regard to prosody unless the hearing signers are very proficient; otherwise fluency would be a confounding factor. Brentari et al. (2012b) asked if hearing status or language experience (L1 versus L2) matter for prosody when the signers are highly proficient. Could there be an "accent" that is possibly a carry-over from co-speech gesture?

To answer this question, Brentari et al. (2012b) analyzed the narratives of three groups: two groups of hearing signers who were interpreters that were certified at the highest level by the Registry of Interpreters for the Deaf in order to isolate whether language experience or hearing status has more of an effect on prosody (see Figure 7.7) – hearing L1 signers (CODAs) and hearing L2 signers – and a third group of deaf L1 signers. The signers retold a short episode of a *Simpsons* television program to another proficient ASL signer. Nine prosodic cues were annotated in the narratives. The manual cues for duration of signs, transition, pause, holds, and drop-hands were analyzed along with the non-manual cues for eyeblinks and position of

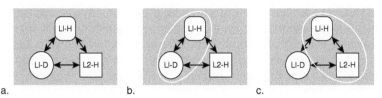

a.   b.   c.

Figure 7.7 Schema of the hypotheses considered in Brentari et al.
(2012b): (a) no effect of American English co-speech gesture on ASL; (b)
an effect of language experience (L1 versus L2) on the prosodic patterns
found; (c) an effect of hearing status (deaf versus hearing) on the prosodic patterns found. (Reprinted with permission from Brentari, et al.
(2012b). "Can experience with co-speech gesture influence the prosody
of a sign language? Sign language prosodic cues in bimodal bilinguals,"
Bilingualism: Language and Cognition, 15(2), pp. 402–412. © Cambridge
University Press.)

the brows, head, and torso. The results show that both hearing status
and language experience have different effects on prosody. Two significant effects of hearing status were found. The first related to the
duration of signs. All three groups show (I)ntonational-phrase-final
lengthening, but the two hearing groups (L1 and L2) show less of
a distinction between I-phrase final and (U)tterance-final boundaries
than the L1 deaf group. Phrase-final lengthening may be exploited in
different prosodic positions by the deaf L1 signers. The second difference was in the use of the non-manual cue of torso position. Shifts in
torso position can be used in sign quotation (Davidson et al., 2015), as
well as to mark I-phrases (see Chapter 4). Both hearing groups of
signers (L1 and L2) used torso shifts more often as a prosodic marker
for I-phrases than the deaf L1 signers did, and both groups of hearing
signers made more frequent use of torso shift than deaf signers to
accompany their quotations (54 percent for L1-D versus for 95 percent
for L1-H, and 83 percent for L2-H signers). These results suggest that
the hearing signers may exaggerate the use of torso shift to some
degree when compared with deaf signers. There was one clear difference in prosody based on language experience (L1 versus L2). The L2
signers had significantly longer pauses at utterance boundaries than
either of the L1 groups. This has been found in L2 learners of spoken
Russian as well (Riazantseva, 2001) and may reflect the need for extra
time in utterance formulation.

To sum up, L2 acquisition differs from L1 acquisition in the order of
parameter acquisition. Child L1 signers make more errors on

handshape, while L2 learners make the most errors with movement. All learners make the fewest errors on POA. Iconicity also appears to play a more important role in sign language acquisition for L2 than L1 learners. Mastery of prosodic structure occurs late in both L1 and L2 acquisition, and even the most proficient hearing signers (L1 and L2) may show a type of accent in their prosodic structure, which may be due to their experience with co-speech gesture.

7.4 THE CRITICAL PERIOD FOR LANGUAGE ACQUISITION AND THE "PHONOLOGICAL BOTTLENECK"

What we have been discussing so far are typical cases of L1 and L2 acquisition, where L1 acquisition implies exposure from birth and L2 is acquired when an L1 is already mastered; we now turn to the second major issue of this chapter, namely atypical cases of sign language acquisition and changing plasticity in the brain with respect to L1 acquisition. Based on the previous section of this chapter we now have a good idea of what typical acquisition of sign language phonology looks like, so we can ask what happens when the L1 age of acquisition (AoA) is delayed. This occurs due to a variety of circumstances in which a deaf child does not have full access to a language until after school age or even into adolescence. In work on spoken language addressing the critical period, most of the evidence comes from bilinguals, since that is the only sizable population there is to study. For example, Weber-Fox and Neville (1996) used event-related potential (ERP) to study differences in neural organization in early and late bilingual language learners. Heterogeneity in both L1 and L2 AoA is a unique feature of sign language communities (Mayberry & Lock, 2003).

A fundamentally important outcome of this work on sign language populations with different L1 and L2 AoA shows that a delay in L1 language acquisition has multiple effects on psycholinguistic processing in adulthood, particularly in morphology (Meier & Newport, 1991; Mayberry et al., 2002; Mayberry & Lock, 2003). The crucial question has been whether the unique and life-long effects are truly associated with a lack of language in early life, or if these effects are due to a constellation of social and other factors.

The deaf community has many members who have had atypical language acquisition experiences, and linguistic effects can be separated from nonlinguistic ones. Sign language research can help adjudicate two competing theoretical explanations of AoA effects on phonological representations. Maturation-based accounts (Penfield & Roberts, 1959; Lennenberg, 1967; Newport, 1990; Mayberry & Eichen, 1991; Mayberry, 2007) argue that infants are uniquely skilled at performing the perceptual kinds of analyses that lead to native-like phonological acquisition (Werker, 1989). They predict that AoA effects will be greater for a late L1 learner compared to a late L2 learner because infant language experience organizes perceptual space into the linguistic categories that are necessary for subsequent language acquisition. By contrast, experience-based accounts (Flege, 1999; McCandliss et al., 2002; Munakata & Pfaffly, 2004; Seidenberg & Zevin, 2006) predict that AoA effects will be reduced for the late L1 learner relative to the late L2 learner, because in L1 learners there is no previously acquired phonological system to interfere with learning. Newport (1990) has proposed a maturational account of the critical theory hypothesis that is compatible with both biological and experiential explanations, which she calls "less is more." It underscores the fact that, even while a Chomskyian language acquisition device may be maximally sensitive at birth, there is also the fact that the child's cognitive resources become more and more stressed as she matures, which results in less resources available to devote to language acquisition.

A key to resolving the debate between the maturation and experiential accounts described above is the finding that AoA effects on sign language processing are especially large in L1 cases where little or no sign language was acquired prior to adolescence. These effects are unlike the well-documented AoA effects for an L2, since learning a spoken or signed L2 at older ages can lead to near-native proficiency depending upon factors, such as the grammatical relationship of the L2 to the L1 and the degree of education undertaken in the L2 (Flege, et al., 1999; Birdsong & Molis, 2001; Hakuta et al., 2003). Mayberry and colleagues have done a great deal of work on the critical period for language acquisition in late L1 signers, and in the next section I will highlight only a few of the studies on this important topic.

Later AoA is associated with lexical errors made during off-line processing tasks that are linked to the phonological form of signs and not to the sentence's meaning (Newport, 1990; Emmorey et al., 1995; Boudreault & Mayberry, 2006). This is sometimes called the "phonological bottleneck." Mayberry and Fischer (1989) and Mayberry and Eichen (1991) conducted two studies using shadowing tasks in ASL narratives and sentences to address the type of lexical error produced – phonological versus semantic errors. Signers were instructed to copy verbatim the signing of the televised narrator while simultaneously watching the stimuli – called "shadowing." Native signers appear to process sign language phonology automatically such that they can direct their attention to the processing and retention of meaning, while non-native signers seem unable to process phonology automatically. Rather, they must allocate relatively more attention to the tasks of phonological identification and the integration of phonological shape with lexical meaning, so that they have proportionately less attention available for the processing and integration of meaning.

An example of a phonological error on the sentence shadowing task might be: WE ATE TOO MUCH TURKEY **SLEEP** POTATO (phonological error) instead of WE ATE TOO MUCH TURKEY **AND** POTATO. The signs **SLEEP** and **AND** are phonologically related because they have the same handshape and the same type of local movement, but they are not semantically related. An example semantic error on this task might be: ABOUT MIDNIGHT, MANY **CHILDREN** CAME MY HOME, instead of ABOUT MIDNIGHT, MANY **FRIENDS** CAME MY HOME where CHILDREN and FRIENDS are semantically, but not phonologically, related in ASL. As Figure 7.8 shows, as the AoA increases, the proportion of semantic errors decreases while the proportion of phonological errors increases. As Mayberry and Fischer (1989: 753) have said, "To know a language means to be able to see through its phonological forms to lexical meaning, automatically."

Mayberry and Witcher (2005) studied priming effects in lexical access via reaction time (RT), as shown in Figure 7.9, for native signers, early learners who were exposed to ASL between age 4 and 8, and late learners who were exposed to ASL between age 9 and 13. Facilitation is in positive RT values and inhibition is in negative RT values, where the baseline of the sign recognition for stimulus pairs that are unrelated linguistically is set at zero. Native signers show more facilitation in semantic than phonological priming, while early learners show priming for both phonological and semantic priming. Late learners show a strong inhibition effect for phonological priming, which supports the concept of a phonological bottleneck. Mayberry and Witcher (2005) suggest two possible explanations for why phonological processing is different in the late L1 learners. First, their phonological system may be less differentiated than that of early learners; their knowledge of ASL phonology may include fewer contrastive segments so that signs may be harder to distinguish given only phonological form. Their lexical neighborhoods would be more populated, thereby slowing sign recognition (Slowiaczek & Pisoni, 1986). Additionally, AoA

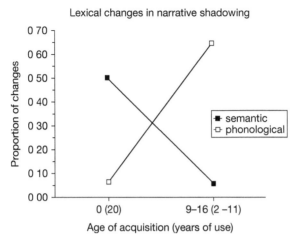

Figure 7.8 Evidence for the "phonological bottleneck." Effects of late L1 acquisition showing that as age of acquisition of an L1 increases, the number of phonological errors increases and semantic errors decrease. (Reprinted by permission from Mayberry, R. & Fischer, S., *Memory & Cognition*, "Looking through phonological shape to lexical meaning: The bottleneck of non-native sign language processing," 1989.)

may affect the mapping of phonological units onto the lexicon (Pallier et al., 2001).

Two additional studies indicate late L1 signers process the parameters of a sign differently than native signers or L2 learners. Morford and Carlson (2011) studied the responses of native deaf, late L1 who acquired ASL between 10 and 18 years of age, and proficient hearing L2 signers who acquired ASL between 16 and 26 years of age in a monitoring task, where a target sign was shown with a specific handshape or POA followed by a block of signs where the signers had to press a key when they saw the targeted handshape or POA. The native signers' responses indicate that they identify both the handshape and the POA of the target sign at roughly the same speed. The hearing L2 signers first identified the target handshape, followed by POA. The late L1 deaf signers produced responses that indicated that handshape was clearly the primary basis for their responses, and fewer than 25 percent of their key press responses shared POA. In addition, while native signers anticipate the movement parameter on the basis of location and handshape cues in the input, the non-native signers show

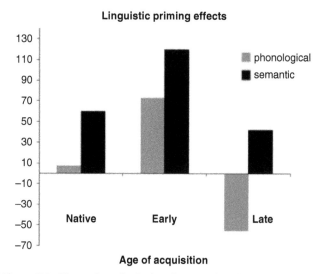

Figure 7.9 Mean phonological and semantic priming effects for ASL sign recognition as a function of age of acquisition. Sign recognition facilitation is expressed as milliseconds faster (positive) than baseline. Sign recognition inhibition is expressed as milliseconds slower (negative) than baseline. (Reprinted with permission from Mayberry, R. & Witcher, P., "What age of acquisition effects reveal about the nature of phonological processing" (Tech. Rept. No. 17, 3), (2005), University of California, San Diego, Center for Research in Language.)

little evidence of integrating phonological cues, relying instead on handshape alone to guide their lexical search. Other differences between late L1 and L2 signers come from categorical perception (CP). Late L1 signers overdiscriminate compared to native signers. In a CP study by Morford et al. (2008), both the non-native and L2 signers showed greater within-category discrimination compared to the native signers, suggesting that there may be a window of opportunity to develop strong phonemic boundaries, which comes along with the associated loss of within-category discrimination.

Hall et al. (2012) studied the same three types of ASL signers as in Morford and Carlson (2011), plus a group of hearing non-signers, and they employed a phonological similarity task. The hearing L2 signers performed more like native signers than the late L1 deaf signers did, and the late L1 deaf signers and the non-signers performed more similarly to each other than to the native signers. The late L1 deaf ASL signers and the non-signers were sensitive to certain phonetic, visual, or somatosensory features that both the native and L2 signers were not sensitive to, but it was not obvious to the researchers which ones these features might have been.

To sum up, late AoA has a wide range of lasting effects on language competence as a whole, and particularly individuals who learn a sign language as an L1 later in life demonstrate weaker phonological processing and word retrieval skills than native signers or proficient L2 signers, which inhibits automatic access to meaning.

7.5 CONNECTION BETWEEN SIGN LANGUAGE PHONOLOGY AND READING

We now bring all of the work presented in this chapter so far to bear on the question of reading. A high level of literacy is necessary to succeed in contemporary society, yet the deaf community as a group has significantly lower levels of literacy than their hearing counterparts. Many deaf students graduate from secondary school with a fourth-grade reading level or less (Allen, 1986). As a field, deaf education has been working on this problem for many decades. Because late L1 learners experience a severe phonological bottleneck with respect to ASL, as we have just discussed, we ask a two-pronged question in this section:

(1) How does this phonological processing issue in late L1 signers interact with learning to read, and how do native signing deaf readers differ from late(r) L1 signers in this regard?
(2) Does experience with sign language phonology prepare deaf children to make grapheme (English) phonology connections? Would exposing all deaf children to ASL phonology place deaf children in a better position of readiness to access the spoken phonological code?

In this section I am going to be explicitly referring to two "phonological" codes. When talking about the topic of reading, most work refers to the English one as the phonological code, but ASL has a phonological code as well, as we have described throughout this volume. It is becoming increasingly clear that in deaf bilinguals both the ASL and English phonological codes are activated when reading via a mechanism known as cross-modal activation. In other words, deaf readers are potentially engaging two types of visual representations – a sign language phonological representation and an orthographic representation of a spoken language – as well as auditory and articulatory representations of the spoken language that they receive via residual hearing, hearing aids, or cochlear implants.

7.5.1   The Use of Spoken and Signed Phonological Codes in Deaf Readers

Do deaf readers engage spoken or signed phonological codes? There have been a variety of different answers to this question, and it appears that many tests of "phonological awareness," which typically involves phoneme identification, are not necessarily the best indicators of the use of a phonological code in this context. Hall and Bavelier (2010) have proposed the Multiple-Coding Hypothesis. This view of memory encoding posits that as many codes as possible are used to maintain words in memory. For example, Waters and Doehring (1990) found that orally educated deaf readers did not use phonological codes during word recognition, but they did in a recall task. The Multiple-Coding Hypothesis predicts that deaf people viewing sign language and hearing people listening to speech may rely preferentially on one or more of the multiple activated codes for different types of word-based activities, such as memory versus recognition. In addition, deaf readers may rely on codes that are more readily available to them, such as orthographic, semantic, tactile, and phonological codes of their respective sign languages, including fingerspelling (Treiman & Hirsh-Pasek, 1983; Lichtenstein, 1998; McQuarrie & Parrila, 2009).

In answering the question concerning whether deaf readers use spoken phonological codes, Bélanger et al. (2012) might say that spoken phonology is probably not a crucial factor for deaf readers, based on their study of word recognition in high- and low-skilled French Canadian deaf readers. Their hypothesis was that if good reading skills require the use of French phonological codes during visual word recognition (Hanson & Fowler, 1987; Perfetti & Sandak, 2000; Luckner & Handley, 2008), then only the group of skilled deaf readers would show phonological effects. The analysis showed no statistical difference between the high- and low-reading groups and phonological priming, nor in phonological similarity in a second recall task. So what does this mean? Should we therefore conclude that spoken phonology is used by both or neither of the groups of deaf readers? One possibility is that there are different aspects of the phonological code – one for accessing features, another one for segments, another for syllable well-formedness, and still another for word phonotactics – and the type of phonological code addressed in this study of French deaf readers, which was segmental in nature, may not be one that deaf readers heavily rely upon. In addition, and this has not been studied and is speculation on my part, there might be language-particular differences in the types of phonological information that deaf readers use, based on the level of transparency between the phonology and orthography.

Hirshorn et al. (2015) would most likely agree with Bélanger et al. (2012) for native signers, but not for orally trained deaf readers. This study investigated the factors that correlated with reading abilities in non-signing (oral) deaf and native-signing deaf readers who were college students. The set of tasks controlled for "shallow" (spoken-orthographic transparency, such as *hat* versus *rat*) and "deep" (spoken-orthographic opacity, such as *toe* versus *bow*) aspects of spoken and written codes, as well as memory tasks, both serial and free memory recall tasks (Figure 7.10). For the native signers, the free memory recall task was the only task with a significant correlation with reading skill. These authors conclude that the native signer readers are most likely using semantic information rather than phonological information in reading. The strongest correlate with reading skill in the oral deaf group was English phonological knowledge, which included phonological judgment, syllable identification, and phoneme manipulation tasks, where the participant had to make a new word with the initial sound of one word and the rime of another (e.g., using *bird* and *toe* to make *bow*). Moreover, when high- and low-skilled readers of oral and signing groups were analyzed separately, again, there was no significant difference between them, showing that both groups are using some type of information from spoken phonological representation.

Emmorey et al. (2013) would argue that at least one type of spoken phonology code is accessed by deaf readers, especially the one related to syllable awareness. The study by Emmorey et al. (2013) discussed earlier in this chapter found that spoken language phonology was engaged when words were fingerspelled to deaf signers, but this was also true when words were presented as print. In a functional magnetic resonance imaging (fMRI) study, they tested hearing and deaf readers during phonological and semantic judgment tasks. The semantic task required participants to respond to the question "Can it be touched?" when words were presented, and the phonological task was to respond to the question "Does the word on the screen have one syllable or two?" Phonological processing engaged bilateral frontal and parietal cortices in both deaf and hearing readers, but

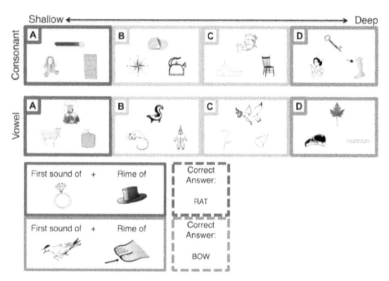

Figure 7.10   Sample items from the phoneme judgment task (top) and
phoneme manipulation task (bottom). Items with black borders are
"shallow" items while items with gray borders are "deep" items.
(Reprinted and cropped from *Frontiers in Psychology*, 6, Hirshorn, et al.,
"The contribution of phonological knowledge, memory, and language
background to reading comprehension in deaf populations," 2015. [doi
.org/10.3389/fpsyg.2015.01153] Used under a CC BY 4.0 license.)

activation was greater for deaf readers in the left pre-central gyrus,
which is associated with motor control of spoken articulators, and in
the intra-parietal sulcus bilaterally. The authors attribute these findings of hyper-activation in the cerebral region associated with motor
control as reflecting increased phonological processing demands for
deaf compared to hearing readers, since the deaf participants were
less accurate as well, as shown by the results on phonological task –
76 percent (deaf) versus 95 percent (hearing) accuracy. Other possible
explanations include the possibility that the hyper-activation could
reflect the particular type of experience with spoken language phonology in deaf readers as it relates to cognitive resources. Since tasks
with speech-based codes are demanding for deaf readers, perhaps
more of their resources are directed toward the phonological task.
They would therefore be less likely to engage in semantic processing
during phonological tasks. Hearing readers, in contrast, may automatically activate phonological and semantic codes during both tasks

when the tasks are relatively easy, resulting in greater functional overlap for these processes.

This would resonate with the concept of the "phonological bottle-neck" as well, since as predicted hearing readers seem to automatically be able to jump to semantic processing, while the deaf readers spend more resources on phonological processing. Another possible explanation suggested by MacSweeney et al. (2009) is that, in comparison to hearing individuals, deaf individuals may rely more on articulatory than acoustic representations of speech for phonological processing tasks. Emmorey and colleagues also considered the possibility that the areas of hyperactivity observed in deaf, compared to hearing, readers might reflect sub-manual articulation of ASL signs, but this possibility was dismissed for several reasons. First, only half of the English words in their study had ASL sign translations, and it is not clear why signers would activate ASL sign translations only during the phonological task and not during the semantic task. Moreover, during debriefing no participant indicated a sign-based strategy for performing either task. Finally, parietal activation during overt sign production is left-lateralized and is most often centered in the superior (rather than the inferior) parietal lobe (Corina & Knapp, 2006; Emmorey, et al., 2007).

In a more recent fMRI study, Emmorey et al. (2016) pursued this thread of syllable awareness further with low- and high-skilled deaf adult readers who profess not to use speech much in their daily lives. The better readers were more accurate on the semantic and phonological tasks, and accuracy on the in-scanner phonological task (syllable judgment) correlated with vocabulary and reading scores; however, pre-scanner phonological awareness of English was not correlated with any of these reading measures. Post hoc comparisons of the ten most and ten least skilled deaf readers revealed increased activation within the left inferior frontal gyrus and left middle temporal cortex for better readers when reading words for meaning. Again, reading ability was significantly correlated with the accuracy of syllable judgments during scanning ($r = 0.55$, $p < 0.005$), but not with the phonological awareness test. The authors suggest that skilled deaf readers are better able to access higher-level syllabic information about words, such as syllable count, but not sub-syllabic segmental information about initial or final consonants, which is a typical type of item of phonological awareness.

Sterne and Goswami (2000) also found that skilled deaf child readers with a mean reading age = 7.2 years (mean chronological age = 11.8 years) exhibited equal syllable awareness to their hearing peers, but much poorer rhyme awareness. They concluded that rhyme judgments may not be relevant for reading, but that syllabification is relevant. They did not find a correlation within the left pre-central gyrus (BA 6), indicating that task accuracy was not associated with the use of covert articulation per se, just as Emmorey et al. (2013) and MacSweeney et al. (2009) proposed, but rather with access to and encoding of abstract syllabic structure.

All of these studies suggest that what is generally called "phonological coding" could be a constellation of skills, including syllable awareness, rhyming, and segment identification, with syllable awareness more relevant than some of the skills typically tested in phonological awareness assessments.

7.5.2 Cross-Modal Activation

Of the three codes mentioned at the beginning of this chapter – sign language phonological representation, spoken language phonological representation, and orthographic representation of the spoken language – what is the cross-activation of these codes? In this section we address cross-modal activation; that is, how language presented in one modality affects processing of a language in another modality, particularly in bimodal bilinguals.[4] These could be CODAs (see glossary) who are hearing and highly proficient in a signed and a spoken language, or deaf signers who are bilingual in spoken (or written) English. As we saw above, print and fingerspelling both seem to activate spoken phonological codes, but a deeper exploration of this question has been taken up more recently, and it is easy to see how it might be relevant for reading. In Chapter 6 we briefly discussed bimodal bilinguals when talking about tip-of-the-tongue (TOT) and tip-of-the-finger (TOF) phenomena. Pyers et al. (2009) concluded that since TOT/TOFs are more frequent in both bimodal and unimodal bilinguals than in monolinguals, they must be related to the lemma level rather than to a level that involves overlapping or competing phonological content between the two languages, since ASL and English share no overlapping phonology.

The three different groups of bilinguals typically enlisted in these studies – unimodal bilinguals (spoken-spoken), hearing bimodal bilinguals (CODAs), and deaf bimodal bilinguals – all experience cross-modal

---

[4] For examples of this type of work on unimodal bilinguals, see Thierry and Wu (2007) and Wu and Thierry (2010, 2012).

activation.[5] Unimodals experience L1 speech effects on L2 print. Bimodal bilinguals experience effects of speech and sign on print, and print and speech on sign. However, the three groups may differ in the relative strength and availability of various routes that processing might take, and bimodal bilinguals help us understand the range of possible activation networks. For example, CODAs employ code blending (simultaneously producing a signed word and an English word) rather than code mixing (temporally interspersing words from the L1 while producing L2 sentences). An example of a code blend is given in (1). Signers don't typically turn off their voices when producing an ASL sign in the middle of a sentence.

(1) *I'm pretty [sure] they were [hearing].*
         sure   hearing

The preference for code blending over code switching implies that dual lexical retrieval is less costly than inhibiting one language, and evidence from picture-naming tasks suggests that simultaneous production of translation equivalents does not incur a processing cost (Emmorey et al., 2014). For bimodal bilinguals, releasing an inhibited language appears to be "cost free," but applying inhibition to a nontarget language is not, which is what unimodal bilinguals have to do all the time since words in two spoken languages cannot be articulated at the same time.

Cross-modal activation of sign on printed English words is apparent in deaf and hearing bimodal bilinguals in work by Morford et al. (2011, 2014). They found that unrelated English word pairs with phonologically related ASL translations elicited slower reaction times to a question of whether the two words are related in meaning (RTs; slower "no" responses) than word pairs that had phonologically unrelated ASL translations. Phonological similarity was defined as sharing a minimum of two formational parameters. For example, BIRD and DUCK are phonologically related because they have the same movement and POA and are semantically related; MOVIE and PAPER are phonologically related because the handshape and POA are the same, but they are semantically unrelated. The RT interference effect was especially prominent for participants with lower levels of English-reading comprehension, suggesting that deaf bimodal bilinguals with lower proficiency in English rely more on lexical links to the ASL translation equivalents. This finding was replicated by Ormel et al.

---

[5] All spoken languages studied thus far in cross-modal activation studies have an associated written system.

(2012) with deaf readers proficient in NGT and by Kubus et al. (2015) with deaf readers proficient in DGS. Emmorey et al. (2017) also obtained similar results of ASL's effect on written language. In their ERP study, half of the English target words used as stimuli had phonologically related ASL translations and the other half did not. The words with phonologically related ASL translations of the English target words elicited a priming effect (in the form of a weaker N400 component), while pairs with phonologically unrelated translations did not, suggesting that the ASL translations produce phonological interference.

Cross-modal activation of written language on a sign language has been found as well. Hosemann et al. (2013) recorded ERPs from deaf native signers of DGS while viewing signed sentences containing a prime and target sign whose German translations rhymed and were also orthographically similar, e.g., LAST WEEK MY HOUSE THERE MOUSE HIDE. Their analysis indicated a priming effect (again, in the form of a weaker N400 component) for target signs that were orthographically and phonologically related in German.

Summing up this section, there is activation of both languages in bilinguals, and one of the widely accepted views about the advantages of bilingualism is the ability to inhibit one language (L1) while using another L2 (Bialystok et al., 2009). The work presented here on hearing and deaf bimodal bilinguals could be very important for showing how knowing two languages can boost processing as well. The work on bimodal bilinguals is also very relevant in the discussion in this section concerning literacy in deaf children, to which we turn next.

7.5.3 Phonological Readiness for Reading in Deaf Children

The above studies are very informative about the outcomes of different language experiences and skills of phonology in an L1 and L2 on reading; however, all the processing studies just described, except one – Sterne and Goswami (2000) – were conducted with adults whose patterns have been established over many years.

The work on phonological processing in children, like that of the adults discussed in Chapter 6, suggests that the cortical locations for phonological processing would be the superior temporal gyrus (STG) and inferior frontal cortex (IFC), possibly bilaterally. Petitto and colleagues have been investigating the sensitivities in the infant brain to phonological input for both spoken and signed languages, with the goal of reading readiness. Using functional near infrared spectroscopy (fNIRS), Petitto et al. (2012) found interesting developmental timing differences in brain activation in younger (4–6 months) versus older (10–12 months) hearing infants acquiring a spoken language. Left STG activation was observed early and remained stable, while left inferior frontal cortex showed greater increase in neural activation in older babies, notably at the precise age when babies enter the first-word milestone. The authors suggest that this may be a first-time focal brain correlate that may mediate a universal behavioral milestone in early language acquisition at the one-word stage. In addition, a difference was observed in the bilingual and monolingual babies: older bilingual babies were more resilient to non-native phonological contrasts at a time when monolingual babies can no longer make such discriminations.[6]

Building on Petitto's work, Stone (2017) and Stone et al. (2017) used fNIRS over the STG and IFC regions bilaterally to test two hypotheses. The first, the "peaked sensitivity" hypothesis, predicts that in early infancy hearing infants exposed to spoken language and deaf infants exposed to sign language would show equal sensitivity to information related to rhythmic-temporal patterning in visual signed language. The second, the "Experience Dependent" hypothesis, predicts that only sign-exposed babies would show a particular type of sensitivity to sign language syllables. Sign-exposed and sign-naïve infants at 6–8 months were tested using fNIRS on sign pseudo-syllables produced at three speeds and in both natural video presentation and in point-light displays: "slow", 0.5 Hz (almost 2 seconds per syllable), "medium," 1.5 Hz (about 600 milliseconds (ms) per syllable), and "fast" 3.0 Hz (about 200 ms per syllable). This age range was chosen because infants have not yet begun to narrow their phonetic inventories to that of their native language, which typically happens at around 9 months. The peak sensitivity hypothesis was supported because language experience showed no effect; both groups of infants (signed and spoken) differentiated between slower (0.5 and 1.5 Hz) and faster (3.0 Hz) rhythmic-temporal frequencies. No significant differences were found between 0.5 Hz and 1.5 Hz in the regions of interest.

Importantly, this low- versus high-frequency sensitivity dovetails on work concerning a mechanism called "neural entrainment" (Giraud & Poeppel, 2012), which is what happens when low-frequency oscillations (< 8 Hz) in the cerebral cortex become temporally aligned to quasi-rhythmic fluctuations in speech volume (i.e., which is loudness, and, practically speaking, the vowel portion of syllables). It has not been clear if this phenomenon is associated to a language mechanism or specifically tied to the auditory signal.

---

[6] Some researchers interpret this finding as immaturity in the bilingual infants.

Two studies helped to resolve this dilemma. Hwang et al. (2011) demonstrated that signed syllables are slower than spoken syllables but still within the range of cortical entrainment for speech, and, as expected, visual motion in sign language is modulated at lower frequencies than auditory volume in spoken language. This difference is consistent with the slower movements in the articulators for sign (the hands) than for speech (the vocal tract). In a related line of research with adults, Brookshire et al. (2017) performed an electroencephalography (EEG) study on ASL entrainment in signers and non-signers. Since the general, nonlinguistic frequencies preferred by the visual cortex are different than those for speech – around 10 Hz and above – Brookshire et al. (2017) were able to test whether entrainment was primarily motivated by the visual modality or by the language information being processed. If peak coherence to sign language is related to the visual signal itself, it should be observed at the frequencies preferred by the visual cortex at around 10 Hz. Contrary to this prediction, they found that cortical coherence to sign language only emerges below 5 Hz, closer to the rate of syllable production found by Hwang et al. (2011). Although preliminary, this work suggests that cortical entrainment to sign language occurs around the frequencies of syllables, words, and phrases in ASL; therefore, low-frequency oscillatory entrainment may reflect a general cortical mechanism that maximizes sensitivity to informational peaks in *languages*, rather than for general auditory or visual modalities. Moreover, signers and non-signers showed stronger entrainment in the frontal regions when they watched videotaped signed narratives, but signers showed stronger entrainment. This suggests that language-specific knowledge is not necessary for entrainment; however, I would suggest that perhaps non-signers were able to show this effect because their brains have had a lifetime of entrainment practice on co-speech gesture and as a result they are able to transfer this skill to sign language.

How is this work relevant for reading? It is extremely difficult to analyze young infants' capabilities and environments and correlate any of them directly with a goal so distant in the child's future as reading skill, even though the goal of such work on infant perception in spoken language tries to make this multifactorial correlation for prosody, auditory perceptual skill, and word segmentation skills as a predictor of language development. In the absence of the relevant factors, a range of speech and language disorders may be predicted (Cristia et al., 2014). In my opinion, no single factor is going be the explanation for poor reading skills in deaf adults. This said, putting together these facts about neural entrainment, infant sensitivity, the findings from adult deaf readers, and the phonological bottleneck in late L1 signers, we might speculate that if young deaf infants are not exposed to rhythmic, prosodically natural, linguistic input at the syllabic babbling stage and into the first-word stage, a critical window may pass. As a result these children will not be able to use phonological codes effectively when they are confronted with the task of learning to read. Late L1 signers are likely to have missed this crucial window, which makes the task much harder for them.

7.6 CONCLUSIONS

This chapter has provided background on seminal work on phonological acquisition in sign languages. The research does much more than provide L1 data in a new modality; it supports the theoretical proposals for phonological representations as presented in Chapter 1 concerning feature classes, the syllable, and the organization of the lexicon in terms of phonological behavior. This chapter also described several unique populations of signers that provide crucial evidence for the way that language is processed under a range of different circumstances related to differing ages of acquisition.

We then considered the phonological processing patterns of deaf, bimodal bilinguals in cross-modal activation. Adult deaf readers are bimodal bilinguals, and as such, cross-modal activation helps us to understand the complex network of activation that is at work in proficient deaf readers and the way it is related to balanced bilingualism. Skilled deaf readers engage spoken phonological codes and access ASL while reading English. But the weighting and priorities of different sets of bimodal bilinguals may differ.

One of the phonological abilities that has emerged as relevant is the awareness of syllables. Other phonological codes might also be important, but it appears the segmental level and rhyming, as typically assessed in phonological awareness tests, are not as important as syllable structure. What is traditionally thought of as (English) phonological meta-awareness is typically tested using sub-syllabic units such as rhyming and initial and final segment identification, which may be less relevant for deaf readers. We see that the link between English phonology and reading ability is clearer if the kinds of phonological units employed in the study design are broadened to include the syllable. The chapter concludes by discussing the possible relationship between sign language phonology and reading readiness.

7.7 FURTHER READING

Mayberry, R. I., Lock, E., & Kazmi, H. (2002). Development: Linguistic ability and early language exposure. *Nature*, 417(6884), 38.

Meier, R. (2002). The acquisition of verb agreement: Pointing out arguments for the linguistic status of agreement in signed languages. In G. Morgan & B. Woll (eds.), *Directions in Sign Language Acquisition* (pp. 115–41). Amsterdam: John Benjamins Associates.

Mirus, G. R., Rathmann, C., & Meier, R.P. (2001). Proximalization and distalization of sign movement in adult learners. In V.L. Dively, M. Metzger, S. Taub, & A.M. Baer (eds.), *Signed Languages: Discoveries from International Research* (pp. 103–19). Washington, DC: Gallaudet University Press.

Morgan, G., Barrett-Jones, S. & Stoneham, H. (2007). The first signs of language: Phonological development in British sign language. *Applied Psycholinguistics*, 28, 3–22.

Petitto, L. A., Holowka, S., Sergio, L.E., Levy, B., & Ostry, D. J. (2004). Baby hands that move to the rhythm of language: Hearing babies acquiring sign languages babble silently on the hands. *Cognition*, 93, 43–73.

Reilly, J., McIntire, M., & Ursula Bellugi, U. (1990). Faces: The relationship between language and affect. In V. Volterra & C. Erting (eds.), *From Gesture to Language in Hearing and Deaf Children* (pp. 128–41). New York: Springer.

8 Sign Language Phonological Variation and Change

Abstract

This chapter covers factors that affect variation in phonological or prosodic form synchronically and diachronically. Such factors can include grammatical context, phonetic factors such as ease of articulation and perception, as well as a range of sociolinguistic factors, such as age, gender, region, and ethnicity.

8.1 INTRODUCTION

In this final chapter of the volume we address phonological variation and change. A discussion of language in its social context can include many topics, including synchronic variation (phonological differences as seen across groups at the same period of time) and diachronic variation (phonological differences within the same group at different historical periods). One might even include language emergence and language acquisition as well. These topics are divided as they are in this book because we will see that synchronic and diachronic phonological variation have more in common with one another than with language emergence (Chapter 5) or language acquisition (Chapter 7). One might think that because all four cases involve change over time that they would have a core set of common principles. They do have a lot in common in terms of the phonetic pressures involved, but there are many ways in which they are different as well. In the case of language variation and change, there are two equally well-defined forms that happen at two points in time – time-x and time-y – or, in synchronic variation, two conditions – context-x and context-y. Each form is embedded in a well-established, mature linguistic system at both time points or in both sociolinguistic contexts. This is not the case in acquisition or language emergence. Acquisition and emergence are both adding to the system in a more accelerated way than in either synchronic or diachronic change.

There has been great interest in synchronic and diachronic variation since the field of sign language linguistics's earliest days (Woodward, 1973, 1976; Battison, 1974; Frishberg, 1975). Attention to diachronic variation has enjoyed a new burst of scholarly energy in the work by Supalla and colleagues on American Sign Language (ASL) (Supalla & Clarke, 2015), and in work on Italian Sign Language (LIS), which includes synchronic and diachronic aspects of variation together using the "apparent time construct" (Geraci et al., 2011; Labov, 1994, 2001).

In general, the two types of variation – synchronic and diachronic – are subject to the same types of pressures as in spoken languages, such as ease of articulation and ease of perception, and just as in spoken languages, these two principles can be expressed in many different ways. Here we ask the question also posed in Lucas and Bayley (cf. 2010: 452): Do signed and spoken languages differ in fundamental ways when it comes to variation? In what way, if any, is modality reflected in both types of variation? These authors set up this question in terms of grammatical conditioning and sociolinguistic conditioning, and we will do the same. In other words, throughout this chapter we will bear in mind that there are social factors associated with phonological differences that identify who is speaking by their demographics, and there are grammatical factors that are associated with phonological differences that refine the ways in which nouns, adjectives, and verbs are identified.

There are fundamentally two functions that language variation accomplishes: It can refine the system (grammatical conditioning), and it can communicate about the identity of its users (sociolinguistic conditioning). Lucas and Bayley (2010) and Fenlon et al. (2013) both point out that grammatical factors are consistent predictors of variation in sign languages, perhaps more than any of the social ones. There might be two reasons for this. It could be due to the visual modality (Lucas and Bayley suggested this reason). However, I would like to add that because sign languages are still young, they may also still be a bit more deeply involved in "building" mode compared to spoken languages – perhaps not in the dramatic way that we see in acquisition or language emergence, but in small ways that still make new distinctions that were not present before. As you have read in previous chapters, in sign languages morphological distinctions are often accomplished by altering one or more phonological features.

8.1.1   Sources of Data

In this section, the sources available for work on variation will be described. The problem for work on any type of variation – synchronic or diachronic – is having enough material that is tagged or annotated. For both synchronic and diachronic variation, annotation of video data must be done manually, and this is very time consuming. The materials listed at the end of the chapter are mostly video collections; a small portion of these collections have been annotated in various ways for specific research questions. The best type of data source for diachronic analysis is a target sign produced naturally on film, which captures the particular phonetics of a given form in a particular linguistic and social context, but this is possible in only a minority of cases.

There are an increasing number of synchronic sources for work on variation, which take the form of dictionaries, lexical "sign banks," and some tagged, naturally occurring data sets consisting of narratives and conversations. The corpus collected by Lucas et al. (2001) is the largest study of ASL sociolinguistic variation to date, which reports on phonological, lexical, morphological, and syntactic variation in ASL, based on videotaped conversations between native signers from seven locations in the United States, from three different age groups. A later project included both White and African American signers. The British Sign Language (BSL) and Auslan corpora are also quite large and based on a number of discourse types. Much of the work described below will be based on these three sets of data. Particularly in the case of synchronic variation, it is important to have a large enough sample to make inferences across a particular geographic area, social group, or demographic factor.

The situation is somewhat different for studies of historical change. A formidable obstacle to the study of phonological change in sign languages is the paucity of sources in most sign languages. Sign languages have been considered to be languages only since around 1960, and general acceptance of this fact by the academic community, broadly defined, took considerably more time. Perhaps ASL, French Sign Language (LSF), and BSL are more fortunate than most sign language communities, because these sign languages have benefited from historical documentation going back to the 1700s. The texts on LSF, ASL's ancestor, and on early BSL, include dictionaries and other materials for teaching the language, which have been preserved in the case of LSF since the first French school for the deaf in Paris was founded in 1761 (Lane, 1984), and in the BSL case since the first British school for the deaf was established in 1760 (Deuchar, 1984). Two hundred and fifty years is a short period of time when compared with the history of spoken languages, which can have written records that traverse thousands of years, but this is much better than most sign language documentation.

For ASL, sign varieties included Martha's Vineyard Sign Language, discussed in Chapter 5 on language emergence (Groce, 1985), and a few other varieties that existed in the early colonies, plus a formidable individual influence from Laurent Clerc, the first superintendent of the American School for the Deaf in Hartford, Connecticut, established in 1817. Clerc was French and used LSF. Prior to 1817 we have LSF materials, but little else in terms of raw material on ASL.

From 1912 to 1915 the National Association of the Deaf (the NAD) created a set of films for the purpose of demonstrating sign language in a variety of functions – lectures, prayers, songs, and theatrical performance of poetry. These films were an important, creative, and effective way of protesting the intended consequences of the Milan Congress of 1880, where a group of (mostly European) educators of the deaf voted on a set of pedagogical principles favoring speech over sign language as a language of instruction. The aftermath of the Milan Congress in Europe was profound because most educational systems in Europe are controlled at the country-wide level by their Ministers of Education, so any decision was immediately expected to be carried out at all schools in a given country. The situation was somewhat better in the United States, where each state controls education policies, and so the NAD created these remarkable films, taking advantage of this new technology, to convince school boards and state legislators that ASL has the same range of functions of any other language; as a result these films are crucially important to the deaf community (Padden & Humphries, 2005).

Historical sources come in three types – text, drawings, photos, and film. One valuable historical source in ASL is Long (1918), a dictionary that not only includes descriptions of how signs are made but also photographs. Text descriptions are helpful in some ways, such as a description for the 1918 ASL sign ANGRY (Michaels, 1923). A description is less helpful, however, than a drawing or photograph of someone producing a sign, as in Figure 8.1, which is a contemporary signer reproducing the descriptions of Michaels (1923) and Stokoe et al. (1965), as well as a current version of the sign ANGRY. In these examples we can see a change that might not be evident from a prose description, regarding the one- versus two-handedness of the word and the specific place on the torso where the sign occurs. In 1918, ANGRY was one-handed and produced close to the waist at the signer's ipsilateral side (Long, 1918; Figure 8.1, left), but it became more centralized and two-handed, as reported in Stokoe et al. (1965) and Frishberg (1975; Figure 8.1, center). Currently, there is synchronic variation between the two-handed form and a one-handed variant (Battison, 1974; Padden & Perlmutter, 1987; Figure 8.1, right).

ANGRY, 1917
one-handed variant

ANGRY, 1975 & current
two-handed variant

ANGRY, 1975 & current
one-handed variant

Figure 8.1 Variants of the ASL sign ANGRY (cf. Frishberg, 1975): (left) one-handed (Long, 1918); (middle) centralized, two-handed form as described in Stokoe et al. (1965); and (right) a contemporary, one-handed variant as described in Battison (1974) and Padden & Perlmutter (1987)

8.1.2 Language Variation, Change, and Emergence

Because there are always a number of factors in play, in historical change and variation we might see opposing pressures ultimately create cases that do what looks like a reversal over time, demonstrating that the variants do not add or reduce complexity but rather seek to maintain an equilibrium of complexity in the system as a whole. The variation of one and two-handed forms of ANGRY shows this: forms go from one-handed to two-handed and then create a synchronic variation between the one and two-handed variants. A case of this in spoken languages is the phenomena of word-final devoicing in the history of German and Yiddish. Old High German did not have final devoicing (700–1050), Middle High German did have it, and subsequently Modern Yiddish, one particular variety related to Middle High German, does not have it (Wetzels & Mascaró, 1977), as shown in (1).

(1) *Historical change and its reversal in German-related varieties: word-
    final devoicing*
    voiced > unvoiced > voiced
    a. Old High German did not have final devoicing (700–1050)
        "wheel" *rad* stays *rad;* "advice" *rat* stays *rat*
    b. Middle High German had final devoicing (1050–1350)
        "wheel" & "advice" *both* pronounced *rat;*
    c. Modern Yiddish does not have final devoicing (1800s)
        "wheel" *rad* stays *rad;* "advice" *rat* stays *rat*

Language emergence and, to some extent, language acquisition, are heavily engaged in expanding the phonological system's linguistic possibilities in addition to reorganizing them. This emphasis on the system's elaboration and expansion makes sign language emergence different than language change, which reorganizes complexity, but is not building a new system in so dramatic a fashion as language emergence. Moreover, language emergence (as discussed in Chapter 5) is also similar to sociolinguistic variation insofar as the variation in language emergence begins with the individual system, then slowly expands to micro-communities in families or in a school setting (Horton, in preparation).

8.2 SYNCHRONIC VARIATION

Sociolinguistic, synchronic variation can appear in any of the components of a grammar, but in sign languages phonetic and phonological factors have been the most extensively studied thus far, and these are the cases that will be discussed here. Examples of such work include Lucas (1995), Bayley et al. (2000, 2002), Lucas et al. (2001, 2002, 2003), and McCaskill et al. (2011) for ASL. For British, Australian, and New Zealand Sign Language (BANZSL) there are several important studies as well, including Schembri and Johnston (2007), Schembri et al. (2009, 2018), and McKee and Kennedy (2006). For LIS, see Radutzky (1989) and Geraci et al. (2011). Sign language phonology involves the inventory and distributional rules for the five parameters: handshape, place of articulation (location), movement, orientation, and non-manual behaviors, in addition to frequency. As in other chapters of this book, I cannot be exhaustive, and have chosen only a few examples to pursue in depth here.

8.2.1   Synchronic Variation Based on Linguistic Factors

Ceil Lucas and colleagues (see above references) have outlined several features constituting variation in the American deaf community as a whole, and for Black ASL as well. The features first noticed by this team have been a springboard for work on a number of other sign languages. Handshape assimilation, sign lowering, and "handedness" (one- versus two-handed variants) have all been discussed. In three of the phonological phenomena examined in the large-scale study described below – metathesis, sign lowering, and one- versus two-handed signs – grammatical category has been found to be the most significant factor in synchronic variation.

8.2.1.1   Handshape

Bayley et al. (2002) and Fenlon et al. (2013) analyzed assimilation of the high-frequency 1-handshape in a wide range of contexts. Both studies found main effects of grammatical category, which interact with the preceding and following sign, as well as effects for region, age, and class in ASL, and region in BSL. The first-person pronoun, I/me, undergoes assimilation to the handshape of an adjacent sign most frequently (Figure 8.2) followed by other pronouns. This process has already been mentioned in Chapter 4, on interfaces, with regard to the prosodic word (P-word). Liddell and Johnson (1989) observed this phenomenon of assimilation in their work on sign language phonology, and Sandler (1999b) proposed that the combination of the assimilated pronoun + verb is a P-word, which cliticizes the pronoun. Within the constituents of the P-word, the verb is considered to be the prominent sign and since the pronoun is, by default, then not prominent, it is more likely to be the undergoer of assimilation.

8.2.1.2   Place of Articulation

Lucas et al. (1995) analyzed the rule of *metathesis* of place of articulation (POA), which allows the order of a sign's places of contact to be high to low, or low to high, as in the sign DEAF (Figure 8.3). She found that only grammatical function and discourse genre were statistically significant predictors for which signs could undergo metathesis. The citation form (i.e., the form one would find in a dictionary) has top contact first (Figure 8.3, left) and the non-citation forms have either bottom contact first (Figure 8.3, center) or a single contact alone (Figure 8.3, right). Predicate adjectives favor citation forms, and

I (1-handshape)   COOK   I (assimilated B-handshape)   COOK

Figure 8.2   The ASL sentence translated into English as *I cook*: (left) the first-person pronoun (the circled handshape) is articulated as the citation form with the 1-handshape; (right) the first-person pronoun is articulated with B-handshape of the following sign COOK (i.e., assimilation)

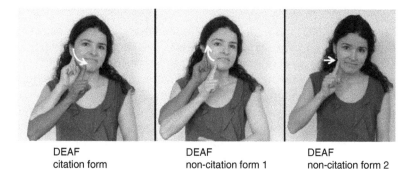

DEAF
citation form

DEAF
non-citation form 1

DEAF
non-citation form 2

Figure 8.3   The ASL sign DEAF in citation (+cf) and non-citation (−cf) forms: (left, +cf) higher contact followed by lower contact; (middle, −cf1) undergoing the rule of metathesis, lower contact followed by higher contact; (right, −cf2) single contact

compound forms with the sign DEAF favor a non-citation form (e.g., DEAF SCHOOL). The other significant factor, discourse genre, shows that non-citation forms tend to occur more in narratives than in conversation.

Lucas et al. (2001) also investigated the phenomenon of sign lowering, which displaces forms with a forehead POA to a place lower on the face. We described this phenomenon in Chapter 2, when describing the modality-specific effects of ease of articulation (Grosvald & Corina, 2012a, 2012b; Tyrone & Mauk, 2010; Mauk &Tyrone, 2012). Lucas et al. (2001) found that older signers, rural signers, native signers, women, and African Americans all favor the citation form (Figure 8.4, left); i.e., they are more linguistically conservative, while younger, urban, non-native, and male signers of the "Mainstream" variety of ASL tend to favor the non-citation form (Figure 8.4, right).[1]

Schembri et al. (2009) also found this same lowering phenomenon in Auslan and NZSL to be associated with grammatical category and with frequency as well – i.e., more frequent signs, and especially more frequent nouns and verbs, are more likely to favor the non-citation form. They also found that gender and region were significant predictors (see the next section), with young women from urban areas leading language change. Schembri and colleagues relate this to the Labovian Principle, which states that women are more likely to innovate when the new form is not stigmatized (Labov, 1990, 2001).

---

[1] We use the term "Mainstream ASL" as a placeholder, since we do not have a full description of this variety.

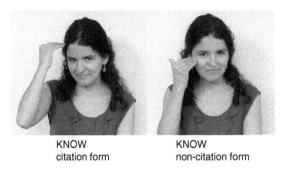

KNOW
citation form

KNOW
non-citation form

Figure 8.4 The ASL sign KNOW: (left, +cf) the place of contact is high on the forehead; (right, –cf) undergoing the phonological rule of displacement – the place of contact is lower on the cheek

In summary, many factors seem to influence synchronic variation – the sign's grammatical category and frequency, its prominence, as well as social factors such as region or sign variety. It is not surprising that there would be a great deal of variation among deaf signers, given the diversity of home life and school experience, and the differing ages at which they acquired a sign language (see Chapter 7 on acquisition). Despite these differences, it is quite remarkable that, even in the large studies described above seeking to be representative of several social factors, such as region, age, and gender, the consistent effect of grammatical function in variation shows that the BSL and ASL communities are indeed, at least to some extent, homogeneous.

8.2.2 Synchronic Variation Based on Sociolinguistic Factors

The examples of phonological variation above were based primarily on frequency or grammatical factors, such as lexical or morphological class, and secondarily on sociolinguistic factors. For social factors, it appears that region can affect lexical choice in a number of forms, as in spoken languages, but there are also at least three other phonological or prosodic elements that are affected by external factors, such as age, gender, and racial/ethnic groups.

The variety of signing termed "Black ASL," has been investigated in the 1970s and 1980s (Woodward, 1976; Woodward et al., 1976; Woodward & DeSantis, 1977; Aramburo, 1989). More recently, in their large study of this variety, McCaskill et al. (2011) localized several features that constitute variation between "Mainstream ASL" and Black ASL, as used in six Southern states. We address several features of variation in Black ASL in the following sections, along with other sociolinguistic factors, such as age and gender.

8.2.2.1   Signing Space

McCaskill (2011) and colleagues found that Black ASL signers exhibited a significant tendency to favor the citation form with regard to the phenomena of sign lowering, discussed in the previous section. In addtion, Black ASL signers were more likely to use a larger signing space than Mainstream ASL signers. (Signing space goes beyond the idea of POA, but for our purposes here I have grouped them together.) In Figure 8.5 we see the same sign LIGHT produced by a young Black and young Mainstream ASL signer in a narrative context. The young Black female signer on the left signs LIGHT higher and farther away from the body than the young Mainstream female signer on the right.

Mulrooney (2002) also found clear evidence of a gender effect in the signing space used in fingerspelling, whereby men were more likely to produce fingerspelled words outside of the usual fingerspelling POA (near the ipsilateral shoulder) than women.

8.2.2.2   One- versus Two-Handed Signs

Two-handed signs may undergo a process of "Weak Drop," a process that has been discussed in ASL and NGT, whereby signs delete the nondominant hand. Type 1 signs (i.e., the movement and handshape are the same on both hands) undergo this process most frequently

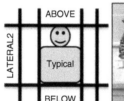

Figure 8.5   (left) The grid used in McCaskill et al. (2011) to determine if a sign was produced in "typical" signing space or not, and the two forms of LIGHT produced by a young Black ASL signer (middle) and a young Mainstream ASL signer (right). Black ASL signers tended to use a larger signing space than Mainstream signers. (Used with permission from The Structure and History of Black American Sign Language project, NSF Grant # BCS0813736.)

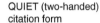

QUIET (two-handed)   QUIET-cf (one-handed)
citation form   Weak Drop form

Figure 8.6   The ASL sign QUIET: (left) two-handed form citation form;
(right) one-handed form due to the phonological rule of Weak Drop.
(Reprinted from *A Prosodic Model of Sign Language Phonology*, by Brentari,
D., Copyright (1998), with permission from MIT.)

(Battison, 1974, 1978; Padden & Perlmutter, 1987), but Type 2 and
Type 3 two-handed signs can do so as well under specific conditions (Brentari, 1998; van der Kooij, 2001). In Figure 8.6 we see
the sign QUIET in its citation form, and as a one-handed variant
that has undergone Weak Drop. Black ASL signers were found to
be significantly less likely than Mainstream ASL signers to use
the one-handed form (McCaskill et al., 2011). This is true for
signs that are two-handed in their citation form (in Black ASL
they resist Weak Drop) and for one-handed signs, such as INFORM
(see Figure 1.7), where a second hand would be added in Black
ASL.

8.2.2.3   Phrasal Rhythm

Brentari et al. (2018) also found sociolinguistic effects of phrasal
rhythm for age and gender. They studied sign language narratives of
twenty-three individuals, including older and younger signers,
Mainstream ASL and Black ASL signers (the data are from the Black
ASL project on which McCaskill's large-scale study was based). They
used a modified version of the normalized Pairwise Variability Index
for spoken languages (Ramus et al., 1999; Grabe et al., 2002) to quantify phrasal rhythm. In spoken languages, this measure plots the
standard deviation of vowel length against the standard deviation of
the space between vowels, which, for speech, are the consonants.
Brentari et al. (2018) plotted the standard deviation of lexical movements against the standard deviation of the space between the lexical
movements – i.e., the transitions. They found that younger signers and

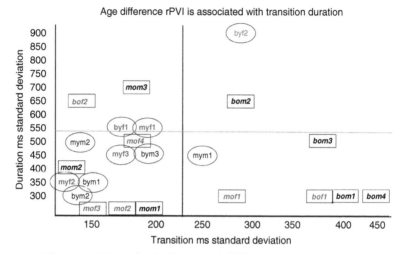

Figure 8.7   Normalized pairwise variability index plotted for Sign Variety ((m)ainstream, (b)lack), Age (older (squares), younger (circles)), and Gender ((m)ale, (f)female) for twenty-three individuals. Standard deviation of transition duration is plotted on the x-axis and standard deviation of sign duration is plotted on the y-axis. (cf. Brentari et al., 2018)

male signers have a relation of lexical movement duration to transition movement duration that is more equal, while older signers and female signers have more of a mismatch between sign duration and transition duration. They also found that the variation in transition duration explains the age effect (older signers have more variation in transition duration than younger signers), while sign duration explains the gender effect (females have more variation in sign duration than males). For this limited data set from narratives, the results are as shown in Figure 8.7, where a black vertical line shows the halfway point for transition times and the gray horizontal line shows the halfway point for sign duration. Regarding age effects for phrasal rhythm, the range is from 0–450 ms so the halfway point is about 225 ms, and we see that this effect is primarily seen in the variation in transition length. Only 2 younger signers (circles) have standard deviations for transition duration above 225 ms (to the right of the vertical black line as 225 ms); 8 are below 225 ms. For older signers (squares), 6 have standard deviations of transition duration above 225 ms; 7 are below 225 ms.

Regarding the gender effect, this effect is primarily seen in the variation in sign length. The range spans from 250–900 ms, so the halfway point is about 550 ms. This effect is primarily seen in the variation in sign length. Only 2 males (black) have standard deviations for sign length above 550 ms (above the horizontal line at 550 ms); 10 are below 550 ms. For females (gray), 4 have standard deviations of sign duration above 550 ms, while 7 are below 550 ms.

In summary, there are some social factors that are associated with variation. Signing space and handedness are associated with Black ASL, and in general this variety seems to be more phonologically conservative. Prosody – specifically the cues of duration of transitions and lexical movements – is affected by age and gender.

8.3 DIACHRONIC CHANGE

Most of the work on diachronic change is on ASL, due to the factors I mentioned earlier in this chapter concerning sources of data and scholarly interest. For some sign language corpora there has been an attempt to gather signs from multiple generations of signers – e.g., BSL, LIS, Sign Language of the Netherlands (NGT), and German Sign Language (DGS). These multi-generational studies stand between synchronic variation and historical change. Bailey (2002) proposes that these are examples of the "apparent time hypothesis," which suggests that variation in the linguistic system used by speakers of different ages at a single point in time can indicate a change in progress; however, at this point we can't really tell if the variation is a historical change in progress or if it is simply age-related; that is, as individuals age they might also change their signing style across the life span.

In this section we will first discuss what has happened in ASL over the approximately 200 years that sources have been available. As always, we will focus on the phonological phenomena involved in historical change, not lexical or syntactic phenomena.

8.3.1   Frishberg's Contribution

An important historical study of phonological change is Frishberg (1975). Her comparisons include forms from the time that Thomas Gallaudet went to Paris in 1815, commissioned to explore methods for deaf education for the newly formed American colonies. He returned to the United States accompanied by Laurent Clerc, a deaf graduate of the Paris School for the Deaf that was established in 1761. Clerc was superintendent of the American School for the Deaf for forty years from 1817 to 1858. He taught children and deaf educators his variety of LSF, which Frishberg refers to as Old French Sign Language (O-FSL). Lane (1984) provides us with a captivating narrative of the French origins of ASL, the early days of the American School for the Deaf, and about the American deaf community at that time.

At the time of Frishberg's work, very little was known about the indigenous varieties of sign language used by American deaf people, but we now know that there were several varieties. One variety was used in Martha's Vineyard (Groce, 1985), another was used in Henniker, New Hampshire, and still another in the Sandy River Valley of Maine. All three were what we would now call village sign languages (as described in Chapter 5), where a relatively high concentration of congenitally deaf individuals in the larger community was sufficient to form and sustain a sign variety (Lane et al., 2000).

Frishberg's primary sources were Schuyler Long's dictionary (1918), already mentioned, and the films made by the National Association of the Deaf in 1913. She compared these early ASL forms to what she calls (M)odern ASL – lexical entries found in Stokoe et al. (1965), *A Dictionary of American Sign Language on Linguistic Principles (DASL)*. Currently, in 2018, we must consider *DASL* a historical source as well, since there has been as much time between the publication of Long (1917) and Stokoe et al. (1965) as between *DASL* and today, approximately fifty years. Her general findings will be summarized below and can also be found in Frishberg (1975) and Klima and Bellugi (1979).

One clear tendency that was noted by Frishberg is that lexical information becomes more focused on the hands over time, while body movements, facial expressions, and environmental contacts tend to be reduced. In O-FSL, COMPARE was produced with the head turning from side to side to gaze at imaginary objects in the two hands, which were held up in front of the signer. In M-ASL, the movements of the hands rocked from side to side, and the head was stationary (Figure 8.8). In O-FSL the sign CONSIDER had a head movement to indicate consideration, while in M-ASL the movement had been displaced to a circular movement of the handshape of the sign.

The location of signs can also be displaced in regular ways in the signing space. Frishberg referred to the "line of bilateral symmetry" (Klima & Bellugi, 1979:73), which has also informed what Brentari (1998) calls the "fundamental signing position," where the hands are bent at the elbows and palms are facing each other, based on the

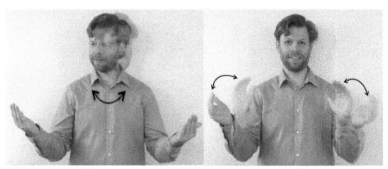

O-FSL COMPARE
(movement of head)

ASL 1965 COMPARE
(movement of the hands)

Figure 8.8 Phonological changes from Old French Sign Language (O-FSL) to Modern ASL (ca. 1965) showing a move towards concentration of lexical information on the hands in the sign COMPARE

definition by Luttgens et al. (1992). Signs tend to move toward this midline. Examples of this displacement, as seen in Figure 8.9, are SWEETHEART and HELP.

The third tendency is that handshapes, movements, and locations of two-handed signs become more symmetrical. Recall from Chapter 1 the four types of signs:

(2)   *The four types of signs (cf. Battison, 1978)*
- Type 0: one-handed forms (e.g., BSL NAME and AFTERNOON in Figure 1.4),
- Type 1: two-handed forms where the handshapes and movements are the same or mirror images on the two hands (e.g., BSL BROTHER and PAPER in Figure 1.4),
- Type 2: two-handed forms where the handshapes are the same on both hands, and one hand (the dominant hand) moves while the other (the non-dominant hand) is stable (e.g., BSL UNSURE in Figure 1.4), and
- Type 3: two-handed forms where the handshapes are different on both hands, and one hand moves while the other is stable (e.g., BSL GAY in Figure 1.4).

If the two hands have different moving handshapes in a sign, one handshape will assimilate to the other and the movements will become more alike. Frishberg observed that handshapes and movements in two-handed signs tend to become alike over time – i.e., they tend to become more symmetrical. The historical changes for the sign

ASL 1918 HELP
contact at the elbow

ASL 1965 HELP
contact at the ulnar side of
the hand (i.e., at the midline)

ASL 1918 SWEETHEART
POA at the heart

ASL 1965 SWEETHEART
POA at the midline

Figure 8.9 Phonological changes from Old French Sign Language (O-FSL) to Modern ASL (ca. 1965) showing displacement of lexical information toward the midline in the ASL sign HELP (top) and SWEETHEART (bottom)

WHISKEY demonstrate this (Figure 8.10). First, in the 1918 version, the nondominant hand is a stationary fist (Type 3; Figure 8.10, left). Next, the nondominant hand assimilates to the dominant one – a Type 2 form, where the handshape is the same on both hands, but one hand does not move (Figure 8.10, center). Finally, the movement becomes more symmetrical: the nondominant hand moves like the dominant hand. In contemporary ASL, the handshapes and movements are the same on both hands (Type 1, Figure 8.10, right). We can understand what is occurring via the process of assimilation. First partial assimilation takes place (handshape alone), then total assimilation (handshape and movement).

ASL 1918 WHISKEY   ASL 1965 two variants of WHISKEY

Figure 8.10   A Type 3, Type 2, and Type 1 two-handed version of the ASL
sign WHISKEY: (left) Type 3 form with no assimilation; (center) Type 2
form with assimilation of handshape; (right) Type 1 version with
assimilation of both handshape and movement. (Reprinted from
A Prosodic Model of Sign Language Phonology, by Brentari, D., Copyright
(1998), with permission from MIT.)

A fourth tendency in phonological change is for multi-part signs
to undergo handshape assimilation. Frishberg refers to this as
fluidity of signs, whereby compounds tend to become simple and
unitary, losing either the first or second element. I repeat
a compound from Chapter 1 here. The compound THINK^SELF,
meaning "decide for oneself" (Figure 8.11), is composed of two
stems – THINK and SELF – but instead of the full forms, each
with independent movements, the compound consists of just
one syllable (a single movement). The handshape assimilation
here is regressive (the thumb of SELF assimilates regressively),
and the two sign movements are reduced to one. The motivation
for this is given in Chapters 1 and 2.

This type of change is also seen elsewhere in the lexicon, in
nativized forms from fingerspelling, such as the sign NO, where
-N- and -O- were fingerspelled handshapes with different selected
fingers -N- 👌 and -O- 👌 produced in a sequence, which has become
a fluid change from an open to closed variant of a two-fingered
handshape. When a pronoun is cliticized to a verb this happens as
well (see Figure 8.2). Both of these diachronic changes move
toward simplification. They obey the SELECTED FINGER CON-
STRAINT (SFC), discussed in Chapter 1, and follow the preference

Figure 8.11   (Repeated from Figure 1.1.) The two ASL stems THINK (left) and SELF (center) which form the compound THINK^SELF or *decide for oneself* (right). The compound (right) has two morphemes but just one syllable, just one movement. (Reprinted from *A Prosodic Model of Sign Language Phonology,* by Brentari, D., Copyright (1998), with permission from MIT.)

for P-words to be monovalent and monosyllabic, as described in Chapter 4.

Lastly, Frishberg reported that there is a tendency for lexical signs to change toward more arbitrary forms and away from iconic or mimetic origins. Frishberg observes that, in a number of cases she has described, iconicity is sacrificed for economy of form or increased perceptual ease. While this is certainly the case, please see Chapter 3 on iconicity and Chapter 5 on language emergence for a perspective on iconicity that allows it to continue to flourish in the language and to cooperate with phonology, rather than be in competition with it.

Frishberg's observations and generalizations were inspirational. She did not have the terminology made available 15–20 years later, but the kind of evidence that she brought to light strengthens many of the arguments about sign language phonology. I cannot overstate the originality and importance of Frishberg's work.

8.3.2   Further Developments in ASL Historical Studies

In the last ten years, Ted Supalla has worked tirelessly to make available to the public the film sources to which Frishberg had access, and to add many others between 1920 and 1960. Supalla and Clarke (2015) describe a multifaceted effort to re-format the videos and to spread the word within the deaf community to look for old family films that would help in ASL historical reconstruction. Supalla and Clarke call this "ASL archeology," because it involves not only using the sources

Figure 8.12 Three historical variants of the ASL sign WHO: (left) circling the whole face from 1918; (center) the index finger circling the mouth with the thumb extended; (right) a common contemporary form with repeating small bending movements of the index finger. (The contemporary image is used with the permission of Ted Supalla. Video clips of the 1918 images are in the public domain, and are available via the Historical Sign Language Database (HSLDB) at http://hsldb .georgetown.edu/films/tablefilm.php?source=hotchkiss&glossid=10 and http://hsldb.georgetown.edu/films/tablefilm.php? source=cloud&glossid=82.)

but also working with families to find them in the first place, working with the delicate old film stock, cataloguing them, and making them available. These scholars also emphasize that these resources are a part of the deaf community's legacy, and they require careful curatorial stewardship on the part of those interested in these materials. During this process, Supalla and colleagues have also published video articles that are extremely helpful in bringing these sources to life by describing the small historical changes and interspersing the relevant historical film clips, allowing viewers on the *Deaf Studies Digital Journal* to understand how these dynamic changes occurred.[2] Here I elaborate on just one of the examples described in this detailed work, the ASL sign WHO, also mentioned in Rimor et al. (1984).

Michaels (1923) describes WHO in the following way: "1. Pass the index finger around the face. 2. Look left and right a little." I now turn your attention to the following variants of WHO shown in Figure 8.12. In the NAD films of that period, there is a whole-face WHO using the index finger (also the first part of the modern sign LOOK-LIKE; Figure 8.12, left), and one with the index finger circling the mouth with the thumb extended (Figure 8.12, center). A common contemporary form is

---

[2] http://dsdj.gallaudet.edu/

Figure 8.13   Historically related ASL signs (left) WHICH, WITH, and
BOSS/CHIEF, which is also used as the "comparative" morpheme –ER in
O-FSL and in ASL. (WITH reprinted from *A Prosodic Model of Sign Language
Phonology*, by Brentari, D., Copyright (1998), with permission from MIT.
WHICH and BOSS/CHIEF printed with permission from Valli, C. (2006).
The Gallaudet Dictionary of American Sign Language. Gallaudet University
Press.)

shown in Figure 8.12, right. If we consider ease of articulation as
a motivation for historical change, Supalla has reconstructed the path
of these earlier signs for WHO to the contemporary form. From Figure
8.12 (left) to Figure 8.12 (center) there are two notable differences: the
movement is reduced and the thumb is extended. Between Figure 8.12
(center) and Figure 8.12 (right), three more changes have occurred: (i)
orientation changes from palm-toward-the-face to palm-toward-the-
midline, (ii) the extended thumb makes contact with the chin, when
previously it did not, and (iii) the movement reduces further to a trilled
bending of the index finger, either at the MCP joint (knuckle) or at the
PIP joint (distal joint).

Supalla (2010) also traces the grammaticalization of the modern ASL
comparative morphemes for -ER and -EST from early LSF and ASL
sources. Based on Stokoe (1965) we know that the sign was functioning as a bound morpheme during this time period. This form was
grammaticalized from various lexical items that were present in
O-FSL (Pélissier, 1856) meaning WITH or OR, and even two-sign constructions meaning WHICH and MORE THAN. Three related forms in
ASL are shown in Figure 8.13.

The historical examples described above all show phonological
tendencies that can be explained in terms of ease of articulation or
ease of perception; however, at least some of these diachronic changes
might be a bit more opaque than those seen in synchronic variation.
Supalla's description of WHO, for example, and of the relationships

between boss and –ER require careful analysis. Nonetheless, they follow the historical trends outlined in Hopper and Trauggott (1993) for spoken languages, as well as those seen in other items that have undergone grammaticalization in sign languages, such as agentive ER – from the lexical item for PERSON in ASL (WRIT-ER, TEACH-ER, REPAIR-ER; see Aronoff et al., 2005).

Other historical changes are similar to those seen in synchronic variation. Displacement of POA is a broad set of changes that include POA lowering (Figure 8.4) and centralization to the midline (Figure 8.9). Simplification of handshape and movement via assimilation (Figures 8.10 and 8.11) are also seen in both diachronic and synchronic variation.

8.4 COMBINING SYNCHRONIC AND DIACHRONIC SOURCES

We now turn to research that employs alternative ways to study possible historical change in progress by employing experimental work on gestural transmission and cross-sectional sampling of various age groups. The processes we have been discussing involve principles of ease of articulation and ease of perception, as well as the loss of iconicity. Van der Kooij (2002) has also suggested that some historical changes reference the phonological system as well. She observed that by reducing the number of POAs, which may have originally referenced iconic places on the body, to centralized POAs (such as SWEETHEART in Figure 8.9), the phonological system is exerting feature economy. (We discussed this also in Chapter 5 on the emergence of phonology.)[3]

Rimor et al. (1984) were the first to address this question experimentally in ASL. These experiments involved techniques of serial transmission and a speeded discourse. Five target signs were used: OLD, WHO, COMPARE, BLIND, and HELP. In the first experiment, a sign/mimed story was videotaped by a model and subsequently transmitted and videotaped across three iterations. The set of five signs just mentioned was compared across multiple productions using citation forms as a baseline, and this was compared with more reduced forms. The speeded discourse experiment involved having signer and non-signer groups reproduce the model's story at two speeds faster than normal – twice as fast and as fast as possible. The results of the two experiments strongly suggest that synchronic

---

[3] See the debate between Moreton (2008) and Yu (2011) as it pertains to spoken languages.

variation and diachronic change stem from the same natural phonetic processes that favor ease of articulation and ease of perception. The changes found in discourse produced at faster speeds were found to be similar to historical change: reductions occurred in both signs and nonlinguistic pantomime, for both signers and non-signers, implicating the work of natural phonetic processes. For example, changes in signs included two- to one-handed forms for BLIND and reduction in the movement for WHO.

Another type of experiment to address changes over time in sign language form has been carried out by Motamedi et al. (2017). They employed an artificial language experiment to try to determine how strategies for expressing grammatical arguments are used across five "generations" of participants in a laboratory setting – particularly agent and patient arguments. The participants were hearing people without sign experience who were asked to use silent gesture. Three main strategies were identified for expressing agents and patients: *lexical*, assigning a particular label to the agent and patient; *body*, using shifts of the body to indicate the agent and patient; and *indexing*, using locations in signing space to track the agent and patient. Pairs of interlocutors in generations 1 and 5 favored the lexical strategy. Pairs in generations 2 and 4 tended to use a body strategy, where agent and verb are simultaneously inferred through the participant's use of their own body. Pairs in generation 3 favored the indexing strategy. This work has focused primarily on strategies to convey meaning (morphological or morpho-syntactic), rather than on phonology, but such experimental work, like Rimor et al. (1984), suggests that gesturing participants make use of similar representational resources to those used in natural sign languages (Meir et al., 2007; Padden et al., 2010). In future work artificial language experiments could also address phonological transmission.

Another research approach used to understand phonological change is cross-sectional sampling of various age groups using the apparent time hypothesis. This approach was used in LIS. Elena Radutzky spent years compiling a LIS dictionary, and then studied LIS through the same historical lens as Frishberg, attending to qualitative difference in vocabulary signed by older and younger signers, which was the basis for her dissertation (Radutzky, 1989). LIS and ASL have occurred within very different social and cultural contexts within the last one hundred years, differences that might lead one to expect more variation in LIS than in ASL. Fontana et al. (2017) and Geraci et al. (2011) outline some important differences between the social and cultural contexts for ASL and LIS. As Geraci states (2011: 529),

LIS is not formally recognized by the government, and this lack of formal recognition has consequences in the educational system. Deaf children are now generally mainstreamed, and there is no guarantee that LIS will be used in their education. Interpreting, not to mention bilingual/bimodal education, is still the exception rather than the rule. In general, LIS is rarely used in institutional settings and is mostly used in private exchanges and informal gatherings.

ASL, in contrast, is used in formal settings, and in primary and secondary residential school settings, at Gallaudet University, as well as in "hearing" universities, as more signing deaf students avail themselves of interpreters at the undergraduate and graduate levels.

We will review the findings of Radutzky (1989) and a more recent study of LIS variation (Geraci et al., 2011) here. In large part, both of these projects found that differences between older and younger signers were similar to those found in historical change in ASL, but there were a few exceptions. Recall that synchronically collected, cross-generational studies are not the same as using sources from different historical periods, since the older signers may simply have changed their signing style across their lifespan.

Radutzky made a number of observations similar to those of Frishberg. First, there was loss of face and body movements in forms produced by younger signers. The LIS signs for SLEEP, SHOWER, and SONG all used to contain body movements and have since lost them. Regarding movement in two-handed signs, even signs with different handshapes on both hands tended to have movements that reproduce or mirror one another. There are different handshapes on the two hands of both the ASL FULL and the LIS sign BOTTLE, but in older signers the nondominant hand remains static, while in younger signers the two hands move in a symmetrical fashion, either across the midline (ASL FULL) or away from the horizontal plane between the two hands (LIS BOTTLE; see Figure 8.14).

Movements generally also tend to be concentrated on the hands and the fingers in the signs produced by younger signers, just as was found in Frishberg (1975), with movements of the whole arm becoming movements of the wrist or fingers. This type of movement change would be called "distalization" in the Prosodic Model (Brentari, 1998). Finally, Radutzky found a tendency toward monosyllabicity by the younger signers, just as Frishberg did for ASL historically, and in the general lexicon of ASL as a whole as was discussed earlier in several chapters of this book.

With regard to POA, Radutzky found, as did Frishberg (1975), that signs become more centralized over time, and with this centralization comes finer distinctions in handshape.

ASL FULL(1)   ASL FULL(2)   LIS BOTTLE(1)   LIS BOTTLE(2)
stable H2   symmetrical movement   stable H2   symmetrical movement

Figure 8.14   The ASL sign FULL and Italian Sign Language sign BOTTLE. Both signs have undergone change, whereby the two hands move in a symmetrical fashion across the midline in ASL FULL (left) or away from each other in LIS BOTTLE (right). (The ASL images are printed with permission from Valli, C. (2006). *The Gallaudet Dictionary of American Sign Language*. Gallaudet University Press, and the LIS images are printed with permission from *Dizionario bilingue elementare della Lingua dei Segni Italiana*, Edizioni **LIS**ME.DI.A.)

LIS older form BIRTHDAY   LIS younger form BIRTHDAY

Figure 8.15   Form of BIRTHDAY used by (left) older and (right) younger signers of LIS. (LIS images are printed with permission from *Dizionario bilingue elementare della Lingua dei Segni Italiana*, Edizioni **LIS**ME.DI.A.)

Radutzky and Frishberg note the loss of grasp and other types of precise contact, which they treat as a property of "fluidity." Both find that signs produced with a grasp or a very precise place of articulation in older signers are often produced without the grasp or with a brushing contact in younger signers. Examples include LIS BIRTHDAY (Figure 8.15) where there is loss of grasping the ear, or change in contact as in ASL WRISTWATCH.

LIS older form SIGN LANGUAGE   LIS younger form SIGN LANGUAGE

Figure 8.16   Form of SIGN LANGUAGE used by (left) older and (right) younger signers of LIS showing a change to a relatively more marked handshape. (LIS images are printed with permission from *Dizionario bilingue elementare della Lingua dei Segni Italiana,* Edizioni **LIS**ME.DI.A.)

Finally, regarding handshape, Radutzky found, as did Frishberg (1975), that handshapes become finer (more marked) in the high-acuity signing space. Radutzky reported a general refinement of hand-shape, where signs produced by older signers with a full B-hand are now produced with a more marked handshape (e.g., SIGN LANGUAGE; Figure 8.16). As Radutzky notes, in modern LIS the three-handshape is quite common.

Radutzky also noted that both she (for LIS) and Frishberg (for ASL) confirmed Siple's prediction diachronically in the lexicon of LIS: signs on the face tend to become one-handed, while off the face they tend to become two-handed. We have already discussed this finding for BSL as well, in Chapter 2; Fenlon et al. (2014b) found that 81.7 percent (517/633) of BSL signs produced at the head and neck are one-handed compared to 59.9 percent (169/282) produced at the trunk and arm.

Geraci and colleagues sought to replicate Radutzsky's findings in a systematic way so as to be able to distinguish variables that might be responsible for specific types of variation. They did so by having the same type of strict data collection principles as the large sociolinguistics projects in the United States, Australia, and in the United Kingdom, sampling from 165 signers across 10 Italian cities from 3 age groups, balanced for gender. The phono-logical behaviors that were analyzed in Geraci et al. (2011) are shown in (3).

(3)   *Patterns of phonological change reported in Geraci et al. (2011; illus-*
      trations of the signs also found there)

- loss of [contact]: e.g., [+contact] "older" to [–contact] "younger" (e.g., BIRTHDAY)
- POA toward [neutral space]: e.g., [–neutral space] "older" to [+neutral space] "younger" (e.g., UNDERSTOOD; the POA has moved from the forehead area to neutral space)
- handshape assimilation: (a) the nondominant hand of two-handed signs assimilates to the handshape of the dominant hand (e.g., WEEK: H2 ⟨⟩ +H1 ⟨⟩ becomes H2 ⟨⟩ +H1 ⟨⟩); and (b) in compounds, the handshape of one stem partially or totally assimilates to the handshape of the other stem (e.g., INTELLIGENT: 1st handshape ⟨⟩ +2nd handshape ⟨⟩ becomes 1st handshape ⟨⟩ or ⟨⟩ +2nd handshape ⟨⟩)

The middle and older groups of signers were combined in the analysis as the "older" group, and for the factors studied, age was indeed a main predictor for the use of the forms with the changes as indicated in (3). The older and younger forms of signs were almost equally split in the older group of signers (49%/51% younger), while the younger forms of sign were more prevalent in younger signers (33%/66% younger forms). Males slightly favored the older forms, while females slightly favored the younger forms.

8.5 CONCLUSIONS

These variation studies confirm, to a large extent, what we know about variation in spoken languages and what has been described about sign language phonological structure; namely, the effects of the "channel" are very powerful – those facilitated by the associated phonetic systems. These phonetic pressures explain many of the examples we have seen here where change has occurred, and we find that in signed as in spoken languages the effects of age and historical change behave in this way; however, some changes push back against "channel" forces. For example, deaf Black ASL and Mainstream signers of the same age have been signing everyday for the same amount of time, yet Black ASL has resisted the tendencies that favor ease of articulation in several ways that take more effort, such as maintaining larger signing space, two-handed signs remaining two-handed, and signs articulated using the citation form's POA higher in the signing space rather than the lowered form. Moreover, the work on ASL and BSL variation concurs that grammatical category is an important predictor of variation in sign languages at this stage in the historical development of these languages. It is also clear that variation and change are grounded in the phonology as van der Kooij has suggested, as the system becomes more economical in its use of features over time.

8.6 FURTHER READING

Frishberg, N. (1975). Arbitrariness and iconicity: Historical change in American Sign Language. *Language*, 51, 696–719.

Geraci, C., Battaglia, K., Cardinaletti, A., Cecchetto, C., Donati, C., Giudice, S., & Mereghetti, E. (2011). The LIS corpus project: A discussion of sociolinguistic variation in the lexicon. *Sign Language Studies*, 11, 528–74.

Lucas, C., Bayley, R. & Valli, C. (2001). *Sociolinguistic Variation in American Sign Language: Sociolinguistics in Deaf Communities*, Vol. VII. Washington, DC: Gallaudet University Press.

Schembri, A., Fenlon, J., Cormier, K., & Johnston, T. (2018). Sociolinguistic typology and sign languages. *Frontiers in Psychology*, 9, 200.

Supalla, T., & Clarke, P. (2015). *Sign Language Archeology*. Washington, DC: Gallaudet University Press.

8.7 FURTHER CORPUS INFORMATION

British Sign Language, BSL: www.bslcorpusproject.org/

Australian Sign Language, Auslan: www.auslan.org.au/about/corpus/

New Zealand Sign Language, NZSL: 138 signers; 50 hours of conversation

Sign Language of the Netherlands, NGT: www.ru.nl/corpusngt/

German Sign Language, DGS: www.sign-lang.uni-hamburg.de/dgs-korpus/index.php/dgs-korpus.html

Swedish Sign Language: www.ling.su.se/english/research/research-projects/sign-language/swedish-sign-language-corpus-project-1.59270

ASL:

- Lucas, C., Bayley, R. & Valli, C. (2001). *Sociolinguistic Variation in American Sign Language: Sociolinguistics in Deaf Communities*, Vol. VII. Washington, DC: Gallaudet University Press.
- the Boston University Corpus http://asl-lex.org/; www.bu.edu/asllrp/ncslgr-for-download/download-info.html

- Black ASL corpus: http://blackaslproject.gallaudet.edu
  /BlackASLProject/Welcome.html
- the sign and gesture archive, SAGA, not yet publicly available:
  https://digitalhumanities.uchicago.edu/projects/SAGA
- Asian Sign Bank (several sign languages in Asia): http://cslds.org
  /asiansignbank/
- LIS corpus: not yet publicly available (see Geraci et al., 2011)

Glossary

amodal properties of language: properties of language that are exhibited in both signed and spoken languages

auditory cortex: An area in the temporal lobe of the brain typically used to process pitch and volume of sound (see also Heschl's gyrus), particularly as it is used in speech

autosegmental phonology: a nonlinear model of phonological representation created by John Goldsmith in 1976

bimodal bilingual: a person who uses two languages, one of which is a spoken language and one of which is a signed language

categorical perception: the ability to perceive distinct categories from a series of equally spaced stimuli (acoustic or visual), accompanied by a peak of discrimination in the same place as the break between categories

citation form: the form of a sign listed in a dictionary or the form produced when asked, "What is the sign for 'x'?"

code blends: a linguistic structure containing portions that come from two different languages and that are expressed at the same time

CODA: literally "child of deaf adult"; a hearing child of deaf parents

communication modality: the signal, articulatory, and perceptual systems used in language, and their potential effects on phonological form. It may be auditory, visual, or tactile

community sign language: an emerging language that originates from a situation in which many deaf people are brought together, such as at a school for the deaf

core lexicon: in a sign language, the component of the lexicon that includes signs that are found in a dictionary and are considered to be native

correspondence: (i) the relationship between phonological and morphological units; (ii) the tendency for languages to prefer that phonological forms have a single meaning

critical period: also sometimes called the "sensitive" period(s) during which it is easier to acquire language structures; most often in childhood and early adolescence

cross-modal activation: during a lexical decision task, when a signed word (visual) activates a spoken word (acoustic) or the reverse

Dependency model of sign language phonology: the model of sign language phonology developed by Harry van der Hulst in the 1990s

diachronic variation: variation seen within the same group at different historical periods

Dispersion theory: a sub-field of Optimality Theory that is concerned with how the features of a phonological system come to be organized as a whole around principles such as symmetry and alignment

distalization: a change in a sign's citation form's movement to a joint that is further away from the center of the body

early learner: a language learner who acquires a particular language before entering school

entrainment: the association between the periodic cycles of neural activity and the periodic cycles of the speech stream or sign stream. Neural entrainment occurs when low-frequency oscillations (< 8 Hz) in the cerebral cortex become temporally aligned to quasi-rhythmic fluctuations in speech volume or sign volume

event-related potential (ERP): a measured electrical response measured in micro-volts on the scalp that is the direct result of a specific sensory, cognitive, or motor event

feature: the smallest phonological unit; the primitive of a phonological system. This definition remains neutral as to whether a feature is distinctive (has a minimal pair associated with it), active (is used in rule), or prominent (is morphological)

foreign lexicon: the component of a sign language lexicon that includes non-native vocabulary items that have been borrowed from another language

goodness of fit: a study where participants choose the best form for a given meaning

Hand Tier model of sign language phonology: the model of sign language phonology developed by Wendy Sandler in the late 1980s

Heschl's gyrus: a convolution of the temporal lobe that is the cortical center for hearing and runs obliquely outward and forward from the posterior part of the lateral sulcus

Hold-Movement model of sign language phonology: the model of sign language phonology developed by Robert Johnson and Scott Liddell during the 1980s

homesign: a system of visual communication developed by a deaf individual who has not been exposed to regular input in a signed, written, or spoken language

hybrid forms (gesture-language): a signed form that includes some material that is clearly categorical and linguistic and some that is analogue and gestural

iconic enhancement: a property of a sign that increases the form's resemblance to its real-world referent along at least one dimension

iconicity: a set of strategies for mapping reference (signified) and form (signifier) in a non-arbitrary way. It is also the adjectival form of "icon," which is one of three types of semiotic sign (icon, index, symbol) that involves direct or indirect mapping of the world onto a particular structure, linguistic or otherwise

intonational phrase (I-phrase): the prosodic unit most closely aligned with the morpho-syntactic clause

inferior frontal sulcus (IFS): One of the areas of the brain implicated in sign language phonology, which is more activated by pseudo-signs than attested signs

KODA: a CODA who is still a child (cf. "kid"; see also CODA)

language ecology: a set of social or demographic characteristics that comprise a particular group or subgroup of a linguistic community, such as proportion of deaf members, age of the community, urban, literate, live in extended families, etc.

language emergence: the trajectory a sign language follows in historical time as it moves from a gesture system through homesign and eventually to a sign language

language medium: the peripheral systems used in a language: visual-gesture or auditory-vocal (see also communication modality)

language variation: a core concept of sociolinguistics and historical linguistics that addresses why features of language vary across time, context, and language user

late learner: a language learner who acquires language after the sensitive (critical) period

mora: an abstract unit of subsyllabic weight. In sign languages, each component of a movement (of the hand, wrist or arm) adds a mora

motherese: a manner of talking to children characterized by enhanced prosodic and phonological features, and in sign language, also enhanced iconicity

movement migration: when a sign's movement is produced in a different place than the citation form's – either closer to (proximalization) or farther away from (distalization) the center of the body

native signer: deaf and hearing children who have deaf signing parents or family members

one-handed sign: a sign produced by one hand, typically the dominant hand of the signer

parameter: one of five classes of features of a sign: handshape, movement, place of articulation, orientation, and non-manual features

phonological contrast: a key concept in phonology based on the opposition found in the system. Contrasts can be distinctive (based on a minimal pair), active (used in a phonological rule), or prominent (used in the morphological system)

phonological phrase (P-phrase): a prosodic unit that is larger than a phonological word and smaller than an intonational phrase

priming study: an experimental design used to study lexical access: first a pre-stimulus that is controlled for a target property is presented and then the stimulus is shown. The differences in reaction response times or size of the response can determine which features inhibit and which features enhance lexical access.

Prosodic model of sign language phonology: the model of sign language phonology developed by the author of this book in the 1990s

prosodic word (P-word; sometimes called phonological word): a prosodic unit that is larger than a syllable and foot and smaller than a phonological phrase

proximalization: a type of movement migration in which a signed movement of a citation form migrates proximally; that is, it moves to a joint that is closer to the center of the body

recall: an experimental design in which participants are presented with stimuli and then, after a delay, are asked to remember as many of the stimuli as possible

segment: an abstract phonological unit of time. The definition of a segment has changed over time to mean its properties as timing units. Currently, a sign language segment is an abstract unit of time, just as it is in spoken languages.

sonority: salience in the visual or acoustic signal upon which a signed or speech stream constructs syllables. In sign languages larger and more complex movements are more sonorous than smaller, simpler movements.

spatial lexicon: one of the three main components of a sign language lexicon, which uses space in an iconic fashion. The spatial lexicon includes spatial verbs and classifier predicates.

Superior temporal gyrus or sulcus (STG or STS): areas in the temporal lobe of the brain implicated in phonology (signed or spoken).

syllable: one of the most basic prosodic units in phonology, based on a nucleus and margins. In sign languages syllables are based on number of sequential movements in a sign – one movement equals one syllable.

synchronic variation: phonological differences within the same group at different historical periods

timing unit: synonym of the term "segment"

triadic comparison: an experimental design in which participants are asked to look at three items and choose the one that is least like the other two

two-handed sign: a sign produced by both hands

useful field of vision (UFOV): the visual area over which information can be extracted at a brief glance without eye or head movements

village sign language: an emerging language that originates in a situation where there is a high incidence of genetic deafness, and which results in a community with an atypically high proportion of deaf members (4 percent or more)

References

Abner, N., Flaherty, M., Stangl, K., Coppola, M., Brentari, D., & Goldin-Meadow, S. (2019). The noun-verb distinction in established and emergent sign systems. *Language, 95* (2), 230–267.

Abu-Zhaya, R., Seidl, A., & Cristia, A. (2017). Multimodal infant-directed communication: How caregivers combine tactile and linguistic cues. *Journal of Child Language, 44*, 1088–1116.

Allen, J. S. & Miller, J. L. (2001). Contextual influences on the internal structure of phonetic categories: A distinction between lexical status and speaking rate. *Perception & Psychophysics, 63* (5), 798–810.

Allen, T. (1986). A study of the achievement patterns of hearing-impaired students: 1974–1983. In A. N. Schildroth & M. A. Karchmer (eds.), *Deaf Children in America* (pp. 161–206). San Diego, CA: College-Hill.

Andrews, S. (1992). Frequency and neighborhood effects on lexical access: Lexical similarity or orthographic redundancy? *Journal of Experimental Psychology, 15* (5), 802–814.

Ann, J. (1993). A linguistic investigation of the relationship between physiology and handshape. Doctoral dissertation, University of Arizona, Tucson, AZ.

Ann, J. (2006). *Frequency of Occurrence and Ease of Articulation of Sign Language Hand Shapes: The Taiwanese Example*. Washington, DC: Gallaudet University Press.

Anderson, D. & Reilly, J. (2002). The MacArthur communicative development inventory: Normative data for American Sign Language. *Journal of Deaf Studies and Deaf Education, 7* (2), 83–106.

Aparicio, M., Gounot, D., Demont, E., & Metz-Lutz, M. N. (2007). Phonological processing in relation to reading: An fMRI study in deaf readers. *Neuroimage, 35*, 1303–1316.

Aramburo, A. (1989). Sociolinguistic aspects of the black deaf community. In C. Lucas (ed.), *The Sociolinguistics of the Deaf Community* (pp. 103–119). San Diego, CA: Academic Press.

Aristodemo, V. (2013). The complexity of handshapes: Perceptual and theoretical perspective. Masters thesis, Università Ca'Foscari Venezia, Venice.

Aronoff, M., Meir, I., Padden, C., & Sandler, W. (2003). Classifier complexes and morphology in two sign languages. In K. Emmorey (ed.), *Perspectives* on *Classifiers in Signed Languages* (pp. 53–84). Mahwah, NJ: Lawrence Erlbaum Associates.

Aronoff, M., Meir, I., & Sandler, W. (2005). The paradox of sign language morphology. *Language*, *81*, 301–344.

Aslin, R. N. & Pisoni, D. B. (1980). Effects of early linguistic experience on speech discrimination by infants: A critique of Eilers, Gavin and Wilson (1979). *Child Development*, *51*(1), 107–112.

Aslin, R. N., Saffran, J. R., & Newport, E. L. (1998). Computation of conditional probability statistics by 8-month-old infants. *Psychological Science*, *9*, 321–324.

Bailey, G. (2002). Real and apparent time. In J. K. Chambers, P. Trudgill, & N. Schilling-Estes (eds.), *The Handbook of Language Variation and Change* (pp. 312–322). Oxford: Blackwell.

Baker, A. E. & Woll, B. (eds.) (2009). *Sign Language Acquisition*. Amsterdam: John Benjamins.

Baker, C. & Padden, C. (1978). Focusing on the non-manual components of American Sign Language. In P. Siple (ed.), *Understanding Language through Sign Language Research* (pp. 27–57). New York, NY: Academic Press.

Baker, S. A., Idsardi, W. J., Golinkoff, R. M., & Petitto, L. A. (2005). The perception of handshapes in American Sign Language. *Memory & Cognition*, *33*, 887–904.

Baker, S. A., Golinkoff, R. M., & Petitto, L. A. (2006). New insights into old puzzles from infants' categorical discrimination of soundless phonetic units. *Language Learning and Development*, *2*, 147–162.

Baker-Shenk, C. (1983). A micro-analysis of the nonmanual components of questions in American Sign Language. PhD thesis, University of California, Berkeley, CA.

Barakat, R. (1975). Cistercian sign language: A study in non-verbal communication. *Cistercian Studies Series*, 11. Kalamazoo, Michigan: Cistercian Publications.

Barberà Altimira, G. (2012). The meaning of space in Catalan Sign Language (LSC): Reference, specificity and structure in signed discourse. PhD dissertation, Universitat Pompeu Fabra, Barcelona, Spain.

Bartels, C. (1999). *The Intonation of English Statements and Questions: A Compositional Interpretation*. New York, NY: Garland.

Battison, R. (1974). Phonological deletion in American Sign Language. *Sign Language Studies*, *5*, 5–19.

Battison, R. (1978). *Lexical Borrowing in American Sign Language*. Silver Spring, MD: Linstok Press. Reprinted. 2003, Burtonsville, MD: Sign Media, Inc.

Baus, C., Carreiras, M., & Emmorey, K. (2013). When does iconicity in sign language matter? *Language and Cognitive Processes*, *28*, 261–271.

Bavelier, D., Brozinsky, C., Tomann, A., Mitchell, T., Neville, H., & Liu, G. (2001). Impact of early deafness and early exposure to sign language on the cerebral organization for motion processing. *Journal of Neuroscience*, *21*, 8931–8942.

Bayley, R., Lucas, C., & Rose, M. (2000). Variation in American Sign Language: The case of DEAF. *Journal of Sociolinguistics*, 4, 81–107.

Bayley, R., Lucas, C., & Rose, M. (2002). Phonological variation in American Sign Language: The case of 1 handshape. *Language Variation and Change*, 14, 19–53.

Beckman, M. E. & Venditti, J. J. (2011). Intonation. In J. Goldsmith, J. Riggle, & A. Yu (eds.), *Handbook of Phonological Theory* (2nd ed., pp. 485–532). Oxford: Wiley/Blackwell.

Bélanger, N. N., Baum, S. R., & Mayberry, R. I. (2012). Reading difficulties in adult deaf readers of French: Phonological codes, not guilty! *Scientific Studies of Reading*, 16, 263–285.

Benedicto, E. & Brentari, D. (2004). Where did all the arguments go? Argument-changing properties of classifiers in ASL. *Natural Language and Linguistic Theory*, 22, 743–810.

Berent, I. (2013). *The Phonological Mind*. Cambridge: Cambridge University Press.

Berent, I., Bat-El, O., Brentari, D., Dupuis, A., & Vaknin-Nusbaum, V. (2016). The double identity of linguistic doubling. *Proceedings of the National Academy of Sciences*, 113, 13702–13707.

Berent, I., Bat-El, O., & Vaknin-Nusbaum, V. (2017). The double identity of doubling: Evidence for the phonology/morphology split. *Cognition*, 161, 117–128.

Berent, I., Dupuis, A., & Brentari, D. (2013). Amodal aspects of linguistic design: Evidence from sign language. *PLOS ONE*, 8, 1–17.

Berent, I., Dupuis, A., & Brentari, D. (2014). Phonological reduplication in sign language: Rules rule. *Frontiers in Psychology*, 5, 560.

Berent, I., Lennertz, T., Jun, J., Moreno, M. A., & Smolensky, P. (2008). Language universals in human brains. *Proceedings of the National Academy of Sciences*, 105, 5321–5325.

Berent, I., Marcus, G. F., Shimron, J., & Gafos, A. I. (2002). The scope of linguistic generalizations: Evidence from Hebrew word formation. *Cognition*, 83, 113–139.

Berent, I., Steriade, D., Lennertz, T., & Vaknin, V. (2007). What we know about what we have never heard: Evidence from perceptual illusions. *Cognition*, 104, 591–630.

Best, C. T., Mathur, G., Miranda, K. A., & Lillo-Martin, D. (2010). Effects of sign language experience on categorical perception of dynamic ASL pseudosigns. *Attention, Perception, & Psychophysics*, 72, 747–762.

Bialystok, E., Craik, F. I. M., Green, D. W., & Gollan, T. H. (2009). Bilingual minds. *Psychological Science in the Public Interest*, 10, 89–129.

Birdsong, D. & Molis, M. (2001). On the evidence for maturational constraints in second-language acquisition. *Journal of Memory and Language*, 44, 235–249.

Bishop, M. (2010). Happen can't hear: An analysis of code-blends in hearing, native signers of American Sign Language. *Sign Language Studies*, 11, 205–240.

Blevins, J. (1993). The nature of constraints on the nondominant hand in ASL. In G. Coulter (ed.), *Phonetics and Phonology Vol. 3* (pp. 43–62). New York, NY: Academic Press.

Bloomfield, L. (1933). *Language*. New York, NY: Henry Holt and Co.

Bochner, J. H., Christie, K., Hauser, P. C., & Searls, J. M. (2011). When is a difference really different? Learners' discrimination of linguistic contrasts in American Sign Language. *Language Learning*, 61, 1302–1327.

Bodomo, A. (2006, April). The structure of ideophones in African and Asian languages: the case of Dagaare and Cantonese. In *Selected Proceedings of the 35th Annual Conference on African Linguistics: African Languages and Linguistics in Broad Perspectives* (pp. 203–213). Harvard, MA: Harvard University Press.

Boersma, P. (2003). The odds of eternal optimization in Optimality Theory. In D. Eric Holt (ed.), *Optimality Theory and Language Change* (pp. 31–65). Dordrecht: Kluwer.

Bolinger, D. (1983). Intonation and gesture. *American Speech*, 58, 156–174.

Bonvillian, J. D., Orlansky, M. D., & Folven, R. J. (1990). Early sign language acquisition: Implications for theories of language acquisition. In V. Volterra & C. Erting (eds.), *From Gesture to Language in Hearing and Deaf Children* (pp. 219–232). Berlin, Heidelberg: Springer.

Bonvillian, J. & Siedlecki, T. (1993). Young children's acquisition of the location aspect of American Sign Language signs: Parental report findings. *Journal of Communication Disorders*, 29, 13–35.

Bookheimer, S. (2002). Functional MRI of language: New approaches to understanding the cortical organization of semantic processing. *Annual Review of Neuroscience*, 25, 151–188.

Bosworth, R. G. & Dobkins, K. R. (1999). Left hemisphere dominance for motion processing in deaf signers. *Psychological Science*, 10, 256–262.

Bosworth, R. G. & Emmorey, K. (2010). Effects of iconicity and semantic relatedness on lexical access in American Sign Language. *Journal of Experimental Psychology: Learning, Memory, and Cognition*, 36, 1573.

Bosworth, R., Wright, C., Bartlett, M., Corina, D., & Dobkins, K. (2003). Characterization of the visual properties of signs in ASL. In A. Baker, B. van den Bogaerde, & O. Crasborn (eds.), *Cross-Linguistic Perspectives in Sign Language Research* (pp. 265–282). Hamburg: Signum Press.

Boudreault, P. & Mayberry, R. I. (2006). Grammatical processing in American Sign Language: Age of first-language acquisition effects in relation to syntactic structure. *Language and Cognitive Processes*, 21, 608–635.

Boutora, L. & Karypidis, C. (2007). Are French Sign Language handshapes perceived categorically? Cognitextes (poster presented at the AFLICO conference 2007).

Boyes-Braem, P. (1981). Features of the hand shape in ASL. Doctoral dissertation, University of California, Berkeley, CA.

Boyes Braem, P. (1990a). *Einführung in die Gebärdensprache und ihre Erforschung*. Hamburg: Signum.

Boyes Braem, P. (1990b.) Acquisition of handshape in American Sign Language: A preliminary analysis. In V. Volterra & C. Erting (eds.), *From Gesture to Language in Hearing and Deaf Children* (pp. 107–127). Heidelberg: Springer-Verlag.

Boyes Braem, P. (1999). Rhythmic temporal patterns in the signing of early and late learners of German Swiss Sign Language. *Language and Speech*, *42*, 177–208.

Boyes Braem, P. (2001). Functions of the mouthing component in the signing of deaf early and late learners of Swiss German Sign Language. In D. Brentari (ed.), *Foreign Vocabulary in Sign Language* (pp. 1–47). Mahwah, NJ: Lawrence Erlbaum Associates.

Brand, R. J., Baldwin, D. A., & Ashburn, L. A. (2002). Evidence for "motionese": Modifications in mothers" infant-directed action. *Developmental Science*, *5*, 72–83.

Brand, R. J., Shallcross, W. L., Sabatos, M. G., & Massie, K. P. (2007). Fine-grained analysis of motionese: Eye gaze, object exchanges, and action units in infant-versus adult-directed action. *Infancy*, *11*, 203–214.

Bregman, A. S. (1990). *Auditory Scene Analysis*. Cambridge, MA: MIT Press.

Brennan, M. (2005). Conjoining word and image in British Sign Language (BSL): An exploration of metaphorical signs in BSL. *Sign Language Studies*, *5*, 360–382.

Brentari, D. (1988). Backwards verbs in ASL: Agreement re-opened. In L. MacLeod, G. Larson, & D. Brentari (eds.), *Proceedings from the Chicago Linguistic Society 24,Vol. 2, Parasession on Agreement in Grammatical Theory* (pp. 16–27). Chicago, IL: Chicago Linguistic Society.

Brentari, D. (1990a). Theoretical foundations in American Sign Language phonology. Doctoral dissertation, University of Chicago, Chicago, IL.

Brentari, D. (1990b). Licensing in ASL handshape change. In C. Lucas (ed.), *Sign Language Research: Theoretical Issues* (pp. 57–68). Washington, DC: Gallaudet University Press.

Brentari, D. (1993). Establishing a sonority hierarchy in American Sign Language: The use of simultaneous structure in phonology. *Phonology*, *10*, 281–306.

Brentari, D. (1998). *A Prosodic Model of Sign Language Phonology*. Cambridge, MA: MIT Press.

Brentari, D. (2002). Modality differences in sign language phonology and morphophonemics. In R. Meier, D. Quinto, & K Cormier (eds.), *Modality* in *Language and Linguistic Theory* (pp. 35–64). Cambridge: Cambridge University Press.

Brentari, D. (2005). The use of morphological templates to specify handshapes in sign languages. *Linguistische Berichte*, *13*, 145–177.

Brentari, D. (2006). Effects of language modality on word segmentation: An experimental study of phonological factors in a sign language. In L. Goldstein, D. Whalen, & C. Best (eds.), *Papers in Laboratory Phonology VIII* (pp. 155–164). Berlin: Mouton de Gruyter.

Brentari, D. (2010). *Sign Languages: A Cambridge Language Survey*. Cambridge: Cambridge University Press.

Brentari, D. (2011). Sign language phonology: ASL. In J. Goldsmith (ed.), *A Handbook of Phonological Theory* (pp. 615–639). New York, NY: Basil Blackwell.

Brentari, D. (2016). Sign language phonology. In G. Gertz & P. Boudreault (eds.), *The SAGE Deaf Studies Encyclopedia*. Washington, DC: Sage Publishers.

Brentari, D. (2018). Modality and contextual salience in co-sign vs. co-speech gesture. *Theoretical linguistics*, *44* (3–4), 215–226.

Brentari, D. & Crossley, L. (2002). Prosody on the hands and face: Evidence from American Sign Language. *Sign Language and Linguistics*, 5, 105–130.

Brentari, D., Coppola, M., Cho, P. W., & Senghas, A. (2017). Handshape complexity as a pre-cursor to phonology: Variation, emergence, and acquisition. *Language Acquisition* 24(4),283–306. doi:10.1080/10489223.2016.1187614.

Brentari, D., Coppola, M., Jung, A. & Goldin-Meadow, S. (2013). Acquiring word class distinctions in American Sign Language: Evidence from handshape. *Language Learning and Development*, *9(2)*, 130–150.

Brentari, D., Coppola, M., Mazzoni, L., & Goldin-Meadow, S. (2012a). When does a system become phonological? Handshape production in gesturers, signers, and homesigners. *Natural Language & Linguistic Theory*, *30*, 1–31.

Brentari, D, Falk, J., Giannakidou, A, Herrmann, A., Volk, E., & Steinbach, M. (2018). Production and comprehension of prosodic markers in sign language imperatives. *Frontiers in Psychology*, Special issue on Visual Language (W. Sandler & C. Padden, eds.)

Brentari, D., Falk, J., & Wolford, G. (2015b). The acquisition of prosody in American Sign Language. *Language*, *91*, e144–e168.

Brentari, D., González, C., Seidl, A., & Wilbur, R. (2011). Sensitivity to visual prosodic cues in signers and nonsigners. *Language and Speech*, *54*, 49–72.

Brentari, D., Hill, J., & Amador, B. (2018). Variation in phrasal rhythm in sign languages: Introducing "rhythm ratio". *Sign Language & Linguistics*, *21*, 41–76.

Brentari, D., & Padden, C. (2001). A language with multiple origins: Native and foreign vocabulary in American Sign Language. In D. Brentari, (ed.),

Foreign Vocabulary in Sign Language: A Cross-Linguistic Investigation of Word Formation (pp. 87–119). Mahwah, NJ: Lawrence Erlbaum Associates.

Brentari, D. & Poizner, H. (1994). A phonological analysis of a deaf Parkinsonian signer. *Language and Cognitive Processes*, *9*, 69–100.

Brentari, D., Poizner, H., & Kegl, J. (1995). Aphasic and Parkinsonian signing: Differences in phonological disruption. *Brain and Language*, *48*, 69–105.

Brentari, D., Nadolske, M. A., & Wolford, G. (2012b). Can experience with co-speech gesture influence the prosody of a sign language? Sign language prosodic cues in bimodal bilinguals. *Bilingualism: Language and Cognition*, *15*, 402–412.

Brentari, D., Renzo, A. D., Keane, J., & Volterra, V. (2015a). Cognitive, cultural, and linguistic sources of a handshape distinction expressing agentivity. *Topics in Cognitive Science*, *7*, 95–123.

Broca, P. (1861/1960). Remarques sur le siège de la faculté du langage articulé, suivies d'une observation d'aphémie (perte de la parole). Bulletins de la Société Anatomique (Paris), 6, 330–357, 398–407. In G. Von Bonin, (ed.), *Some papers on the cerebral cortex*. Translated as "Remarks on the seat of the faculty of articulate language followed by an observation of aphemia" (pp. 49–72). Springfield, IL: Charles C. Thomas.

Brookshire, G., Lu, J., Nusbaum, H. C., Goldin-Meadow, S., & Casasanto, D. (2017). Visual cortex entrains to sign language. *Proceedings of the National Academy of Sciences*, *114*, 6352–6357.

Browman, C. P., & Goldstein, L. (1989). Articulatory gestures as phonological units. *Phonology*, *6*, 201–251.

Browman, C. P., & Goldstein, L. (1992). Articulatory phonology: An overview. *Phonetica*, *49*, 155–180.

Bybee, J. (1994). A view of phonology from a cognitive and functional perspective. *Cognitive Linguistics*, 5, 285–305.

Bybee, J. (2003). *Phonology and Language Use* (Vol. 94). Cambridge/New York: Camberidge: Cambridge University Press.

Campbell, R., Martin, P., & White, T. (1992). Forced choice recognition of sign in novice learners of British Sign Language. *Applied Linguistics*, *13*, 185–201.

Cardin, V., Orfanidou, E., Kästner, L., Rönnberg, J., Woll, B., Capek, C. M., & Rudner, M. (2015). Monitoring different phonological parameters of sign language engages the same cortical language network but distinctive perceptual ones. *Journal of Cognitive Neuroscience*, *28*, 20–40.

Carreiras, M., Gutiérrez-Sigut, E., Baquero, S., & Corina, D. (2008). Lexical processing in Spanish sign language (LSE). *Journal of Memory and Language*, *58*, 100–122.

Carrigan, E. & Coppola, M. (2017). Successful communication does not drive language development: Evidence from adult homesign. *Cognition*, *158*, 10–27.

Carstairs McCarthy, A. (2001). ASL "syllables" and language evolution: A response to Uriagereka. *Language*, 77, 343–349.

Caselli, N. K., & Pyers, J. E. (2017). The road to language learning is not entirely iconic: Iconicity, neighborhood density, and frequency facilitate acquisition of sign language. *Psychological Science*, 28, 979–987.

Caselli, N. K., Sehyr, Z. S., Cohen-Goldberg, A. M., & Emmorey, K. (2017). ASL-LEX: A lexical database of American Sign Language. *Behavior Research Methods*, 49, 784–801.

Chase, C. & Jenner, A. R. (1993). Magnocellular visual deficits affect temporal processing of dyslexics. *Annals of the New York Academy of Sciences*, 682, 326–329.

Cheek, A., Cormier, K., Repp, A., & Meier, R. P. (2001). Prelinguistic gesture predicts mastery and error in the production of early signs. *Language*, 77, 292–323.

Chomsky, N. (1957). *Syntactic Structure*. The Hague: Mouton.

Chomsky, N. & Halle, M. (1968). *The Sound Pattern of English*. Harper & Row.

Church, R. B. & Goldin-Meadow, S. (1986). The mismatch between gesture and speech as an index of transitional knowledge. *Cognition*, 23, 43–71.

Clark, H. & R. Gerrig (1990). Quotation as demonstration. *Language*, 66, 764–805.

Clements, G. N. (1985). The geometry of phonological features. *Phonology*, 2, 225–252.

Clements, G. N. (1990). The role of the sonority cycle in core syllabification. In M. Beckman (ed.), *Papers in Laboratory Phonology I: Between the Grammar and Physics of Speech* (pp. 282–333). Cambridge: Cambridge University Press.

Clements, G. N. (2001). Representational economy in constraint-based phonology. In T. A. Hall (ed.), *Distinctive Feature Theory* (pp. 71–146). Berlin: Mouton de Gruyter.

Clements, G. N. & Hume, E. (1995). The internal organization of speech sounds. In J. Goldsmith, (ed.), *Handbook of Phonological Theory* (pp. 245–306). Oxford: Basil Blackwell.

Conlin, K., Mirus, G., Mauk, C., & Meier, R. (2000). The acquisition of first signs: Place, handshape and movement. In C. Chamberlain, J. Morford, & R. Mayberry (eds.), *Language Acquisition by Eye* (pp. 51–69). Mahwah, NJ: Lawrence Erlbaum Associates.

Coppola, M., & Brentari, D. (2014). From iconic handshapes to grammatical contrasts: Longitudinal evidence from a child homesigner. *Frontiers in Psychology*, 5, 830.

Corina, D. (1990). Reassessing the role of sonority in syllable structure: Evidence from a visual-gestural language. In M. Ziolkowski, M. Noske & K. Deaton (eds.), *Proceedings for the Annual Meeting of the Chicago Linguistic Society, 26; Vol. II: The Parasession on the Syllable in Phonetics and Phonology* (pp. 33–43). Chicago, IL: Chicago Linguistic Society.

Corina, D. P. (1999). On the nature of left hemisphere specialization for signed language. *Brain and Language*, *69*, 230–240.

Corina, D. P., Jose-Robertson, L. S., Guillemin, A., High, J., & Braun, A. R. (2003). Language lateralization in a bimanual language. *Journal of Cognitive Neuroscience*, *15*, 718–730.

Corina, D. P., & Knapp, H. P. (2006). Lexical retrieval in American Sign Language production. *Papers in Laboratory Phonology*, *8*, 213–240.

Corina, D. P., McBurney, S. L., Dodrill, C., Hinshaw, K., Brinkley, J., & Ojemann, G. (1999). Functional roles of Broca's area and SMG: Evidence from cortical stimulation mapping in a deaf signer. *Neuroimage*, *10*, 570–581.

Cormier, K., Schembri, A. C., & Tyrone, M. E. (2008). One hand or two? Nativisation of fingerspelling in ASL and BANZSL. *Sign Language & Linguistics*, *11*, 3–44.

Cormier, K., Quinto-Pozos, D., Sevcikova, Z., & Schembri, A. (2012). Lexicalisation and de-lexicalisation processes in sign languages: Comparing depicting constructions and viewpoint gestures. *Language & Communication*, *32*, 329–348.

Coulter, G. (1993). *Current Issues in American Sign Language Phonology*. San Diego, CA: Academic Press.

Crasborn, O. (2001). Phonetic implementation of phonological categories in Sign Language of the Netherlands. Doctoral dissertation, LOT, Utrecht.

Crasborn, O. (2012). Phonetics. In R. Pfau, M. Steinbach, & B. Woll (eds.), *Sign Language: An International Handbook* (pp. 4–20). Berlin: Walter de Gruyter.

Cresdee, D., & Johnston, T. (2014). Using corpus-based research to inform the teaching of Auslan as a second language. In D. McKee, R. Rosen, & R. McKee (eds.), *Signed languages as second language: International perspectives on teaching and learning* (pp. 85–110). Basingstoke: Palgrave Macmillan.

Crasborn, O. & van der Kooij, E. (1997). Relative orientation in sign language phonology. In J. Coerts & H. de Hoop (eds.), *Linguistics in the Netherlands 1997* (pp. 37–48). Amsterdam: John Benjamins.

Cristia, A. (2011). Fine-grained variation in caregivers'/s/predicts their infants'/s/category. *The Journal of the Acoustical Society of America*, *129*, 3271–3280.

Cristia, A., Seidl, A., Junge, C., Soderstrom, M., & Hagoort, P. (2014). Predicting individual variation in language from infant speech perception measures. *Child Development*, *85*, 1330–1345.

Croft, W. (1990). *Typology and Universals. (Cambridge Textbooks in Linguistics)*. Cambridge: Cambridge University Press.

Cutting, J. E., & Rosner, B. S. (1974). Categories and boundaries in speech and music. *Perception & Psychophysics*, *16*, 564–570.

Cuxac, C., & Sallandre, M. (2007). Iconicity and arbitrariness in French Sign Language: Highly iconic structures, degenerated iconicity and diagrammatic iconicity. *Empirical Approaches to Language Typology*, *36*, 13.

Dachkovsky, S. (2007). Linguistic vs. paralinguistic intonation in sign language. Presentation at the Max Planck Institute for Psycholinguistics.

Dachkovsky, S., Healy, C., & Sandler, W. (2013). Visual intonation in two sign languages. *Phonology*, *30*, 211–252.

Davidson, K. (2015). Quotation, demonstration, and iconicity. *Linguistics and Philosophy*, *38*, 477–520.

Dell, F., & Elmedlaoui, M. (1985). Syllabic consonants and syllabification in Imdlawn Tashlhiyt Berber. *Journal of African Languages and Linguistics*, *7*, 105–130.

Demey, E. & van der Kooij, E. (2008) Phonological patterns in a dependency model: Allophonic relations grounded in phonetic and iconic motivation. *Lingua*, *118*, 1109–1138.

Deuchar, M. 1984. *British Sign Language*. London: Routledge & Kegan Paul.

Devlin, J. T., Matthews, P. M., & Rushworth, M. F. (2003). Semantic processing in the left inferior prefrontal cortex: A combined functional magnetic resonance imaging and transcranial magnetic stimulation study. *Journal of Cognitive Neuroscience*, *15*, 71–84.

Diehl, R. L., Lotto, A. J., & Holt, L. L. (2004). Speech perception. *Annual Review of Psychology*, *55*, 149–179.

Diffloth, G. (1972). Notes on expressive meaning. *Proceedings from the 8th Annual Meeting of the Chicago Linguistic Society* (pp. 440–447). Chicago, IL: Chicago Linguistic Society.

Dingemanse, M., Schuerman, W., Reinisch, E., Tufvesson, S., & Mitterer, H. (2016). What sound symbolism can and cannot do: Testing the iconicity of ideophones from five languages. *Language*, *92*, e117–e133.

do Carmo, P., Mineiro, A., Branco, J. C., de Quadros, R. M., & Castro-Caldas, A. (2013). Handshape is the hardest path in Portuguese Sign Language acquisition: Towards a universal modality constraint. *Sign Language & Linguistics*, *16*, 75–90.

Downing, L., Hall, T. A., & Raffelsiefen, R. (2004). *Paradigms in Phonological Theory*. Oxford: Oxford University Press.

Dronkers, N. F., Redfern, B. B., & Knight, R. T. (2000). The neural architecture of language disorders. In M. Gazzaniga (ed.), *The New Cognitive Neurosciences* (pp. 949–960). Cambridge, MA: MIT Press.

Dronkers, N. F., Redfern, B. B., & Ludy, C. A. (1995). Lesion localization in chronic Wernicke's aphasia. *Brain and Language*, *51*, 62–65.

Dudis, P. G. (2004). Depiction of events in ASL: Conceptual integration of temporal components. Doctoral dissertation, University of California, Berkeley.

Dunbar, E. & Dupoux, E. (2016). Geometric constraints on human speech sound inventories. *Frontiers in Psychology.* doi:10.3389/fpsyg.2016.01061.

Duncan, S. (2005). Gesture in signing: A case study from Taiwan Sign Language. *Language and Linguistics*, 6, 279–318.

Dye, M. W., Hauser, P. C., & Bavelier, D. (2009). Is visual selective attention in deaf individuals enhanced or deficient? The case of the useful field of view. *PloS one*, 4(5), e5640.

Eccarius, P. (2008). A constraint-based account of handshape contrast in sign languages. Doctoral dissertation, Purdue University, West Lafayette, IN.

Eccarius, P. & Brentari, D. (2007). Symmetry and dominance: A cross-linguistic study of signs and classifier constructions. *Lingua*, 117, 1169–1201.

Eccarius, P. & D. Brentari. (2008). Contrast differences across lexical substrata: Evidence from the ASL handshape. In N. Adams, A. Cooper, F. Parrill, & T. Weir (eds.) *Proceedings from the 44th Annual Meeting of the Chicago Linguistic Society, vol. 2* (pp. 187–201). Chicago, IL: Chicago Linguistic Society.

Eccarius, P. & Brentari, D. (2010). A formal analysis of phonological contrast and iconicity in sign language handshapes. *Sign Language & Linguistics*, 13, 156–181.

Eimas, P. D. (1963). The relation between identification and discrimination along speech and non-speech continua. *Language and Speech*, 6(4), 206–217.

Ekman, P. (1993). Facial expression and emotion. *American Psychologist*, 48, 384.

Emmorey, K. (1999). Do signers gesture? In L. Messing & R. Campbell (eds.) *Gesture, Speech, and Sign* (pp. 133–159). New York, NY: Oxford University Press.

Ekman, P. & Friesen, W. V. (1971). Constants across cultures in the face and emotion. *Journal of Personality and Social Psychology*, 17, 124.

Ekman, P. & Friesen, W. V. (1978). *The Facial Action Coding System: A Technique for the Measurement of Facial Action.* Palo Alto, CA: Consulting Psychological Press.

Emmorey, K., Bellugi, U., Friederici, A., & Horn, P. (1995). Effects of age of acquisition on grammatical sensitivity: Evidence from on-line and off-line tasks. *Applied Psycholinguistics*, 16, 1–23.

Emmorey, K., Giezen, M. R., Petrich, J. A., Spurgeon, E., & Farnady, L. O. G. (2017). The relation between working memory and language comprehension in signers and speakers. *Acta Psychologica*, 177, 69–77.

Emmorey, K., Grabowski, T., McCullough, S., Damasio, H., Ponto, L., Hichwa, R., & Bellugi, U. (2004). Motor-iconicity of sign language does not alter the neural systems underlying tool and action naming. *Brain and Language*, 89, 27–37.

Emmorey, K. & Herzig, M. (2003). Categorical versus gradient properties of classifier constructions in ASL. In K. Emmorey (ed.), *Perspectives on Classifier Constructions in Signed Languages* (pp. 222–246). Mahwah, NJ: Lawrence Erlbaum Associates.

Emmorey, K., Kosslyn, S. M., & Bellugi, U. (1993). Visual imagery and visual-spatial language: Enhanced imagery abilities in deaf and hearing ASL signers. *Cognition, 46*, 139–181.

Emmorey, K., McCullough, S., & Brentari, D. (2003). Categorical perception in American Sign Language. *Language and Cognitive Processes, 18*, 21–45.

Emmorey, K., Mehta, S. & Grabowski, T. (2007). The neural correlates of sign versus word production. *NeuroImage, 36*, 202–208.

Emmorey, K., Mehta, S., McCullough, S., & Grabowski, T.J. (2014). How sensory-motor systems impact the neural organization for language: Direct contrasts between spoken and signed language. *Frontiers in Psychology*, 5, doi:10.3389/fpsyg.2014.00484.

Emmorey, K., Mehta, S., McCullough, S., & Grabowski, T. J. (2016). The neural circuits recruited for the production of signs and fingerspelled words. *Brain and Language, 160*, 30–41.

Emmorey, K., Weisberg, J., McCullough, S., & Petrich, J. A. (2013). Mapping the reading circuitry for skilled deaf readers: An fMRI study of semantic and phonological processing. *Brain and Language, 126*, 169–180.

Emmorey, K., Xu, J., & Braun, A. (2011). Neural responses to meaningless pseudosigns: Evidence for sign-based phonetic processing in superior temporal cortex. *Brain and Language, 117*, 34–38.

Engberg-Pedersen, E. (1993). *Space in Danish Sign Language*. Hamburg: Signum Press.

Ergin, R. (2017). Central taurus sign language: A unique vantage point into language emergence. Doctoral dissertation, Tufts University.

Ergin, R. & Brentari, B. (2017). Handshape preferences for objects and predicates in Central Taurus Sign Language. In M. LaMendola & J. Scott (eds.), *Proceedings of the 41st Annual Boston University Conference on Language Development* (pp. 222–235). Somerville, MA: Cascadilla Press.

Erting, C.J., Prezioso, C., & Hynes, M. G. (1990). The interactional context of mother-infant communication. In V. Volterra, & C. Erting (eds.), *From Gesture to Language in Hearing and Deaf Children* (pp. 97–106). Berlin: Springer Verlag.

Etxeberria, U. & Irurtzun, A. (2015). The emergence of scalar meanings. *Frontiers in Psychology*, 6, 141.

Fenlon, J., Cooperrider, K., Keane, J., Brentari,D., & Goldin-Meadow, S. (2019). Comparing sign language and gesture: Insights from pointing. *Glossa: A Journal of General Linguistics*, 4(1). DOI: http://doi.org/10.5334/gjgl.499.

Fenlon, J., Cormier, K. & Brentari, D. (2017). The phonology of sign languages. In S.J. Hannahs & A. Bosch (ed.), *Routledge Handbook of Phonological Theory* (pp. 453–475). New York, NY: Routledge.

Fenlon, J., Cormier, K., Rentelis, R., Schembri, A., Rowley, K., Adam, R., & Woll, B. (2014a). *BSL SignBank: A Lexical Database of British Sign Language* (1st ed.). London: Deafness, Cognition and Language Research Centre, University College London.

Fenlon, J., Schembri, A., Rentelis, R., & Cormier, K. (2013). Variation in handshape and orientation in British Sign Language: The case of the "1"hand configuration. *Language & Communication, 33*(1), 69–91.

Fenlon, J., Schembri, A., Rentelis, R., Vinson, D., & Cormier, K. (2014b). Using conversational data to determine lexical frequency in British Sign Language: The influence of text type. *Lingua, 143*, 187–202.

Fiez, J. A. (1997). Phonology, semantics, and the role of the left inferior prefrontal cortex. *Human Brain Mapping, 5*, 79–83.

Fischer, S. (1978). Sign language and creoles. In P. Siple (ed.), *Understanding Language Through Sign Language Research: Perspectives in Neurolinguistics and Psycholinguistics* (pp. 309–331). New York, NY/San Francisco, CA/London: Academic Press.

Fischer, S. & Gough, B. (1978). Verbs in American Sign Language. *Sign Language Studies, 7*, 17–48.

Flege, J. E. (1999). Age of learning and second-language speech. In David Birdsong (ed.), *Second Language Acquisition and The Critical Period Hypothesis* (pp. 101–131). Mahwah, NJ: Lawrence Erlbaum.

Flege, J. E., Yeni-Komshian, G. H., & Liu, S. (1999). Age constraints on second-language acquisition. *Journal of Memory and Language, 41*, 78–104.

Flemming, E. (1995). Auditory representations in phonology. Doctoral dissertation, University of California, Los Angeles.

Flemming, E. (1996). Evidence for constraints on contrast: The dispersion theory of contrast. *UCLA Working Papers in Phonology, 1*, 86–106.

Flemming, E. (1997). Phonetic optimization: Compromise in speech production. *University of Maryland Working Papers in Linguistics, 5*, 72–91.

Flemming, E. (2002). *Auditory Representations in Phonology.* New York, NY: Routledge.

Flemming, E. (2017). Dispersion theory and phonology. In M. Aronoff (ed.), *Oxford Encyclopedia of Linguistics.* Oxford: Oxford University Press.

Fogel, A. (1981). The ontogeny of gestural communication: The first six months. In R.E. Stark (ed.), *Language Behavior in Infancy and Early Childhood* (pp. 17–44). New York, NY: Elsevier Science Ltd.

Fontana, S., Corazza, S., Braem, P. B., & Volterra, V. (2017). Language research and language community change: Italian sign language 1981–2013. *Sign Language Studies, 17*, 363–398.

Fowler, C. A., 2004. Speech as a supramodal or amodal phenomenon. In G. Calvert, C. Spence, & B. E. Stein (eds.), *Handbook of Multisensory Processes* (pp. 189–201). Cambridge, MA: MIT Press.

Friedman, L. A. (1976). Phonology of a soundless language: Phonological structure of the American Sign Language. Doctoral dissertation, University of California at Berkeley, Berkeley, CA.

Friedman, L. A. (ed.). (1977). *On The Other Hand: New Perspectives on American Sign Language*. New York, NY: Academic Press.

Frishberg, N. (1975). Arbitrariness and iconicity: Historical change in American Sign Language. *Language*, 51, 696–719.

Fromkin, V. A. (1973). Introduction. In V. A. Fromkin (ed.), *Speech Errors as Linguistic Evidence* (pp. 11–45). The Hague: Mouton.

Fuks, O. (submitted) Two styles of infant-directed signing in Israeli sign language. *Language, Learning & Development*.

Geraci, C. (2009). Epenthesis in Italian Sign Language. *Sign Language & Linguistics* 12(1), 3–51.

Geraci, C., Battaglia, K., Cardinaletti, A., Cecchetto, C., Donati, C., Giudice, S., & Mereghetti, E. (2011). The LIS corpus project: A discussion of sociolinguistic variation in the lexicon. *Sign Language Studies*, 11, 528–574.

Geraci, C., Bayley, R., Cardinaletti, A., Cecchetto, C., & Donati, C. (2015). Variation in Italian Sign Language (LIS): The case of wh-signs. *Linguistics*, 53, 125–151.

Giezen, M. R. & Emmorey, K. (2017). Evidence for a bimodal bilingual disadvantage in letter fluency, *Bilingualism: Language and Cognition*, 20(1),42–48.

Giraud, A. L. & Poeppel, D. (2012). Cortical oscillations and speech processing: Emerging computational principles and operations. *Nature Neuroscience*, 15, 511.

Goffman, L., Gerken, L., & Lucchesi, J. (2007). Relations between segmental and motor variability in prosodically complex nonword sequences. *Journal of Speech, Language, and Hearing Research*, 50, 444–458.

Göksel, A. & Kelepir, M. (2013). The phonological and semantic bifurcation of the functions of an articulator: HEAD in questions in Turkish Sign Language. *Sign Language & Linguistics*, 16, 1–30.

Goldinger, S. D., Luce, P. A., & Pisoni, D. B. (1989). Priming lexical neighbors of spoken words: Effects of competition and inhibition. *Journal of Memory and Language*, 28, 501–518.

Goldin-Meadow, S. (2003). *The Resilience of Language: What Gesture Creation in Deaf Children Can Tell Us about How All Children Learn Language*. New York, NY: Psychology Press.

Goldin-Meadow, S. & Brentari, D. (2017). Gesture, sign, and language: The coming of age of sign language and gesture studies. *Behavioral and Brain Sciences*, 40.

Goldin-Meadow, S., McNeill, D., & Singleton, J. (1996). Silence is liberating: Removing the handcuffs on grammatical expression in the manual modality. *Psychological Review*, 103, 34.

Goldin-Meadow, S. & Mylander, C. (1983). Gestural communication in deaf children: Noneffect of parental input on language development. *Science*, 221, 372–374.

Goldinger, S. D., Luce, P. A., Pisoni, D. B., & Marcario, J. K. (1992). Form-based priming in spoken word recognition: The roles of competition and bias. *Journal of Experimental Psychology: Learning, Memory, and Cognition*, 18, 1211–1238.

Goldsmith, J. (1976). Autosegmental phonology. Doctoral dissertation, MIT, Cambridge, MA. [Published New York: Garland Press, 1979].

Goldsmith, J. (1992). Tone and accent in Llogoori. In D. Brentari, G. Larson, & L. MacLeod (eds.), *The Joy of Syntax: A Festschrift in Honor of James D. McCawley* (pp. 73–94). Amsterdam: John Benjamins.

Goldsmith, J. (2001). Probabilistic models of grammar: phonology as information minimization. *Phonological Studies*, Vol. 5. Tokyo: The Phonological Society of Japan (Kaitakusha).

Goldsmith, J. (2002). Probabilistic models of grammar: Phonology as information minimization. *Phonological Studies*, 5, 21–46.

Goldsmith, J. & Larson, G. (1990). Local modeling and syllabification. In *Papers from the 26th Annual Regional Meeting of the Chicago Linguistics Society: Parasession on the Syllable in Phonetics and Phonology*. Chicago Linguistics Society, 129–141.

Gollan, T. H. & Acenas, L. A. (2004). What is a TOT? Cognate and translation effects on tip-of-the-tongue states in Spanish–English and Tagalog–English bilinguals. *Journal of Experimental Psychology: Learning, Memory, and Cognition*, 30, 246–269.

Golston, C. & Yang, P. (2001). White Hmong loanword phonology. In C. Féry, A. D. Green, & R. van de Vijver (eds.), *Proceedings of HILP 5* (pp. 40–57). Potsdam: University of Potsdam.

Gómez, D. M., Berent, I., Benavides-Varela, S., Bion, R. A. H., Cattarossi, L., Nespor, M., & Mehler, J. (2014). Language universals at birth. *Proceedings of the National Academy of Sciences*, 111(16), 5837–5341.

Gordon, M. (2006). *Syllable Weight: Phonetics, Phonology, Typology*. New York, NY: Routledge.

Grabe, E. & Low, E. L. (2002). Durational variability in speech and the rhythm class hypothesis. *Papers in Laboratory Phonology 7*, Berlin: Mouton.

Green, D. M. (1971). Temporal auditory acuity. *Psychological Review*, 78, 540.

Grenoble, L., Baglini, R., & Martinović, M. (2015). Verbal gestures in Wolof. In R. Kramer, E. C. Zsiga, & O. Tlale Boyer (eds.), *Selected Proceedings of the 44th Annual Conference on African Linguistics (ACAL 44)* (pp. 110–121). Somerville, MA: Cascadilla Press.

Grigely, J. (1996). *Textualterity: Art, Theory, and Textual Criticism*. Ann Arbor, MI: University of Michigan Press.

Groce, N. E. (1985). *Everyone Here Spoke Sign Language: Hereditary Deafness on Martha's Vineyard*. Cambridge, MA: Harvard University Press.

Grosjean, F. & Lane, H. (1976). How the listener integrates the components of speaking rate. *Journal of Experimental Psychology: Human Perception and Performance*, 2, 538–543.

Grosvald, M. & Corina, D. (2012a). Perception of long-distance coarticulation: An event-related potential and behavioral study. *Applied Psycholinguistics*, 33(1), 55–82.

Grosvald, M. & Corina, D. (2012b) The perceptibility of long-distance coarticulation in speech and sign: A study of English and American Sign Language. *Sign Language and Linguistics*, 15, 73–103.

Grote, K. & Linz, E. (2003). The influence of sign language iconicity on semantic conceptualization. In W. Müller & O. Fischer (eds.), *From sign to signing: Iconicity in Language and Literature, Vol. 3*. Amsterdam: John Benjamins.

Gruber, J. (1965). Studies in lexical relations. Doctoral dissertation, Massachusetts Institute of Technology, Cambridge, MA.

Haiman, J. (1978). Conditionals are topics. *Language*, 54, 564–589.

Haiman, J. (1980). The iconicity of grammar: Isomorphism and motivation. *Language*, 56, 515–540.

Hakuta, K., Bialystok, E., & Wiley, E. (2003). Critical evidence: A test of the critical-period hypothesis for second-language acquisition. *Psychological Science*, 14, 31–38.

Hall, M. & Bavelier, D. (2010). Working memory, deafness and sign language. In M. Marschark & P. E. Spencer (eds.), *The Handbook of Deaf Studies, Language and Education, Vol. 2*. (pp. 458–472). Oxford: Oxford University Press.

Hall, M. L., Ferreira, V. S., & Mayberry, R. I. (2012). Phonological similarity judgments in ASL: Evidence for maturational constraints on phonetic perception in sign. *Sign Language & Linguistics*, 15, 104–127.

Halle, M. (1959). *The Sound Pattern of Russian*. The Hague: Mouton.

Halle, M. & Vergnaud, J. R. (1987). *An Essay on Stress*. Cambridge, MA: MIT Press.

Hanson, V. L. & Fowler, C. A. (1987). Phonological coding in word reading: Evidence from hearing and deaf readers. *Memory & Cognition*, 15, 199–207.

Hara, D. (2003). A complexity-based approach to the syllable formation in sign language. Doctoral dissertation, University of Chicago, Chicago, IL.

Harnad, S. (1987). *Categorical Perception: The Groundwork of Cognition*. Cambridge: Cambridge University Press.

Harris, M., Clibbens, J., Chasin, J., & Tibbitts, R. (1989). The social context of early sign language development. *First Language*, 9, 81–97.

Hart, B. & Risley, T. R. (1995). *Meaningful Differences in the Everyday Experience of Young American Children*. Baltimore, MD: Brookes Publishing.

Hayes, B (1989). Compensatory lengthening in moraic phonology. *Linguistic Inquiry* 20, 253–306.

Herrmann, A. (2015). The marking of information structure in German Sign Language. *Lingua*, 165, 277–297.

Herrmann, A. & Pendzich, N-K. (2014). Nonmanual gestures in Sign Languages. In C. Müller, A. Cienki, E. Fricke, S. H. Ladewig, D. McNeill, & J. Bressem (eds.), *Handbook Body – Language – Communication* (pp. 1249–1260). Berlin/Boston, MA: De Gruyter Mouton.

Hickok, G., Bellugi, U., & Klima, E. S. (1996). The neurobiology of sign language and its implications for the neural basis of language. *Nature, 381*(6584), 699–702.

Higgins, D. (1923). *How to Talk to the Deaf.* St. Louis, MO: Higgins.

Hildebrandt, U. & Corina, D. (2002). Phonological similarity in American Sign Language. *Language and Cognitive Processes, 17,* 593–612.

Hillis, A. E., Wang, P., Barker, P., Beauchamp, N., Gordon, B. & Wityk, R., (2000). Magnetic resonance perfusion imaging: A new method for localizing regions of brain dysfunction associated with specific lexical impairments? *Aphasiology, 14*(5–6), 471–483.

Hillyard, S. A. & Picton, T. W. (1979). Conscious perception and cerebral event-related potentials. In J. E. Desmedt (ed.), *Cognitive Components in Cerebral Event-Related Potentials and Selective Attention. Progress in Clinical Neurophysiology, Vol. 6.* (pp. 1–52). Basel: Karger.

Hirsh, I. J. & Sherrick Jr, C. E. (1961). Perceived order in different sense modalities. *Journal of Experimental Psychology, 62,* 423.

Hirshorn, E., Dye, W. M., Hauser, P., Supalla, T., & Bavelier, D. (2015). The contribution of phonological knowledge, memory, and language background to reading comprehension in deaf populations. *Frontiers in Psychology, 25.* https://doi.org/10.3389/fpsyg.2015.01153.

Hockett, C. (1955). *A Manual of Phonology.* Baltimore, MD: Waverly Press.

Hockett, C. (1960). The origin of speech. *Scientific American, 203,* 89–96.

Hockett, C. F. (1978). In search of Jove's brow. *American Speech, 53,* 243–313.

Hohenberger, A., Happ, D., & Leuninger, H. (2002). Modality-dependent aspects of sign language production: Evidence from slips of the hands and their repairs in German Sign Language. In R. Meier, D. Quinto, & K. Cormier (eds.), *Modality in Language and Linguistic Theory* (pp. 112–142). Cambridge/New York, NY: Cambridge University Press.

Holm, J. (2000). *An Introduction to Pidgins and Creoles.* Cambridge/New York, NY: Cambridge University Press.

Holzrichter, A. & Meier, R. P., (2000). Child-directed signing in American Sign Language. In C. Chamberlain, J. Morford, & R. Mayberry (eds.), *Language Acquisition by Eye* (pp. 25–40). Mahwah, NJ: Lawrence Erlbaum Associates.

Hömke, P., Holler, J., & Levinson, S. (2017). Eye blinking as addressee feedback in face-to-face conversation. *Research on Language and Social Interaction, 50,* 54–70.

Hopper, P. & Traugott, E. (1993) *Grammaticalization.* Cambridge: Cambridge University Press.

Horton, (2018). Conventionalization of shared homesign systems in Guatemala: Lexical & morpho-phonological dimensions. Doctoral dissertation, University of Chicago.

Horton, L., Goldin-Meadow, S., Coppola, M., Senghas, A., & Brentari, D. (2015). Forging a morphological system out of two dimensions: Agentivity and number. *Open Linguistics*, 1, 596–613.

Hosemann, J., Altvater-Mackensen, N., Herrman, A., & Mani, N. (2013). Cross-modal language activation. Does processing a sign (L1) also activate its corresponding written translations (L2)? Presented at the 11th Theoretical Issues in Sign Language Research Conference, London.

Humphries, T., Kushalnagar, P., Mathur, G., Napoli, D. J., Padden, C., & Rathmann, C. (2014). Ensuring language acquisition for deaf children: What linguists can do. *Language*, 90, e31–e52.

Humphries, T., & MacDougall, F. (2000). "Chaining" and other links: Making connections between American Sign Language and English in Two Types of School Settings. *Visual Anthropology Review*, 15, 84–94.

Hwang, S-O. (2011). Windows into sensory integration and rates in language processing: Insights from signed and spoken languages. Doctoral dissertation, University of Maryland, College Park.

Hwang, S-O, Tomita, N., Morgan, H., Ergin, R., Ilbasaran, D., Seegers, S., Lepic, R., & Padden, C. (2017). Of the body and the hands: Patterned iconicity for semantic categories. *Language and Cognition*, 9, 573–602.

Hyman, L. (1985). *A Theory of Phonological Weight*. Dordrecht: Foris.

Idsardi, W. (1992). The computation of prosody. Doctoral dissertation, MIT, Cambridge, MA.

Inkelas, S. (2011). The phonology-morphology interaction. In J. Goldsmith, J. Riggle, & A. Yu (eds.), *Handbook of Phonological Theory* (2nd ed., pp. 68–102). Oxford: Wiley/Blackwell.

Iskarous, K. & Goldstein, L. (2018). The dynamics of prominence profiles: From local computation to global patterns. In D. Brentari & J. Lee (eds.), *Shaping Phonology* (pp. 153–177). Chicago, IL: University of Chicago Press.

Israel, A. & Sandler, W. (2011). Phonological category resolution: A study of handshapes in younger and older sign languages. In R. Channon & H. van der Hulst (eds.), *Formational Units in Sign Languages* (pp. 177–202). Berlin: De Gruyter / Ishara Press.

Itô, Junko. (1986). Syllable theory in prosodic phonology. Doctoral dissertation, University of Massachusetts, New York (Published 1989, Garland Press).

Itô, J. & Mester, A. (1995a). The core-periphery structure of the lexicon and constraints on re-ranking. In J Beckman, S. Urbanczyk, & L. Walsh (eds.), *University of Massachusetts Occasional Papers in Linguistics [UMOP] Vol. 18: Papers in Optimality Theory* (pp. 181–209). Amherst, MA: GLSA.

Itô, J. & Mester, A. (1995b). Japanese phonology. In J. Goldsmith, J. Riggle, & A. Yu (eds.), *Handbook of Phonological Theory* (2nd ed., pp. 817–838). Oxford: Wiley/Blackwell.

Jackendoff, R. (1996). The architecture of the linguistic-spatial interface. In P. Bloom, M. A. Peterson, L. Nadal, & M. E Garrett (eds.), *Language and Space* (pp. 1–30). Cambridge, MA: MIT Press.

Jackendoff, R. (1972). *Semantic Interpretation in Generative Grammar.* Cambridge, MA: MIT Press.

Jakobson, R. (1971/1990). Shifters verbal categories, and the Russian verb. In *Selected Writings II* (pp.130–147). The Hague: Mouton. [also in L.R. Waugh & M. Monville-Burston (eds.) *On Language* (pp. 386–392). Cambridge, MA: Harvard University Press.]

Jakobson, R., Fant, G., & Halle, M. (1952). *Preliminaries to Speech Analysis: The Distinctive Features and their Correlates.* Cambridge, MA: MIT Press.

Jantunen, T. (2006). The complexity of lexical movements in FinSL. In M. Suominen, A. Arppe, A. Airola, O. Heinamaki, M. Miestamo, U. Määttä, J. Niemi, K. K. Pitkaänen & K. Sinnemäki (eds.), *A Man of Measure: Festschrift in Honour of Fred Karlsson on His 60th Birthday* (pp. 335–344). Turku: The Linguistic Association of Finland (Special Supplement to SKY Journal of Linguistics; vol. 19, 2006).

Jantunen, T. (2007). Tavu suomalaisessa viittomakielessä. [The syllable in Finnish Sign Language; with English abstract] *Puhe ja kieli*, 27, 109–126.

Jantunen, T, & Takkinen, R. (2010). Syllable structure in sign language phonology. In D. Brentari (ed.), *Sign Languages* (pp. 312–331). Cambridge: Cambridge University Press.

Japan Institute for Sign Language Studies (ed.). (1997). *The Japanese-Japanese Sign Language Dictionary.* Tokyo: Federation of the Deaf.

Johnson, J. S. & Newport, E. L. (1989). Critical period effects in second language learning: The influence of maturational state on the acquisition of English as a second language. *Cognitive Psychology*, 21, 60–99.

Johnson, K. & Hume, E. (2003). Phonetic explanation in phonology: Overview of the symposium. In M.J. Solé, D. Recasens, & J. Romero *Proceedings of the 15th International Congress of Phonetic Sciences* (pp. 359–361). Barcelona: Casual Productions.

Johnston, T. (1989). Auslan: The sign language of the Australian deaf community. Doctoral dissertation, University of Sydney, Sydney.

Johnston, T. (2002). BSL, Auslan and NZSL: Three signed languages or one? In A. Baker, B. van den Bogaerde, & O. Crasborn (eds.), *Cross-Linguistic Perspectives in Sign Language Research: Selected Papers from TISLR 2000* (pp. 47–69). Hamburg: Signum Verlag.

Johnston, T. & Schembri, A. C. (1999). On defining lexeme in a signed language. *Sign Language & Linguistics*, 2, 115–185.

Jusczyk, P. W., Houston, D. M., & Newsome, M. (1999). The beginnings of word segmentation in English-learning infants. *Cognitive Psychology*. 39, 159–207.

Jusczyk, P. W., Rosner, B. S., Cutting, J. E., Foard, C. F., & Smith, L. B. (1977). Categorical perception of nonspeech sounds by 2-month-old infants. *Perception & Psychophysics*, *21*, 50–54.

Kantor, R. (1980). The acquisition of classifier handshapes in American Sign Language. *Sign Language Studies*, 28, 193–200.

Kaschube. D. (1967). *Structural Elements of Crow.* University of Colorado Press.

Keane, J. (2014). Towards an articulatory model of handshape: What fingerspelling tells us about the phonetics and phonology of handshape in American Sign Language. Doctoral dissertation, University of Chicago, Chicago, IL.

Keane, J. & Brentari, D. (2016). Fingerspelling: Beyond handshape sequences. In M. Marschark & P. Siple, (eds.), *The Oxford Handbook of Deaf Studies in Language: Research, Policy, and Practice* (pp. 146–160). New York, NY/Oxford: Oxford University Press.

Keane, J., Brentari, D. & Riggle, J. (2015). Segmentation and pinky extension in in ASL fingerspelling. In E. Raimy & C. Cairns (eds.), *The Segment in Phonology and Phonetics* (pp. 103–128). Hoboken, NJ: Wiley-Blackwell.

Kegl, J. (1985). Locative relations in American Sign Language word formation, syntax and discourse. Doctoral dissertation, MIT, Cambridge, MA.

Kegl, J. & Iwata, G. (1989). Lenguaje de Signos Nicaragüense: A pidgin sheds light on the "Creole?" ASL. In R. Carlson, S. DeLancey, S. Gildea, D. Payne, & A. Saxena (eds.), *Proceedings of the Fourth Meetings of the Pacific Linguistics Conference* (pp. 266–294). Eugene, OR: Department of Linguistics, University of Oregon.

Kelly, A. (1995). Fingerspelling interaction: A set of deaf patterns and her daughter. In C. Lucas (ed.), *Sociolinguistics in Deaf Communities, vol 1* (pp. 62–73). Washington, DC: Gallaudet University Press.

Kendon, A. (1980). The sign language of the women of Yuendumu: A preliminary report on the structure of Warlpiri sign language. *Sign Language Studies*, *27*, 101–112.

Kendon, A. (1984). Knowledge of sign language in an Australian aboriginal community. *Journal of Anthropological Research*, *40*, 556–576.

Kendon, A. (1985). Iconicity in Warlpiri Sign Language. In P. Bouissac, M. Herzfeld, & R. Posner (eds.), *Iconicity: Essay on the Nature of Culture.* Tübingen: Stauffenburger Verlag.

Kendon, A. (1987). Speaking and signing simultaneously in Warlpiri sign language users. *Multilingua-Journal of Cross-Cultural and Interlanguage Communication*, *6*, 25–68.

Kendon, A. (1988). Parallels and divergences between Warlpiri sign language and spoken Warlpiri: Analyses of signed and spoken discourses. *Oceania*, *58*, 239–254.

Kendon, A. (2004). *Gesture: Visible Action as Utterance.* Cambridge: Cambridge University Press.

Kimmelman, V., Sáfár, A., & Crasborn, O. (2016). Towards a classification of weak hand holds. *Open Linguistics*, 2, 211–234.

Kiparksy, P. (1982). Lexical phonology and morphology. In I. S. Yang (ed.), *Linguistics in the Morning Calm* (pp. 3–91). Seoul: Hanshin Press.

Kita, S., Ingeborg, V. G., & van der Hulst, H. (2014). The non-linguistic status of the symmetry condition in signed languages. *Sign Language & Linguistics*, 17, 215–238.

Kita, S. & Özyürek, A. (2003). What does cross-linguistic variation in semantic coordination of speech and gesture reveal? Evidence for an interface representation of spatial thinking and speaking. *Journal of Memory and Language*, 48, 16–32.

Kisch, S. (2012). Demarcating generations of signers in the dynamic sociolinguistic landscape of a shared sign-language: The case of the Al-Sayyid Bedouin. In Ulrike Zeshan & Connie de Vos(eds.), *Sign Languages in Village Communities: Anthropological and Linguistic Insights* (pp. 87–125). Boston, MA: De Gruyter.

Klima, E. & Bellugi, U. (1979). *The Signs of Language*. Cambridge, MA: Harvard University Press.

Kluender, K. R. & Kiefte, M. (2006). Speech perception within a biologically-realistic information-theoretic framework. In M. A. Gernsbacher & M. Traxler (eds.), *Handbook of Psycholinguistics* (pp. 153–199). London: Elsevier.

Kohlrausch, A., Püschel, D., & Alphei, H. (1992). Temporal resolution and modulation analysis in models of the auditory system. *The Auditory Processing of Speech: From Sounds to Words*, 10, 85.

Krahmer, E. & Swerts, M. (2007). The effects of visual beats on prosodic prominence: Acoustic analyses, auditory perception and visual perception. *Journal of Memory and Language*, 57, 396–414.

Kubus, O., Villwock, A., Morford, J. P., & Rathmann, C. (2015). Word recognition in deaf readers: Cross-language activation of German Sign Language and German. *Applied Psycholinguistics*. 6, 831–854.

Kuhl, P. K. & Miller, J. D. (1975). Speech perception by the chinchilla: Voiced-voiceless distinction in alveolar plosive consonants. *Science*, 190, 69–72.

Kuramada, M. Brown, Bibyk, S., Pontillo, D., & Tanenhaus, M. (2014). Is it or isn't it: Listeners make rapid use of prosody to infer speaker meanings. *Cognition* 133, 335–342.

Kusters, A. (2017). *Innovation in Deaf Studies: The Role of Deaf Scholars*. Oxford: Oxford University Press.

Labov, W. (1990). The intersection of sex and social class in the course of linguistic change, *Language Variation and Change*, 19: 205–254.

Labov, W. (1994). Principles of Linguistic Change. Volume I: Internal Factors. Oxford: Blackwell.

Labov, W. (2001). *Principles of Linguistic Change. Volume 2: Social Factors*. Oxford/Cambridge, MA: Blackwell.

Ladd, D. R. (1996). *Intonational Phonology*. Cambridge: Cambridge University Press.

Ladd, D. R. (2014). *Simultaneous Structure in Phonology*. Oxford: Oxford University Press.

Laks, B., Calderone, B., & Celata, C. (2018). French liaison in the light of corpus phonology: From lexical information to patterns of usage variation. In D. Brentari & J. Lee (eds.), *Shaping Phonology: Essays in Honor of John Goldsmith*. Chicago, IL: University of Chicago Press.

Landau, L. & Lifshitz, E. (1987). *Fluid Mechanics*. In *Course of Theoretical Physics*, 2nd ed. (pp. 378–382). Oxford: Pergamon Press.

Lane, H. (1984). *When the Mind Hears*. New York, NY: Random House.

Lane, H., Boyes-Braem, P., & Bellugi, U. (1976). Preliminaries to a distinctive feature analysis of handshapes in American Sign Language. *Cognitive Psychology, 8,* 263–289.

Lane, H., Pillard, R., & French, M. (2000). Origins of the American deaf-world: Assimilating and differentiating societies and their relation to genetic patterning. *Sign Language Studies, 1,* 17–44.

Lang, G. (2008). *Making Wawa: The Genesis of Chinook Jargon*. Vancouver, BC: University of British Columbia Press.

Launer, P. B. (1982). "A plane" is not "to fly": Acquiring the distinction between related nouns and verbs in American Sign Language. Doctoral dissertation, City University of New York, New York.

Lenneberg, E. H. (1967). *Biological Foundations of Language*. NewYork, NY: Wiley.

Lepic, R., Börstell, C., Belsitzman, G., & Sandler, W. (2016). Taking meaning in hand: Iconic motivations in two-handed signs. *Sign Language & Linguistics* 19, 37–81.

Lewin, T. (2010). Colleges see 16% increase in study of sign language. *The New York Times*.

Liberman, A. M., Cooper, F. S., Shankweiler, D. P., & Studdert-Kennedy, M. (1967). Perception of the speech code. *Psychological Review, 74,* 431–461.

Liberman, A. M., Harris, K. S., Hoffman, H. S., & Griffith, B. C. (1957). The discrimination of speech sounds within and across phoneme boundaries. *Journal of Experimental Psychology, 54,* 358.

Lichtenstein, E. H. (1998). The relationships between reading processes and English skills of deaf college students. *The Journal of Deaf Studies and Deaf Education, 3,* 80–134.

Liddell, S. (1984) THINK AND BELIEVE: Sequentiality in American Sign Language. *Language, 60,* 372–392.

Liddell, S. (2003). *Grammar, Gesture, and Meaning in American Sign Language*. Cambridge: Cambridge University Press.

Liddell, S., & Johnson, R. E. (1986). American Sign Language compound formation processes, lexicalization, and phonological remnants. *Natural Language & Linguistic Theory, 4,* 445–513.

Liddell, S., & Johnson, R. E. (1989). American Sign Language: The phonological base. *Sign Language Studies, 64*, 195–277.

Liddell, S. & Metzger, M. (1998). Gesture in sign language discourse. *Journal of Pragmatics, 30*, 657–697.

Lieberth, A. K. & Gamble, M. E. B. (1991). The role of iconicity in sign language learning by hearing adults. *Journal of Communication Disorders, 24*, 89–99.

Lillo-Martin, D. & Meier, R. P. (2011a). On the linguistic status of "agreement" in sign languages. *Theoretical Linguistics, 37*, 95–141.

Lillo-Martin, D. & Meier, R. P. (2011b). Response to commentaries: Gesture, language, and directionality. *Theoretical Linguistics, 37*, 235–246.

Loehr, D. (2007). Aspects of rhythm in gesture and speech. *Gesture, 7*, 179–214.

Long, J. S. (1918). *The Sign Language: A Manual of Signs, Being a Descriptive Vocabulary of Signs Used by the Deaf of the United States and Canada.* Gallaudet College. Des Moines, IA: R. Henderson.

Lu, J. & Goldin-Meadow, S. (2017). Combining categorical and gradient information in sign and spoken communication. Paper presented at the 11th International Symposium on Iconicity in Language and Literature. University of Brighton.

Lu, J., Jones, A., & Morgan, G. (2016). The impact of input quality on early sign development in native and non-native language learners. *Journal of Child Language, 43*, 537–552.

Lucas, C. (1995). Sociolinguistic variation in ASL: The case of DEAF. *Sociolinguistics in Deaf Communities, 1*, 3–25.

Lucas, C. & Bayley, R. (2010). Variation in American Sign Language. In D. Brentari (ed.), *Sign Languages* (pp. 451–75). Cambridge: Cambridge University Press.

Lucas, C., Bayley, R., Rose, M., & Wulf, A. (2002). Location variation in American Sign Language. *Sign Language Studies* 2(4). 407–440.

Lucas, C., Bayley, R., & Valli, C. (2001). *Sociolinguistic Variation in American Sign Language: Sociolinguistics in Deaf Communities*, Vol. VII. Washington, DC: Gallaudet University Press.

Lucas, C., Bayley, R., & Valli, C. (2003). *What's Your Sign for PIZZA? An Introduction to Variation in American Sign Language.* Washington, DC: Gallaudet University Press.

Luckner, J. L., & Handley, C. M. (2008). A summary of the reading comprehension research undertaken with students who are deaf or hard of hearing. *American Annals of the Deaf, 153*, 6–36.

Luttgens, K., Deutsch, H., & Hamilton, N. (1992). *Kinesiology: Scientific Basis of Human Motion. 8th edition.* Dubuque, IA: Brown and Benchmark.

MacNeilage, P. F. (2008). *The Origin of Speech.* Oxford: Oxford University Press.

MacNeilage, P. F., & Davis, B. L. (1993). Motor explanations of babbling and early speech patterns. In *Developmental Neurocognition: Speech and Face Processing in the First Year of Life* (pp. 341–352). Dordrecht: Springer.

MacSweeney, M., Brammer, M. J., Waters, D., & Goswami, U. (2009). Enhanced activation of the left inferior frontal gyrus in deaf and dyslexic adults during rhyming. *Brain, 132*, 1928–1940.

MacSweeney, M., Campbell, R., Calvert, G. A., McGuire, P. K., David, A. S., Suckling, J., & Brammer, M. J. (2001). Dispersed activation in the left temporal cortex for speech-reading in congenitally deaf people. *Proceedings of the Royal Society of London B: Biological Sciences, 268*, 451–457.

MacSweeney, M., Campbell, R., Woll, B., Giampietro, V., David, A., McGuire, P. K., Calvert, G. A., & Brammer, M. J. (2004). Dissociating linguistic and nonlinguistic gestural communication in the brain. *Neuroimage* 22, 1605–1618.

MacSweeney, M., & Cardin, V. (2015). What is the function of auditory cortex without auditory input? *Brain, 138*, 2468–2470.

MacSweeney, M., Goswami, U., & Neville, H. (2013). The neurobiology of rhyme judgment by deaf and hearing adults: An ERP study. *Journal of Cognitive Neuroscience, 25*, 1037–1048.

MacSweeney, M., Waters, D., Brammer, M. J., Woll, B., & Goswami, U. (2008). Phonological processing in deaf signers and the impact of age of first language acquisition. *Neuroimage, 40*, 1369–1379.

Maddieson, I. (1984). *Patterns of Sounds*. Cambridge/New York, NY: Cambridge University Press.

Maddieson, I., Bhattacharya, T. Smith, E., & Croft, W. (2011). Geographical distribution of phonological complexity. *Linguistic Typology*, 15, 267–279.

Mak, J. & Tang, G. (2012). Movement types, repetition, and feature organization in Hong Kong Sign Language. In H. van der Hulst & R. Channon (eds.), *Formational Units in the Analysis of Signs* (pp. 315–337). Nijmegan: Ishara Press.

Mandel, M. (1981). Phonotactics and morphophonology in American Sign Language. Doctoral dissertation, University of California, Berkeley, CA.

Mann, W., Marshall, C. R., Mason, K., & Morgan, G. (2010). The acquisition of sign language: The impact of phonetic complexity on phonology. *Language Learning and Development, 6*, 60–86.

Marentette, P. F. & Mayberry, R. I. (2000). Principles for an emerging phonological system: A case study of early ASL acquisition. In C. Chamberlain, J. Morford, & R. Mayberry (eds.), *Language Acquisition by Eye* (pp. 71–90). Mahwah, NJ: Lawrence Erlbaum Associates.

Markwardt, F. C. (1989). *Peabody Individual Achievement Test – Revised Manual*. Circle Pines, MI: American Guidance Service.

Marr, D. (1982). *Vision*. San Francisco, CA: W.H. Freeman.

Marschark, M. (2009). *Raising and Educating a Deaf Child: A Comprehensive Guide to the Choices, Controversies, and Decisions Faced by Parents and Educators*. Oxford: Oxford University Press.

Marshall, C. R. & Morgan, G. (2015). From gesture to sign language: Conventionalization of classifier constructions by adult hearing learners of British Sign Language. *Topics in Cognitive Science*, 7(1), 61–80.

Martinez del Rio, A. (2018). Distribution of structure within the handshape and movement parameters in ASL: A comparison of complexity based approaches. ms, University of Chicago.

Masataka, N. (1992). Motherese in a signed language. *Infant Behavior & Development*, 15, 453–60.

Mathur, G. & Rathmann, C. (2010a). Verb agreement in sign language morphology. In Diane Brentari (ed.), *Sign Languages* (pp. 173–196). Cambridge: Cambridge University Press.

Mathur, G. & Rathmann, C. (2010b). Two types of nonconcatenative morphology in signed languages. In G. Mathur & D.J. Napoli (eds.), *Deaf around the World: The Impact of Language* (pp. 54–82). Oxford/New York, NY: Oxford University Press.

Mauk, C. E. & Tyrone, M. E. (2012). Location in ASL: Insights from phonetic variation. *Sign Language & Linguistics*, 15, 128–146.

Mayberry, R. I. (2007). When timing is everything: Age of first-language acquisition effects on second-language learning. *Applied Psycholinguistics*, 28, 537–549.

Mayberry, R., Del Giudice, A. A., & Lieberman, A. M. (2011). Reading achievement in relation to phonological coding and awareness in deaf readers: A meta-analysis. *The Journal of Deaf Studies and Deaf Education*, 16, 164–188.

Mayberry, R. I. & Eichen, E. B. (1991). The long-lasting advantage of learning sign language in childhood: Another look at the critical period for language acquisition. *Journal of Memory and Language*, 30, 486–512.

Mayberry, R. I. & Fischer, S. D. (1989). Looking through phonological shape to lexical meaning: The bottleneck of non-native sign language processing. *Memory & Cognition*, 17, 740–754.

Mayberry, R. I. & Lock, E. (2003). Age constraints on first versus second language acquisition: Evidence for linguistic plasticity and epigenesis. *Brain and Language*, 87, 369–384.

Mayberry, R. I., Lock, E., & Kazmi, H. (2002). Development: Linguistic ability and early language exposure. *Nature*, 417(6884), 38.

Mayberry, R. I. & Witcher, P. (2005). *What Age of Acquisition Effects Reveal about the Nature of Phonological Processing* (Tech. Rept. No. 17, 3). San Diego, CA: University of California, San Diego, Center for Research in Language.

Maye, J. & Gerken, L. A. (2000a). Distributional cues to phonemic categories. In *Proceedings of the 20th Boston University Conference on Language Development*. Boston, MA: Cascadilla Press.

Maye, J., & Gerkin, L. (2000b). Learning phoneme categories without minimal pars. In S.C. Howell, S.A. Fish, & T. Keith-Lucas(eds.). *BUCLD* 24 (pp. 522–533). Somerville, MA: Cascadilla Press.

Maye, J. & Gerken, L. A. (2001). Learning phonemes: How far can the input take us? *Proceedings of the 21st Boston University Conference on Language Development*. Boston, MA: Cascadilla Press.

McCandliss, B. D., Fiez, J. A., Protopapas, A., Conway, M., & McClelland, J. L. (2002). Success and failure in teaching the [r]-[l] contrast to Japanese adults: Tests of a Hebbian model of plasticity and stabilization in spoken language perception. *Cognitive, Affective, & Behavioral Neuroscience*, *2*, 89–108.

McCarthy, J. (2001). *A Thematic Guide to Optimality Theory in Phonology*. Cambridge/New York, NY: Cambridge University Press.

McCarthy, J. & Prince, A. (1994). The emergence of the unmarked: optimality in prosodic morphology. ms. Rutgers University Community Repository.

McCarthy, J. & A. Prince. (1995). Faithfulness and reduplicative identity. In J Beckman, S. Urbanczyk, & L. Walsh (eds.), *University of Massachusetts Occasional Papers in Linguistics [UMOP]* Vol. 18: Papers in Optimality Theory (pp. 249–384). Amherst, MA: GLSA.

McCaskill, C., Lucas, C., Bayley, R., & Hill, J. (2011). *The Hidden Treasure of Black ASL: Its History and Structure*. Washington, DC: Gallaudet University Press.

McClave, E. Z. (2000). Linguistic functions of head movements in the context of speech. *Journal of Pragmatics*, *32*, 855–878.

McCullough, S. & Emmorey, K. (1997). Face processing by deaf ASL signers: Evidence for expertise in distinguishing local features. *Journal of Deaf Studies and Deaf Education*, 212–222.

McCullough, S. & Emmorey, K. (2009). Categorical perception of affective and linguistic facial expressions. *Cognition*, *110*, 208–221.

McGurk, H. & MacDonald, J. (1976). Hearing lips and seeing voices. *Nature*, *264*, 746.

McIntire, M. (1977). The acquisition of American Sign Language hand configurations. *Sign Language Studies*, 16, 247–266.

McIntire, M. L. & Reilly, J. (1996). Looking for frogs in the narrative stream: Global and local relations in maternal narratives. *Journal of Narrative and Life History*, *6*, 65–86.

McKee, D. & Kennedy, G. (2006). The distribution of signs in New Zealand Sign Language. *Sign Language Studies*, 6, 372–390.

McNeill, D. (1992). *Hand and Mind: What Gestures Reveal about Thought*. Chicago, IL: University of Chicago Press.

McQuarrie, L. & Parrila, R. (2009). Phonological representations in deaf children: Rethinking the "functional equivalence" hypothesis. *Journal of Deaf Studies and Deaf Education*, *14*, 137–154.

McQueen, J. (1996). Word spotting. *Language and Cognitive Processes*, 11, 695–699.

McQueen, J. M. & Cutler, A. (1998). Spotting (different kinds of) words in (different kinds of) context. *Proceedings of the Fifth International Conference on Spoken Language Processing*, *6*, 2791–2794.

Meir, I. (2002). A cross-modality perspective on verb agreement. *Natural Language & Linguistic Theory, 20*, 413–450.

Meir, I. (2010). Iconicity and metaphor: Constraints on metaphoric extension of iconic forms. *Language, 86*, 865–986.

Meir, I., Padden, C. A., Aronoff, M., & Sandler, W. (2007). Body as subject. *Journal of Linguistics, 43*(3), 531–563.

Meir, I., Sandler, W., Padden, C., & Aronoff, M. (2010). Emerging sign languages. In M Marschark & P. Spencer (eds.), *Oxford Handbook of Deaf Studies, Language, and Education, vol 2* (pp. 267–280). Oxford: Oxford University Press.

Meier, R. (1993). A psycholinguistic perspective on phonological segmentation in sign and speech. In G. Coulter (ed.), *Current Issues in ASL Phonology* (pp. 169–188). San Diego, CA: Academic Press.

Meier, R. (2002a). Why different, why the same? Explaining effects and non-effects of modality upon linguistic structure in sign and speech. In R. P. Meier, Kearsy Cormier, & David Q. Quinto-Pozos (eds.), *Modality and Structure in Signed and Spoken Languages* (pp. 1–25). Cambridge: Cambridge University Press.

Meier, R. (2002b). The acquisition of verb agreement: Pointing out arguments for the linguistic status of agreement in signed languages. In G. Morgan & B. Woll (eds.), *Directions in Sign Language Acquisition* (pp. 115–141). Amsterdam: John Benjamins Associates.

Meier, R. (2006). The form of early signs: Explaining signing children's articulatory development. In M. Marschark, B. Schick, & P. Spencer *Advances in the Sign Language Development of Deaf Children* (pp. 202–230). Oxford: Oxford University Press.

Meier, R. (2012). Language and modality. In R. Pfau, M. Steinbach, & B. Woll (eds.), *Sign Language: An International Handbook* (pp. 574–601). Berlin: Mouton de Gruyter.

Meier, R. P., Mauk, C. E., Cheek, A., & Moreland, C. J. (2008). The form of children's early signs: Iconic or motoric determinants? *Language Learning and Development, 4*(1), 63–98.

Meier, R. & Newport, E. (1991). Language acquisition by deaf children, *American Scientist, 79*, 60–70.

Michaels, J. (1923). *A Handbook of the Sign Language of the Deaf.* Atlanta, GA: Southern Baptist Convention.

Mielke, J. (2005). Modeling Distinctive Feature Emergence. In J. Alderete, C. Han, & A. Kochetov (eds.), *Proceedings of the 24th West Coast Conference on Formal Linguistics* (pp. 281–289). Somerville, MA: Cascadilla Proceedings Project.

Miller, G. A. & Nicely, P. E. (1955). An analysis of perceptual confusions among some English consonants. *The Journal of the Acoustical Society of America, 27*, 338–352.

Mirus, G. R., Rathmann, C., & Meier, R. P. (2001). Proximalization and distalization of sign movement in adult learners. In V. L. Dively,

M. Metzger, S. Taub, & A. M. Baer (eds.), *Signed Languages: Discoveries from International Research* (pp. 103–119). Washington, DC: Gallaudet University Press.

Mithun, M. (1984). The evolution of noun incorporation. *Language, 60,* 847–894.

Mohay, H., Milton, L., Hindmarsh, G., & Ganley, K. (1998). Deaf mothers as language models for hearing families with deaf children. In A. Weisel (ed.), *Issues Unresolved: New Perspectives on Language and Deafness* (pp. 76–87). Washington, DC: Gallaudet University Press.

Moreton, E. (2008). Analytic bias and phonological typology. *Phonology, 25,* 83–127.

Morford, J. P. & Carlson, M. L. (2011). Sign perception and recognition in non-native signers of ASL. *Language Learning and Development, 7,* 149–168.

Morford, J. P., Grieve-Smith, A. B., MacFarlane, J., Staley, J., & Waters, G. (2008). Effects of language experience on the perception of American Sign Language. *Cognition, 109,* 41–53.

Morford, J. P. & Kegl, J. A. (2000). Gestural precursors to linguistic constructs: How input shapes the form of language. In D. McNeill (ed.), *Language and Gesture* (Vol.2, pp. 358–387). Cambridge: Cambridge University Press.

Morford, J. P., Kroll, J. F., Piñar, P., & Wilkinson, E. (2014). Bilingual word recognition in deaf and hearing signers: Effects of proficiency and language dominance on cross-language activation. *Second Language Research, 30,* 251–271.

Morford, J. P., Wilkinson, E., Villwock, A., Piñar, P., & Kroll, J. F. (2011). When deaf signers read English: Do written words activate their sign translations? *Cognition, 118,* 286–292.

Morgan, G., Barrett-Jones, S., & Stoneham, H. (2007). The first signs of language: Phonological development in British Sign Language. *Applied Psycholinguistics, 28,* 3–22.

Motamedi, Y., Schouwstra, M., Culbertson, J., & Smith, K, Kirby, S. (2017). The cultural evolution of complex linguistic constructions in artificial sign languages. *Proceedings of the 39th Annual Meeting of the Cognitive Science Society.*

Mous, M. (2007). *A Sketch of Iraqw Grammar.* Leiden: Leiden University, Centre of Linguistics.

Mufwene, S. (2013). Language as technology: Some questions that evolutionary linguistics should address. In T. Lohndal (ed.), *In Search of Universal Grammar. From Old Norse to Zoque.* Amsterdam: John Benjamins.

Mulrooney, K. J. (2002). Variation in ASL fingerspelling. In P. M. Chute & C. Lucas (eds.), *Turn-Taking, Fingerspelling, and Contact in Signed Languages* (pp. 3–23). Washington, DC: Gallaudet University Press.

Munakata, Y. & Pfaffly, J. (2004). Hebbian learning and development. *Developmental Science, 7*(2), 141–148.

Nänny, M. & Fischer, O. (2002). *Iconicity in Language and Literature 3.* Amsterdam/Philadelphia, PA: John Benjamins.

Neidle, C., Kegl, J., MacLaughlin, D. Bahan, B., & Lee, R. (2000). *The Syntax of American Sign Language. Functional Categories and Hierarchical Structure.* Cambridge, MA: MIT Press.

Nespor, M. & Sandler, W. (1999). Prosody in Israeli Sign Language. *Language and Speech, 42,* 143-176.

Nespor, M. & Vogel, I. (1986). *Prosodic Phonology.* Dordrecht: Foris.

Neville, H. J., Bavelier, D., Corina, D., Rauschecker, J., Karni, A., Lalwani, A., Braun, A., Clark, V., Jezzard, P., & Turner, R. (1998). Cerebral organization for language in deaf and hearing subjects: Biological constraints and effects of experience. *Proceedings of the National Academy of Sciences, 95* (3), 922-929.

Neville, H., Coffey, S., Lawson, D., Fischer, A., Emmorey, K., & Bellugi, U. (1997). Neural systems mediating American Sign Language: Effects of sensory experience and age: Effects of sensory experience and age of acquisition. *Brain and Language, 57,* 285-308.

Neville, H. J. & Lawson D. (1987a) Attention to central and peripheral visual space in a movement detection task: An event-related potential and behavioral study. I. Normal hearing adults. *Brain Research/ Cognitive Brain Research, 405,* 253-267.

Neville, H. J. & Lawson D. (1987b). Attention to central and peripheral visual space in a movement detection task: An event-related potential and behavioral study. II. Congenitally deaf adults. *Brain Research/Cognitive Brain Research, 405,* 268-283.

Neville H. J. & Lawson D. (1987c). Attention to central and peripheral visual space in a movement detection task. III. Separate effects of auditory deprivation and acquisition of a visual language. *Brain Research/ Cognitive Brain Research, 405,* 284-294.

Nevins, A., Pesetsky, D., & Rodrigues, C. (2009). Evidence and argumentation: A reply to Everett (2009). *Language, 85,* 671-681.

Newman, A. J., Supalla, T., Fernandez, N., Newport, E. L., & Bavelier, D. (2015). Neural systems supporting linguistic structure, linguistic experience, and symbolic communication in sign language and gesture. *Proceedings of the National Academy of Sciences, 112,* 11684-11689.

Newport, E. L. (1982). Task specificity in language learning? Evidence from American Sign Language. In E. Wanner & L. A. Gleitman (eds.), *Language Acquisition: The State of the Art* (pp. 450-486). Cambridge: Cambridge University Press.

Newport, E. L. (1990). Maturational constraints on language learning. *Cognitive Science, 14,* 11-28.

Newport, E. L. & Supalla, T. (2000). Sign language research at the millennium. In K. Emmorey & H. Lane (eds.), *The Signs of Language Revisited: An Anthology to Honor Ursula Bellugi and Edward Klima* (pp. 103-114). Mahwah, NJ: Lawrence Erlbaum Associates.

Nittrouer, S. & B. Pnnington. (2010). New approaches to the study of childhood language disorders. *Current Directions in Psychological Science* 19, 308–313.

Nobe, S. (2000). Where do most spontaneous representational gestures actually occur with respect to speech. In D. McNeill (ed.), *Language and Gesture* (Vol. 2, pp. 186–198). Cambridge: Cambridge University Press.

Norris, D., McQueen, J. M., Cutler, A., & Butterfield, S. (1997). The possible word constraint in the segmentation of continuous speech. *Cognitive Psychology*, 34, 191–243.

Nyst, V. (2010). Sign languages in West Africa. In D. Brentari (ed.), *Sign Languages* (pp. 405–432). Cambridge: Cambridge University Press.

Occhino, C. (2017). An introduction to embodied cognitive phonology: Claw-5 handshape distribution in ASL and Libras. *Complutense Journal of English Studies*, 25, 60–103.

Occhino, C., Anible, B., Wilkinson, E., & Morford, J. P. (2017). Iconicity is in the eye of the beholder. *Gesture*, 16, 100–126.

Ohala, J. J. (1990). Alternatives to the sonority hierarchy for explaining segmental sequential constraints. In M. Ziolkowski, M. Noske, & K. Deaton (eds.), *Proceedings for the Annual Meeting of the Chicago Linguistic Society, 26. Vol. II: The Parasession on the Syllable in Phonetics and Phonology* (pp. 319–338). Chicago, IL: Chicago Linguistic Society.

Ohala, J. J. & Kawasaki, H. (1984). Prosodic phonology and phonetics. *Phonology*, 1, 113–127.

Okrent, A. (2002). A modality-free notion of gesture and how it can help us with the morpheme vs. gesture question in sign language linguistics, or at least give us some criteria to work with. In R. P. Meier, D. G. Quinto, & K. A. Cormier, (eds.), *Modality and Structure in Signed and Spoken Languages* (pp. 175–198). Cambridge: Cambridge University Press.

Orfanidou, E., Adam, R., Morgan, G., & McQueen, J. M. (2010). Recognition of signed and spoken language: Different sensory inputs, the same segmentation procedure. *Journal of Memory and Language*, 62, 272–283.

Orlansky, M. & Bonvillian, J. (1984). The role of iconicity in early sign acquisition. *Journal of Speech and Hearing Disorders*, 28, 47–63.

Ormel, E., Hermans, D., Knoors, H., & Verhoeven, L. (2012). Cross-language effects in written word recognition: The case of bilingual deaf children. *Bilingualism: Language and Cognition*, 15, 288–303.

Ortega, G. & Morgan, G. (2015). Phonological development in hearing learners of a sign language: The influence of phonological parameters, sign complexity, and iconicity. *Language Learning*, 65, 660–688.

Ortega, G., Sumer, B., & Ozyürek, A. (2014). Type of iconicity matters: Bias for action-based signs in sign language acquisition. In P. Bello, M. Guarini, M. McShane, & B. Scassellatie (eds.), *36th Annual Conference of the Cognitive Science Society* (pp. 1114–1119). Austin, TX: Cognitive Science Society.

Oxford, W. (2013). A contrast-based model of merger. In S. Keine & S. Sloggett (eds.), *Proceedings of NELS 42, Volume 2* (pp. 95–106). Amherst, MA: GLSA.

Padden, C. (1983). Interaction of morphology and syntax in American Sign Language. Doctoral dissertation, University of California, San Diego. Published 1988, New York: Garland Press.

Padden, C. (2006). Learning to fingerspell twice. In B. Schick, M. Marschark, & P. Spencer (eds.), *Advances in the Sign Language Development of Deaf Children* (pp.189–201). New York, NY/Oxford: Oxford University Press.

Padden, C. & Humphries, T. (2005) *Inside Deaf Culture*. Cambridge, MA: Harvard University Press.

Padden, C. A. (1988). Grammatical theory and signed languages. In F. J. Newmeyer (ed.), *Linguistics: The Cambridge Survey: Volume 2, Linguistic Theory: Extensions and Implications* (pp. 250–266). Cambridge: Cambridge University Press.

Padden, C. A. & Humphries, T. (1990). *Deaf in America: Voices from a Culture*. Cambridge, MA: Harvard University Press.

Padden C. A., Meir, I., Aronoff, M., & Sandler, W. (2010). The grammar of space in two new sign languages. In D. Brentari (ed.), *Sign Languages: A Cambridge Language Survey* (pp. 570–592). Cambridge: Cambridge University Press.

Padden, C. A. & Perlmutter, D. M. (1987). American Sign Language and the architecture of phonological theory. *Natural Language & Linguistic Theory*, 5, 335–375.

Padden, C. A., & Ramsey, C. (1998). Reading ability in signing deaf children. *Topics in Language Disorders*, 18, 30–46.

Pallier, C., Colomé, A., & Sebastián-Gallés, N. (2001). The influence of native-language phonology on lexical access: Exemplar-based versus abstract lexical entries. *Psychological Science*, 12, 445–449.

Pan, Z. & Tang, G. (2017). Deaf children's acquisition of the phonec features of handshape in Hong Kong Sign Language (HKSL). Paper presented at the Conference on Formal and Experimental Approaches to Sign Theory (FEAST). University of Reykjavik, Iceland.

Patel, R. & Brayton, J. T. (2009). Identifying prosodic contrasts in utterances produced by 4-, 7-, and 11-year-old children. *Journal of Speech, Language, and Hearing Research*, 52, 790–801.

Peirce, C. S. (1958) *Collected Papers of Charles Sanders Peirce, 1931-1935*. Cambridge, MA: Harvard University Press.

Pélissier, P. (1856). *Iconographie des signes*. Paris: Dupont.

Penfield, W. & Roberts, L. (1959). *Speech and Brain-Mechanisms*. Princeton, NJ: Princeton University Press.

Pendzich, Nina-Kristin. (2017). Lexical nonmanuals in German Sign Language (DGS). Doctoral dissertation. Georg-August-Universität Göttingen, Göttingen.

Perfetti, C. A. & Sandak, R. (2000). Reading optimally builds on spoken language: Implications for deaf readers. *Journal of Deaf Studies and Deaf Education*, 5, 32–50.

Perlmutter, D. (1992). Sonority and syllable structure in American Sign Language. *Linguistic Inquiry*, 23, 407–442.

Perniss, P., Lu, J. C., Morgan, G., & Vigliocco, G. (2017). Mapping language to the world: The role of iconicity in the sign language input. *Developmental Science*, 21(2), e12551.

Perniss, P., Thompson, R., & Vigliocco, G. (2010). Iconicity as a general property of language: Evidence from spoken and signed languages. *Frontiers in Psychology*, 1, 227.

Petitto, L. A., Berens, M. S., Kovelman, I., Dubins, M. H., Jasinska, K., & Shalinsky, M. (2012). The "Perceptual Wedge Hypothesis" as the basis for bilingual babies' phonetic processing advantage: New insights from fNIRS brain imaging. *Brain and Language*, 121, 130–143.

Petitto, L. A., Holowka, S., Sergio, L. E., Levy, B., & Ostry, D. J. (2004). Baby hands that move to the rhythm of language: Hearing babies acquiring sign languages babble silently on the hands. *Cognition*, 93, 43–73.

Petitto, L. A., Langdon, C., Stone, A., Andriola, D., Kartheiser, G., & Cochran, C. (2016). Visual sign phonology: Insights into human reading and language from a natural soundless phonology. *Wiley Interdisciplinary Reviews: Cognitive Science*, 7, 366–381.

Petitto, L. A. & Marentette, P. F. (1991). Babbling in the manual mode: Evidence for the ontogeny of language. *Science*, 251, 1493–1496.

Petitto, L. A., Zatorre, R. J., Gauna, K., Nikelski, E. J., Dostie, D., & Evans, A. C. (2000). Speech-like cerebral activity in profoundly deaf people processing signed languages: Implications for the neural basis of human language. *Proceedings of the National Academy of Sciences*, 97, 13961–13966.

Pfau, R. (2016). Non-manuals and tones: A comparative perspective on suprasegmentals and spreading. *Linguística Revista de Estudos Linguísticos da Universidade do Porto*, 11, 19–58.

Pfau, R. & Quer, J. (2010). Nonmanuals: Their prosodic and grammatical roles. In D. Brentari (ed.), *Sign Languages: A Cambridge Language Survey* (pp. 381–402). Cambridge: Cambridge University Press.

Pfau, R. & Steinbach, M. (2004) On grammaticalization: Do sign languages follow the well-trodden paths? Presentation at the Theoretical Issues in Sign Language Research conference, Barcelona, Spain.

Pierrehumbert, J. (2001). Exemplar dynamics: Word frequency, lenition and contrast. In J. Bybee & P. Hopper (eds.), *Frequency Effects and Emergent Grammar* (pp. 137–158). Amsterdam: John Benjamins.

Pierrehumbert, J. & Hirschberg, J. (1990). The meaning of intonational contours in discourse. In P. Cohen, J. Morgan, & M. Pollack (eds.), *Intentions in Communication* (pp. 271–311). Cambridge, MA: MIT Press.

Pinedo Peydró, F. J. (2000). *Diccionario de la lengua de signos espanola*. Madrid: CNSE.

Plato. *Cratylus*. Translation by C.D.C. Reeve, (1998), Indianapolis, IN: Hackett Publishing.

Poeppel, D. & Idsardi, W. (2011). Recognizing words from speech: The perception-action-memory loop. In G. Gaskell & P. Zwitserlood (eds.), *Lexical Representation* (pp. 171–196). Mouton de Gruyter.

Poizner, H. (1983). Perception of movement in American Sign Language: Effects of linguistic structure and linguistic experience. *Perception & Psychophysics*, 33, 215–231.

Poizner, H., Bellugi, U., & Tweney, R.D. (1981). Processing of formational, semantic, and iconic information in American Sign Language. *Journal of Experimental Psychology: Human Perception and Performance*, 7, 1146.

Poizner, H., Brentari, D., Kegl, J., & Tyrone, M. (2000). The structure of language as motor behavior: Evidence from signers with Parkinson's disease. In K. Emmorey & H. Lane (eds.), *The Signs of Language Revisited: An Anthology to Honor Ursula Bellugi and Edward Klima* (pp. 509–532). Mahwah, NJ: Lawrence Erlbaum Associates.

Poizner, H., Klima, E., & Bellugi, U. (1987). *What the Hands Reveal about the Brain*. Cambridge, MA: MIT Press.

Poldrack, R. A., Wagner, A. D., Prull, M. W., Desmond, J. E., Glover, G. H., & Gabrieli, J. D. (1999). Functional specialization for semantic and phonological processing in the left inferior prefrontal cortex. *Neuroimage*, 10, 15–35.

Price, C. J., Moore, C. J., Humphreys, G. W., & Wise, R. J. S. (1997). Segregating semantic from phonological processes during reading. *Journal of Cognitive Neuroscience*, 9, 727–733.

Prince, A. & Smolensky, P. (1993). *Optimality Theory*. Technical Report #2 of the Rutgers Center for Cognitive Science, Rutgers, NJ.

Pustejovsky, J. (1995). *The Generative Lexicon*. Cambridge, MA: MIT Press.

Puupponen, A., Wainio, T., Burger, B., & Jantunen, T. (2015). Head movements in Finnish Sign Language on the basis of motion capture data: A study of the form and function of nods, nodding, head thrusts, and head pulls. *Sign Language & Linguistics*, 18, 41–89.

Pyers, J., Gollan, T. H., & Emmorey, K. (2009). Bimodal bilinguals reveal the source of tip-of the-tongue states. *Cognition*, 112, 323–329.

Quer, J. (2005). Context shift and indexical variables in sign languages. In E. Georgala & J. Howell (eds.), *Proceedings of Semantics and Linguistic Theory (SALT) 15* (pp. 152–168). Ithaca, NY: CLC Publications.

Quer, J. (2012). Negation. In R. Pfau, M. Steinbach, & B. Woll (eds.), *Sign Language: An International Handbook* (pp. 316–338). Berlin: Mouton de Gruyter.

Radutzky, E. J. (1989). La lingua italiana dei segni: Historical change in the sign language of deaf people in Italy. Doctoral dissertation, New York University, New York.

Ramachandran, V. S. & Hubbard, E. M. (2001). Synaesthesia – a window into perception, thought and language. *Journal of Consciousness Studies*, 8, 3–34.

Ramsey, C. (1997). *Deaf Children in Public Schools: Placement, Contexts, and Consequences*. Washington, DC: Gallaudet University Press.

Ramus, F., Nespor, M., & Mehler, J. (1999). Correlates of linguistic rhythm in the speech signal. *Cognition*, 73, 265–292.

Rathmann, C. & Mathur, G. (2012). Verb agreement. In R. Pfau, M. Steinbach, & B. Woll (eds.), *Sign Language: An International Handbook* (pp. 136–57). Berlin: DeGruyter.

Ratliff, M. (1992). *Meaningful Tone: A Study of Tonal Morphology in Compounds, Form Classes, and Expressive Phrases in White Hmong*. Dekalb, IL: Northern Illinois University Press.

Redd, Nola Taylor. (2012). "How Fast Does Light Travel? | The Speed of Light." *Space.com*, Space.com, 7 Mar. 2018, www.space.com/15830-light-speed.html.

Reh, M. (1983). Krongo: A VSO language with postpositions. *Journal of African Languages and Linguistics*, 5, 45–55.

Reilly, J., McIntire, M., & Anderson, D. (1994). Look who's talking! Point of view and character reference in mothers' and children's ASL narrative. Paper presented at the Boston University Conference on Language Development (BUCLD).

Reilly, J., McIntire, M., & Bellugi, U. (1991). Baby face: A new perspective on universals in language acquisition. In P. Siple & S. Fischer (eds.), *Theoretical Issues in Sign Language Research: Psychology* (pp. 9–23) Chicago, IL: University of Chicago Press.

Reilly, J., McIntire, M., & Ursula Bellugi, U. (1990). Faces: The relationship between language and affect. In V. Volterra & C. Erting (eds.) *From Gesture to Language in Hearing and Deaf Children* (pp. 128–41). New York, NY: Springer.

Riazantseva, A. (2001). Second language proficiency and pausing a study of Russian speakers of English. *Studies in Second Language Acquisition*, 23, 497–526.

Riedl, T. R. & Sperling, G. (1988). Spatial-frequency bands in complex visual stimuli: American Sign Language. *JOSA A*, 5, 606–616.

Rimor, M., Kegl, J., Lane, H., & Schermer, T. (1984). Natural phonetic processes underlie historical change & register variation in American Sign Language. *Sign Language Studies*, 97–119.

Roberson, D. & Davidoff, J. (2000). The categorical perception of colors and facial expressions: The effect of verbal interference. *Memory & Cognition*, 28, 977–986.

Rubach, J. & Booij, G. E. (1990). Edge of constituent effects in Polish. *Natural Language & Linguistic Theory*, 8(3), 427–463.

Russo, T. (2005) A cross-cultural, cross-linguistic analysis of metaphors in two Italian Sign Language registers. *Sign Language Studies*, 5, 333–359.

Sáfár, A. & Crasborn, O. (2013). A corpus-based approach to manual simultaneity. In L. Meurant, A. Sinte, M. Van Herreweghe, & M. Vermeerbergen (eds.), *Sign Language Research, Uses and Practices: Crossing Views on Theoretical and Applied Sign Language Linguistics* (pp. 179–203). Berlin: Mouton de Gruyter.

Sáfár, A. & Kimmelman, V. (2015). Weak hand holds in two sign languages and two genres. *Sign Language & Linguistics*, *18*, 205–237.

Sagey, E. (1986). The representation of features and relations in non-linear phonology. Doctoral dissertation, Massachusetts Institute of Technology, Cambridge, MA.

Sanders, N. & Napoli, D. J. (2016a). Reactive effort as a factor that shapes sign language lexicons. *Language*, *92*, 275–297.

Sanders, N. & Napoli, D. J. (2016b). A cross-linguistic preference for torso stability in the lexicon. *Sign Language & Linguistics*, *19*(2), 197–231.

Sandler, W. (1986). The spreading hand autosegment of American Sign Language. *Sign Language Studies*, *50*, 1–28.

Sandler, W. (1989). *Phonological Representation of the Sign: Linearity and Nonlinearity in American Sign Language*. Dordrecht: Foris.

Sandler, W. (1993). A sonority cycle in American Sign Language. *Phonology*, *10*, 243–279.

Sandler, W. (1999a). The medium and the message: Prosodic interpretation of linguistic content in Israeli Sign Language. *Sign Language & Linguistics*, *2*, 187–216.

Sandler, W. (1999b). Cliticization and prosodic words in a sign language. In T. A. Hall & U. Kleinhenz (eds.), *Studies on the Phonological Word* (pp. 223–55). Amsterdam: John Benjamins.

Sandler, W. (2009) Symbiotic symbolization by hand and mouth in sign language. *Semiotica*, *174*, 241–75.

Sandler, W. (2010). Prosody and syntax in sign languages. *Transactions of the Philological Society*, *108*, 298–328.

Sandler, W. (2012a). Visual prosody. In R. Pfau, M. Steinbach, & B. Woll (eds.), *Sign Language: An International Handbook* (pp. 55–77). Berlin: De Gruyter Mouton.

Sandler, W. (2012b). Dedicated gestures and the emergence of sign language. *Gesture*, *12*(3), 265–307.

Sandler, W. (2014). Emergence of phonetic and phonological features in sign language. *Nordlyd*, *41*, 183–212.

Sandler, W. (2016). What comes first in language emergence? In N. Enfield (ed.), *Dependency in Language: On the Causal Ontology of Language Systems. Studies in Diversity in Linguistics 99* (pp. 67–86). Berlin: Language Science Press.

Sandler, W., Aronoff, M., Meir, I., & Padden, C. A. (2011a). The gradual emergence of phonological form in a new language. *Natural Language & Linguistic Theory*, *29*, 503–543.

Sandler, W. & Lillo-Martin, D. (2006). *Sign Language and Linguistic Universals.* Cambridge/New York, NY: Cambridge University Press.

Sandler, W., Meir, I., Dachkovsky, S., Padden, C., & Aronoff, M. (2011b). The emergence of complexity in prosody and syntax. *Lingua*, 121(13), 2014–2033.

Sandler, W., Meir, I., Padden, C., & Aronoff, M. (2005). The emergence of grammar: Systematic structure in a new language. *Proceedings of the National Academy of Sciences*, 102, 2656–2665.

Sapir, E. (1921). *An Introduction to the Study of Speech.* New York, NY: Harcourt, Brace.

Savage-Rumbaugh, E. S. (1986). *Ape Language: From Conditioned Response to Symbol.* New York, NY: Columbia University Press.

Schane. S. (1984). The fundamentals of particle phonology. *Phonology Yearbook*, 1, 129–155.

Schein, J. D. (1989). *At Home among Strangers: Exploring the Deaf Community in the United States.* Washington, DC: Gallaudet University Press.

Schembri, A., Fenlon, J., Cormier, K., & Johnston, T. (2018). Sociolinguistic typology and sign languages. *Frontiers in Psychology*, 9, 200.

Schembri, A. & Johnston, T. A. (2007). Sociolinguistic variation in the use of fingerspelling in Australian Sign Language: A pilot study. *Sign Language Studies*, 7, 319–347.

Schembri, A., Jones, C., & Burnham, D. (2005). Comparing action gestures and classifier verbs of motion: Evidence from Australian Sign Language, Taiwan Sign Language, and nonsigners' gestures without speech. *Journal of Deaf Studies and Deaf Education*, 10, 272–290.

Schembri, A., McKee, D., McKee, R., Pivac, S., Johnston, T., & Goswell, D. (2009). Phonological variation and change in Australian and New Zealand Sign Languages: The location variable. *Language Variation and Change*, 21, 193–231.

Schermer, T. (1990). In search of a language: Influences from spoken Dutch on Sign Language of the Netherlands. Doctoral dissertation, University of Amsterdam, Amsterdam.

Schermer, T. (2001). The role of mouthings in Sign Language of the Netherlands: Some implications for the production of sign language dictionaries, in P. Boyes Braem & R. Sutton-Spence (eds.), *The Hands are the Head of the Mouth: The Mouth as Articulator in Sign Languages* (pp. 273–284). Hamburg: Signum.

Schick, B. (1990). The effects of morphosyntactic structure on the acquisition of classifier predicates in ASL. In C. Lucas (ed.), *Sign Language Research: Theoretical Issues* (pp. 358–374). Washington, DC: Gallaudet University Press.

Schlehofer, D. & Tyler, I. J. (2016). Errors in second language learners' production of phonological contrasts in American Sign Language. *International Journal of Language and Linguistics*, 3, 30–38.

Schlenker, P. (2018a). Visible meaning: Sign language and the foundations of semantics. *Theoretical Linguistics*.

Schlenker. P. (2018b). Gesture projection and cosuppositions. *Linguistics and Philosophy*, 41, 295–365.

Schlenker, P. & Lambert, J. (2017). Iconic plurality in ASL. Paper presented at the Formal and Experimental Approaches to Sign Theory Conference (FEAST). Reykjavik, Iceland.

Scott, S. K. & Johnsrude, I. S. (2003). The neuroanatomical and functional organization of speech perception. *Trends in Neurosciences*, 26, 100–107.

Sehyr, Z. S. & Cormier, K. (2015). Perceptual categorization of handling handshapes in British Sign Language. *Language and Cognition*, 8, 501–532.

Sehyr, Z. S. & Cormier, K. (2016). Perceptual categorization of handling handshapes in British Sign Language. *Language and Cognition*, 8, 501–532.

Sehyr, Z. S., Petrich, J., & Emmorey, K. (2016). Fingerspelled and printed words are recoded into a speech-based code in short-term memory. *The Journal of Deaf Studies and Deaf Education*, 1–16.

Seidenberg, M. S. & Zevin, J. D. (2006). Connectionist models in developmental cognitive neuroscience: Critical periods and the paradox of success. *Attention & Performance XXI: Processes of Change in Brain and Cognitive Development*, 585–612.

Selkirk, E. (2011). The syntax-phonology interface. In J. Goldsmith, J. Riggle, & A. C. L. Yu (eds.), *The Handbook of Phonological Theory*, 2nd Edition. (pp. 435–84). Oxford: Wiley-Blackwell.

Senghas A. (1995). Children's contribution to the birth of Nicaraguan Sign Language, Doctoral dissertation, Massachusetts Institute of Technology, Cambridge, MA.

Senghas, A. (2010). The emergence of two functions for spatial devices in Nicaraguan sign language. *Human Development* 53: 287–302.

Senghas, A. (2005). Language emergence: Clues from a new Bedouin sign. *Current Biology*, 15, R463–R465.

Senghas, R., Senghas, A., & Pyers, J. (2005). The emergence of Nicaraguan Sign Language: Questions of development, acquisition, and evolution. In J. Langer, C. Milbrath, & S. Parker (eds.), *Biology and Knowledge Revisited: From Neurogenesis to Psychogenesis* (pp. 287–306). Mahwah, NJ: Lawrence Erlbaum Associates.

Sevcikova, Z. (2014). Categorical versus gradient properties of handling handshapes in British Sign Language (BSL). Doctoral dissertation, University College London, London.

Sherer, T. (1994). *Prosodic Phonotactics*. Doctoral dissertation, University of Massachusetts, Amherst.

Shintel, H., Nusbaum, H. C., & Okrent, A. (2006). Analog acoustic expression in speech communication. *Journal of Memory and Language*, 55, 167–177.

Shport, I. A. & Redford, M. A. (2014). Lexical and phrasal prominence patterns in school-aged children's speech. *Journal of Child Language, 41,* 890–912.

Siegel, G. M., Clay, J. L., & Naeve, S. L. (1992). The effects of auditory and visual interference on speech and sign. *Journal of Speech, Language, and Hearing Research, 35,* 1358–1362.

Singleton, J. L., Morford, J. P., & Goldin-Meadow, S. (1993). Once is not enough: Standards of well-formedness in manual communication created over three different timespans. *Language, 69,* 683–715.

Siple, P. (1978). Visual constraints for sign language communication. *Sign Language Studies, 19,* 97–112.

Slowiaczek, L. M. & Pisoni, D. B. (1986). Effects of phonological similarity on priming in auditory lexical decision. *Memory & Cognition, 14,* 230–237.

Smith, A., Johnson, M., McGillem, C., & Goffman, L. (2000). On the assessment of stability and patterning of speech movements. *Journal of Speech, Language, and Hearing Research, 43,* 277–286.

Spencer, P. E., Bodner-Johnson, B. A., & Gutfreund, M. K. (1992). Interacting with infants with a hearing loss: What can we learn from mothers who are deaf? *Journal of Early Intervention, 16,* 64–78.

Sperling, G. (1980). Bandwidth requirements for video transmission of American Sign Language and finger spelling. *Science, 210,* 797–799.

Starr, C., Evers, C., & Starr, L. (2005). *Biology: Concepts and Applications.* Pacific Grove, CA: Thomson Brooks/Cole.

Sterne, A., & Goswami, U. (2000). Phonological awareness of syllables, rhymes, and phonemes in deaf children. *The Journal of Child Psychology and Psychiatry and Allied Disciplines, 41,* 609–625.

Stokoe, W. (1960). *Sign Language Structure: An Outline of the Visual Communication Systems of the American Deaf.* Buffalo, NY: University of Buffalo (Occasional Papers 8).

Stokoe, W. Casterline, D., & Croneberg, C. (1965). *A Dictionary of American Sign Language on Linguistic Principles.* Washington, DC: Gallaudet College Press.

Stone, A. (2017). Neural systems for infant sensitivity to phonological rhythmic-temporal patterning. Doctoral dissertation, Gallaudet University, Washington, DC.

Stone, A., Kartheiser, G., Hauser, P. C., Petitto, L. A., & Allen, T. E. (2015). Fingerspelling as a novel gateway into reading fluency in deaf bilinguals. *PloS One, 10,* e0139610.

Stone, A., Petitto, L. A., & Bosworth, R. (2018). Visual sonority modulates infants' attraction to sign language. *Language Learning and Development, 14,* 130–148.

Strickland, B., Geraci, C., Chemla, E., Schlenker, P., Kelepir, M., & Pfau, R. (2015). Event representations constrain the structure of language: Sign language as a window into universally accessible linguistic biases.

Proceedings of the National Academy of Sciences of the United States of America, 112(19), 5968–73.

Strutt, R. & William, J. (1896). *The Theory of Sound* (2nd ed.). London: MacMillan & Co.

Supalla, T. (1982). Structure and acquisition of verbs of motion and location in American Sign Language. Doctoral dissertation, University of California, San Diego.

Supalla, T. (2009). Sign language archeology. *Deaf Studies Digital Journal*, 1, 1–5.

Supalla, T. (2010). Using etymology to link ASL to LSF. *Deaf Studies Digital Journal*, 2, 1–7.

Supalla, T. & Clarke, P. (2015). *Sign Language Archeology*. Washington, DC: Gallaudet University Press.

Supalla, T. & Newport, E. L. (1978). How many seats in a chair? The derivation of nouns and verbs in American Sign Language. In P. Siple (ed.), *Understanding Language through Sign Language Research* (pp. 91–132). New York, NY: Academic Press.

Swingley, D. (2009). Contributions of infant word learning to language development. *Philosophical Transactions of the Royal Society of London B: Biological Sciences*, 364, 3617–3632.

Sze, F. (2008). Blinks and intonational phrases in Hong Kong Sign Language. In J. Quer (ed.), *Signs of the Time: Selected Papers from TISLR 2004* (pp. 83–107). Hamburg: Signum.

Takkinen, Ritva (1995). Phonological acquisition of sign language: A deaf child's developmental course from two to eight years of age. Doctoral dissertation, University of Helsinki, Helsinki.

Takkinen, Ritva (2003). Variation of handshape features in the acquisition process. In A. Baker., B. van den Bogaerde, & O. Crasborn (eds.), *Cross-Linguistic Perspectives in Sign Language Research* (pp. 81–91). Hamburg: Signum.

Tang, G., Brentari, D., González, C., Sze, F. (2010). Crosslinguistic variation in the use of prosodic cues: The case of blinks. In Brentari, D. (ed.), *Sign Languages: A Cambridge Language Survey* (pp. 519–542). Cambridge: Cambridge University Press.

Taub, S. (2001). *Language from the Body: Iconicity and Metaphor in American Sign Language*. Cambridge: Cambridge University Press.

Taylor, C. L. & Schwarz, R. J. (1955). The anatomy and mechanics of the human hand. *Artificial Limbs*, 2, 22–35.

Tent, Jan (1993). Phonetic symmetry in sound systems. Symmetry. *Culture and Science*, 4, 345–368.

Thelen, E. (1991). Motor aspects of emergent speech: A dynamic approach. In N. A. Krasnegor, D. M. Rumbaugh, R. L. Schiefelbusch, & M. Studdert-Kennedy (eds.), *Biological and Behavioral Determinants of Language Development* (pp. 339–362). Hillsdale, NJ: Erlbaum.

Thierry, G. & Wu, Y. J. (2007). Brain potentials reveal unconscious translation during foreign-language comprehension. *Proceedings of the National Academy of Sciences*, 104, 12530–12535.

Thompson, R., Emmorey, K., & Gollan, T. H. (2005). "Tip of the fingers" experiences by deaf signers: Insights into the organization of a sign-based lexicon. *Psychological Science*, 16, 856–860.

Thompson, R. L., Vinson, D. P., & Vigliocco, G. (2009). The link between form and meaning in American Sign Language: Lexical processing effects. *Journal of Experimental Psychology: Learning, Memory, and Cognition*, 35, 550.

Thompson, R. L., Vinson, D. P., & Vigliocco, G. (2010). The link between form and meaning in British Sign Language: Effects of iconicity for phonological decisions. *Journal of Experimental Psychology: Learning, Memory, and Cognition*, 36, 1017.

Thompson, R., Vinson, D., Woll, B, & Vigliocco, G. (2012). The road to language learning is iconic: Evidence from British Sign Language. *Psychological Science* 23, 1443–1448.

Trager, G. L. (1958). Paralanguage: A first approximation. *Studies in Linguistics Occasional Papers*, 13, 1–12.

Traxler, C. B. (2000). The Stanford Achievement Test, 9th Edition: National norming and performance standards for deaf and hard-of-hearing students. *Journal of Deaf Studies and Deaf Education*, 5, 337–348.

Treiman, R. & Hirsh-Pasek, K. (1983). The role of phonological recoding for deaf readers. Paper Presented at the Annual Conference of the American Psychological Society, Anaheim, CA.

Trubetzkoy, N. (1939). *Grundzu¨ge der phonologie [Principles of Phonology]*. Göttingen: Vandenhoeck and Ruprecht (trans. 1969, University of California Press, Berkeley).

Truckenbrodt, H. (1999). On the relation between syntactic phrases and phonological phrases. *Linguistic Inquiry*, 30, 219–255.

Truckenbrodt, H. (2012). The interface of semantics with phonology and morphology. In C. Maienborn, K. von Heusinger, & P. Portner (eds.), *Handbook of Linguistics and Communication Sciences, Vol 3: Semantics* (pp. 2039–2069). Berlin: Mouton de Gruyter.

Tyrone, M. E., Kegl, J., & Poizner, H. (1999). Interarticulator co-ordination in deaf signers with Parkinson's disease. *Neuropsychologia*, 37, 1271–1283.

Tyrone, M. E. & Mauk, C. E. (2010). Sign lowering and phonetic reduction in American Sign Language. *Journal of Phonetics*, 38, 317–328.

Tyrone, M. E., & Mauk, C. E. (2016). The phonetics of head and body movement in the realization of American Sign Language signs. *Phonetica*, 73, 120–140.

Tyrone, M. E., Nam, H., Saltzman, E., Mathur, G., & Goldstein, L. (2010). Prosody and movement = in American Sign Language: A task-dynamics approach. Paper presented at the *5th International Conference on Speech Prosody*, Chicago.

Välimaa-Blum, R. (2005). *Cognitive Phonology in Construction Grammar*. Berlin: Mouton.

Valli, C. (2006). *The Gallaudet Dictionary of American Sign Language*. Washington, DC: Gallaudet University Press.

van den Bogaerde, B. (2000). Input and interaction in deaf families. Doctoral dissertation, University of Amsterdam, Utrecht: LOT (Netherlands Graduate School of Linguistics).

van der Hulst, H. (1993). Units in the analysis of signs. *Phonology*, 10(2), 209–241.

van der Hulst, H. (1995). The composition of handshapes. *University of Trondheim, Working Papers in Linguistics*, 1–18. Dragvoll, Norway.

van der Hulst, H. (2000). Modularity and modality in phonology. In N. Burton-Roberts, P. Carr, & G. Docherty (eds.), *Phonological Knowledge: Its Nature* (pp. 207–244). Oxford: Oxford University Press.

van der Hulst, H. & van der Kooij, E. (2006). Phonetic implementation and phonetic pre-specification in sign language phonology. In L. Goldstein, D. Whalen, & C. Best (eds.), *Papers in Laboratory Phonology, 8* (pp. 265–286). Berlin/New York, NY: Mouton de Gruyter.

van der Hulst, H. & van der Kooij, E. (in press). Phonological structure of signs: Theoretical perspectives. In J. Quer, R. Pfau & A. Herrmann (eds.), *The Routledge Handbook of Theoretical and Experimental Sign Language Research*. London: Routledge.

van der Kooij, E. (2001). Weak drop in Sign Language of the Netherlands. In V. Dively, M. Metzger, S. Taub, & A.M. Baer (eds.), *Signed Languages. Discoveries from International Research* (pp. 27–42). Washington, DC: Gallaudet University Press.

van der Kooij, E. (2002). *Reducing Phonological Categories in Sign Language of the Netherlands: Phonetic Implementation and Iconic Motivation*. Utrecht: LOT (Netherlands Graduate School of Linguistics).

van der Kooij, E. & van der Hulst, H. (2005). On the internal and external organization of sign language segments: Some modality-specific properties. In M. van Oostendorp & J. van de Weijer (eds.), *The Internal Organization of Phonological Segments* (pp. 153–180). Berlin: Mouton de Gruyter.

Veditz, G. W. (1913). *The Preservation of Sign Language*. B/W film, part of NAD Gallaudet Lecture Films series commissioned by National Association of the Deaf (1910–1920).

van 't Veer. B. (2015). *Building a Phonological Inventory Feature Co-occurrence Constraints in Acquisition*. Utrecht: LOT.

Vigliocco, G., Vinson, D. P., Woolfe, T., Dye, M. W., & Woll, B. (2005). Words, signs and imagery: When the language makes the difference. *Proceedings of the Royal Society B, 272*, 1859–1863.

Vihman, M. M. (1996). *Phonological Development: The Origins of Language in the Child*. Cambridge, MA: Blackwell.

Vogt-Svendsen, M. (1981). Mouth position & mouth movement in Norwegian Sign Language. *Sign Language Studies, 33*, 363–376.

Wallin, L (1992). Polysynthetic signs in Swedish Sign Language. Doctoral dissertation, University of Stockholm.

Waters, G. & Doehring, D. (1990). The nature and role of phonological information in reading acquisition: Insights from congenitally deaf children who communicate orally. *Reading and Its Development: Component Skills Approaches*, 323–373.

Waugh, L. R. (2000). Against arbitrariness: Imitation and motivation revived, with consequences for textual meaning. In P. Violi (ed.), *Phonosymbolism and Poetic Language* (pp. 25–56). Turnhout: Brepols.

Weber-Fox, C. M. & Neville, H. J. (1996). Maturational constraints on functional specializations for language processing: ERP and behavioral evidence in bilingual speakers. *Journal of Cognitive Neuroscience*, 8, 231–256.

Wedel, A. (2004). Self-organization and categorization in phonology. Doctoral dissertation, University of California, Santa Cruz.

Wernicke, C. (1874). *Der Aphasische Symptomencomplex*. Breslau: Cohn and Weigert;

Werker, J. F. (1989). Becoming a native listener. *American Scientist*, 77, 54–59.

Wetzels, L, & Mascaró, J. (1977). The typology of voicing and devoicing. *Language* 77, 207–244.

Whalen, D. H., Best, C. T., & Irwin, J. R. (1997). Lexical effects in the perception and production of American English/p/allophones. *Journal of Phonetics*, 25, 501–528.

Whitworth, C. (2011). Features and natural classes in ASL handshapes. *Sign Language Studies*, 12(1), 46–71.

Wilbur, R. (1994). Eyeblinks & ASL phrase structure. *Sign Language Studies*, 84, 221–240.

Wilbur, R. (1997). A prosodic/pragmatic explanation for word order variation in ASL with typological implications. In M. Verspoor, K. D. Lee, & E. Sweetser (eds.), *Lexical and Syntactical Constructions and the Constructions of Meaning* (pp. 89–104). Amsterdam/Philadelphia, PA: John Benjamins Associates.

Wilbur, R. (1999a). Stress in ASL: Empirical evidence and linguistic issues. *Language and Speech*, 42, 229–250.

Wilbur, R. (1999b). Metrical structure, morphological gaps, and possible grammaticalization in ASL. *Sign Language & Linguistics*, 2, 217–244.

Wilbur, R. (2000). Phonological and prosodic layering of nonmanuals in American Sign Language. In K. Emmorey & H. Lane (eds.), *The Signs of Language Revisited: Festschrift for Ursula Bellugi and Edward Klima* (pp. 213–244). Mahwah, NJ: Lawrence Erlbaum Associates.

Wilbur, R. (2008). Complex predicates involving events, time and aspect: Is this why sign languages look so similar? In J. Quer (ed.), *Signs of the Time: Selected Papers from TISLR 2004* (pp. 219–250). Hamburg: Signum.

Wilbur, R. B. (2010). The semantics–phonology interface. In D. Brentari (ed.), *Sign Languages: A Cambridge Language Survey* (pp. 357–382). Cambridge: Cambridge University Press.

Wilbur, R., Klima, E., & Bellugi, U. (1983). Roots: The search for origins of signs in ASL. *Proceedings from the 19th annual meeting of the Chicago Linguistic Society*, 314–336.

Wilbur, R. & Patschke, C. (1999). Syntactic correlates of brow raise in ASL. *Sign Language & Linguistics*, 2, 3–41.

Wilbur, R. B. & Patschke, C. (1998). Body leans and the marking of contrast in American Sign Language. *Journal of Pragmatics*, 30, 275–303.

Wilbur, R. & Zelaznik, H. (1997). *Kinematic Correlates of Stress and Position in ASL*. Chicago, IL: Paper presented at the Linguistic Society of America.

Wilcox, S. (1992). *The Phonetics of Fingerspelling*. Amsterdam: John Benjamins.

Wilcox, P. (2001). *Metaphor in American Sign Language*. Washington, DC: Gallaudet University Press.

Wilcox, P. (2005). What do you think? Metaphor in thought and communication domains in American Sign Language. *Sign Language Studies*, 5(3), 267–291.

Wilcox, S. (2004). Gesture and language: Cross-linguistic and historical data from signed languages. *Gesture*, 4, 43–73.

Wilcox, S. & Occhino, C. (2016). Constructing signs: Place as a symbolic structure in signed languages. *Cognitive Linguistics*, 27, 371–404.

Wilcox, S., Rossini, P. & Pizzuto, E. (2010). Grammaticalization in sign languages. In D. Brentari (ed.), *Sign Languages: A Cambridge Language Survey* (pp. 332–354). Cambridge: Cambridge University Press.

Williams, J. & Newman, S. (2016a). Phonological substitution errors in L2 ASL sentence processing by hearing M2L2 learners. *Second Language Research*, 32, 347–66.

Williams, J. & Newman, S. (2016b). Impacts of visual sonority and handshape markedness on second language learning of American Sign Language. *Journal of Deaf Studies and Deaf Education*, 21, 171–186.

Williamson, K. (1989). Tone and accent in Ịjọ. In H. van der Hulst & N. Smith (eds.), *Pitch Accent Systems* (pp. 253–278). Dordrecht: Foris.

Wilson, M. (2002). Six views of embodied cognition. *Psychonomic Bulletin & Review*, 9, 625–636.

Woods, D. L., Herron, T., Kang, X., Cate, A. D., & Yund, E. W. (2011). Phonological processing in human auditory cortical fields. *Frontiers in Human Neuroscience*, 5, 42.

Woodward, J. (1973). *Implicational Lects on the Deaf Diglossic Continuum*. Washington, DC: Georgetown University Press.

Woodward, J. (1976). Black southern signing. *Language in Society*, 5, 211–8.

Woodward, J., & Desantis, S. (1977). Negative incorporation in French and American sign language. *Language in Society*, 6, 379–388.

Woodward, J., Erting, C., & Oliver, S. (1976). Facing and hand (l) ing variation in American Sign Language phonology. *Sign Language Studies, 10*(1), 43–51.

Wu, Y. J. & Thierry, G. (2010). Chinese-English bilinguals reading English hear Chinese. *The Journal of Neuroscience,* 30, 7646–7651.

Wu, Y. J. & Thierry, G. (2012). Unconscious translation during incidental foreign language processing. *NeuroImage,* 59, 3468–3473.

Wurm, S. A. & Mühlhäusler P. (1985). *Handbook of Tok Pisin (New Guinea Pidgin).* Canberra, A.C.T.: Department of Linguistics, Research School of Pacific Studies, Australian National University.

Xiang, M., Wang, S-P., & Cui, Y-L. (2015). Constructing covert dependencies – the case of wh-in-situ processing. *Journal of Memory and Language, 84,* 139–166.

Xu, Z. (2007). Inflectional morphology in optimality theory. Doctoral dissertation. State University of New York at Stony Brook.

Yang, C. (2017). *The Price of Linguistic Productivity: How Children Learn to Break the Rules of Language.* Cambridge, MA: MIT Press.

Yip, M. (1988). The obligatory contour principle and phonological rules: A loss of identity. *Linguistic Inquiry, 19,* 65–100.

Yu, A. C. L. (2011). On measuring phonetic precursor robustness: A response to Moreton. *Phonology,* 28, 491–518.

Zeshan, U. (2003). Indo-Pakistani Sign Language grammar: A typological outline. *Sign Language Studies,* 157–212.

Zeshan, U. (2006). Sign languages of the world. *Encyclopedia of Language and Linguistics.* Boston, MA: Elsevier.

Zeshan, U. & de Vos, C. (2012). *Sign Languages in Village Communities: Anthropological and Linguistic Insights.* Berlin: Mouton, de Gruyter.

Zhao, W., Ziyi P., & Tang, G. (2017). The perception of handshapes in the Hong Kong Sign Language. *Presentation at the conference on Formal and Experimental Approaches to Sign Theory (FEAST).*

Index

Lightning Source UK Ltd.
Milton Keynes UK
UKHW011507030622
403870UK00018B/513

9 781107 534094